CW01337948

About the Author

Glen Oglaza is an award-winning television news reporter and political correspondent with more than twenty-five years' experience with ITN and Sky News. At ITN, he covered many of the biggest stories of the 1980s and 1990s, was part of the award-winning ITN teams covering the fall of the Berlin Wall, the plight of the Kurds in the wake of the first Gulf War, and the massacre in Dunblane. He was BAFTA nominated for his coverage of the London poll tax riot. As a political correspondent, he covered the governments of Tony Blair, Gordon Brown and David Cameron.

When I Stories

From the Front Line of Television News
Reporting for ITN

Glen Oglaza

When I Stories
From the Front Line of Television News
Reporting for ITN

Pegasus

A CIP catalogue record for this title is
available from the British Library.

ISBN 978-1-80468-090-2

Pegasus is an imprint of
Pegasus Elliot Mackenzie Publishers Ltd.
www.pegasuspublishers.com

First Published in 2024

Pegasus
Sheraton House Castle Park
Cambridge England

Printed & Bound in Great Britain

Dedication

For Maddie and Seb

Acknowledgements

So many people have helped me over so many years. You know who you are, so just a few special mentions.

My sister Sue, for all the typing, fantastic support and keeping me to deadline. Elaine Wadsworth and all at Pegasus. The late and much lamented Tony Cartledge and all at Metro Radio. All those at ITN and Sky News who were such a pleasure to work with. The camera crews and VT editors who taught me so much. Sandy Gall, who first aroused my interest in becoming a television news reporter. Andy Reeds and all at Crown Media, so much unsung talent. Marion, for all the good times. My parents, for putting up with me! Most of all this is for my children. This is some (but by no means all!) of what we got up to. And you, dear reader. I hope you enjoyed sharing my reminiscences.

Finally, apologies if I've forgotten or misremembered anyone or anything although, as I kept and still keep a diary, this is unlikely.

Introduction

As news reporters, we are in the storytelling business, the eye witnesses to history, writing, it's said, 'the first draft of history'. Our stories are restricted to facts, and we need to be not only accurate but also accessible, explaining often complex situations in ways that are easy to absorb, in language that is as clear as possible.

I love telling stories, and over the years, I have often reminisced about some of the things we got up to covering some of the biggest stories in the world. So many people have told me I should write them down.

"But who," I replied, "would want to read them?"

The reply was, "Well, I would for a start" often enough for me to finally attempt to put pen to paper.

I don't know who first coined the term 'when I stories'.

I first heard it from the legendary ITN cameraman, Paul Carleton. In the pub, of course. He was being disparaging. He had more 'when I stories' than most people have had hot dinners, but he would not be telling them as to do so was somehow socially unacceptable. It would lack class.

In my new, post-ITN and Sky News life, I use them all the time to illustrate and drive home points I need my students (CEOs, military officers, executive MBA students) to take on board. Many of them have also asked, "When are you going to write a book?"

To begin at the beginning, but where is the beginning?

I'm sure you don't want to know about my childhood, whether I loved or hated school (mostly the latter), how and why I went completely off the rails as a teenager. Do you want to know how I woke up one day and realised I had to break out of what was clearly becoming a downward spiral and get my life back on track? How I took three A levels in nine months and was offered a place at several universities? Probably not.

But Aberdeen University must get a special mention, as being a student there turned my life around. I threw myself into student life, even being elected union president with a record number of votes, thanks to a brilliant campaign run by my friends Nigel Nuttall and Andy Wanowski, who had also been one of my best friends at school. Being elected president meant I got paid for a sabbatical year which boosted my income from the student grant. Yes, kids, we got a grant paid by the government, which also paid the tuition fees. We were so lucky.

After five very happy years in Aberdeen, I emerged with a very respectable MA Honours degree.

I also somehow managed to clean up the academic glittering prizes, 'Best Student in English' for both my final two years, the 'Seafield Medal for Best English Scholar', and the 'Dougherty Prize' for best essay, which was on French symbolist poetry! I couldn't quote you a single line of Verlaine or Rimbaud these days !

During my years at ITN and later at Sky News, I kept a diary. Without it, this book and the sequel, *More When I Stories*, would not have been possible. My memory is good, but not that good!

CHAPTER 1

Starting out: Radio Days. Margaret Thatcher's Second Landslide. The Miners' Strike. Radio Pranks

I had a brilliant time at Metro Radio, Newcastle, which I joined in April 1982. Not only reporting and writing and reading news bulletins, but also hosting a radio phone-in during the miners' strike, producing and presenting a weekly documentary strand (one of which, on testing cosmetic products on animals, won an award at The New York Radio Awards) and even presenting a weekly travel/holiday show.

The highlight of 1983 was, of course, the general election, Margaret Thatcher's second landslide. I worked from nine a.m. until three thirty a.m. the following morning, a general election pattern that would become horribly familiar.

It was an incredible result. The Tory vote actually fell by two per cent and yet the Conservatives won a staggering landslide of seats. Labour's vote share was their worst ever, at twenty-eight per cent, but they still got more than two hundred seats, while the new kids on the block, the Liberal-SDP alliance, won twenty-five per cent of the vote but got only two dozen seats. Shirley Williams and Bill Rogers were defeated. Tony Benn's demise was also a surprise, so too the defeat of Enoch Powell.

The election also saw success for a certain Tony Blair in Sedgefield.

Other highlights of the year included covering the Durham Miners' Gala and my first interviews with Labour Party deputy leader, Roy Hattersley, and the first of many, many interviews with Neil Kinnock. Other political interviews that year included the Conservative Party Chairman John Gummer who, as I wrote in my diary, came across as incredibly smug, Tony Benn (the first of many), Keith Joseph and David Mellor, nearly ten years before his fall from grace. There were also the stories which set the tone in the north-east: shipbuilding, coal mining and steel.

1983 also saw my second opportunity to get up close and personal with the British army following my earlier work in Northern Ireland. Exercise Lionheart was held on Lüneburg Heath in northern Germany, an old Panzer training area. We landed at Gütersloh where I was met by a handsome Jeremy Irons lookalike British army officer straight out of central casting and his CO, Colonel Hollands, all six foot six of him! I stayed in a rusty Second World War Nissan hut and had great fun with Howitzers and tanks and rode, for the first of many times, in an APC (Armoured Personnel Carrier). It was also the first of many stays in the Normandy barracks in Paderborn.

For me, as for many others, 1984 was dominated by the miners' strike. Northumberland miners were the first in the country to vote for a strike. I was often on the picket lines, where the mood, jovial at first, became more sour as the strike wore on. There were many interviews with miners' leaders including Arthur Scargill, who was sometimes friendly but usually hostile.

On one occasion, the NCB boss, Ian McGregor, who was quite elderly at the time, was accidentally pushed to the ground when a low wooden fence which was holding back angry miners gave way. This presented the classic dilemma of what to do as a journalist. My future ITN colleague, Nick Owen, then working for Tyne Tees Television, and others rushed forward to help the injured McGregor, but my instinct was to carry on reporting the story live. Sometimes you need to be hard-hearted.

On another day on the picket line, I was wearing a contraption on my back with a huge aerial which allowed me to broadcast live. The striking miners began a chant of, 'Beam me up, Scottie!' The *Star Trek* reference singing could clearly be heard in the background to my live reports.

I split up with my long-term girlfriend, Jackie. She kept our dog, Purdey, a black Labrador. Jackie had turned up with her after going home to Perthshire one weekend.

"What a lovely dog," I said. "Whose is it?"

"She's yours."

Purdey was named after the gun not the Joanna Lumley character from *The Avengers*. She had been trained as a gun dog at the Queen's estate at Balmoral. The only problem was that when the gun went off, she ran in the opposite direction. She hated loud bangs. But she was trained to within an inch of her life. I never had to use a dog lead, she walked to heel all the time.

One day, I was delivering the weekly student newspaper around the university. I'd often pick up the papers from the train from Inverness, where they were printed.

The grass quad at King's College, the oldest part of the university dating from 1495, was so immaculately groomed it looked like it had been trimmed with nail scissors. As I was dropping off the papers at King's College library one day, Purdey decided to leave a large deposit on the immaculate lawn.

"Whose dog is that?" came an angry voice from the porters' lodge.

I, of course, walked off in the opposite direction disowning the lovely dog. And of course, she ran straight over to me.

"Oh it's you Glen, that's OK."

Which taught me a very early lesson in always befriending everyone, from the highest to the lowest and everyone in between.

I know this might sound unkind but, after the initial shock, I missed my dog more than I missed the girlfriend.

My reaction was to throw myself into work. One of the pleasures of running a holiday/travel show is you get lots of freebies to distribute around the newsroom. All that was required was to produce an interesting, colourful piece of radio as a result. So it was that in October I found myself in the United States. One day, we were in Orlando, mesmerised by the size of the white-sneakered American tourists. They were enormous. So much so that one of the other journalists on the trip, a very proper and respectable columnist from Bristol, kept running up behind them and snapping their backsides. He was doing this next to a bandstand when the band suddenly struck up 'Roll out the Barrel'. Cue collapse of British journalist party in fits of giggles. But while we were having fun, on October 12th an IRA bomb exploded the Grand Hotel in Brighton. I was flying over New York in a helicopter at the time, the start of my lifelong love affair with helicopters.

Over the following years, I met Martin McGuiness several times in Northern Ireland, and bizarrely, for a drink in the bar of the Grand Hotel, Brighton during a Labour party conference. This exemplified his rehabilitation but was strange to say the least.

Just a few days later, having returned to the UK, I was in Northern Ireland, getting up close and personal with the British army once again. This included my first trip in a tiny Gazelle helicopter. The days were sober, the evenings far less so. Never venture into a sergeants' mess unless you have hollow legs!

On our final night, I joined a group of young officers to watch Sandy Gall's return to Afghanistan documentary, *Allah against the Gunships*, two years on. Their main interest was in the weapons and tactics used, they wanted to see a good firefight. They were disappointed, but I was inspired. This is what I wanted to do, going to dangerous places and shining a light on under-reported conflicts.

In March 1985 the miners went back to work, defeated but still immensely proud. People who are not from mining communities don't understand, but the closing of a pit in a mining village can have catastrophic consequences. With no money coming in, everyone in the village suffers. And they did suffer. Our job was to report those consequences.

The year also saw me interviewing many more senior politicians including Peter Walker, Tom King (stern), Nigel Lawson, Michael Meacher (who I found rather swivel-eyed), and Jack Cunningham to name but a few. Although we didn't have such a position or title, I was, in effect, Metro's political editor, with political stories usually falling to me to cover.

From an early age, I'd been very interested in politics, one of the taboo subjects at home around the dinner table, along with sex and religion. Nowadays, of course, these are mostly what we talk about along with football for those who are interested.

In June, thirty-nine people died and hundreds were injured when a wall collapsed at Heysel Stadium during the European Cup Final between Liverpool and Juventus. I was reading the news, as usual. The way the studio was set up at Metro, I sat opposite the DJ. Mostly, they spent their time while I was reading the news every hour preparing for their next segment. On the day of the Heysel Stadium disaster, the DJ had very obviously not been listening to the news because the first song he played after the bulletin was 'The Walls came Tumbling Down' by the Style Council. He simply couldn't understand why I was calling him every name under the sun, mostly referring to the inadequate size of his brain and wit.

Sometimes, the DJs would prank us for fun, like the individual who thought it was hilarious to crawl under the desk and try to set fire to my scripts (everything was on paper back then) as I was reading them. So, I'd be reading the news in my serious news reading voice while kicking him under the able and trying to grab his cigarette lighter.

Our brilliant head of news, Tony Cartledge, who taught me so much, had a bad habit of not reading his scripts before presenting the hourly news. He was an excellent newsreader, but we had tried many times to get him to at least glance through his scripts beforehand, as we all did, just to check for any difficult pronunciations. The BBC in London had a pronunciation unit. If we weren't sure how to pronounce a name, or if we were arguing about it, we'd phone them pretending to be a BBC radio station and get a definitive answer. Our chance came when the news included a report on two Russian cosmonauts who had successfully returned to Earth. They had impossibly long names. We sat in a huddle in the newsroom, waiting to see how badly Tony would slur and stumble his way through this story. When you're broadcasting the news, you're always reading a few words ahead of the words coming out of your mouth. So it was that Tony read, "The two cosmonauts..." Slight pause, here come the names. "Who were both Russian."

Of course, it wasn't all work. I had two fantastic nights when Bruce Springsteen played at St James' Park. I had to do some work on the first night, vox popping Springsteen fans but the second night was spent just enjoying the concert. Many years later, I enjoyed another free concert by The Boss at Wembley Stadium, courtesy of ITN. There was also the night we went to see Dire Straits. One of the DJs at the radio station was friends with the band, and after a concert at St James' Park, they played for about one hundred of us at a tiny nightclub called Julie's on the Newcastle quayside for hours, jamming a version of 'Johnny B Goode' and generally just messing around.

CHAPTER 2

Joining ITN

In 1986 I said goodbye to Metro Radio. Local radio was the place to learn your trade, sometimes make mistakes, hone your skills and find your voice. We had done innumerable reports for national radio, IRN and LBC, for which we were paid extra. I had spent a very happy four years in Newcastle but was spurred into action after interviewing Brian Redhead, presenter of Radio Four's *Today* programme, who had said, "It's time for you to come to London to play with the big boys."

I'd learnt so much from Tony Cartledge and my wonderful colleagues at Metro. I'd learnt so much about what makes a story news. When I'd first left university, several people were kind enough to offer me advice and took the time to see me, one of them was Peter Carey, the then editor of *Panorama*. Another was Melvin Bragg. Peter asked me which was the most important story: three hundred people dead in a ferry disaster in the South China Sea, two policeman shot dead in Paris, or a police officer stabbed in Birmingham. Naively, I said, "Well, three hundred people dead, of course." He told me how wrong I was. All news is fundamentally parochial. Our audience, our British audience, cares far more about a stabbing of a police officer in Birmingham than whatever's happening in the South China Sea.

I left Metro Radio in October. Drink was taken! I worked for a few weeks at Capital Radio in London on a news programme called *The Way It Is*, led by the excellent Matthew Bannister. I had worked on the show, with Metro's blessing, for six weeks earlier in the year.

Optimistically, though without much expectation, I'd applied for a job at ITN. To my amazement, a letter arrived on my birthday, October 18th, telling me I'd got it!

My first day at ITN was on the 29th December 1986. We were to launch the first British international television news, for Superchannel, the first pan-European news. Portacabins had been hoisted onto the roof of the ITN building in Wells Street. These were to be our home. The keen young team, led by experienced ITN hands, Nigel Dacre (brother of Paul!) and Bill Taylor, included ex-BBC newscaster Sue Carpenter, financial reporter Ed Mitchell, foreign editor Angela Thomae and my soon-to-be good friends, fellow tyros Artemis Pittas, Victor Van Amorengen and Helen Symoniedes. John Suchet was the main presenter. First, though, we had to grapple with ITN's Basys news computer system.

At that time, with satellite and cable television still in its infancy, terrestrial television news had huge audiences. The nation really would gather around television sets to watch the BBC *Nine O'Clock News* or ITN's *News at Ten*, the highest-rated news programme in Britain with regular audience figures of ten to fifteen million. For many years, *News at Ten* was ITV's top-rated programme for ABC1 viewers until it was overtaken by, er, Cilla's *Blind Date*! The commercial break halfway through *News at Ten* pretty much paid for ITN's news coverage. The times, and resources, were good.

Superchannel launched at the end of January 1987, and on February 2nd we broadcast the first Pan-European television news, an historic day we were told in the history of broadcasting, which was suitably celebrated long into the night.

For the next few months, I covered stories from all over the world without leaving the studio. All the big foreign stories, and some domestic UK politics.

A lot of stories that year were from the Middle East. One of our triumphs was to get amateur pictures from the Palestinian refugee camp Bourj el-Barajneh two weeks before ITN's veteran Middle East correspondent, Brent Sadler, got into the camp for a world exclusive report.

I covered stories like the Pope's two-week tour of South America, the Iran-Iraq war, French President Jacques Chirac's bi-lateral in Moscow, and stories in South Korea, Pakistan Australia, the USA, China and others too numerous to recall. And Margaret's Thatcher's third election victory — and all without leaving the building, simply using pictures and interviews coming into ITN HQ in Wells Street. I wanted to be out reporting, but it was invaluable experience, learning the art of telling stories for television news.

I also occasionally presented, but I was desperate to get out there to do some proper reporting. So I was given the opportunity to do a reporting shift for *News at Ten*, the most popular news programme in Britain.

I was young enough, keen enough and hungry enough to grasp the opportunity with both hands.

My first ITN shift was on April 18th. I reported on pictures from the Philippines for the lunchtime news and Argentina for the late news. On my second day, a Sunday, I had the lead story, a coup attempt in Buenos Aires. I got it done with less than sixty seconds to spare. This would also become a familiar pattern.

There were fulsome congratulations in the newsroom, especially from Mike Nolan, the sometimes gruff and often very funny Australian foreign news editor and the best-on-the-road fixer/producer of his generation.

Veteran ITN reporter Terry Lloyd ambled over.

"Glen mate." Pause. "Crap."

I knew then that we would get along very well, and so we did, until his untimely death in Iraq in 2003. Terry was a great reporter, but also an immensely warm human being. The two are, of course, inseparable. Empathy is a quality shared by all the best reporters.

Humility is also a key component of the best reporters, that self-doubt which lies behind the apparent arrogance of being able to walk into any situation and 'own' the story.

Humility is a lesson best learnt early. When I first started in radio, I was well aware that I knew very little. By the time I arrived at ITN, I knew how to tell a story but I also recognised that I had an enormous amount to learn about how to do that for television. And the way you learn is from the people you work with, the camera crews and picture editors who'd been doing it for years.

The first time I was sent to Belfast for ITN was with cameraman, Mike Inglis, and sound recordist, Ray Cheeseman, both very experienced and who'd worked in Northern Ireland many times. They took me on a tour, showing me the Falls Road, Shanklin Road, the Divas Flats etc. The stories we covered while we were there were largely driven by them. I got the information from the usual sources, the police, the army, by simply talking to people and trying to find witnesses and, of course, by talking to local reporters, the people who really know the story. In my case, this largely meant Eamonn Mallie, a font of knowledge and good advice.

When this goes wrong, it can do so spectacularly. There are two stories of young ITN reporters whose arrogance was their undoing. In the first case, the reporter had had the temerity to try to tell a very experienced cameraman how to do his job! On the way back from the story, the cameraman stopped the car at the nearest train station and said, "Right you! Out!" The hapless reporter had to get the train back to London. The second case was even worse. This time, the cameraman (a different one) pulled over onto the hard shoulder of the M25 and dumped the reporter beside the motorway. Needless to say, neither reporter lasted long at ITN.

I was sent to Warrington in 1993 when IRA bombs killed two children and injured more than fifty people. I was dispatched because it was felt the relatively inexperienced reporter covering the story was causing problems. I was greeted by producer, Rob Davidovitz, with the words, "Thank God you're here."

The reporter, notorious for having a short temper, had upset just about everyone, Rob told me, including at one point shouting at the manager of a local supermarket at the scene of the blasts, "You people got what you deserved!" Absolutely incredible. He was lucky that his behaviour never got back to the bosses back at ITN. Nether Rob nor I was going to 'snitch'. As it was, his bad temper proved to be his undoing sometime later.

Back in 1987 and for the next few months I was doing double shifts for ITN and the ITN news for Superchannel. On one not entirely untypical day, I reported on the breaking of diplomatic relations between France and Iran and got the lead story on both channels including *News at Ten*.

For most of the year, ITN used me the same way as ITN Superchannel, to voice foreign stories, although I did manage to escape in June, to cover an EU summit in Brussels (the first of SO many). Real foreign reporting at last. It was my first live TV interview, my first foreign PTC (piece to camera) for my news package, and I got to work alongside Jon Snow, one of the truly great reporters. We worked until late and drank until even later. After midnight we were in the Grand Place, when Jon decided, for some reason, to start punching the air above his head (he's very tall, so about eight feet in the air!) shouting, "Viva la revolution!"

ITN veteran, Bill Taylor, was a fine chief sub for Superchannel news, but could often be brusque to say the least. For example, one day in July he accosted me.

"Straighten your tie, get your jacket on and get down to reception. There's some MP or other there. Take him to the board room and give him a drink."

I was doing more and more ITN reporter shifts, often getting the lead story. I was also presenting 'newsflashes', which we now call breaking news, breaking into the ITV programmes. After one, an American helicopter attack on an Iranian ship the Americans claimed was laying mines in the Straits of Hormuz, Alastair Burnet, that giant of television news, congratulated me. It was, he said, "Very good. I reached for my tin hat."

In August, in Hungerford, Michael Robert Ryan shot dead sixteen people, including his own mother, before shooting himself. I wasn't sent until a couple of days later. I was to work for the first time with cameraman, Paul Carleton, and his sound recordist, Tony Hemmings. I'd been warned by the news desk that they've been working flat out and probably hadn't had much sleep. So, I turned up all bright-eyed and bushy-tailed in Hungerford on a warm, sunny August day. Arriving at the hotel where the crew was staying, I phoned Paul in his room.

"I'm downstairs," I said.

"So what?" came the not very helpful reply.

For once, I read the situation quickly. "Well," I said. "I've got a jug of Pimm's all ready for you."

Despite the horror of the story, the three of us spent a pleasant hour on the hotel terrace overlooking a croquet lawn beyond which cows were grazing in a field. Beyond that was a line of trees and rising from behind the trees were hot air balloons. The local hot air ballooning club was having its annual meeting. After a jug or two of Pimm's, they were in a better mood and ready to work again. It was my first encounter with Carleton and Hemmings, with whom I was to cover many stories in the years ahead.

In October I escaped to Orange County Virginia to stay with my university friend, Anne Etchison. Anne was a teacher and thought it would be a good idea for me to go to her school and talk to her teenage students. So I decided to put up a map of Europe and show them where London was.

The questions were fabulous. Did I have a Lamborghini? Did I live in a castle? Ann later explained that a Lamborghini was the only foreign car they'd ever heard of, and I was the only foreigner they'd ever met, and they'd also heard an Englishman's home is his castle. One little boy, thirteen years old, mop of blond hair, baseball cap worn backwards, came up to me afterwards.

"Your accent is awesome. You've got to teach me to talk like that because the girls around here really go for that stuff."

The King's Cross fire in November was literally at the end of the road, ITN having moved into shiny new offices in Gray's Inn Road. More than thirty people were dead (we later learnt the total was thirty-one), and dozens injured.

The smell was indescribable. It was the smell of smoke, but what else? More than one hundred and fifty firefighters were deployed that night, many of them were sitting in the street, exhausted, shell-shocked. One described it to me simply as, "Hell."

I spent part of the following year covering the public inquiry, which went on for three months.

Sometimes, even the most accomplished media performers could do with some proper media training advice. In December, I interviewed Bob Geldof. The interview lasted forty minutes and was basically a monologue, I barely got a word in! Which was very amusing and entertaining, but had to be edited down to one minute thirty seconds for the news.

Compare and contrast with an interview I did that year with Prime Minister Margaret Thatcher. She was reputed to have walked into one of her first television interviews as Conservative Party leader, slammed a pile of papers onto the desk, and said, "There are my answers. Now what are your questions?"

She seemed to approach her interview with me in the same frame of mind, largely ignoring my questions and delivering the messages she was there to deliver. The last time I had met her was some years earlier in Newcastle, when she had called me, 'a moaning Minnie'. She'd been there to announce new jobs with a tech company, Press Production Systems, which was opening in the area. At the time, the site was an industrial wasteland, what these days we would call a brownfield site. There is a famous image of Mrs Thatcher striding across this wasteland which made the next day's front pages. Unemployment in the north-east at the time was the highest in mainland Britain so, of course, our questions were all about jobs. She fixed me with that steely gaze and said. "Now stop being a moaning Minnie. Stop it."

Moaning Minnies was the headline in most newspapers the next morning.

CHAPTER 3

1988: Klosters. Baby Doreen Mason. Lockerbie

The year started very well. On January 4th, I got the job as a full-time staff ITN reporter. There were three of us newbies: myself, Jo Andrews and Robert Hall. Three of us had been chosen from a field of twenty-three. I was later told that Nigel Hancock, the head of Home News, had decided the three he wanted weeks before. A lot of champagne disappeared that evening. It was slightly terrifying, with a steep learning curve ahead even though I had already been doing reporting shifts for months. I was very excited, but also driven by a fear of failure. A daunting but exhilarating prospect.

One of my first interviews as a fully-fledged ITN reporter was with the acting genius, Ian McKellen, long before his Gandalf days, at an AIDS rally in Hyde Park. We also interviewed half the cast of Eastenders, Peter Tatchell (always good value) and others, but McKellen stood out for his warmth, humanity, empathy and humility. He was clearly destined for greatness.

An ITN friend hosted a New Year party at his home in Hammersmith. The doorbell rang and a female guest, also an ITN colleague, answered it. "Did anyone order a taxi to go to Wimbledon?"

At that moment, out host's eighteen-year-old daughter appeared at the top of the stairs and screamed at her father, "And how could you have an affair with that total bitch? You've fucked up all our lives. I hate you."

Stunned silence. And then, from the woman at the front door. "Er, did anyone order a taxi to Wimbledon?"

In March we were in Klosters in Switzerland with the Royal reporters, some of Fleet Street's finest, otherwise known as the Crested Reptiles. Prince Charles had been involved in an avalanche in the Alps, which had killed his friend, Major Hugh Lindsay. Another friend, Patti Palmer-Tomkinson, was in intensive care. The job was madness. It involved finding out where Prince Charles was at any given time. His team used diversionary tactics so, for example, they would send convoys of limousines in different directions to throw us off the scent. I was still a comparative novice but had a very experienced field producer, John Toker, working with me. At one point, three limousines set off from outside the prince's hotel. Do we follow them or not? John's helpful contribution was, "It's up to you." So we did. After a lunatic car chase involving several leading members of Her Majesty's press, the police threw up a roadblock to stop us and allow Prince Charles to escape.

We found him later, entirely by chance, in Davos. A scoop, but one entirely due to luck.

The newspapers are not immune to blatant invention, I'd learnt this lesson early on. Attending a conference of The National Union of Students in Blackpool many years earlier, there'd been a mad Trot motion to set up a collection for the IRA. It was dismissed out of hand by the NUS executive, and of course, was not even debated. That didn't stop the *Daily Mail* from running a half page story under the headline: Students collect money for the IRA.

On this occasion the *Sun* claimed that a local official was blaming Prince Charles for the accident. I found him, and he told me he hadn't spoken to the *Sun* or any other newspaper.

The Crested Reptiles were a breed apart. The loudest of them was the corpulent James Whitaker of the *Daily Mirror*, known as 'the big red tomato'. With a fabulous bass-baritone voice, the joke doing the rounds was that the avalanche had been caused by his screaming at a rival (from the *Daily Express*) in his booming voice calling him a complete (expletive deleted!).

I was still riding my luck. In March I covered the funeral of Corporal Derek Wood of the Royal Signals, who had been murdered in Belfast. Paul Carleton took some excellent, sensitive shots of the funeral service, which included a three-volley gun salute. I couldn't think of anything to say at that point, so I said nothing. Our story was very well received back at base. Mervyn Hall, the senior news editor, said keeping silent during the gun salute was 'masterful'!

Merv had a nickname for everyone. Mine was 'Double', short for double-glazing, a play on words (sort of) on my surname. Just to show how

Chinese whispers can work, some months later a Channel 4 news producer earnestly asked me if I'd been a double-glazing salesman before becoming a reporter!

In May, we covered the P&O Ferries dispute, which involved bouncing between Dover, Calais and Zeebrugge. It was my first interview with union leader and left-wing firebrand, Len McCluskie.

A couple of years earlier, I had interviewed another union leader called Len. Len Murray. This resulted in a most peculiar story. A friend of mine was visiting friends in Oldham who said, "Shall we go for a Glen Oglaza?" My astonished friend asked them what on earth they were talking about. It turns out that they'd seen me interviewing Len Murray and decided that their new slang word for curry should be changed from a Ruby to a Len, and then they'd changed it again to a Glen Oglaza. And thus, my greatest claim to fame: I'd become Oldham slang for a curry.

But I digress. Back to the P&O strike. Hugh Thompson, ITN cameraman Nigel's father and an ITN legend in his own right, had clearly covered too many wars. His comment on the strike was, "Why don't they just mine the harbour?"

From the P&O dispute, we went straight to something far more serious. In the Dutch town of Roermond, close to the German border, the Provisional IRA had detonated a car bomb, an attack on RAF personnel. Three people had been killed and another three injured. They had also shot dead two Australian tourists, who they claimed they had mistaken for off-duty British soldiers.

I committed the cardinal sin of getting separated from my camera crew. BBC reporter, Carole Walker, rescued me by giving me a lift to the TV station where my crew had gone to feed our material. This was untypical of BBC reporters to say the least. Normally the rivalry with the BBC was extremely intense.

There's a famous story which exemplifies this, from the Turkish invasion of Cyprus in 1974. ITN reporter, Michael Nicholson, and his team had broken down on the road near Nicosia. Despondent, they were stranded beside their car. The rival BBC team drove past jeering and making suitably rude gestures. A few minutes later, Nicholson and co heard the drone of C-130 aircraft. Looking up, they saw hundreds of Turkish paratroopers descending. In a scene now famous in the annals of ITN, Nicholson strode over to the first paratrooper, hand outstretched and said, "Michael Nicholson, ITN. Welcome to Cyprus." Needless to say, the BBC lot looked like whipped dogs the next time our team saw them.

Thanks Carole. I still owe you a big favour.

In August, we were in Canterbury to cover the Lambeth Conference, the Church of England debate on the ordination of women bishops. As we were feeding our story for *News at Ten* from our satellite dish in the car park, the Archbishop of Canterbury, Robert Runcie, appeared. He was fascinated by the technology. Our engineer told him, "It goes up there to your boss, and if he approves, it gets sent back down to ITN in London." There was a pause. I wondered how the archbishop was going to react to this blasphemy. Fortunately, he found it very funny and laughed heartily.

As an aside, ITN like almost everywhere else was incredibly non-PC at that time. To give just one example, we had an Indian sound recordist, the only non-white person in the camera crews' department. Eric was highly educated, erudite and could recite Coleridge's 'Kubla Khan' (In Xanadu did Kubla Khan A stately pleasure dome decree) in its entirety, his party-piece. Without a hint of malice, the crews called him 'Ethnic Eric', or 'Ethnic' for short. In fact, only popular people were afforded nicknames.

"Oi, Ethnic, fancy a cup of tea?"

"Come on, Ethnic, we're late." And so on.

And sexism was rife. There was a reporter notorious for grabbing the bottom of every attractive girl who passed his desk. Some of the more ambitious young women would try to use this to their advantage. There were two attractive blondes who went on to have hugely successful careers in broadcasting. They would come to work wearing incredibly short skirts, and when they went to see one of the bosses in his office, would enter backwards on their knees. OK, they didn't exactly do that, but they would sashay in, sit down and cross their legs in a way that Sharon Stone would recognise. It worked on the more libidinous, with others it would backfire. They shared my view: I'm not actually looking for a sex slave, what I want is good, incisive and succinct writing. Ok?

Not that I was impervious to the charms of the opposite sex. I was young and single and living the life. Legendary ITN studio director, Diane Edwards-Jones, was notoriously potty-mouthed. She once instructed a presenter to tell the Chancellor of the Exchequer, Geoffrey Howe, to, "Tell that little fucker Howe to stop fucking fidgeting!"

The chancellor heard that on the talkback and said, "Oh, does she mean me?"

Another instruction to a floor manager was, "Tell that fucker in purple to move to his left a bit." This was also overheard, by the Archbishop of Canterbury!

Di once said to me, "You're a randy little fucker, aren't you?" I'm pretty sure it was not meant as a compliment!

ITN paid for me to go to a Bruce Springsteen concert. The Boss and Sting were headlining an Amnesty International concert at Wembley. There was a gantry just beneath the front of the stage meant only for photographers and cameramen. Needless to say, that is where I positioned myself. An hour before the concert was due to start, *News at Ten* dropped the story. But we got a clear instruction from the news desk. 'You guys should stay and enjoy the concert anyway.' They didn't have to ask twice!

In November, ITN *World News* broadcast for the last time on the doomed Superchannel. The next year, Sky News would launch and change the face of television news in the UK forever.

Roy Aston and Christine Mason were convicted of the manslaughter of their baby, Doreen. It was an horrific case, one of many that I covered at the Old Bailey. They had smashed their baby's head against a wall to stop her crying. The mother, Christine Mason, was a particularly pathetic sight in court, just repeating, "I want my babby back." ITN foreign editor, Maggie Eales, herself a mother, asked me how I could possibly cover such an awful story. Being young, single and blasé, I replied that it was just another story. Years later, when I had children of my own, and even to this day, I can't even read about child abuse without crying let alone reporting on it.

I'd produced a five-minute backgrounder for *News at Ten* for the baby Doreen case but, on the day of the verdict, Lockerbie happened. Of course, my piece was dropped, though a shorter version had run on the evening news at 5:45. ITN chartered a plane to get a team to Lockerbie. I was included. When we got there, the town resembled the aftermath of a battle. In this small, Scottish border town, bits of metal like shrapnel were scattered everywhere. So too were human remains.

Pan Am flight 103 had been blown apart by a terrorist bomb. Everyone onboard had been killed. Two hundred and fifty-nine souls. We came across bodies still strapped into their seats. Burnt body parts were everywhere. In Sherwood crescent, eleven people were killed when the aircraft's flaming fuel tanks had landed, creating a huge crater.

Putting aside any emotion and our profound horror, we had a job to do. The money shot was the plane's cockpit, lying in a field, the most famous image of the disaster. For three days, our camera crews, with Paul Carleton prominent among them, ran rings around the friendly Dumfries and Galloway police, until officers were drafted in from the Strathclyde force. They were all about six foot five tall and we were used to separating Celtic and Rangers fans. They weren't taking any nonsense from us.

CHAPTER 4

1989: Hillsborough. The Year of Revolutions: The Fall of the Berlin Wall.
The Velvet Revolution. Alexander Dubcek. Romania

Sometimes, working in television news can be very frustrating. By January 2nd we'd been in Lockerbie for nearly two weeks. I was to file a report for *News at Ten* with another coming from Frankfurt where, it was believed, mailbags had got onto flight 103 unchecked.

After much debate at ITN in London, it was decided that there would be just one package, which would be pulled together by a reporter back in London. Apart from the fact that it is always better to have a package from a reporter at the scene, and that I could easily have incorporated the Frankfurt material into a piece from Lockerbie, the resulting package for *News at Ten* was poor. It allowed producers in London to have more control, but it began with library pictures (something of a cardinal sin in TV news) and contained factual inaccuracies (even worse).

There's nothing for it in these circumstances but to get the team together to eat, drink and commiserate. And then drink some more. Tomorrow is another day, and the news never stops. And of course, the next day was as busy as ever, out with RAF search teams to look for wreckage which was spread over a large area. The day after, I found myself doorstepping Margaret Thatcher yet again, as Paul Carleton and Tony Hemmings filmed the Lockerbie Memorial Service. She was reasonably forthcoming, as was the Labour leader, Neil Kinnock. Prince Charles was less so. You're not supposed to doorstep royals, but that doesn't stop us from trying.

Covering the news can be grim, and sometimes heart-breaking. But there are also moments of levity. Back from Lockerbie, we were sent to the beautiful Chatsworth house in Derbyshire to interview the Duke of Devonshire about his new, self-sufficient water pumping station. We conducted the interview in the magnificent state apartment created for King William the Third and Queen Mary. Throughout the five-minute interview, the elderly duke farted nonstop, a long continuous wet flatulence. We made a fantastic effort to keep a straight face. Although it was only a light 'And Finally' story for a quiet Sunday, cameraman Nigel Thompson drove like a maniac to central TV to feed our piece in time. Whatever the story, however trivial, we always gave it our all and always made the deadline.

In February, we returned to Klosters. Prince Charles was returning a year after the avalanche which had killed his friend, Major Hugh Lindsay. Nigel Thompson was one of the best cameramen in the world, and very clever. One of the bonds between us was that we were born on the same day. He was also rather fond of the drink. Once again, the game was to find out where Charles would be the next day. We were in a restaurant in Klosters one evening, drinking the Swiss wine, fleisch. After several bottles, Nigel was stripped to the waist and demanding, "More flesh!" Suddenly, there was a hush in the restaurant. Prince Charles and his entourage appeared from a private dining room at the back of the restaurant where they'd been having dinner. His equerry came over to our table. He thought, mistakenly, that we had discovered where Prince Charles was dining but had left him in peace. Our reward was vital information.

"Thank you. Tomorrow we'll be skiing the Gotschnagrat", the main mountain overlooking Klosters. The next morning, we had a scoop. No one else knew he was there. The only problem was that I was so hungover that I couldn't say the word Gotschnagrat!

On that trip, I also got to indulge in one of my favourite pastimes, flying around in a helicopter, a Swiss air ambulance Jet Ranger. We touched down on top of a mountain where I interviewed a very attractive Swiss doctor, Elsa Rauch. I told her, as I told everyone, to look at me and not at the camera.

"Oh," she said. "But I like to look at you."

When the camera crew picked themselves up and stopped laughing, we carried on filming, but for the rest of the time we were there they made a point of coming up to me several times a day and declaring in a faux Swiss accent, "Oh but I like to look at you."

During that return to Klosters, I also experienced yet again the tabloids' need to invent stories. At one point while he was out skiing, Prince Charles had got slightly ahead and stopped, looking over his shoulder and waiting for his friends to catch up. This was captured on long lens cameras and carried in the newspapers the next day with the caption: Prince Charles gazing at the spot where his friend died. In fact, they were three valleys away from where the avalanche had actually happened.

April 15th 1989, and those shocking images from the FA cup semi-final at Hillsborough between Liverpool and Nottingham Forest. We got the first available train to Sheffield. An ITN cast of thousands descended, including Jon Snow, sports reporter, Mark Austin, senior producers Andy Tilley and John Toker, and a lot of camera crews. We filmed gut-wrenching pictures from the stadium, and of the injured arriving at Hallamshire hospital. Despite our large (and highly talented) presence on the ground, the news report was pulled together in London, without a single package from Sheffield, a decision presumably based on the sheer volume of material arriving at ITN HQ.

The next day, I filed the report on why it had happened and what had gone wrong, while Mark Austin covered the visit of Prime Minister Margaret Thatcher.

Ninety-seven people had died in horrific circumstances, crushed to death, pushed against the fences around the pitch. It began to emerge that the police had allowed thousands of ticketless Liverpool fans into the stadium at the Leppings Lane end. They had simply opened the gates, and those pushing from the back to get onto the terraces had caused the crush so fatal to those at the front.

There were moving pictures from Anfield with a hundred thousand people passing through Liverpool's stadium, laying flowers around the goalmouth at the Kop end.

Two days after the disaster, on Monday, Prince Charles and Diana, Princess of Wales, visited the Sheffield hospitals. As well as those who had lost their lives, more than seven hundred had been hospitalized. Once again, I found myself doorstepping members of the royal family with the usual result.

We reconstructed the route Liverpool fans had taken to get to the game and tried to build a picture of what had gone wrong. Although we'd finished in plenty of time for *News at Ten*, we had to wait for graphics to be fed to us from London, even though it would have made more sense to drop in the graphics at ITN HQ. Something to do with a shortage of picture editors back at base. In the end, we made the top of *News at Ten* by the skin of our teeth. The amiable Robin Elias, senior *News at Ten* producer who had been with us during our edit in Sheffield, said, "I will never, ever, criticise anyone on the road again." An admirable sentiment which did not, of course, stand the test of time!

After editing for *News at Ten*, we were unceremoniously thrown out of our hotel. Every hotel room in Sheffield had been booked for the snooker. The ITN travel office found us another one — in Barnsley!

On Tuesday, three days after the disaster, relatives of the deceased visited the Leppings Lane end terrace. The press was not allowed in, but we sent cameraman Alan Downes up in a cherry picker to get exclusive topshots. The images were extremely moving. Also visiting the terrace, was Lord Justice Taylor, whose subsequent report would lead to the banning of fences and all-seater football stadia.

It began to emerge that the south Yorkshire police were culpable, to say the least. ITN producer John Toker, himself a scouser, commented, "It's just the usual scallies trying to bunk in." This was normal practice at the time, we all did it as kids. I knew how to climb into several first division stadiums. But this was on an altogether different scale, not just a few kids trying to get in for nothing. The police had been at the very least negligent.

The cherry picker was a brilliant idea and we used it for several more days to get exclusive pictures. Amazingly, no one else (including the BBC) thought to hire one.

The following weekend we were moved to tears, first by the one-minute silence, one week after the disaster, at 3.06p.m. on Saturday, and then by the memorial service in the Anglican cathedral on Sunday. 'Abide with me' gets me every time.

Hillsborough also taught me, once again, how the tabloids sometimes operate. The criticism of the *Sun*'s outrageous, hurtful and false reporting of Hillsborough has been widely covered. My own experience was far less dreadful than those lies. There had been reports of fighting at a pub near the stadium, so we went to investigate. The pub landlady told us that the fans had been loud, a few glasses had been smashed, but there had been no fighting. Crucially, she also told us that they were Nottingham Forest not

Liverpool fans. The *Sun* the next morning, carried a story: Liverpool fans smashed up pub.

Later that week, we interviewed the man in charge of the gates at Hillsborough, Jack Stone. This involved finding him in a pub and buying a lot of drinks, proper old-school journalism. He had an amazing story to tell, in particular that the police had ordered the gates to be opened so that they could get out to restore order, not to relieve the crush outside. They had ignored the warnings that opening the gates would let in thousands of fans. The police thought they could control that influx. They were wrong with such appalling and fatal consequences.

Jack Stone would not go on camera, but after much persuasion, he gave us an excellent on-camera interview a week later, and even posed for pictures in front of the now infamous Leppings Lane end gates.

I stayed in Sheffield for much of May and June covering Lord Justice Taylor's inquiry. At times it was very fraught, as I had to interview the relatives of those who'd died. Among them, Trevor Hicks stood out. He'd been at the game, and almost unimaginably, had lost his two teenage daughters, Sarah and Victoria. Somehow, he managed to provide clear and dispassionate testimony to the inquiry. Brave man. Very. He was also strong enough, and angry enough, to give us an interview for *News at Ten* afterwards. Later, during the trial of the police match commander, David Duckenfield, Trevor Hicks recalled how he'd been told to, "Shut your f***ing prattle", by a police officer when he had tried to draw attention to the unfolding disaster.

Away from the inquiry, life went on. On the day, May 3rd, that we'd interviewed Jack Stone, John Toker and I went out to celebrate our scoop after *News at Ten*. After something of a pub and club crawl, we found ourselves in the middle of Sheffield at three a.m. The city was closed, except for somewhere called the 'Blues Club'. Two taxi drivers separately assured us that it was very dangerous there. "Full of Jamaicans, drugs, and you'll get robbed." What the hell, we went for it anyway. It was a bar and it was open. When we walked in, the place went silent. Here were two white men in suits, almost certainly the plod. But the barman was friendly, the few Rastas present went back to playing dominoes and pool, so we stayed for a couple of beers before calling it a night.

Football, too, went on. Liverpool beat Everton 3–2 after extra time to win the FA cup final at Wembley. Of course, we were all rooting for Liverpool, for once.

The highlight, though, was a Liverpool defeat. At Anfield, on May 26th, Arsenal won the league in the most incredible circumstances. I was editing the lead story on Hillsborough for *News at Ten* with picture editor Ron Lakeman, who was even more of a Gunners fan than me, while we watched the game on the TV in the hotel room where we were editing. It was the very last game of the season. Arsenal needed to win by two clear goals to take the title from hot favourites, Liverpool, who'd been undefeated since January and, having won the FA cup, were going for the double. Somehow we did it, winning 2–0 with the winning goal scored by Danny Thomas in the final minute of the game. While I was jumping around the room punching the air, Ron was unable to contain himself and ran down to the hotel reception like a madman and kissed all the receptionists, both male and female.

That's enough Arsenal (ed).

For much of the summer of 1989 I bounced around towns and cities in the north of England, in itself an education, covering assorted industrial disputes, including those of the NUR and NALGO, the snappily-titled National and Local Government Officers Association. Remember them? At the time, Britain's largest white-collar union, in 1993 NALGO was one of the three unions which merged to form UNISON.

In Liverpool I covered the dockers' strike and the bizarre trial of comedian Ken Dodd, who was accused of tax evasion because he liked to keep his cash (a lot of it!) at his home. He was acquitted of all charges. There was absolute mayhem when he emerged from court with his cheeky-chappy grin. Cameraman Mick James got some great shots as he managed to get to the front of the mad media scrum. Afterwards, we tried to find Ken Dodd to get an interview, but he had gone to ground. He did, however, give an interview to the new kids on the block, Sky News, an interview which was strongly rumoured to be part of a News International buyout.

Sometimes I'd be the one pulling together the news package in London, much to the chagrin, no doubt, of those in the field, at the scene. One such occasion was the IRA bomb at the Royal Marines music school in Deal, Kent in September. Despite a large ITN team on the ground, including three of our top reporters, my friend and colleague Peter Sharp did the report in London for the early evening news, and I pulled it together for *News at Ten*.

As summer gave way to autumn, rumblings were afoot in Europe. Something was going on in Germany!

I'd been sent to Unna Masson, near Dortmund on September 8th where the IRA had shot dead a British soldier's wife, Heidi, the wife of Staff Sergeant Clive Hazell. I was still riding my luck. I got to the scene just in time to see the bullet-ridden car being taken away by the police, but there was no sign of my freelance camera crew. Fortunately for me, the BBC crew had also failed to turn up. I eventually found my crew relaxing at WDR TV in Dortmund. Bloody useful they were sitting around there! The next day, with the crew suitably chastised and fully briefed, we fed from ZDF in Düsseldorf, which was a lot more successful. So too was our coverage of Heidi's memorial service (another one, sadly) the following Sunday.

And then came the news that was to transform Europe.

Sometimes, you can work all day for nothing as your story is overtaken by events or by a bigger story happening elsewhere. To give just two examples: In March 1989 I was in Cherbourg, where a ship had capsized spilling its potentially lethal cargo of insecticide into the English Channel. Working with cameraman Sebastian Rich, sound recordist Roger Dove and ITN's Paris producer Barbara Gray, we got some tremendous shots and had a good story to tell, but never made it to air. At the last moment, our story was dropped for an interview with Defence Secretary Tom King on the big story of that day: Two senior RUC officers had been assassinated in Northern Ireland.

I was the victim of a more comical example many years later when, as Sky News political correspondent, I had travelled to Stockholm with Prime Minister David Cameron in February 2012 for a summit with Scandinavian leaders. The evening we arrived, the England football manager, Fabio Capello, resigned. Sky News went Capello-tastic. For more, see February 2012 in *More When I Stories*.

But I digress. Back to Germany. It is September 10th, 1989. After the memorial service for Heidi Hazell, which we filmed discreetly and as unobtrusively as possible from a distance with no requests for any interviews, reports started coming in that Hungary was to open its border with Austria at midnight, allowing thousands of East Germans who had gathered there to escape to the West. We were covering another story, in Dortmund, and set off for the long drive to Passau, arriving at eleven p.m. It was quiet. It wasn't until three a.m. that the first East German family crossed the border, Gerhart and Nicol Meyer and their two children. The media were there in force. We spent hours at the border as car after car went through. Joyful scenes. We fed our material from the ORF (Austrian TV) ground station in Passau. We also managed to interview the prime minister of Bavaria. We didn't sleep. Sleep is for wimps!

We found a family willing to be our story, an example of the one illustrating the many. Joachim and Marina Lehmann and their children Stefan, nine, and Anna, eight, were from East Berlin. We helped them unload their funny little Trabant car, then drove them to Munich airport in our two Mercedes saloons, at times at two hundred kilometres an hour. Faster than I'd ever driven before, or ever want to again.

We flew the Lehmanns to Berlin where, at the airport, they were reunited with their West Berlin family members. They ran towards each other across the airport concourse into each other's arms. It was incredibly emotional. Cameraman Phil Bye, a hardened veteran of war zones but a sensitive soul, filmed these moving scenes until he, like me, was reduced to tears.

Although we thought the story of our family would make one piece for *News at Ten*, it had been so well received that the next morning, ITN wanted updates for every news bulletin. So we took pictures of the Lehmann family in their cousin's flat, a toyshop, a Mercedes showroom. The money shot, though, was of the family of four gazing from their new home in West Berlin across to their old home in communist East Berlin.

To celebrate, we went for dinner and were joined by Paris producer Barbara Gray who had just arrived in Berlin and a team from *Channel 4 News*, led by correspondent Nik Gowing. At one point and apropos of nothing, Nik leant across the table and asked me completely out of the blue, "Have you read my book?"

"No, I'm afraid I haven't. Not yet," was my diplomatic answer.

Being Channel 4, I'd assumed it would be something very pointy-headed. In fact he was referring to his novel, *The Wire*, a thriller set mostly in Poland. I hadn't read it then, but I have since. Recommended.

I was working with a Belgian freelance camera crew. Later that day, we were trying to park our vehicle, a Renault Espace, in a multistorey car park. The cameraman leaned across and spoke to the German driver who had just parked in the space next to the one we were trying to get into. Suddenly, to my horror, the whole crew were giving Nazi salutes and shouting, 'Sieg Heil'.

"What are you doing?" I asked.

They explained that he'd asked the German driver to move over slightly so that we could fit in, but the driver had replied, "I must park between ze white lines."

By the end of September I was back in London. I'd been asked by Gareth Parry of the *Guardian* to co-write a book about Hillsborough. Now, literary agents Curtis Brown were struggling to find a publisher, despite their earlier confidence. They were being told that books about football don't sell. I was speechless. Not only was it not a 'book about football', but it was bound to sell well even if only in Liverpool and Sheffield.

Nothing to do with the news, but I spent most of October cruising in the Caribbean. My sister was working as an officer on a cruise ship and I got a ninety-five per cent discount: a two-thousand-dollar-cruise for just a hundred dollars. We went to Puerto Rico, the Dominican Republic, the US Virgin Islands, Jamaica, Grand Cayman, the Yucatan Peninsula of Mexico with its incredible Mayan ruins, and the island of Cozumel, as well as spending some time misbehaving in Miami. Just to enter the spirit of things I took part in an evening of competitive games. One of them involved who could be the quickest to remove their pants. So, I dived behind a lifeboat, removed my trousers, took off my pants, put my trousers back on and emerged triumphantly holding my underwear in the air. Of course, all the other contestants were American and had simply removed their trousers. I came last.

Another game was to imitate James Bond saying, My name is Bond. James Bond. Double O Seven licensed to kill." I did this in my best Roger Moore voice (I do a mean Roger Moore impression). All the others were drawling the words in broad American accents. The prize was a bottle of champagne, and I was already deciding whether to drink it right away or give it to someone as a present when the results came through. I came last again. How was that possible?

Back from the Caribbean and suitably refreshed, tanned, and with batteries recharged, the next stop was Prague, the beautiful capital of Czechoslovakia, in early November. I'd been there as a child on a family holiday, and again as a teenager but not since. Several thousand East German refugees were camped inside the West German Embassy. The grounds of the embassy were packed, with more people flooding in. Erich Honecker had resigned as GDR leader in October and been replaced by Egon Krenz who appeared to be trying to walk a reforming path. It wasn't helping. There were huge demonstrations in several East German cities, the largest in Leipzig on October 30th. They culminated in an estimated one million people marching in East Berlin in early November, but they were simply demanding reforms. Few if any could foresee what was about to happen.

I was working with a freelance Czech crew, cameraman Csaba, who spoke no English and sound recordist Gabor, a Hungarian physicist who had never been anywhere near television equipment or a TV station in his life. It was hard work, but their enthusiasm made up for their shortcomings. They were also convinced that Hungary was on the brink of 'democracy and freedom'.

The next day we drove up to Karlovy Vary (formerly Carlsbad). It was a hair-raising, terrifying white-knuckle ride. Csaba drove like a lunatic, tailgating and flashing everyone to get out of his way. From Karlovy Vary, we headed to the small border town of Cheb where East German refugees were crossing the border into Czechoslovakia. It was a strange human tide, a sense of desperation overridden by hope and expectation.

Only later did someone from the company from whom I'd hired the crew ask me, "How was Csaba's driving?" and told me that Csaba was not really a professional cameraman at all (I'd worked that out for myself!). He was, in fact, a professional rally driver!

Next morning, November 6th, I left Csaba and Gabor at the border and walked across the Iron Curtain, No Man's Land, in the pouring rain. Quite an experience. I felt like a character in a John le Carré novel. I was supposed to meet a WTN cameraman, but there was no sign of him. There was one phone box and a long line of East Germans waiting to use it. After queuing for an hour, I called WTN in Frankfurt and the ITN foreign desk to discover that the cameraman had been sent back to Frankfurt, leaving me stranded.

After a series of taxis and trains, I flew from Nuremberg, arriving in Frankfurt in the evening. A wasted day, but I still managed to record a piece to camera at Frankfurt airport with the latest information provided by the foreign desk and, with producer Mary Amthor, cut a more than passable package for *News at Ten*.

After a bit of sleep, it was back to Berlin to film our lovely family, the Lehmanns. Marina had found a job and we interviewed her at work. The children had found a school, and seemed very happy. Joachim had a job at a chocolate factory. Talk about landing on your feet! It was my first visit to a chocolate factory. I love the stuff.

On November 8th, we flew from Berlin to the quiet university town of Bonn, at the time the rather unlikely capital of West Germany, to cover Chancellor Helmut Kohl's State of the Nation speech. There was no hint in the speech of what was about to happen. Egon Bahr of the SPD was among the people I interviewed that day. He had been the architect of Willy Brandt's 'Ostpolitick'. He referred to the mass demonstrations in Leipzig and other East German cities, and to the flood of refugees coming to the West, but he too seemed to have no idea of the seismic, tectonic change that was about to happen.

Our plan was to return to Bavaria the next day to film at the over-crowded, makeshift refugee centres.

I was woken at one a.m. after just one hour's sleep for the second consecutive night by the ITN Foreign Desk. There had been a ferry disaster in Hamburg. We set off an hour later. In fact, the ferry was called the 'Hamburg', and was limping into Bremerhaven. We got there in time to film and talk to the shaken passengers, sixty Brits among them, disembarking from a ferry with a hole the size of a double-decker bus in its side.

We sent our package, which led the lunchtime news, and had a quick lunch with my old friend Ben Brown, who was now working for the BBC. We also led the five forty early evening news, but then it happened: East German leader, Egon Krenz had declared the entire East German border open. He had had little choice after East Berlin party leader, Günter Schabowski, prematurely announced that the GDR government would allow East Germans unlimited access to West Germany immediately. Thousands took advantage, pouring past unprepared, uninformed and perplexed border guards.

We were to fly to Berlin at seven a.m. Mike Nolan on the foreign desk had suggested we drive overnight, but we were all sleep-deprived and decided that would be too dangerous. A mistake, as it turned out. What Mike knew, and we didn't, was that half of ITN was about to descend on Berlin. News editor and resident in-house wit Owen Smith, a scouser and one of the funniest men I'd ever met who really should have had a career in stand-up, put up a huge sign in the main ITN newsroom: *Will the last person going to Berlin please turn off the lights*.

After several phone calls with Head of Foreign News, Maggie Eales, in the early hours of the morning, we were diverted to Helmstadt on the internal German border to cover the thousands of people crossing the frontier. This had been my idea. If, as Maggie had told me, ITN was heading to Berlin en masse, we'd just get caught up in a huge ITN operation. We needed to find another angle, another way of telling the story.

Maggie couldn't get hold of me at first. Remember, this was in the days before mobile phones, so she was calling my hotel room. When she eventually got hold of me, after one of our Belgian cameramen had tracked me down, I told her I'd gone for a walk. In fact, I was in bed with a beautiful Belgian who I won't name to spare her blushes. Maggie wasn't fooled, and thereafter, 'he's gone for a walk' became a euphemism at ITN for what *Private Eye* calls 'Ugandan affairs!

I was familiar with the frontier post at Helmstadt. As a child and into early adulthood, I'd crossed here several times on family holidays. Now, it was unrecognisable. The border guards were still there, but they were no longer the stern-faced sentinels demanding to see our papers. Those severe faces were transformed into wide, beaming smiles as thousands of people laughed, cheered, sang, hugged and swigged from bottles of champagne. It was very emotional, and of course, provided great pictures.

I did a sententious (and probably slightly pompous) piece to camera, paraphrasing American President George Bush, about 'the end of the old order in Europe'.

As we fed out package that evening, we saw the astonishing live pictures from Berlin: they were dancing on top of the Berlin Wall. In retrospect, although we had some superb material, which was very well received back in London and had run as story three after Bill Neely in West Berlin and Ian Glover-James in East Berlin, we should have headed straight to Berlin and made the story our own. Of course, we had no idea that we would be witnessing such incredible scenes.

We wasted no more time and headed to Berlin. There were huge traffic jams going both ways across the border at Helmstadt. It took us two hours to get across. East to west, there was a thirty-mile traffic jam, but everyone was joyful, smiling and waving (and possibly very drunk!), sounding their horns, joy unconfined. My Belgian cameraman got some more great shots.

The streets of West Berlin were packed, East Berliners in their funny little Trabants and Wartburgs and their dowdy clothes, such a contrast to the fashionable West Berliners in their top-of-the-range Mercedes. They were one national family, and yet so very different.

We filmed at Berlin's exhibition centre, which had become the country's biggest refugee centre. Six hundred beds in the centre had been provided by the BAOR (British Army of the Rhine). We interviewed Housing Minister, Rita Hermanns, who turned up an hour late. Her reason/excuse? She had been caught up in the euphoria and had been dancing in the streets.

At the Brandenburg Gate, the bizarre spectacle of four ITN presenters (Jon Snow, Trevor McDonald, Alastair Stewart and John Suchet) interviewing one another live. This was a trend begun by the American networks, to send their main anchors to the big story. And they were there, Peter Jennings, Dan Rather, Tom Brockaw all anchoring from Berlin. We had four presenters apparently anchoring simultaneously and interviewing one another! From behind them, I could see that the very tall Jon Snow had been told to stand with his legs very wide apart so that he wouldn't tower over the other three! Meanwhile, fellow reporter David Chater and I were doing all the work! For the first time, I walked along the top of the Berlin Wall.

Early the next morning, I was filming part of the wall being torn down with cameraman John Martin and sound recordist Roger Dove, and people were now moving freely into West Berlin. More tears, more hugs, more champagne. At Invalidenstrasse, the Welsh Fusiliers were handing out tea and soup, so we interviewed the British Commandant, Berlin, Major-General Robert Corbett who, despite the obligatory British military stiff upper lip, was clearly as moved and excited as the rest of us. We also filmed at Spandau, where Rudolf Hess, Hitler's deputy, had been imprisoned until his death in 1987.

Berlin was a party town. Before the fall of the wall, and surrounded by hostile East Germany, it had seemed to epitomise 'eat, drink and be merry, for tomorrow we die'. So, work done and several drinks later, we decided to enjoy Berlin's fabled nightlife. A small group of us, including my friend ITN (and later Sky News) cameraman, Paul Dickie, headed off to a club someone (with a sense of humour!) had recommended. It was a gay bar! Being gay in West Berlin seemed to involve a lot of muscles, leather, tattoos, chains and moustaches! We quickly fled! We bumped into my Belgian crew, Dirk, Immanual and the lovely Ingrid Bertrand in somewhere called 'Big Sexyland'. The least said about that place the better.

By November 14th the plan was for the most of the ITN team to return to London, until we heard strong rumours that the wall was to come down in front of the Brandenburg Gate. The money shot!

With camera crew Paul Dickie and John Hunt, I headed across to East Berlin, followed by producer Sue Tinson, reporter, Ian Glover-James, cameraman Paul Carleton, and sound recordist Bernie Clancey. We stayed in the Grand Hotel. It was only too easy to imagine Hitler and his entourage descending the huge central staircase.

The wine list at the Grand Hotel was a tome, more than fifty pages long. It included a 1939 Château Lafite for, if I remember correctly, five thousand dollars. Could we see it? The waitress, all black leather boots and peroxide blonde hair, and no doubt the daughter of some apparatchik, frowned.

"We haff GDR vine."

"How about a Merlot?"

"We haff GDR vine." Paul Carleton lived on red wine. He rarely seemed to eat,

"OK," he said. "We'll try your GDR wine please."

It was almost undrinkable. Carleton, who has a frightfully posh upper middle class accent, told her that he had travelled the world and that, "My dear, your GDR wine is the finest I have ever tasted." He was upgraded to the Bach suite, the best in the hotel. The old charmer!

Next morning, we crossed Checkpoint Charlie (more childhood memories, I had crossed it several times), filmed at Potsdamer Platz and walked along the top of the wall next to the Brandenburg Gate. People were chipping away at the wall to collect souvenirs with small hammers which an enterprising Berliner was selling. The lovely ITN presenter Carol Barnes had arrived at Berlin and asked me to get her a piece of the wall. I began chipping away. As my hand went back, the hammer seemed to disappear into thin air. A German policeman had removed it from my grasp with a disapproving look. The cops had been walking behind everyone else removing their hammers. I guess there was no fixed penalty yet in force for this particular act of vandalism. Otherwise, I might have had to stump up some Deutschmarks.

The rumour persisted that the section of the wall next to the Brandenburg Gate was about to come down. There were also rumours that Russian leader Mikhail Gorbachev was coming to Berlin. British Foreign Secretary Douglas Hurd was definitely on his way. So, Carol and I and our camera crews were told to stay in Berlin.

To pass the time, I was asked to do a feature piece, an 'And Finally', on the smelly East German cars now cramming the streets of West Berlin. This was easy enough but I referred to 'two-stroke Skodas'. I liked the alliteration. The only problem was that they weren't Skodas! Trabants and Wartburgs, yes, but no Skodas. No one had noticed before the package was aired. *News at Ten* supremo Nick Pollard (who was later to be a superb Head of News at Sky News and, later still, boss at BFBS), who was running the operation at Berlin hadn't spotted it. Nor had anyone else, including several senior producers who had packed our edit room to review it before we sent it to London. Nor did anyone back at ITN. But the chairman of Skoda back in the UK did, and was demanding an apology and threatening to sue.

Shit! Shit! Shit! Bugger! Bugger!

I was mortified, and wanted to phone my bosses, Dave Mannion and Nigel Hancock, to apologise but Pollard wisely advised me not to. If any of our bosses wanted to talk to me they would call. Otherwise, he said, lie low, it will blow over. I was later told that the Skoda boss was offered and accepted lunch, a tour of ITN and our profound apologies.

That didn't stop the camera crews from taking the mickey in time-honoured fashion. John Martin thereafter and to this day referred to me as 'Glen O'Skoda', and still calls me 'Skode'.

More importantly, the wall by the Brandenburg Gate finally came down. Paul Carleton clambered onto the top of a large van to film it. At one point, he slipped and fell off, banging his chest on the edge of the van's roof on his way down. Undeterred and unflinchingly, he clambered back up and carried on filming, even though it later emerged that he had broken a rib. I would have been a pitiful wreck, howling in pain!

And so, back to London on November 17th where I watched on TV the huge demonstrations in Prague. Our reporter covering them was a veteran of several wars. He was superb at getting into inaccessible, dangerous places, and very good at reporting conflict. But his scriptwriting left something to be desired, and political analysis was completely beyond him. The foreign desk phoned to see if my Czech visa had expired. Unfortunately, it had. There had, incidentally, been absolutely no mention by anyone of my Skoda cock-up. Phew!

The next day, I was not off to Prague but Colchester, and a horribly familiar story: a soldier and his wife had been injured by an IRA car bomb. This led the news all day until the late evening, when three soldiers were killed by a landmine in Northern Ireland. Also horribly familiar.

At one point, crime correspondent Colin Baker, who was also something of a legend, appeared and probably could have taken over the story (something we call being 'big footed', it's horrible when it happens), but he graciously bowed out.

After three frustrating days, my Czech visa finally came through. Except for a pause to watch the House of Commons being televised for the first time (it's now hard to imagine PMQs without TV cameras, but that was how it had been until November 1989), I researched the situation in Czechoslovakia, reading up and making phone calls. The plan was for me and my team to cover the rest of the country, with a separate team covering the events in Prague.

We flew to Vienna, cameraman Alan Downes, sound recordist John Boyce, picture editor Bill Frost and I, and drove to the Slovakian capital, Bratislava. We had to wait for over three hours at the Austrian-Czech border in a snow blizzard, very John Le Carré. We pushed in and generally made a nuisance of ourselves. If we hadn't, we could have been stuck there for days.

Although the world's (and ITN's) attention was mostly focused on Prague, and specifically on Wenceslas Square, in the Slovakian capital tens of thousands of people were also congregating in the city's main square, calling for the overthrow of the government and an end to Communist rule.

Part of our mission was to secure an interview with Czechoslovakia's former leader, Alexander Dubček.

Following The Prague Spring of 1968 and the Soviet response to send in the tanks to restore order, Dubček was thrown out of the Communist Party and forced to work for over twenty years, in the Forestry Service. He remained a popular figure among both Slovaks and Czechs. Dubček and his wife, Anna, continued to live in a comfortable villa in a nice neighbourhood in Bratislava.

In 1988, Dubček had been allowed to travel to accept an honorary doctorate from Bologna University, and while he was there, gave an interview with Italian Communist Party daily newspaper *L'Unità*, his first press interview since 1970.

Our task was to get the first television interview with him.

Dubček supported the Public against Violence (VPN) and the Civic Forum, but power still hung in the balance. It was by no means certain that the revolution would succeed. People were nervous, fearing that the Soviet tanks might once again roll in.

Indeed, in our hotel I'd greeted the receptionists in my best but very limited Polish, which is very similar to Czech. Several times after that, as I approached reception, I heard them whispering to one another, "Be careful, he speaks Polish".

It took two weeks of meetings every day with anyone who had any connection to Dubček, most fruitfully through intermediaries with Dr Jan Čárnogurský, Václav Havel's constitutional adviser and an old friend of our target. It took them the two weeks to decide that they trusted me (and ITN), and he sent a message that Dubček would do the interview.

We had recruited a brilliant interpreter/fixer, Martin Petrik. Martin had two degrees, in maths and physics, and two brains! The revolution had begun with student demonstrations in Prague and Bratislava and they were soon supported by factory workers in their tens of thousands. We had gone to the university to find out what was going on from some English language speakers, and we found Martin.

For the modest sum of a hundred dollars a day, he would arrive at my hotel room at six thirty every morning to tell me what the newspapers and radio news were saying, which allowed me to then phone the foreign desk and show off!

Things were moving apace. Jan Čárnogurský had been released from prison. I had managed to chat to Dubček's wife, Anna, and had become friends with interpreter Susanna, whose father, George Veres, was a journalist who'd been banned from journalism since 1968 and was one of Dubček's closest friends. These were my 'Dubček watchers', the people I was hoping would get me an interview with the former Czechoslovakian leader. The anti-government protests in Bratislava were growing. The entire Central Communist Party of Czechoslovakia resigned, and the government in Prague abolished Clause Four of the country's constitution, the 'leading role' of the Communist Party. Just two weeks of intensive opposition had ended forty-five years of repression.

While we had been waiting for Dubček, we had been busy covering the story of the Velvet Revolution, including a general strike. With John Boyce and our interpreter, Martin, I went to film in some factories, and we found ourselves being invited into a workers' meeting in the Dimitrov Factory, where they made the notorious plastic explosive Semtex, the terrorists' favourite. That, in itself, was quite a scoop!

On November 30th, the Russians announced that they were to withdraw all their troops from Czechoslovakia. In other words, the Soviet occupation was over. I went to the local Red Army Headquarters to meet the Bratislava commander, the very charming Colonel Soktov who said he'd have to get permission to give us a filming facility and an interview. I was allowed in, but the crew were told to wait by the guardroom at the front gate. It was ten o'clock in the morning but the colonel produced bottles of vodka. We spent an amusing time together exchanging tall stories, but he wouldn't let the camera crew in. By the time I returned to them, I was somewhat the worse for wear. They filmed me walking, or rather staggering, back towards them!

Finally, on December 3rd Dubček agreed to an interview, encouraged by his wife, Anna, my notes and, crucially, a note recommending us from his friend George Veres. He had a pile of requests from other news organisations, but had decided to do just one interview, and it was to be with us the next day. Scoop City!

The interview itself, at Dubček's house, was the first he'd given for twenty-one years, and it showed. To say he didn't exactly speak in soundbites would be something of an understatement. I had with me one of ITN's most senior and respected cameramen, Alan Downes, and sound recordist John Boyce. In those days, we worked on tape, each of which lasted twenty minutes after which they had to be changed. I asked Dubček the first question, something very open along the lines of, "What do you think of what is happening in your country ? Is it a genuine revolution and will it succeed?"

Twenty minutes later, Alan had to call, "Tape change", and halt the interview while he out a new tape in the camera.

Dubček had only reached 1971 (something about shoe production! Really!), having started in 1968. It was a long interview even though we had a fantastic interpreter, Jan, who was translating almost simultaneously. Dubček felt like that thing he was, an old-style communist leader, albeit a humane and reforming one, trying to come to terms with seismic changes frankly beyond the comprehension of any party leader who had been nurtured and risen to power during the Soviet Communist era.

It was exhausting!

More importantly, it was very long, and as ever, we were on a tight deadline to get the interview edited down and packaged. Back at the TV studio in Bratislava, which VT editor Bill Frost (another ITN legend) had made his own, we set to work. The only way into and out of the building was by climbing scaffolding at the back. The police were guarding the front, and inside the place was crawling with secret police. Bill did a fantastic job, and we sent a four-minute piece to lead that night's *News at Ten*.

Bill Frost, by the way, was a mad Spurs fan, despite being Irish! He also has a tremendous sense of humour and mischief. So when, a few days after our interview, Dubček was due to address a crowd of between one hundred thousand and two hundred and fifty thousand (estimates vary) enthusiastic supporters in Bratislava, they chanted as they were waiting for him, "We want Dubček".

All of them, that is, except for a group of twenty or thirty people gathered around Bill Frost who was leading them in a chant of, "Where's Glenn Hoddle?"

Our fixer/interpreter, Martin, was completely perplexed by this, having no idea who the Spurs and England footballer was (or, for that matter, what football is).

He'd also been the victim of Bill's sense of humour one morning when, as he was telling me what the Czech press was reporting about the progress of the revolution, Bill suddenly asked him, "Yes, that's all very well, but did Spurs win?"

Martin, a very serious and conscientious soul, looked crestfallen. He'd been asked a question he didn't understand, let alone know the answer to!

A good interpreter is vital, and Martin was first class. I'm reminded of the story of the senior British army officer in Bosnia who was being obstructed by a local town mayor and his flunkies.

"Look", he said. "Tell him if he doesn't do it heads will roll."

Which was translated as, "He says if you don't do what he's telling you to do he'll cut off your heads and roll them down that hill over there!" Full compliance was quickly forthcoming!

Martin got his revenge on December 6th, the day the border between Czechoslovakia and Austria was officially opened. It was a short drive to Vienna, but travel to the Austrian capital had, of course, been forbidden. So the whole of Slovakia, or so it seemed, decided to go to Vienna for breakfast. Thousands of cars were driving past us, their occupants leaning out of the windows giving the V for victory salute and shouting, 'svoboda' (freedom). I'd given Martin the day off so that he too could celebrate. As we were filming, I spotted him in a car full of friends, tooting the horn and making a lot of noise. I said to Alan and John, "Look, there's Martin. Let's get a 'svoboda' from him and stick him on the telly."

As Martin and his friends passed us, driving very slowly, they leaned out of the windows and gave us a rousing chorus of, "Where's Glenn Hoddle?"

Dubček might have become president of the new Czechoslovakia, but he considered the revolution a chance to continue the work he had started twenty years earlier, misjudging the mood of the country. People wanted absolutely nothing to do with any form of communism, not even Dubček's liberal version. He was also out-of-step with the mood in his native Slovakia. Dubcek supported the continuation of a united Czechoslovakia, but his Slovak countrymen wanted their own country which, of course, is what subsequently came to pass.

He was, however, elected chairman of the Federal Assembly (the Czechoslovak parliament) on 28th December 1989, and re-elected in 1990 and 1992. He died that November.

A few days later, we were beside the Danube, the border between Austria and Slovakia, on the Slovakian side where there was a rusty barbed wire fence, literally an Iron Curtain. A week earlier, we would not have been allowed to film there. We'd have been arrested as spies, just as we would have been if we'd been caught filming some of the shots we took in East Germany that summer. Now, we could take our viewers behind the Iron Curtain.

Beside the fence lay a spent bullet cartridge. Had someone been shot at by border guards as they tried to swim to freedom in the West? I still have the cartridge at home. It sits next to a small, Slovakian fabric lapel flag from that time. I hope to God he or she got safely across the river.

As a postscript to this, the ITV documentary programme, *World in Action*, did an interview with Dubček in January, 1990, which they trailed as, 'his first interview' since 1968. I asked my ITN bosses to point out to them that this wasn't the case, but no one did. I guess it wasn't worth the trouble, or maybe it just depended on your definition of 'interview'. A long news package for *News at Ten*, or a stand-alone interview filling an entire programme.

For twenty-four hours we basked in the praise for our world exclusive Dubček interview, but then it was time to fly home. The foreign desk called: could I cover Neil Kinnock's visit to Germany? The crew had to get home, family commitments, but the foreign desk would find me another, probably freelance. So, I bade farewell to my great team Alan, John and Bill, and Martin Petrick drove me to Vienna. This time, we crossed the Czechoslovakian-Austrian border in less than two minutes. From Vienna, I flew to Düsseldorf where I discovered, to my delight, that my new cameraman was Paul Carleton. We travelled to Berlin from RAF Wildenrath to RAF Gatow with Neil Kinnock in an RAF Andover, and interviewed the Labour leader on board. At this time, December 1989, Margaret Thatcher's leadership was coming under increasing fire and Neil Kinnock had a good chance of winning the next general election and becoming prime minister. He was loquacious to say the least, which led to the *Daily Mail* and others dubbing him the 'Welsh windbag'. On the many occasions I met him, I always found him to be very open, full of great and often very funny anecdotes, and excellent company.

Kinnock's visit to Berlin involved a seemingly endless round of meetings with German politicians and photo-ops at the Reichstag, the Brandenburg Gate, and in East Berlin. He was clearly excited to be there, and intrigued by the political direction that a unified Germany might take. Officially, unification was to take almost another year (October 3rd 1990), but everyone was looking ahead to the new Germanys' place in Europe and the world.

I teamed up with German freelance cameraman, the marvellously-named Dietmar Hack. We were to go to Leipzig, now something of a 'Hero City', where the anti-East German government protests had begun. To be as inconspicuous as possible, we hired a small car, a Fiat Uno, hoping we'd stand out less than we would if we'd been driving a big, flashy Merc. In fact, once we were on the East German autobahns, still unchanged since they were created by Hitler in the 1930s, we were the fastest thing on the road!

I was used to East Germany being grey, drab and depressing. I'd been several times before. What I hadn't previously noticed was the appalling level of pollution. En route, we stopped at Bitterfeld to film chimneys spewing black smoke. We also covertly filmed Russian soldiers, still very much in evidence.

In Leipzig, we spoke to Edgar Dunstall, one of the leaders of 'New Forum', the group at the forefront of the opposition to the communist government. We came across American reporter, Jack Lawrence, and his crew from ABC who were openly filming on the streets. It seemed our 'secret squirrel' covert filming was no longer necessary.

Leipzig looked like it hadn't changed at all since 1945. As in East Berlin, many buildings still carried the scars of war, peppered by bullet holes. I took a photo of a long residential street, still cobble-stoned and with a single parked car, just one, in a four-hundred-metre stretch. The image seemed to perfectly illustrate the Cold War era. More John Le Carré!

The money shot in Leipzig was the Stasi headquarters. ITN camera crew Eugene Campbell and Chris Angwin had been sent from West Berlin to work with us. The Stasi secret police building, from where the communist regime had kept Leipzig's citizens under the heel, was now a scene of jubilation. Inside, New Forum activists, the self-styled "citizens' committee", were hurling Stasi files out of the windows to a cheering crowd below. It seemed a mistake to destroy the evidence, but everyone was caught up in the spirit of the moment. Liberation! Freedom! Victory!

We found the Stasi boss, Colonel Reinhard Ebbish, now relieved of his duties. To my amazement, he agreed to be interviewed on camera. Together with Eugene's astonishing pictures, this made the story. A mini-scoop. Later, after we'd fed our story for *News at Ten*, the verdict came back from ITN in London: 'sensational'. But not in a pejorative sense. They loved it.

Never fall asleep at dinner with ITN people. We were once at a Chinese restaurant at the south coast of England when one of the team made that mistake. We paid the bill and left him there, telling the waiters to wake him up and tell him we had left without paying. Two minutes later, he ran out of the restaurant in a panic, cursing us. He saw the funny side once he'd calmed down.

On December 14th, we were back at the Grand Hotel in East Berlin. We'd had one of those ITN dinners involving a large team and industrial quantities of alcohol. One of the cameramen, who I won't name to save his blushes, nodded off. We shook him awake and told him with great urgency and absolutely straight faces that Egon Krenz had gone mad and was riding a unicycle on top of the Berlin Wall. He had to go and get the shots right away. He snapped into sober, professional mode, grabbed his camera and rushed out of the door. A moment later he was back. "Bastards!"

We spent more time in Berlin and Leipzig telling the stories of the aftermath of the fall of the Berlin Wall, working with ITN crews and our lovely WTN producer, Mary Amthor, and fantastic interpreter/fixer, Connie Rudat. But the spotlight was moving south, to Romania.

In the wake of Berlin and Czechoslovakia, workers and students in Romania had been organising mass strikes. There was the pivotal moment when communist dictator, Nicolae Ceauşescu, had addressed a crowd from a balcony in Bucharest. Many in the crowd had been hand-picked and bussed in by the Securitate to cheer The Leader. Now though, they booed. It began quietly, but grew in volume and intensity. A perplexed Ceauşescu, his face drained of colour, withdrew back inside. He looked completely bewildered. He may or may not have realised it, but the game was up.

By December 22nd, he had fallen and was under arrest. A dictator removed so quickly, almost in the blink of an eye. The ITN foreign desk was trying to get us and teams from London into Romania, but it was proving to be difficult. The country was in a state of civil war, the bureaucracy had effectively ceased to exist. The ITN circus was en route, more than thirty journalists and camera crews. Some were already in Bucharest and filing tremendous stories.

Finally, finally, on Christmas Eve, we were sent too. As in Czechoslovakia, ITN was already well covered in the capital city, so my task was basically to cover the rest of the country.

I flew to the Hungarian capital Budapest with Paul Carleton and Tony Hemmings, where we were met by producer John Toker, who had hired a Volvo estate promising the hire company that we were planning to film a documentary in Hungary, and good grief, had absolutely no intention of driving to Romania. Perish the thought!

We drove straight to the border town of Szeged. Senior ITN producer Sue Tinson told us she wanted us to do something potentially dangerous the next day, but it was up to us whether or not to do it. The plan was to go to a town called Sibiu, where heavy fighting was continuing. No journalists had got there yet. We were to go in convoy with MSF (Médicins Sans Frontières), even though Red Cross convoys had been shot to pieces. Of course, the answer was Yes.

After just one hour's sleep (this was becoming far too common!), we began Christmas Day 1989 tagging along behind an MSF convoy full of enthusiastic, dedicated and brave people. They drove incredibly slowly, and it took us most of the day to get to Sibiu. The only precaution they had taken was to attach a large steel sheet to the back of one of their coaches, protecting the rear window. The people along the way, and at the dozens of roadblocks were friendly and excited, shouting, "Freedom", "Liberty", and so on, just as they had in Czechoslovakia. But these people were armed, and more than a little nervous.

We arrived in Sibiu as darkness was falling. The MSF aid workers were welcomed as heroes which, in my opinion, they were. We filmed them meeting local doctors, unloading medical supplies and getting briefed on the local situation. Then we were taken to a nearby motorway. There were more than sixty bullet-ridden bodies lying on or beside the road, including that of a two-year-old boy. We were told they had been killed by the Securitate, Ceauşescu's notorious secret police militia. These weren't the first dead bodies I'd seen, but I had never seen so many.

The Securitate were far more than simply secret police or Ceauşescu's Praetorian Guard. They were an army, well-trained and well-armed and designed to be a match for the official Romanian army should the generals ever attempt a military coup.

And on that Christmas Day, Nicolae Ceauşescu and his wife, Elena, were tried and executed, taken behind a building and shot dead by a firing squad, the news and the disturbing images brought to us by ITN reporter Paul Davies and his excellent team in Bucharest.

Boxing Day was spent in hospitals and at the local mortuary. Bodies were laid out in a courtyard with locals peering in from the outside which seemed ghoulish, but they were simply there to see if anyone they knew had been killed. In the main hospital, doctors were treating a Securitate man injured in the fighting. Not surprisingly, he didn't want to talk to us.

Sibiu, in Transylvania and nearly two hundred miles north of Budapest, was the stronghold of Ceauşescu's son, Nico, and those loyal to him. We filmed the aftermath of what had clearly been some heavy fighting. Burnt out cars, a destroyed APC, and too many bullet holes to count. Artillery and mortars had been used, as well as machine guns, as the Securitate and the Romanian army, supplemented by students from the Sibiu Military Academy, fought a pitched battle for control of the city.

In Cluj, my Belgian friend, picture editor Ingrid, was still shaking. She and her team had been caught in the crossfire during a shoot-out between the Securitate and the Romanian army They were in their car in the main town square when they came under fire, her correspondent had been shot and she was lying in his blood as the battle raged. Now, several hours later, she was sobbing on my shoulder.

Our stories from Sibiu and Cluj led the news for the next twenty-four hours, along with reports from Timişoara, where the revolution (if that's what it was) had begun.

Timişoara was a small, ethically Hungarian city in Transylvania. The Securitate had tried to arrest a local cleric, Pastor Lazlo Tokes, but hundreds of people had gathered around his house and prevented his arrest. Tanks had been sent in, people had been killed, but what had begun as a little local difficulty became the spark of a revolution.

Our next task was to find the priest, Pastor Lazlo Tokes, who had escaped and was rumoured to be hiding somewhere in Transylvania. We had learnt that he was in a remote village and was being protected by the army. This in itself was an astonishing development. The loyalty of the army was now in doubt and would lead to crowds in Bucharest chanting, "The army is with us".

We drove up through the Transylvanian hills. The 'road' was so bad and potholed, in places it was little more than a dirt track. I have a photograph of Paul and Tony gleefully holding up the undercarriage of our very robust Volvo, which had been smashed off. Don't tell the hire company in Budapest!

In the industrial Transylvanian steel town of Zalău, high in the mountains, we found a hotel. Zalău is surrounded by a beautiful national park. It is also an ideal bandit country. We had to eat and drink in my room, because there was not enough alcohol in the place and receptionist Mia and her husband, Puiu, did not want the dozens of steel workers in the bar to see us drinking. Everyone here seemed convinced that the priest was in Bucharest.

I was woken the next morning by Puiu knocking on the door with what he had decided was his secret password: "Dracula has arrived!" I sent him to Carleton's room with the same message. Puiu's English was fairly good, but not good enough to employ as our interpreter, so he introduced us to his English teacher, Monica. Eventually, we discovered that Lazlo Tokes was hiding in a small village called Mineu, several miles up another potholed dirt track, very remote. When we got there, we found his wife, Edith, who confirmed his presence but said he was out for the day and would be back at about six p.m. We headed to the nearby town of Cebu Sylvania for drinks with members of the local council of the 'committee for national salvation', who confirmed that Pastor Tokes was indeed being protected by the army, although we had seen no sign of any soldiers in Mineu. When we returned to the village, we did our interview with Lazlo Tokes, the man who had inadvertently kick-started the Romanian revolution.

We stayed that night in a hotel in Cebu Sylvania. There was no running water, and nothing to eat or drink. Dan, from the Committee for National Salvation, came to our rescue, bringing bread and salami, and most importantly, beer and the local *puccine*, which he had purloined from the town's mayor.

Monica, our translator, was taken to giggling spontaneously in the back of the car. When I asked her why she was laughing, she would say it was simply because she was talking to us in English, something that would have been unthinkable just two weeks before. Puiu had also told us that two just weeks earlier he would have been arrested simply for talking to us.

Our Lazlo Tokes world exclusive interview was very well received back in London, and so we richly deserved our New Year's Eve celebration back in the border town of Szeged. We saw in the New Year amid wild scenes. Gypsy bands, dancing, drinking, and with both ethnic Hungarians and Romanians shouting, "Victoria!", and "Libertate Romania!"

Just as a postscript to this amazing year, I'm often asked what was the best story I've ever covered, or who was the most interesting person I've interviewed? I have always found those questions impossible to answer, but the fall of the wall is right up there. ITN won the RTS (Royal Television Society) award that year for coverage of a news event; The Fall of The Berlin Wall. I was among the list of those mentioned in the citation.

After Germany, Czechoslovakia and Romania, we were mischievously looking across to other East European countries. Which might be next to go? Bulgaria, perhaps? Or Albania?

The news spotlight was already moving on. The next seismic change was to come in Moscow.

CHAPTER 5

1990: Towyn. London Poll Tax Riot. Damascus. Kashmir. Saddam invades Kuwait. Thatcher goes. Washington

1990 began with shaking off the hangover from our New Year's Eve party in Szeged before driving to Budapest. I had never spent much time in the Hungarian capital and we had a couple of hours to admire the panoramic Citadel, and from across the Danube, the magnificent parliament building before for our lunchtime flight to Amsterdam via Prague and on to Heathrow and home.

ITN editor-in-chief, Stewart Purvis, phoned with congratulations for our work over the previous few weeks. He'd been at Gatwick airport with champagne to welcome the ITN-chartered plane bringing the team back from Bucharest, but I had 'slipped through the net'.

What a year 1989 had been. What would this new year and this new decade bring?

First, though, some time off to catch up with friends, family and life in general, two weeks of well-earned normality. Dinners and pubs in London, visiting friends in Newcastle, the Lake District and Paris. Decompressing.

For the rest of January I covered stories that will barely be remembered now: in Manchester, Deputy Chief Constable John Stalker and the so-called 'shoot to kill' policy in Northern Ireland; an interview with John Waite, the cousin of Church of England envoy, Terry Waite, who was still being held hostage in Beirut; tennis star John McEnroe being thrown out of the Australian Open for bad behaviour; and a tribunal hearing for former Grenadier Guardsman Winston Lindsay, who was black and was claiming racial discrimination against the British army.

Our esteemed colleague, Trevor McDonald, was the subject of the TV show *This is your Life*!

In early February I was working on the Salman Rushdie story. He was the subject of a fatwa. *The Satanic Verses* had upset the wrong people. Although passions were running high in the Muslim community in Britain as elsewhere, most of the Muslim leaders I interviewed regarded the issuing of a fatwa as monstrously out of proportion.

There was also another interview with Prime Minister Margaret Thatcher when she presented awards for achievement and bravery to one hundred and fifty children, something she did rather well and for more than two hours.

Then, in mid-February, it was back to Germany. On the fight to Berlin, I sat next to the great actor Ben Kingsley, who was on his way to the Berlin Film Festival. He was friendly and very chatty. I was simply star-struck.

The next day, I was crossing Checkpoint Charlie once again, and then driving to Leipzig where we filmed in factories and were invited into factory workers' homes to get a sense of how the new freedom was affecting their lives. Their every move was no longer being watched and recorded by the Stasi and their new freedom allowed them to say whatever they wanted to. Our stories made it to air, just, but we were in the wrong place. In South Africa, Nelson Mandela was released from prison on February 11th, after being incarcerated for twenty-seven years. That story belonged to ITN South Africa correspondent, Jeremy Thompson, but a team had also been sent from London. Sadly, I was not among them, so we watched that famous Walk to Freedom on TV in Germany.

I had been an anti-apartheid activist in my student days, campaigning for Mandela's release. I would have loved so much to have been there.

Our stories from Leipzig, Dresden and East Berlin were just about getting on air, but the news agenda was being dominated by South Africa. We were squeezed out of the news running order two days after Mandela's release, when he addressed a packed football stadium in Soweto. Like just about everyone else in the world, we were watching. In my case, with a sense of awe and a desperate desire to be in Soweto at that moment.

Many years later, I was to meet Nelson Mandela when he was the keynote speaker at a Labour Party conference. Even in old age, his charisma was tangible, almost physical.

At home, the rest of February and March were spent covering a range of domestic stories. In Brighton, the beach was closed after canisters of potassium cyanide had been washed ashore. Britain was hit by severe storms and several people were killed. I spent days on that hardy perennial, the 'weather wrap', pulling together pictures from around the country, updated for each news bulletin.

There had been severe flooding in Towyn, a seaside resort in North Wales. So I spent a few days there covering the story with ITN camera crew Bob Hammond and Paul Dickie. A sea surge had overwhelmed the town's sea defences and hundreds of tons of sea water had gushed through the streets. More than a thousand homes had to be evacuated, thousands of people were unable to return home for months.

The crew got some excellent shots from a helicopter, and we worked all night filming the evacuations. By daylight, we filmed at Bodelwyddan Castle, which had been transformed into the main evacuation centre. The following day, Prince Charles and Diana, Princess of Wales, came to visit what had become a disaster zone. We had met and befriended the Davies family at Bodelwyddan Castle and taken them to inspect their ruined home. Now, we wired them up for their meeting with the Prince of Wales. If we weren't allowed to doorstep members of the royal family, we (and by we, I mean our audience) could at least hear what they were saying. A bit naughty perhaps, but Prince Charles came across as deeply sympathetic. Our story led *News at Ten*.

We spent three more days in Towyn, mostly focusing on the cleaning-up operation, firemen pumping water out of homes as the water level in the town dropped, gas and electricity supplies being restored to areas on the edge of town, and of course, a lot of 'people stories' telling the traumatic experiences they had endured.

On our last day, a Sunday, we filmed the church service at St George's Church, interviewed the vicar and town's mayor, Gareth Parry. Meanwhile, ITN crew Frank Harding and Keith Edwards were getting more dramatic shots from the sea wall, and I had other crews filming other elements: clothes and blankets being donated at the evacuation centres; people returning to their homes to inspect the devastation. We had told the story of Towyn, but it was to take that pretty Welsh seaside town years to fully recover.

I hadn't interviewed Arthur Scargill since the end of the miners' strike. Now, while we were still in Towyn, a story was breaking which claimed that he had, in effect, stolen money from the NUM during the strike. We drove to Sheffield, to the NUM headquarters, and I conducted a long interview with Scargill who was forthcoming and predictably outraged by the allegations. We fed our story for the five forty early evening news, and then took Scargill to Yorkshire Television (YTV) to watch the *Cook Report*, Roger Cook with more shock-horror revelations. Scargill's reaction, off camera, was "What a load of bollocks!"

He did a live interview with Jon Snow into *Channel 4 News*, and I interviewed him again at length for *News at Ten*. We stuck with the Scargill story for a few days. At one point, a fellow ITN reporter turned up demanding to do the package for the lunchtime news. I didn't mind. Producer Chris Jamieson had remarked "He's not a team player", a serious condemnation in our business.

There were plenty of lighter moments, covering the news isn't always doom and gloom. Among our stories from the north of England that March we covered the World Student Games in Sheffield. Protests against the poll tax were increasing around the country. We went to The Morecambe Conservative Club where the local Conservative Association was threatening to resign en masse in protest. There were some marvellous characters straight out of central casting. Alan Bennett would have had a field day!

We were scrambled to Liverpool to film picket lines of ambulance men and women on strike only to discover that no such picket lines existed! But there was a strike, and they had a strike headquarters, so we covered the story from there. Our efforts were cut short when the news desk suddenly sent us to Dublin. The extradition of two suspected terrorists to the UK had been refused by the Irish Supreme Court. We interviewed several of the main politicians involved and other protagonists, but our material was fed into a pull-together edited in London so we were told to fly back to Manchester from where we covered Manchester's failed bid to host the 1996 Olympic Games.

And so March passed, covering stories mostly in the north of England, and most of them strikes and crime stories. Those northerners, it seemed to me, were overly fond of murdering one another!

Three weeks after the floods in Towyn, we returned to see how the town was coping. This was one of those rare things, a follow-up story. All too often, we cover a story and, after the news spotlight moves elsewhere, never return. We spoke to many of the people we'd met three weeks earlier, including the Davies family, the vicar and Towyn's mayor. We also interviewed families who had been moved to Pontins at Prestatyn, now an evacuation centre. Surrounded by barbed wire fences, it looked like a stalag. We decided it had been designed that way, not to deter anyone from breaking in but to keep the Pontin's holidaymakers captive.

At the end of March, we covered Lord Justice Taylor's inquiry into Hillsborough. There were no surprises as we had known for weeks what his conclusions would be.

The poll tax protests were gathering pace. On March 30th, I was in Chingford, Essex, to cover a speech by Norman Tebbit who, like his boss the prime minister, was taking a hard line.

The next day, the protests erupted into a riot in central London. On a warm sunny day, I headed off with my crew, Ted Henley and Dave Prime. Outside Downing Street, most of the protesters were peaceful but a small group of anarchists were clearly intent on trouble. Missiles started flying and the mood turned ugly. The police decided to clear the area, as the main body of the march was still streaming by on its way to Trafalgar Square. But the crowd in Whitehall had grown, and was growing uglier.

I had been in riots abroad, in Europe and in Rawalpindi, where the crowds had parted and swarmed around us, respecting our neutrality. This time, though, we were being treated as the enemy. "*News at Ten*. Lies at Ten", was the chant, as we were shoved, jostled and spat at. Missiles, bottles and bricks, were flying. Mounted police arrived, probably prematurely. The crowd took their arrival as an act of provocation.

In Trafalgar Square, Tony Benn was addressing the rally, oblivious to the riot now building up in Whitehall.

We edited a package for the early evening news. I worked with picture editor Peter Reid in an edit van in Northumberland Street. It had been frightening, and we had been lucky to escape unscathed. Now, the anti-poll tax rioters were rocking our edit van as we worked.

Earlier, I had messaged the news desk that the protest was getting ugly, and this was getting very big. Eventually, the bizarre reply came back. "Please call news desk, we think there's been some trouble in Downing Street." I told the news desk to send as many crews as possible, and soon they were turning up, among them Mike Inglis, Eugene Campbell, Chris Squires and Rob Dukes, who got some fantastic pictures. They were, as ever, incredibly brave and were filming where the violence was at its worst.

By now the street fighting had become serious and the riot police were deploying in force. We did a newsflash at six o'clock, by which time South Africa House in Trafalgar Square was on fire and thousands of rioters were involved in running street battles, which had spread as far as Leicester Square.

At one point, a rioter was threatening my cameraman, Ted Henley, with a piece of scaffolding. I gave him twenty pounds to go away (only 'go away' were not quite the words I used) and he did.

We decided to climb some nearby scaffolding in Trafalgar Square to get a better view and some topshots of what was going on. Meanwhile, Mike Inglis, Ray Cheeseman, Eugene Campbell, Chris Squires and others were right in the thick of it, filming up close the hand-to-hand fighting. The images were astonishing. Probably the most famous of them was a protestor hurling a piece of scaffolding through the open front window of a police car as it sped across Trafalgar Square.

Later that evening, once Trafalgar Square had been cleared by the police and things had calmed down, we drank into the small hours. As far as I was concerned we were toasting the ITN camera crews, who had been absolutely heroic.

We were nominated for a BAFTA award. We should have won given the fantastic work of our camera crews, but the BBC pipped us at the post with their live coverage of the Strangeways prison riot in Manchester. Strangeways was a big story, and it ended right in the middle of the BBC *Six O'clock News*. Back then, live news coverage was fairly rare. It was technically difficult and extremely cumbersome. When ITN had done the first-ever lives from the Great Wall of China, it had involved helicoptering fourteen large flight cases onto the top of the wall. So, by virtue of its live coverage, the BBC picked up the BAFTA.

The next day was a case of, 'Wow! Follow that!' Nursing a dreadful hangover, I covered the aftermath story all day, leading the news. However, the story was already being overshadowed by events in Manchester. The spotlight had moved to Strangeways, where the twenty-five-day prison riot and rooftop protest had begun. One prisoner was killed and nearly two hundred prisoners and prison officers injured.

On April 1st, the day the riot started, initial but unconfirmed reports were suggesting as many as ten people had been killed.

I never did get to Strangeways, ITN was very well covered, but I did get to go to Paris for a story on a new anti-rabies serum, covered a Norwegian ferry disaster, and another prison riot, at Dartmoor where, on April 7th, a hundred prisoners took over the jail's D wing.

We arrived at Dartmoor prison in the early hours of the morning. A fellow reporter, the same one who had been described to me as 'not a team player' in Sheffield the previous month, appeared at midday, apparently expecting to swan in and do the live two-way for the lunchtime news. I was completely relaxed about this, as I knew I would get on air with the story later that day. This time, though, the news desk insisted I do it. We sat down afterwards, after he'd stopped having a hissy fit, cleared the air and worked out a plan to cover the story.

God only knows how producers and news editors cope with some egomaniac reporters. I always (well, almost always!) managed to keep my ego under control.

In the event, it was all over in twenty-four hours. Another Strangeways it was not. We were about to head for home when news broke of another (copycat?) prison riot, this time in Bristol. The prison was literally across the road from my friend Rory McLean's house. Now working for BBC Radio, he had already begun filing reports for Radio Four. What a stroke of luck! We got some excellent shots from Rory's first floor window. At the rear of the prison, we managed to get some shouted interviews with some of the prisoners on the roof.

The Bristol prison protest was even shorter than the one at Dartmoor, it lasted just a few hours. We told the story all day. Before we left, I read a bedtime story to Rory's sons, Jamie and Robin. Jamie, the eldest, is one of my godchildren, although I confess, I am a rather negligent godfather.

A week later, it was back to Sheffield for the Hillsborough inquest. The coroner, Dr Stefan Popper, was incredibly long-winded. Didn't he realise we had deadlines! We got on air for all bulletins, and the next day, visited the stadium with the inquest jury and filmed them discreetly. This was done with the blessing of the police, but I was later told that the coroner was apoplectic when he was told (and saw on the news!) what we had done.

At the end of April, I had been staying with friends in the Lake District when the news desk phoned, early in the morning, absolutely desperate for someone to work that day. I couldn't believe it. I was three hundred miles away and on a break. But they really couldn't find another reporter (obviously better at hiding than I was!) so, instead of a long walk and a leisurely lunch, I had to leave before breakfast and drive back to London. At first, it was a quiet news day, but French TV channel TF1 had got hold of the video of the Ceauşescu trial and execution last Christmas Day, including very disturbing images of Elena Ceauşescu screaming, raging, and pleading for her life. We edited the package for the late news bulletin but it was decided, correctly in my view, not to run it. It was an important historical document, but as a news item seemed needlessly sensationalist.

I took some leave. As well as visiting friends in Scotland, for much of May I was back cruising in the Caribbean, courtesy of my sister. This is not a travelogue or stories from my holidays, but I thought I would share just one story from this cruise. Apart from the obvious beauty of the islands we visited and the Mayan ruins at Chichen Itza and Tulum, there was also onboard entertainment. This was very hit and miss. The crew doing a 'fashion show' was a low point, but also hilarious since I knew them all and most were beyond embarrassed. The highlight was the fabulous Motown group, The Temptations. They performed in a storm, the ship was lurching from side to side. Every few minutes, one of the Temptations fled from the stage to vomit. But they still managed to render a perfect and beautiful 'My Girl'.

I also spent some time in Miami, and drove down to Key West for the first time. I had always been a big fan of Ernest Hemmingway (the writer, not the man), so this was a special treat.

Having recovered from my Caribbean adventure (I think the sign of a good holiday is that you come home spiritually refreshed but physically exhausted!), it was back to Germany on June 1st. A British army major had been shot dead by the IRA. By the time I arrived, my Belgian crew, Michel and Immanuel, had already shot the story. They had managed to get pictures of the IRA getaway car, which no one else had. It had been chased by the police before being abandoned. Fantastic work. There was still much to be done, interviewing eye witnesses and so on, but largely due to their efforts out story led the news all day.

Next morning, we were on an early flight to Paris and a three-hour drive to Joigny, where there had been a fatal bus crash, a British double-decker bus with seventy-six people onboard. At least twelve were feared dead, although the actual figure that later emerged was eleven with another sixty-one injured.

Our task the following day was to try to get an interview with the driver of the bus, John Johnston from Stoke-on-Trent. He had been injured and was in hospital in Auxerre. Several Fleet Street hacks were already there. Although the police had apparently interviewed him for five hours, there was no chance of speaking to him. So we interviewed a senior police officer and a British Embassy official and rushed back to Paris to feed for *News at Ten*.

As soon as we had done so, we had to drive to Brussels to cover a BSE (mad cow disease) story the next day.

From an IRA murder in Germany, to an horrific bus crash in France, to mad cow disease talks in Brussels: the strange life of an on-the-road ITN reporter!

In Brussels I worked with Belgian cameraman Dirk Van Capellan, sound recordist Immanuel, and my friend picture editor Ingrid Bertrand. She had recovered from her terrible experience in Romania, but was still having nightmares.

The talks on mad cow disease dragged on and on, an all-nighter like so many in Brussels. This scuppered our plan to get back to Paris to doorstep Nelson Mandela, who was visiting the French capital.

The talks in the Charlemagne building finally ended at four p.m., twenty-four hours after they had begun. We interviewed British minister, John Gummer, his French opposite number and a spokesman for the European Commission and sent the lead story for the five forty news. Having worked for thirty-four hours nonstop, the crew went home. I wanted to do the same, but the *News at Ten* producer wanted a re-cut to include some elements of the story to be inserted in London, so Ingrid and I carried on working to fulfil his desire.

Later I talked to Ingrid about her hideous experience in Romania. I hadn't realised the full extent of the horror. She had been trapped in heavy crossfire, while her reporter lay dead beside her, shot through the head. She herself had to play dead for six hours. No wonder she was still having nightmares.

As soon as we returned from Brussels, we were back in Bristol. The ALF (Animal Liberation Front) had reportedly carried out an attack and detonated a car bomb. The ALF denied responsibility, but a thirteen-month-old baby in a pushchair had been injured, suffering flash burns and shrapnel wounds. Horrific. We found baby John at the Bristol Royal Infirmary the next day, with his mother Sarah. His father, Jim, turned up a few minutes later with a team from the *Daily Mirror*, who had signed up the family for an exclusive and were far from happy to see us. Despite that, Sarah and Jim gave us their only TV interview, and we had the only TV pictures of baby John. A mini-scoop which led ITN bulletins all day, including *News at Ten*.

Sometimes, even rival news organisations have to work together and pool resources. If, for example, there were two exits to a building and we and the BBC had two crews between us, we would cover both exits and if the person we wanted emerged from one of them, we would share the pictures.

So it was that the next day, I interviewed Dr Max. Hedley of Bristol university, whose car had been blown up. The deadline for the lunchtime news was very tight, so I did a pooled interview for us and three other news organisations: HTV, the BBC and Sky News, which was still in its infancy but slowly growing in stature and credibility. Picture editor Gordon Hickey's fingers worked at lightning speed and we edited our package with just seconds to spare.

From Bristol to Doncaster for a poll tax story, then back to London for Gerry Conlon. He was one of the Guilford Four, wrongly convicted in 1975 of the IRA Guilford pub bombings. Conlon had always protested his innocence. His father, Giuseppe, who was also wrongly convicted, had died in prison in 1980. Now, after fifteen years in jail, a special inquiry had invalidated the forensic and other evidence on which they were convicted. Finally, Conlon was released in October 1990, after the Court of Appeal overturned his conviction. Later, Conlon's lawyer, Gareth Pierce, would also secure the release of the so-called Birmingham Six.

As a footnote, Conlon was very flatteringly portrayed by Daniel Day-Lewis in the 1993 film, *In the name of the Father*.

While most cameramen are professional to a fault, occasionally they need some diplomatic encouragement. ITN's Midlands-based cameraman Frank Harding was old school. He had seen it all. He had also taken some of the most memorable images of the miners' strike, at Orgreave. Frank was notorious for never using a tripod, preferring to work 'off the shoulder'. Unlike the modern, lightweight tripods, back then they were just another heavy piece of kit to carry. I personally hated carrying them, but it was usually the reporter's job to do so. I was always very happy when a cameraman, camera in one hand tripod in the other, would decline my offer to carry the tripod, saying he was 'perfectly balanced'.

Two days after the Conlon story, I met up with Frank and his sound recordist Russell Clements. We were to film Tornado jets taking off from the end of a runway as they flew towards us and over our heads. Great fun. The first two aircraft took off, with us standing at the end of the runway getting the shots (and getting deafened!). Frank had the camera on his shoulder, and I could tell from his movements that the shots might be a bit wobbly. They needed the stability of a tripod. So I went to the back of his car and made a great drama of pretending to blow dust and cobwebs off his tripod.

"Hey Frank. Look what I found."

He took the hint. The resulting video was fantastic.

In late June, a devastating earthquake hit Iran. The foreign desk was trying to get us in, probably on an aid flight. In the meantime, I interviewed a team of rescue workers from International Rescue (the organisation that would much later be led by David Miliband) who were preparing to fly to Tehran. In the end, I didn't go. Instead, I became that reporter based at ITN HQ pulling together the lead story from pictures coming into the building, while the poor buggers doing all the work on the ground (in this case, the team in Iran led by reporter Robert Moore) had to settle for story two. That would change in the following days as the Iran team produced some excellent work.

The IRA detonated a Semtex bomb at the Carlton Club in St James' Street, the original home of the Conservative Party. Cameraman Alan Downes and sound recordist Geoff Moyes were already filming the scene by the time I got there. Around twenty people had been injured when the ground floor of the building collapsed into the basement. Picture editor

Gordon Hickey wove his magic once again, editing a two-minute package in less than ten minutes, and we finished our edit just in time to roll it live at *News at Ten*. The crew quickly set up so I could do a live two-way as an update to end that night's news.

Details emerged, as usual, the next day. Fifteen pounds of Semtex, twenty people confirmed injured. Margaret Thatcher had visited soon after the explosion, and we interviewed Carlton Club chairman, Willie Whitelaw. It was still ITN's lead story.

The backdrop to that summer was Italia '90, The World Cup (football for those who don't know or don't care!). I had been in the newsroom when Ireland had beaten Romania in a penalty shoot-out. Every Irish goal was cheered to the rafters. Ireland lost their next game, a quarter-final, 1–0 to the hosts Italy. Now, on July 4th, it was England's turn to be eliminated in a penalty shoot-out with West Germany. We watched in horror as Stuart Pearce's penalty was saved and Chris Waddle blasted his over the crossbar, a moment which no doubt haunts him to this day.

Perhaps the greatest thing about Italia '90 was the theme music, Luciano Pavarotti's incomparable rendition of 'Nessum Dorma' from Puccini's *Turandot*, roughly translated as: 'None shall sleep… at dawn, I will win! I will win! I will win!'

The following weekend, I was at a friend's wedding at the Bank of England's sports club in East Sheen where the England football team had trained for the 1966 World Cup and where, by happy coincidence, my prep school team also trained. I still have the World Cup winning team's autographs buried somewhere in a drawer.

The foreign desk called. The Iranian news agency was reporting the imminent release of one of the European hostages being held in Beirut. It might be Brian Keenan, or possibly Terry Waite. I was to be one of a large ITN team being assembled to fly either to Cyprus or possibly Damascus. But it definitely, absolutely, would not be today. I was to be on standby for tomorrow.

I was at the wedding, and needless to say, another call came through not long afterwards. "Get to Heathrow now!" I did so, and met up with several other members of the team. The plan was to fly to Tel Aviv, charter a plane to Cyprus and then another onto Damascus. As it turned out, the plan fell apart and we flew direct to Cyprus the next morning. Wedding abandoned needlessly.

So it was that we spent a very pleasant few days at the Palm Beach Hotel in Larnaca. The Syrians did not want to let us into Damascus, despite our best efforts. We did not have mobile phones, inconceivable as that seems nowadays, so the ever innovative camera crews got telephone extensions to run to the side of the swimming pool so that we could make calls and wait for our Syrian visas to come through in maximum comfort.

The latest rumour was that it would indeed be Brian Keenan and that he would be released on Wednesday or Thursday, three days hence. The Syrians were playing silly buggers with our visas. Several times, we were told they were being approved, so we packed and got ready to go when the word came through to stand down again. Although we were having a very pleasant time, this was immensely frustrating. To add to the ITN team, presenter Trevor McDonald arrived with not one but two producers, Nigel Baker and Nigel Dacre, to look after him.

We took their passports to Nicosia to join the ITN pile in the torturous process of applying for visas to Syria. There were seventeen of us for dinner that Tuesday evening, including accountant Chris Grout. This was costing ITN a small fortune.

Finally, the next morning the visas were approved and we all piled onto an ITN-chartered jet to fly from Nicosia to Damascus. The idea was that any hostage released would be taken at once to the Syrian capital. If not, we would try to get to Beirut. We checked into the Damascus Sheraton where senior foreign editor Mike Nolan briefed the team. Basically, little appeared to be moving, just rumours and increasingly feverish speculation.

Mike and I shared a room on that first night, as the hotel was almost full for a wedding apparently costing one million dollars!

From a balcony, I watched this spectacular event with cameraman Sam Keene providing a hilarious running commentary and presenter Zeinab Badawi holding forth with her views on Islam from the point of view of her Sudanese heritage. There were more than eight hundred wedding guests, a Lebanese pop star, Egypt's most famous belly dancer, fire-eaters, jugglers, musicians, singers and more flowers than you could count. There were also several armed bodyguards.

One of our picture editors was the legendary Fred Hickey. I know I use that word a lot, but in this case it's entirely justified. Fred was not only one of the kindest people I have ever met, he was also one of the funniest. Welcoming guests to this sumptuous wedding were members of the bride's family standing in a line. At the end of that line was Fred, shaking hands with every guest in turn, and welcoming them with a cheeky smile! While this was very funny, I was also slightly concerned. Anyone holding such a luxurious, expensive wedding in Damascus at that time and with armed bodyguards was likely to have, at the very least, links with international crime and probably terrorism. Fortunately, traditional Arab hospitality prevailed and Fred was treated as a family member!

The next morning, a Thursday, I moved into my own room and we waited for developments. It now seemed that a hostage release was unlikely, at least for a few days. President Assad was off the Cairo on a state visit, and the continuing Israeli bombing of Hezbollah targets was delaying Keenan's release if, indeed, it was to be Brian Keenan.

A difficult decision for ITN, but it was decided back in London that we should stay. The release might happen over the weekend or early the following week. With camera crew Chris Squires and Rob Dukes, I doorstepped the Syrian Foreign Ministry for several hours until the foreign minister himself told me that nothing would happen that day.

I did, however, have a story to do, an interview with Mrs Sunnie Mann whose husband Jackie Mann, a former Battle of Britain RAF pilot, had been kidnapped in Beirut the previous May by a terrorist group linked to Hezbollah. He was released after more than two years in September 1991. Sunnie was extremely charming and a very good interviewee. We edited a four-minute piece for *News at Ten*.

Friday was another day, anther doorstep. This time, we were waiting for the Irish Ambassador for more than five hours without success and despite the best efforts of Ulster journalist Eamonn Mallie, who was with us in Damascus and had always helped me so much in Northern Ireland.

Finally, after a week on the story we were recalled to London. There had been no hostage release, and we had spent a frustrating few days of doorsteps and dealing with Syrian bureaucracy. We also enjoyed some downtime at the Sheraton and seeing the Syrian capital. I had visited the fabulous Umayyad mosque with Zeinab. She was dressed modestly enough, certainly by Western standards, but some locals near the mosque hissed at her and called her names. An Arabic speaker, she told me they were calling her a 'Western whore'. She was completely unfazed by these fanatics.

Zeinab was also brilliant at haggling for bargains. In a souk, I wanted to buy some colourful handmade baskets. She told me to hang back and look angry while she explained to the stallholder that I was her boss and if she didn't get a good price, I would have her beaten. The chivalrous man let her have them for next to nothing!

It was to be another week before Brian Keenan was finally released after four years in captivity, and another year before journalist John McCarthy was freed in August 1991. After more than five years in captivity. Terry Waite was released three months later, and spoke of being blindfolded, beaten and subjected to mock executions.

Incidentally, I recommend you read John McCarthy and Jill Morrell's book, *Some other Rainbow,* and especially Brian Keenan's, *An Evil Cradling.* Apart from having such an horrific story to tell, he has the Irish gift for literature. It is brilliantly written.

After two days off, I had one of those strange reporter's days, story-less but still with a life-experience bonus. At first, I was in Westminster for a Broadcasting Standards Council press conference, and interviewed Lord Rees-Mogg. Frankly, there wasn't much of a story. News came in of the discovery of an Animal Liberation Front bomb in Tunbridge Wells. We covered the story, filmed all that was relevant, edited for *News at Ten*, only to be told it wasn't wanted. There were too many stories, it was a busy news day. But here's the bonus. With cameraman Alan Downes, I flew down to Tunbridge Wells and back in ITN's shiny new helicopter, call sign GO ITN (with my initials, I treated it as my own personal Squirrel!) low over Central London twice. People pay a lot of money for such a privilege.

In July, we followed up the Scargill story in Paris, of all places, when I was sent to get an interview with Alain Simon, President of the International Miners' Organisation, who had been reluctant to get involved. We doorstepped him at his villa in Le Muy. Initially, he was hostile and a bit aggressive, but eventually gave me a twenty-five-minute interview in perfect English. Working with picture editor Mario at FR3 French TV we sent two minutes for the lunchtime news, then flew back to London to edit for the five forty early evening news and *News at Ten*. Verbal herograms all around. It would have been the lead story, but the IRA had detonated a bomb at the London Stock Exchange. They had given a thirty-minute warning, and thankfully, no one was hurt. But the bomb caused a lot of damage right in the heart of the City of London. It was a huge story, and our story slipped down to story two.

I had suggested that we cover the Kashmir conflict between India and Pakistan. With help from the foreign desk, we had arranged an interview with Pakistan's Prime Minister Benazir Bhutto, and got the green light.

Getting a visa from the Pakistan Embassy was easy, the journey wasn't. I was booked to fly via Paris to Dubai, and then on to Karachi. The flight from Heathrow to Paris was delayed for ninety minutes because one of the runways at Charles de Gaulle airport was closed for repair. As a result, our flight arrived too late for the connection to Dubai. And my luggage had gone AWOL. I phoned the foreign desk. The quickest alternative route was a flight from Gatwick to Karachi, again via Dubai. So I flew back from Paris to Gatwick. It had, in effect, taken six hours to travel the few miles from Heathrow to Gatwick. The whereabouts of my luggage was unknown. Finally, I relaxed on a very comfortable UAE (now Emirates) flight from Dubai to Karachi, and just made the last flight of the day to Islamabad.

The Benazir Bhutto interview went very well. She was insightful, incisive and incredibly charming. I was working with cameraman Paul Carleton and sound recordist Tony Hemmings. Carleton rarely ate, and lived on red wine, Hemmings ate like a horse. So the normal routine at dinner was that Hemmings would finish his meal and look at Paul's almost untouched plate.

"Are you going to eat that, Paul?"

When the negative reply came, Tony would switch plates and scoff the lot.

In Pakistan, which was dry, Tony had improvised in advance. He had hidden a bottle of whisky, a bottle of gin and a bottle of vodka in a silver battery case, which was the prefect height for a bottle of spirits. We would order soft drinks, a coke or a bitter lemon, even an orange Fanta, whatever was available. Our drinks would disappear under the table to be surreptitiously topped up.

Next day, we set off for a five-hour drive in a minibus to Muzaffarabad, capital of Azad Kashmir. Our driver, Orangzeb, was elderly, cheerful and straight out of central casting. We also had an information ministry minder with us.

Azad means 'free', obviously a politically loaded description. With tensions rising, and their armies mobilising on both sides of the border, there were growing fears that the tensions over Kashmir could lead to a nuclear war between India and Pakistan.

Muzaffarabad was noisy and very colourful, with those multicoloured single-decker buses clogging up what passed for roads. We interviewed the leader of the KLF (Kashmir Liberation Front), surrounded by his Mujahideen fighters. We were told there was a Mujahideen training camp on top of a nearby hill. Despite the obvious risks of kidnapping or worse, Paul, Tony and I climbed the hill to find nothing more than a peaceful farm. Either they were very well hidden, or the KLF were fantasising.

After a superb drive through the beautiful Murree Hills, we were back in Muzaffarabad where Benazir Bhutto's press secretary arranged for a technician to be available at the local TV station all night for our benefit. Strange how things work in Pakistan. It took us half the rest of the night to edit our package and send it to London. We had some great pictures. Even though I had been standing next to him the entire time, Carleton once again astonished me with his extraordinary talent. He saw things through his viewfinder that I had not even realised were there.

We fed our package to Karachi at seven twenty a.m., from where it was fed on to London. We finally got our heads down for some sleep at nine fifteen a.m.

After all that, *News at One* programme editor Nigel Dacre said he wasn't sure if he'd have the space to run our story! Happily, *News at Ten* loved it and ran it.

Once we'd had a few hours' sleep we had an hour to kill, so we visited the Faisal Mosque, the largest in the world. We covered a riot in Rawalpindi, not an unusual event in the city at that time, but our main effort was getting travel passes to go to Peshawar to cover the story of Afghan refugees returning home. Pakistani bureaucracy! It took all day, but next morning we were on a flight to Peshawar and the north-west frontier. Oh, and my luggage finally turned up — at British Airways in Karachi.

From the airport at Peshawar we picked up a driver, Jan, who seemed very capable, so we hired him for the duration. Jan knew just how to get the necessary permit to go to the border crossing at Torkham, on the Khyber Pass. Amazingly, he got us through the bureaucracy in half an hour. Normally it took several days. This and one or two other equally unlikely outcomes left us convinced that Jan was definitely a spook. He also got us a pass to visit the refugee camps, also in record time.

The refugee camp we filmed had a rather permanent look about it, with mud houses, shops and other businesses. Many of the children with such beautiful faces were born in the camp and had never seen Afghanistan. The adults told us they couldn't go home until the Mujahideen were in control.

Paul, Tony and I travelled up the Khyber Pass with two frontier police guards. They each looked about ninety years old but were probably a lot younger. They were armed with First World War Lee Enfield rifles!

It was amazing to be there, a place so steeped in history. The winding road eventually led to a sleepy frontier post. The guards on both sides were very relaxed, so I stepped into Afghanistan to do my piece to camera.

In Landi Kotal, a wild frontier town where Afghan Mujahideen mixed with armed local tribesmen, you could buy anything. Hashish was readily available over the counter. Under the counter, you could get anything from heroin to an AK-47. That evening, we drank far too much of the famous Murree Hills gin. This time, we were able to drink openly as we seemed to have landed in the only bar in Pakistan, other than private members' clubs, where you could do so.

On the drive back to Islamabad the next day, we experienced one of those magical moments when we stopped for a cold drink near Attock in the Punjab, where the Kabul River ends its five-hundred-mile journey from the Hindu Kush and empties into the River Indus against the backdrop of the Kala Chitta Mountains. The waters of the two rivers ran blue and rusty brown before merging, a truly magical place.

We fed our package after much grief about the picture quality (the video levels were initially too high, apparently). We got the go-ahead from Head of Foreign News Maggie Eales to go across to India to cover the Indian side of the Kashmir conflict provided it was safe (or at last not too dangerous) and didn't take too long (which I took to mean didn't cost too much).

I had terrible stomach cramps, either caused by something I ate or, more likely, by the overindulgence in the Murree Hills gin. It felt like dysentery. A local doctor prescribed some pills which soon solved the problem.

At the Indian High Commission, First Secretary Yugandra Kumar managed to rush through our visas in twenty-four hours. It normally took days. I had asked the British Embassy to nudge them along, which helped.

I was very excited to visit Srinagar in the Kashmir Valley, India's most northerly city, and the possibility of seeing the golden temple at Amritsar.

In the event we were to see neither, thanks to Saddam Hussein.

After a frustrating delay, our visas were finally approved in New Delhi. First, though, we had to fly to Karachi. Islamabad airport was even more chaotic than usual. All flights to Karachi and Lahore were full for the next week. Thousands (or so it seemed) of people were trying to push their way onto that evening's special flight. We emerged pouring with sweat but triumphant! The flight itself was something else, with people brewing up tea on little gas stoves in the aisles.

We overnighted at a fleapit hotel near Karachi airport, arriving at two a.m. I phoned my mother, it was her birthday. At one point, Carleton snatched the phone from me. "Your son is a debauched drunk who has self-inflicted diarrhoea." My mum thought he was hilarious. If only she knew!

Next morning, we went to see the Indian Consul-General Mani Tripathi, who was incredibly helpful. Not only did he give us our Indian visas but also a letter of authority, contact names in the ministry of External Affairs in Delhi who he would warn of our arrival, and a Mercedes with a consular official to help us persuade Pakistan International Airways to let us onto the one thirty flight to Delhi. It seems India was keen that we told its side of the Kashmir story.

Despite our best efforts, PIA wasn't playing ball, and we spent a frustrating four hours at the airport. The best the airline could do was to reissue our tickets to fly via Bombay (Mumbai) at midnight.

We used the time to make calls to set up the India story. I spoke to the External Affairs Secretary Aftab Seth, who assured me we were expected and that they would try to find some time for us to talk to the Indian prime minister. I had told them that we had interviewed Benazir Bhutto, hoping that would spur them to greater efforts.

We got the midnight flight, arrived in Bombay (now Mumbai) at two thirty a.m., and entered the comedy nightmare of the Bombay customs hall!

The British Raj left a legacy in India, both good and bad. Indian bureaucracy definitely falls into the latter category. The customs officers wanted a two hundred thousand pound cash bond for our camera gear, showing us the relevant regulation in their custom officers' Bible. There was no way they could let us into the country. It took us four hours of cajoling, bargaining, negotiating, and feigning extreme anger. Dozens of otherwise underemployed officials became involved, signing and stamping a bewildering assortment of documents. Paul Carleton bore the brunt of all this. He was the eldest, and they treated him as our leader (which in many ways he was). They recognised the officer class when they saw it!

Eventually, victory! Just when it seemed all was lost, they relented. In part, this was because they had no secure room large enough to impound our kit. They had shallow steel cabinets for confiscated drugs and small arms, but that was about it. I finally persuaded the top man that we really were on our way to interview the Indian prime minister at his personal invitation. Once they had capitulated, we still had an hour of bureaucratic arse-covering. We became a file, a handsome file, full of duly signed forms, covered in stamps, and bound with a splendid bright pink ribbon. I like to think that sometime after that we became a case history for trainee Indian customs officers to study.

We emerged exhausted, and all getting very tired and a little irritable. We bought tickets for a flight to Delhi, and adjourned to the Leela Kempinski Hotel.

To get to the hotel, we drove through the most appalling poverty. People, many of them children, dressed only in loincloths were living in mud by the side of the road. This vision of human misery extended right up to the doors of the five-star hotel. As we entered, we were met with drinks on silver platters provided by a welcome committee of waiters dressed in immaculate pressed whites. The contrast could not have been starker.

We were woken by the news that Iraq had invaded Kuwait. So Saddam Hussein had not been merely sabre-rattling after all. Naturally, the instruction came through from the foreign desk to forget going to Delhi and Srinigar. A few minutes later the foreign desk was on the phone again: "Go. Go. Go to Dubai!"

Three hours later we were in the air, Cathay Pacific to Dubai.

Our first task was to film HMS York of the Armilla patrol, and Friday prayers. Our package, which led *News at One*, was vetted by the official government censor. Middle East correspondent Brent Saddler arrived so, of course, I got big-footed. We vox-popped some Kuwaitis for Brent's five forty package which, however, was not allowed through by the censor.

We only spent five days in Dubai. It was impossible to get to Kuwait. At one point, Brent Saddler suggested a camera crew hire a dingy and get up the coast to Kuwait. He was told to F off in no uncertain terms. I'm still not sure to this day if he was joking.

Paul, Tony and I flew in a de Havilland over the Gulf searching, unsuccessfully, for American warships. We had seriously planned to charter a boat and simply set sail for Kuwait the next day, that was how desperate we were to get to the story. But when we returned to the hotel that evening, we found a very fed up Brent Saddler and producer John Toker. Our feeds to ITN had been cancelled. We were told that editor-in-chief Stewart Purvis didn't want reports from 'in the Gulf' because it implied we were in or very near Kuwait. We were as near as we could get, and all other broadcasters were doing the same. But ITN were happier to pull the pictures together in London. Maybe they just wanted to save money. It was a decision that the foreign desk had strongly opposed, but they were overruled.

So, the next day, we were due to return to London. I found it absolutely incredible that we were being recalled from a potential war zone involving British and American forces. It emerged that this was a financial rather than editorial decision.

On that day, Benazir Bhutto was deposed. Her attempts at reform had finally been thwarted by conservative, military and Islamist opposition and she was being accused of corruption. Her government had been dissolved by Pakistan's president, Ghulam Ishaq Khan, who had made her life as difficult as possible from the moment she had been elected.

My visa for Pakistan was single-entry, so was now invalid!

Although it was good to see friends and family, it was strange to be home in Highgate. I felt I should be in the Middle East. The Americans were sending troops and fighter aircraft to Saudi Arabia. I was definitely in the wrong place.

Although I was supposed to be on leave, I only got one day off before the foreign desk called. It was good to be wanted. We were to go to

Rotterdam on 'my' helicopter 'GO ITN'. Cameraman Peter Wilkinson and I covered the story of illegal oil supplies from Iraq. We filmed at an oil storage depot, and the testing of oil for country of origin.

The real story though, was of a Greek tanker which was suspected of carrying illegal Iraqi crude oil. We learnt from the harbourmaster that it was still forty-five miles out at sea. From Berghaven, on the Hook of Holland we hired a boat and two hours out found the tanker and followed her into port. The captain refused to speak to us. The story was thin, but still of interest back in London.

Now, I was finally supposed to have a week off. It lasted just three days before I was sent to Düsseldorf to cover the trial of two IRA men. Gerard McGergin was long-winded, to say the least. His co-defendant, Gerry Hanratty, was even worse giving the court a two-hour lecture on the history of Irish Republicanism. With Robberechts editor Dirk Heuben, I sent the story for *News at One* and re-cut it for the five forty news and *News at Ten* before flying home again.

The next few weeks were frustrating, working in London not in the Middle East. I watched a particularly strong *News at Ten* with Des Hamill live in Washington, Mark Austin in Saudi Arabia and Sandy Gall in Amman. Things were hotting up.

There were plenty of stories to cover, including going to the top of Europe's tallest office building at the time, in Canary Wharf, with Mrs Thatcher. The prime minister used the opportunity to condemn Saddam Hussein's latest tactic of relocating Westerners, including children, to potential military targets. They were hostages. The Iraqis had the gall to refer to them as 'guests'. We called them Human Shields.

It was still slightly grating to watch the superb reports from Mark Austin in Saudi Arabia, or Bill Neely in Jordan, or Norman Rees in Dubai. Why had ITN pulled us out of the region only to execute a massive U-turn just a few days later and replace us? The answer, of course, was money, a financial rather than editorial decision. I was deeply envious. I had to bite my tongue; my time would come again.

I was involved, sort of, at a distance. I interviewed the Iraq Families Support Group, packaged pictures coming into ITN of Brits who had escaped from Kuwait, and more than once went to the so-called Iraqi Cultural Centre to help the foreign desk try to get visas for Iraq. I even interviewed a 'radio-ham', Eddie Benon, who had been trying to contact someone, anyone, in Kuwait. He thought they'd been frightened into silence.

I was in Zurich with cameraman, Pete Blanchard, in late August for what turned out to be something of a non-story when the foreign desk called. Could I go to Istanbul? You bet!

A fifteen-year-old British boy was reportedly being allowed to leave Iraq, destination Istanbul. Pete and I landed in Istanbul on a Friday, only to be told by the foreign desk that the boy wasn't heading to Istanbul after all, but asking if I could get to the Jordanian capital Amman instead. It turned out that the next available flight wasn't for another forty-eight hours, on the Sunday. I can't tell you how happy I was when the foreign desk said we should wait out in Istanbul and fly out to Amman on the Sunday flight.

Brian Keenan was finally released from his captivity in Beirut after fifty-two months of what must have been dreadful physical suffering and psychological torture. There had been strong rumours from the Iranian news agency for the previous twenty-four hours. It was impossible for anyone with a British passport to get there, but Irish passport-holding reporters Bill Nelly and James Furlong had been dispatched so we were well covered.

While Brian Keenan was enjoying his first moments of freedom, we were being tourists in Istanbul, such an enthralling city so steeped in history. We walked around the huge Grand Bazaar, visited the Blue Mosque and St Sofia, but what tickled me most (and still does) was the New Mosque. Completed in 1665, this was the 'new' one. Byzantium. Constantinople. Istanbul. Thank you, ITN!

Dinner was in an excellent fish restaurant on the Bosphorus, recommended by a local taxi driver. Sometimes, working for ITN could involve hardship, lack of sleep, even an element of danger. But not always.

On Sunday morning, the plan changed, as is the nature of covering the news. American diplomats and their families were coming out of Iraq and into Turkey. WTN and ABC both had cameras at the border and would feed their material to Ankara. We couldn't get a flight to the border, there wasn't one, so Ankara was the place to be. After a gentle Sunday afternoon flight from Istanbul, we checked into the Ankara Hilton and set up at TRT (Turkish Television).

The American diplomats and their families crossed the border the next morning. We got the WTN and ABC pictures in Ankara, from where we sent a package to ITN in London. We were the lead story.

From Ankara, it was off to Cairo for a meeting of the Arab League. I linked up with cameraman Bernie Glancy in the Ramses Hilton. We were tasked to get some 'Cairo shots', so we naturally headed to the Pyramids. We hired a wonderful guide who went by the name of Moses. He was seventy-three, looked ninety-three, and had been a guide for fifty years, so he really knew his stuff. In the Al Azhar Bazaar, around the mosque of the same name, we were the only Westerners. The ancient architecture was decaying but still beautiful and so resonant of earlier times.

The Arab League meeting was pandemonium. The security was ridiculous. We still managed to get some decent enough shots. Mostly, I hung around waiting for the interminable meeting to finish and chatting to other journalists far more knowledgeable about Arab affairs then me.

The meeting ended without a press conference or any agreed resolution. The Arab League was deeply divided. Talking to Egyptians in Cairo, the contrast with Turkey could not have been sharper. In Istanbul and Ankara they were largely indifferent to the invasion of Kuwait, they felt it did not affect them. In Cairo, it was another matter entirely. Egyptians believed war was coming, and that Egypt itself could be dragged into it.

In Libya, Colonel Gaddafi was offering us a free trip to Tripoli where he wanted to announce his own peace initiative. However, because our Middle East correspondent Brent Sadler had gone the previous week and Gaddafi had simply ranted incoherently, Jim Ackhurst on the ITN foreign desk wisely decided that we shouldn't go even though it would cost nothing. It was the right decision but still disappointing as I would have loved to have gone to Tripoli to interview the mad Libyan dictator in his famous tent.

The next morning, the Arab League did call a press conference. They had agreed, but only by majority, to reiterate the decision of the Arab summit of three weeks earlier demanding that Iraqi forces leave Kuwait immediately and unconditionally, and that Iraq pay reparations.

I had a message back at the hotel which should have read: *Please phone Channel 4 Daily*. The breakfast news show on Channel 4. I got the message as: *Please phone Chanel in Delhi*. Did the hotel think I was a perfume salesman?

Back in the UK, in September, there were plenty of other stories to cover, away from the Middle East. In Midhurst, Sussex, a dog in quarantine kennels had been put down after showing symptoms of rabies. Cameraman Peter Wilkinson and I flew there in the ITN helicopter on a very clear day over the Sussex Downs. By the way, why are these hills called 'downs'? The answer lies in the old English word 'dun', meaning hill. I thought I'd share that with you. I knew my English degree would be useful one day!

The following day, we were in Portland for a facility on board HMS Brazen, a type-22 frigate about to leave for the Gulf. Shot by Bob Hammond and edited by Fred Hickey, there was no escaping THE story of the moment. A few days later, back at ITN, I voiced pictures from Kuwait for all news bulletins. One day, I even voiced-up pictures from the Spanish grand prix. I'm not even remotely interested in motor sport and knew next to nothing about it, although some years later I had the pleasure of interviewing Lewis Hamilton and Jenson Button in Downing Street

In Staffordshire, we covered the shooting of Air Chief Marshal Sir Peter Terry, former governor of Gibraltar, an attempted murder by the IRA. He had suffered very serious injuries. We were still there two days later when his wife, Lady Betty Terry, gave a press conference. She was extremely dignified and resilient.

So many of the stories I covered at that time were related to what was happening in Kuwait. At the end of September, we were back in Germany, at Fallingbostel, 7th Armoured Brigade HQ, to film Challenger tanks heading for the Gulf. We followed them on their transporters along the autobahn to Bremerhaven, great pictures, and filmed them being loaded onto ships bound for the Gulf. Surprisingly perhaps, we were the lead story.

I got the lead story again, but from London, a few days later when three Brits made a daring escape from Iraq by boat and again the next day when the three-men-in-a-boat arrived at Heathrow.

The big political story that day, October 5th, was the announcement by Margaret Thatcher and Chancellor of the Exchequer John Major that we were joining the European ERM (the Exchange Rate Mechanism). That was not to end well!

The next day, I packaged pictures of the successful launch of the shuttle Discovery carrying the European satellite, Ulysses. The mission, a five-year voyage around the Sun. Amazing. The next day, it was stories about the US economy, specifically the budget deficit. And after that, an interview with German General Wolfgang Altenberg at RUSI (The Royal United Services Institute) in Whitehall: West German 'traitors' had been exposed in files that the East German Stasi had failed to destroy. The day after, a piece for *News at Ten* on Lester Piggott getting his jockey's licence back. And the next day, the sudden surrender of General Michel Aoun in Beirut.

The strange and very varied life of an ITN reporter. From space, to the US economy, to German spies, to horseracing, to Lebanese politics, all within the same week! You had to become an instant expert on any subject under the sun, and in this case, including the Sun. Researching any subject in those days, life before Google, involved a lot of work, reading up and phoning people to get yourself up to speed. Now, the world is at our fingertips. If I want to know anything about Michel Aoun, Wikipedia has it all.

Mid-October, and another week in Europe. First, to Hanover to cover the departure of a squadron of the Queen's Dragoon Guards leaving for the Gulf, complete with family farewells and a regimental band to send them off. In Luxembourg, we covered a European foreign ministers meeting. Douglas Hurd was in good form talking about Edward Heath's successful visit to Baghdad to get some of the British hostages out.

Other stories that month included an interview with Iraq's ambassador to London which ran at length on *News at Ten*, another Grand Prix, this time in Japan, and on one particularly busy news day, six British soldiers were killed in two separate car bombs in Northern Ireland and Ted Heath returned from Baghdad with thirty-three freed British hostages.

There were also plenty of interviews with senior politicians. I was busy, BUT I wasn't in the Middle East.

November was dominated by the ousting of Margaret Thatcher. Challenged for the Conservative Party leadership, she had ignored sensible advice and travelled to Paris for a summit, confident that she would win. In the first ballot she did, but not by enough. Despite her defiant, "We fight on, we fight to win", on the steps of the Élysée Palace, the writing was clearly on the wall, and her closest supporters knew it.

On November 1st, Geoffrey Howe had resigned, a devastating blow. I doorstepped him, but he wouldn't speak to us. Others were more forthcoming and I interviewed several ministers in the following days including Leon Brittan, William Waldegrave and Ken Clarke more than once. The drama culminated in a tearful Margaret Thatcher leaving Downing Street with her ever-faithful husband Denis as her side.

In the leadership contest which followed, my task was to stick like glue to the favourite, Michael Heseltine. So it was that almost every time you saw him with his campaign manager, Michael Mates, beside him, I'd be just behind or alongside them, microphone poised, while an assortment of cameramen walked backwards in front of us to get the shot.

This was one of the very few occasions when being in shot was justified. I didn't think reporters should ever become part of the story. Not everyone shared this view. There was a famous example of a Channel 4 news correspondent, who I won't name here, walking alongside President Gorbachev on a walkabout in Moscow. Although this wasn't seen on the news, in the edit room, when the editor turned up the volume, all you could hear was this reporter screaming at his cameraman: "Two-shot! Two-shot!"

This same reporter, by the way, was notorious for taking forever to deliver a piece to camera, often taking dozens of attempts before he got it right. Back in the day, a camera crew was a three-man team: cameraman, sound recordist and lighting man. This reporter and crew were filming one day in Cairo in broad daylight, so they had left the lighting man back at the hotel. After dozens of failed attempts to deliver a simple piece to camera, they had to phone the hotel and get the lights as it was getting dark. On another famous occasion, he was on the Green Line in Beirut to report on a temporary ceasefire. As he struggled to deliver his piece to camera, machine gun fire erupted in the background and he had to change the story to, "The ceasefire has broken down"!

I, on the other hand, blessed with having a very good short-term memory, had established a reputation for being a 'one-take wonder', which made the camera crews' lives a lot easier.

Away from the toppling of Margaret Thatcher, there were other stories to cover that November. Crime stories from the Old Bailey, and a lot of domestic politics. Often, this involved doorstepping/interviewing cabinet ministers for stories to be packaged sometimes by ITN's team of political correspondents but usually by political editor Michael Brunson. We called this being 'Brunsonned'. A great political editor, Mike had now become a verb!

There was also, of course, the build-up of armed forces in the Gulf. On November 1st, Iraq offered the wives and families of their Western 'guests' the opportunity to visit them for Christmas, a move dismissed by the government here as 'cynical propaganda'. I spent the day working from the Foreign Office, packaging for all ITN bulletins.

For once, we had a pleasant story to cover when a four-year-old boy from Hemel Hempstead, Simon Jones, turned up safe and well after going missing for eight weeks. Another light story was an auction of classic cars. Great pictures.

In mid-November, I was in Paris for the visit of US Secretary of State James Baker who was meeting not only the French president but also UN Secretary-General Pérez De Cuéllar. Baker's mission was to firm up European support for the impending military operation in Kuwait. Two days later, we were in the Charlemagne building in Brussels for another European foreign ministers' meeting.

Let me digress for a moment. If you want journalists to be happy, provide them with food and water, maybe coffee, and certainly basic toilet facilities. Off the courtyard of the Élysée Palace in Paris was a room specifically for journalists' (non-alcoholic!) refreshments, and toilets. The Charlemagne and other European Community (as it then was) buildings in Brussels were always well supplied with coffee and croissants. And toilets. The same was true of Washington, Berlin, Warsaw, Prague, Rome — in fact, of every capital city I'd worked in, if journalists were there to cover the activities of the prime minister or president. Except for Downing Street, where there was absolutely nothing.

This may sound unimportant, and it is, but the problem was that once you were locked inside Downing Street, standing in the street often for hours and in all weathers, you did not dare leave because that would be the moment the prime minister or the cabinet minister you were waiting for would emerge. So you needed an iron bladder, or to risk going to the nearest pub (thank you the Red Lion and Churchill's cafe) and then have to face the time-consuming palaver of going through the security again at the entrance to Downing Street. Every time there was a change of government and a new prime minister, I would ask them to provide, at the very least, a Portaloo hidden somewhere discreetly. I knew just the place. It never happened, and my colleagues are still being treated just as poorly.

On November 14th, as expected, Michael Heseltine declared his candidacy for the Conservative Party leadership. It came just a day after Geoffrey Howe's demolition of Margaret Thatcher's leadership in the House of Commons. Mild Geoffrey Howe of all people! It was seen as the most crushing indictment of a serving prime minister since Leo Amery's political assassination of Neville Chamberlain in 1940. Thatcher was clearly very vulnerable. Even if she won the leadership contest, she would be irreversibly damaged. Estimates of the strength of Heseltine's support varied considerably. Although the conservative newspapers were to rally behind his bid in the following days, they seemed more intent on replacing Mrs Thatcher rather than enthusiastically supporting Mr Heseltine.

When it came to the vote, on November 21st, Mrs Thatcher won by two hundred and four votes to Heseltine's one hundred and fifty-two. There were sixteen abstentions. Thatcher was just four votes short of the majority required for victory. As noted earlier, she was in Paris and declared herself determined to fight on in the second ballot, due the following week.

Forty-eight hours later, she was gone.

It was a Thursday morning, November 22nd, when Thatcher's bombshell resignation announcement sent shockwaves through newsrooms around the country, and around the world. Apparently, she had been told by half her cabinet and the 'Tory grandees' that she would lose a second vote against Michael Heseltine. She was left with little choice. Whatever one's view of Margaret Thatcher, it seemed almost inconceivable that a serving prime minister with a huge majority and three general election victories behind her could be deposed in this way. ITN was live all day, a sterling performance, all hands on deck.

That evening, in the House of Commons' No Confidence debate, she delivered a command performance of extraordinary bravura. She was on top form, absolutely trashing her opponents. "I'm enjoying this," she shouted, as she swung the handbag one last time. The rivals for the Crown, Michael Heseltine, John Major and Douglas Hurd may have felt uncomfortable, may have shifted in their seats a few times, but they put on a good show of enjoying the Iron Lady's Final Hurrah.

I watched the ensuing political fallout from Egypt, though only out of the corner of my eye as I was focused on the Biblical scenes along the River Nile, unchanged in two thousand years. I was on leave for a week but still in touch with the foreign desk who were trying to get me a visa for Saudi Arabia, with working in Washington as the fallback if that failed, which it did.

Before leaving for the States to work at ITN's Washington bureau for the month of December, I covered the return of British hostages from Kuwait, both from Heathrow and Frankfurt airport arrivals hall. I flew back from Frankfurt with John Burke, who had escaped after hiding out from the Iraqis in Kuwait City for nearly four months. He obviously needed to talk, and he told me all about it for more than four hours on the ground and in the air. It sounded like some sort of *Boy's Own* adventure, but it must have been terrifying.

December was my first time in Washington for ITN. I walked from Union Street station to our bureau on M Street, behind the White House. As I strolled happily along, I began to notice the area I was in. It wasn't pretty. Gangs of youths on street corners, even a couple of burnt out cars. So I marched purposefully, trying to look as if I owned the place. When I got to the bureau, my ITN colleagues were astonished that I had survived. No one walked there, they told me. I was 'lucky to be alive'! And that is what I soon discovered about Washington, which is one of my favourite cities. Stray just two or three blocks from Pennsylvania Avenue and you would find yourself in an urban war zone.

This was the first time I met the cameraman Jon Steele, former US marine and on of ITN's finest. Our first job was to cover a summit between George Bush and the new Prime Minister John Major at Camp David. Maybe I'm easily impressed, but I felt privileged to be there.

For Christmas, we did a story about a new American board game, 'Gulf War'. Truly bizarre and, in my view, completely inappropriate. But it made an amusing package for ITN.

Away from the impending conflict in Kuwait, which now seemed inevitable, we covered other news, including the story of Nancy Cruzan, who had died in hospital in Missouri. She had been on a life support machine since 1983 following a car accident. After a seven-year legal battle which went all the way to the Supreme Court, her parents had won the right to allow her to die. It was a landmark 'right to die' case.

With camera crew Jon Steele and Chris Schlemon, I spent a few days in Norfolk, Virginia. From the giant naval base, American warships were setting off for war. In the freezing cold, we filmed the departure of aircraft carrier Theodore Roosevelt and her escort ships for the Gulf, and the emotional family farewell scenes.

CHAPTER 6

1991: The Gulf War. The Kurds in Northern Iraq. Yugoslavia. Robert Maxwell

The news in the first half of 1991 was dominated by Gulf War One. To explain the nomenclature, Gulf War One was the expulsion of Iraqi forces from Kuwait. Gulf War Two, twelve years later, led to the overthrow of Saddam Hussein.

This is a Western perspective. Viewed from the region, the first Gulf War was the one in the 1980s between Iraq and Iran, which had begun when Iraq invaded Iran in 1980 and lasted for eight years, leaving at least one million dead. Casualty estimates vary as both sides were issuing wildly differing numbers.

In a slight echo of 1989, my first assignment of the year was in Greece, where Albanians were flooding across the border. We had been told that the Albanian refugees would be too frightened to talk to us. In the event, after the long drive with camera crew Mick James and Rob Dukes from Athens to the border town of Filiates, we found them only too happy to tell their stories. The crew did some very fine work, especially considering the short time we had before we had to get back to Athens to feed our story to ITN. We could not have done it without our fixer/interpreter and insanely fast Greek driver, Thomas Papanitroloni. The foreign desk had not managed to get us Albanian visas. The BBC had succeeded and filed from Tirana, but the view from back at base was that our stories from the border were far better. We had been in the right place.

I was still in Greece when Sandy Gall presented *News at Ten* for the last time. I was delighted to have a good story running that night, but I missed the party which had, by all accounts, kept the entire Champagne region in profit for another year!

I spent most of Gulf War One bouncing between Amman and Cairo, and not where the fighting was. I flew to Amman with camera crew John Martin and Roger Dove and picture editor Roger Pitman. Our edit suite at the InterContinental hotel was spectacular, with a four-poster bed and a Jacuzzi. My room was an altogether more modest affair.

The first day was largely spent bedding in, talking to colleagues at ABC, WTN (the television news agency jointly owned by ITN and ABC), the British Embassy, the Jordanian Information Ministry and so on. Reinforcements arrived in the shape of senior producer Angela Frier and camera crew Phil Bye and Jim Dutton. That afternoon, British diplomats came out of Iraq and into Jordan, so we already had a story to tell. The next few days were busy, but we only got on air sporadically. We were not where the story was.

We filmed at the Al-Azraq refugee camp run by the Red Crescent, Pérez De Cuéllar, when he stopped off en route to Baghdad and there was a photo-op with King Hussein of Jordan. We did stories from the border crossing at Al-Ruwayshid. Our driver, Ahmed, needed a day off so his cousin Mustafa drove us there, a driver so fast he bordered on lunacy as we almost crashed several times, racing along the potholed, so-called road through a freezing desert moonscape.

After some bureaucratic nonsense at the border, we got enough excellent pictures and human stories to fill an entire bulletin and braced ourselves for the lunatic drive back to Amman. If I was to be injured in a war zone, I certainly did not want it to be in a bloody car accident!

One day, we hung out at the airport looking for fifty-four-year-old Welshman, Patrick Trigg, who had been held in solitary confinement in Baghdad for a hundred and twenty days during which he had been interrogated many times. We eventually tracked him down at the Marriott Hotel. Tall and gaunt, he gave us an excellent and very moving interview. He turned out to be the last Western hostage to leave Iraq. We cut two minutes for *News at Ten*. The feedback from the foreign desk was that it was OK but a little disappointing. They wanted, and I quote, "More shock-horror torture"!

In the streets of Amman, Palestinians were gleefully burning the American flag. At that time sixty per cent of the population of Jordan was Palestinian, mostly refugees who had fled the conflicts with Israel. With the

UN deadline for Iraq to withdraw from Kuwait looming, King Hussein went on TV to speak to his people.

The speech was broadcast live by CNN. As well as appealing for calm, he said his country was ready to fight if need be. This did not go down well in Washington, where his message was completely misunderstood. Until that misunderstanding was cleared up, Jordan found itself inadvertently on America's list of hostile nations.

On the night of January 16th, the Americans began to bomb targets in Iraq and Kuwait. Saddam Hussein was defiant, but most of his air bases and missile sites were reportedly destroyed in eight hours of almost continuous bombing. From Amman, we covered reaction to the start of the war, which was almost universally anti-American, and Phil and Jim got shots from the border of refugees fleeing from Iraq. We fed our package for *News at Ten* just as the Americans began a second night of intense bombing.

I was woken by producer Angela Frier on the phone at three a.m. Iraq had attacked Tel Aviv and Haifa with Scud missiles. Should she tell the others? I suggested not, as there was nothing we could do about it, but she called them anyway. I got up sleepily and opened my bedroom door to the extraordinary sight of our American colleagues from ABC running up and down the corridor, struggling into their NBC (nuclear, biological and chemical) suits and gas masks, and generally racing around like headless chickens. At the same time, cameraman John Martin, who had the room opposite me, also opened the door to his room to see what was going on. We looked at each other, shrugged, and went back to bed, although I confess I moved my gas mask to within reach.

Colin Baker was reporting for ITN from Tel Aviv. The CNN correspondent there did a live two-way in a gas mask. He was muffled and unintelligible, you could barely make out a word. To compound the absurdity, his producer walked into shot to hand him a piece of paper with the latest information. The producer, who I knew and who was English, was not wearing a gas mask. The edict came from ITN. We were not to do lives wearing a gas mask unless we were actually under attack or an attack was imminent!

The Iraqi attack on Tel Aviv and Haifa was largely ineffective. Fifteen people had been injured, none too seriously.

Senior producer Nigel Baker and cameraman Seb Rich arrived from Baghdad with sensational pictures from beneath the American bombing. It was such a relief to see them both safe and well. Seb, brave as a lion, had been wound up by Middle East correspondent Brent Sadler (they called him 'death or glory!') to such an extent that he had been convinced the Americans were going to nuke Baghdad. I'd had to calm him down days earlier over the phone and explain why using nuclear weapons was simply not going to happen.

They also told of the day the Americans had bombed what they claimed was a chemical weapons facility and the Iraqis said was a milk factory near their hotel. As yellow smoke billowed towards them, their correspondent opened the window, breathed in and declared that he didn't think it was poisonous! Brave? Debatably. Daft? Very. True? Probably.

John Martin, Roger Dove and our wonderful Jordanian fixer Afnan Taha did the border run. Afnan, who was Palestinian, taught me so much about the Palestinian mindset. She was such a pleasure to work with, always positive, even when she was clearly very upset by what was happening. She later married American cameraman Jon Steele.

Nigel and Seb did live two-ways for ITN and the American networks. Surprisingly perhaps, ITN also ran our package from Jordan, speculating on the possibility of Israeli retaliation.

This was part of the reason we were in Amman. Our boss, Nigel Hancock, was convinced Israel would invade Iraq via Jordan. I imagined he had a vision of us riding to war on the back of an Israeli tank!

Over the next few days we covered various events: King Hussein held a press conference; refugees were coming over the border; in the streets they were still merrily burning the Stars and Stripes. But our packages were not making the main ITN bulletins. They were running overnight in the graveyard bulletins. We could not compete with the material coming out of Iraq, known as 'whiz bang pictures' in the business. Chris Hulme on the foreign desk, a man with a deadpan sense of humour, assured me that they had a special bin next to the desk labelled 'Glen Oglaza packages from Jordan'! Thank you so much for that.

We also took the occasional cultural excursion, taking in the King Abdullah and Abu Darwish mosques. Other options in Amman were somewhat limited. Apart from our hotel, there were only three places still open in the city: Romero's Italian (actually Palestinian) restaurant, an Indian called The Kashmir, and rather bizarrely, a tenpin bowling alley. Whenever we had an hour or two off, we became fairly proficient at tenpin bowling!

I felt that although ITN was doing the fantastic job of covering the US bombing in Iraq, all news organisations were becoming obsessed with the military hardware. This was not a Hollywood movie. We weren't putting out the other side enough. The view from the 'Arab street' or the stories of the people who had been under the bombardment and fled their country. This is something we could have been doing from Jordan, but there was very little appetite for the story we were trying to tell.

Brent Saddler and his team pitched up. They had been thrown out of Baghdad, and things picked up a little. Brent was filing from Amman in lieu of Baghdad, and I was getting on air more frequently. It was still relatively soft material though. Refugee stories from the Jordan-Iraq border, a visit by Queen Noor to the Azraq refugee camp, Friday prayers and anti-American demonstrations at the Baqa'a Palestinian camp, interviews with senior Jordanian military officers and so on.

Reporter Marine of TF1 French TV was single-handedly raising the morale of our picture editors. Her modus operandi for asking for our pictures was to stand behind the seated VT editor and rest one of her very ample breasts on his shoulder. It worked every time. Mission accomplished, she would shake her chest from side to side, exclaiming in her sexy French accent, "Oh! You are so lovely to me!"

We had a day off and spent it in Jerash, the best-preserved Roman provincial city in the Middle East. We had it entirely to ourselves. There were no fences, no guides, and no tourists. We simply strolled around at will. There were countless pieces of Roman pottery lying around. Ninety per cent of the site was still unexcavated which, given the magnificent forum, main street, Temple of Artemis etc., was astonishing.

Here was a fairly typical day. We had done a story about an Englishwoman who had opened a rescue centre for horses. It ran at five a.m. and never again saw the light of day. We interviewed the head of the Red Cross in Jordan on the refugees stuck on the Iraqi side of the border. Pooling with La Cinque French TV, we got some very good pictures from the border. Around seven hundred refugees had been allowed to cross from

Iraq into Jordan. They were cold and hungry, with vivid tales of the terrors they'd endured. It was story twenty in the five forty running order. The bulletin ran out of time after story nineteen! But the piece did get a run on *News at Ten*, so the day had ended well.

That same day, January 28th, dozens of Iraqi pilots had flown their fighter aircraft to Iran. It wasn't clear if they intended to defect or to continue the war from Iranian soil. Either way, they were to be thwarted. The Iranians simply impounded their aircraft until the end of the war.

The day after we visited Jerash, Phil, Afnan and I were at the Al-Ruwayshid border post. We went as far as the Iraq checkpoint at Trebeil where we were told in no uncertain terms (at gunpoint) that if we filmed our camera would be smashed and we would be arrested. Near the Red Cross transit camp, we found a Palestinian family stranded and stateless, who were being forced to return to Iraq. Our lovely Afnan was in floods of tears, but there was nothing we could do to help them.

News at Ten producers were keen to run our story. In the end, there wasn't room for it but it did run on CNN, as had so many of our packages. In fact, I was getting on CNN almost as much as on ITN. To state the obvious, and as I was to discover much later when I joined Sky News, being a twenty-four-hour news channel gives you a lot more air time to fill and a lot more freedom.

Iraq issued four visas for an ITN team to return to Baghdad. Five had been due to go. Cameraman Jim Dutton stayed with us in Amman. Unlucky Jim. Or lucky Jim?

Once they'd left, supplies for our Baghdad team arrived in Amman. We had also become something of a staging post. Next morning, we loaded up a truck with a trusted driver. Amazingly, almost always our re-supplies reached their destination in Baghdad. But this time, the driver and fully-laden truck re-appeared. He had been stopped at the border, his car had broken down in Azraq, he had been called up to serve in the army. Three lies in one breathless rush of excuses. However, nothing was missing and on the second attempt with a different driver everything was delivered to the Iraqi capital.

While organising the Baghdad re-supply, we also edited a pull-together piece for ITN. Burnt out trucks on the desert road to Baghdad, and Arab reaction including those of the newspapers in Saudi Arabia and vox pops in

Amman. *News at One* loved it, and so did *News at Ten*. There were plenty of verbal herograms, which lifted our spirits.

I should perhaps explain what the desert between Amman and Baghdad is like. Forget those romantic images of the desert, Saharan sand dunes and so on. This was hard, rocky terrain, just rocks and dust where nothing can grow. The so-called road is barely discernible from the harsh landscape around it, and it is very cold in winter. The drive to the border from Amman took four hours, and the same again on the other side to get to Baghdad. But at night, it glowed with the light of a million stars. Only deep in the bush in Kenya and in the middle of the Sahara desert had I ever seen such a magical, silver sparkling sky.

We had just loaded another truck with a generator, petrol, food and water and sent it on its way to Baghdad when the word came from the Palace, the interview we had been after for some time with Crown Prince Hassan, the King's brother, had been approved. Despite keeping us waiting for four hours, the Crown Prince gave us a long and fascinating interview. He shared the view, widespread in Jordan and much of the Arab world, that the American reaction to the Iraqi seizure of Kuwait was entirely about oil, saying that if Palestine had had oil the Israel-Palestine problem would have been resolved, "In twenty-five days, not twenty-five years". Of course, it remains unresolved to this day.

Scottish producer, John Curran, arrived from London. ITN had been spending very heavily. It was far from cheap to keep all these people on the road. John, it seemed, had been tasked to get things under control and to try to get receipts for everything. Not easy in Arab countries. John had very little experience of working 'on the road' and none of working in the Middle East. I was keen to introduce him to our ABC and WTN colleagues, relevant helpful Jordanians and aid organisations, and generally get him up to speed on the story and how we were running the operation. But he seemed more interested in buying files and paperclips for the office. He kept saying, "I must buy a typewriter." Eventually, I took our main driver Ahmed to one side.

"Take John to buy a typewriter."

"Yes, Mr Glen."

"And Ahmed, try and take all day."

John, a slightly-built, mild-mannered Scot had a great line in Glaswegian menace, for example, if you don't do what he told you to do, "You'll be picking up your teeth with your broken arm!' Sandy Macintyre on the foreign desk was another Scot who'd probably watched too many episodes of *Taggart*.

His favourite: "I've been through harder than you to get INTO a fight!"

The foreign desk said they wanted a story from Jordan but had no idea what! The Americans were telling their citizens to leave Jordan. I made some calls to the British and American embassies and colleagues at ABC and CBS. There didn't appear to be much to it. Instead, we interviewed Indian refugees who had compelling stories about the destruction of Basra. As we edited our package for *News at Ten*, furniture was being moved around our office. A major re-organisation was taking place, John's files and paperclips (and new typewriter!). It was distracting but, bless him, on his typewriter quest he had bought me a gift, a military camouflage pen, which I still have to this day.

Mindful of the mood in his country, on February 6th King Hussein again addressed the nation. What he had to say was very supportive of Iraq and even went so far as to claim that Saddam Hussein was fighting for all Arabs. It was essentially a call-to-arms with a short coda at the end calling for a ceasefire which felt almost like an afterthought. His words were firmly aimed at his domestic audience, but he appeared to have come off the fence with a vengeance. The State Department in Washington was incandescent. Jordan was again, for a short while, considered an enemy.

The following day, we did a package reflecting reaction to the King's inflammatory national address. Incredibly, our packages got on air. I say incredibly because this was the day, February 7th, that the IRA mortar-bombed Downing Street.

That evening, we flew to Cairo to cover a visit by British Foreign Secretary Douglas Hurd. We were due to stay for three days. I was concerned that we wouldn't be able to get back to Amman on the Sunday as Jordan might well have been bombed, invaded or both by then!

It took us most of the day in Cairo to get our press accreditation. It was a Friday, so everywhere was either closed or moving at snail's pace. *News at Ten* wanted a piece on the view from Egypt, both pro and anti the war. Fortunately, Video Cairo had gathered plenty of material so, while camera crew Mike Borer and Paul Dickie went to get shots of Douglas Hurd at the Foreign Ministry and a tremendous soundbite, I beavered away with a freelance editor who was slow (and a little deaf!) but very willing. We fed a very respectable three-minute-twenty package for *News at Ten*.

Back at the Ramses Hilton, a big Thank You fax from ITN was waiting for us. Fax machines, remember those?

Next day, we were in the Presidential Palace for Douglas Hurd's meeting with Egyptian President Hosni Mubarak, a press conference, and a one-to-one interview with Douglas Hurd. Like all the Foreign Secretaries I have had the privilege of meeting and interviewing, he was charming, incredibly articulate, and completely on top of his brief. Pre-Boris Johnson, that is!

There were three of us from ITN. Egyptian TV had a crew of eighteen. I counted them. One man's sole purpose appeared to be holding a screwdriver in case it was needed. Job creation Egypt style.

In the afternoon, our work done, and the tiger (ITN) fed, we went to the Pyramids. Paul and Mike had never been. The site was officially closed because of the war, but we found a hole in the fence. When I had been previously, the place had always been packed with tourists, guides and locals trying to sell souvenir tat. Now, we had the place to ourselves, in silence. It was a magical, mystical, time-travelling moment.

Back in Amman a couple of days later, we did two stories on Palestinians living in Jordan (the majority of the Jordanian population is Palestinian) and the comparative weakness of the Jordanian armed forces. Why, for example, had they been unable to shoot down Iraqi Scud missiles passing over their territory en route for Israel? We also fed Douglas Hurd and King Hussein soundbites for a backgrounder being pulled together in London. In the middle of all that, a busy day, we celebrated the lovely Afnan's birthday and surprised her with a huge chocolate cake and her present, a beautiful rug from Baghdad.

The next day, three days of national mourning began in Jordan after the Americans bombed what Iraq said was a civilian bomb shelter but the Americans claimed was a military command centre. Newspapers were bordered in black, and on the streets, huge demonstrations of people dressed in black and carrying black flags of mourning. We were the lead story for the first time in a while.

That evening, we flew back to Cairo for an Arab League Foreign Ministers meeting. I was once again slightly concerned to be leaving Amman in case the ground war started and the airport closed while we were out of position and unable to get back. I filled out yet another Iraq visa application in order to get myself and the crew to Baghdad in case we were needed there.

The Arab League Foreign Ministers meeting was the usual bunfight. We edited a package on the meeting and the mood in Cairo. The reaction of the bombing in Iraq was muted, in contrast to the uproar in Amman. As we were feeding for the lunchtime news, Radio Baghdad announced that Iraq had agreed to comply with UN Resolution 660 and withdraw from Kuwait. There was great excitement everywhere. ITN went 'open-ended', that is we broadcast continuously on ITV. It turned out to be another lie. The offer carried the by now familiar qualifications and was not the unconditional withdrawal demanded by the Resolution at all. Saddam Hussein was playing games, presumably to delay the start of the ground war. I did a couple of live two-ways, still something of a novelty in those days and a fresh package for the five forty and *News at Ten* reflecting Arab reaction to the latest diplomatic moves.

There was still an appetite for a piece the next day, so we got some more words from President Mubarak and others. When we got to Egyptian TV to feed our package to London, we were told they had no confirmation of our satellite booking from ITN, although the foreign desk had undoubtedly booked the satellite time. I got hold of the boss of Egypt TV who told me that the engineer involved was not only incompetent but also virulently anti-Western and had deliberately blocked our booking. With profuse apologies, she told me she would probably fire him. I was so angry I'd had done far worse to him. Missing a feed was a cardinal sin, even when it was clearly not our fault.

Back in Amman, we got the interview with PLO leader Yasser Arafat, which I had been chasing hard for several days. It was a very good twenty-minute interview. For me, the most memorable thing about that interview was how Arafat took a liking to cameraman Seb Rich who was something of a blond Adonis, and kept inviting Seb to stroke the handle of his famous pearl-handled revolver!

Late February, I was back to Cairo again, this time for the meeting of the Islamic Conference. As so often, evenings were spent in bars and sometimes casinos. On this evening, we were in a casino in our hotel. The place was full of young Kuwaiti men behaving like spoilt rich brats, literally screwing up, to them, worthless Egyptian pounds and throwing them around and generally treating the lovely Egyptian staff like something they'd stepped on. I contained my anger. Our soldiers were going to bleed and die in the desert for these bloody people?

Saddam Hussein announced that he was going on Radio Baghdad with a very important statement on the afternoon of February 21st although our package from Cairo still squeezed onto the bulletins. Far from being conciliatory, Saddam attacked his enemies and said the war would continue 'until victory'. It would not, of course, be his.

ITN editor-in-chief Stewart Purvis came to visit. Dinner that evening was in Romero's, an Italian/Palestinian restaurant and about the only place in Amman that was still open. Stewart was in top form, and seemed very pleased by the way ITN's operation in the Middle East was going. At the end of the meal, I asked for the bill. The waiter, with a big grin, sidled up to me.

"Yes, Mr Glen. A journalist bill?"

"No, no Mustafa. Just a normal bill."

A journalist bill is where the alcohol is 'lost'. My view is that expenses should cover living costs, including alcohol with dinner within reason. A beer or two each. I could hardly get away with that with the boss beside me, so we had to do what we were supposed to do, and pay for the alcohol in cash out of our own pockets. Perish the thought!

Back to Cairo again. The day after Saddam's defiant broadcast, US President George Bush had issued an ultimatum. Leave Kuwait by noon the next day or face the consequences. Coalition ground forces were poised to strike.

My mission in Cairo again was to get reaction from senior Egyptian and Kuwaiti government officials who were now in exile in the Egyptian capital. Mubarak was saying nothing, and the rest were doing the same. They were keeping their heads down.

I got back from Cairo just as our ITN team arrived in Amman from Baghdad, forced to leave once again. It was great to see them all. Brent

Saddler, Angela Frier, cameraman Phil Bye, Jim Dutton (who had managed to get an Iraqi visa after all) and picture editor, Patrick O'Ryan-Roerder, were dirty, dusty but safe and well and full of stories. *News at Ten* wanted me to do a pull-together of Arab reaction from Cairo, Amman and using agency pictures from Yemen and elsewhere, but I was able to join the others for dinner and a proper catch-up in a Chinese restaurant which we had found, another eating establishment in Amman still functioning.

The ground war duly began the next day. Very quickly, the Iraqi military began to collapse. At one thirty in the morning, eleven thirty p.m. in London, I did a live phono (talked live on the phone) to Alastair Burnet at ITN. It was an hour after *News at Ten* came off air, and Alastair had clearly taken some refreshment. Although it was one thirty a.m. in Amman, the InterContinental was a proper journalists' hotel. It had a bar on the top floor that was open twenty-four hours a day, a very bad idea! Producer John Curran came up to the bar. I had a beer in one hand and a whisky in the other when he told me they wanted me live on the phone right now. I thought he was joking. He wasn't.

Collin Baker in Tel Aviv was on immediately before me. It seemed he had also been imbibing. I listened to him and Alastair slurring their way through their two-way. Then it was my turn.

"So, Glen, how is King Saddam Hussein taking the news?"

Ignoring the elevation of the Iraqi dictator to the ruler of Jordan, I knew that even though I was slightly drunk I was going to be fine. Of the three of us, I'm sure I was by far the most sober.

The next morning, we did lives into *Channel 4 Daily* and ITN special bulletins. After one of them, the next guest, MP Greville Janner said "Everything Glen had just said is entirely accurate and absolutely spot on." It's always nice when that happens.

News at Ten decided that this time they did actually want an Arab reaction piece, so I interviewed a couple of academics and Dr Assad Abdul Rahman of the Palestine National Council and we sent a modest one-minute-thirty package.

Within three days, coalition forces had taken Kuwait City. We had all been hard at work in Amman and elsewhere in the region, but ITN cameraman Nigel Thompson and others were providing fantastic coverage of the fighting on the ground in Kuwait. Nigel was 'embedded' with the 7th

Armoured Brigade, The Desert Rats, with whom my uncles had fought at El Alamein and up through Italy during the Second World War.

A word about embedding. That is when a cameraman, sometimes with a reporter, joins a military unit for an operation. They get otherwise unavailable access, we get pictures we wouldn't otherwise get, but we surrender objectivity for accessibility. This is fine provided we have other teams seeing the effects of the outgoing ordnance, not just the shells leaving the tanks. We need to be able to report on the impact those shells are having.

Also, embedding is fine when the operation is going well, and so far they always have. But what will happen when the military unit we are embedded with takes serious casualties? I know soldiers well enough to be sure that having a camera pointed at them in such circumstances will not go down well.

On March 1st, King Hussein of Jordan again addressed the nation. This time his tone was much softer, seeking conciliation. In my view, this was the weakest story of the day by far, but *News at Ten* wanted a package and, to my amazement, it ran.

So too did our story the next day. I'd gone to the Baqa'a refugee camp with WTN cameraman, Yasser, who was Palestinian. Westerners were not welcome, but by then I could pass for anything. I had a deep tan. Indeed, when I was on holiday with my wife Marion, who is also olive-skinned, anywhere in the Mediterranean or north Africa, tourists were forever asking us for directions! So, as long as I kept my mouth shut, we would be OK. We got some good shots and tried to interview a doctor, who was angry and abusive. We had to leave as a hostile mob began to form. As we drove off, they threw rocks at our car. I understood their pain, but I was sick of being treated as the enemy, being accused of murdering their children. Still, it made a good three-minute piece for *News at Ten*.

Cameraman Bernie Glancy became known as Border Bernie. He had volunteered, or been volunteered, to stay at the border with the refugees for days on end. We'd send a car to the border every day to get his excellent material. Sometimes one of us would go, to do a piece to camera or talk to people. On one such occasion, the car pulled up and an arm extended through the rear window holding a glass of cold Chablis. Sandy Gall had arrived!

Towards the end, Bernie returned to Amman. He was covered in dust but was as cheerful as ever. South African picture editor Andy Rex, who was almost as wide as he was tall and it was all solid muscle, span through Bernie's tape at speed with Bernie and the rest of us standing behind him. He ejected the tape and threw it over his shoulder.

"Crap! Unusable!" he said.

Poor Bernie's face was a picture until he noticed Andy's huge grin. Cruel, but also very funny.

We did one last story from Jordan, a mixed bag of Western prisoners being released, UNICEF aid workers and, of all things, the Jordanian economy. Then it was time to go home. The money men had pulled the plug, and ITN was pulling out of Amman, Israel and Bahrain.

Before we left, we had to visit Petra, the ancient capital of the Nabataeans in the Arabah Valley which runs from the Dead Sea to the Gulf of Aqaba. The pink sandstone of the 'Rose City' sparkled in the sun as we emerged from the one-kilometre-walk through the Siq, the narrow gorge just three metres wide that leads directly to the Al-Khazneh (the Treasury), its columns carved into the rock. We walked in through the Siq and rode back out on horseback. Petra is absolutely stunning. There were no tourists, of course, just us and a few sheep and goats. Another opportunity to time travel. We only had three hours there. I resolved to return one day to spend more time in 'the rose red city, half as old as time'. I still haven't. Maybe one day.

After the ceasefire, the Kurds in northern Iraq had risen up, fuelled by the hope that the Saddam Hussein regime would fall. Despite initial successes, in which the Kurdish Peshmerga fighters captured every city in the north, the Americans failed to help them despite initially encouraging them to overthrow the regime. They were brutally suppressed, as were the Marsh Arabs in the south. Although Iraq was not allowed to fly fixed-wing aircraft, they were permitted to use helicopters because the infrastructure of the country was so badly damaged. In particular, too many bridges had been destroyed. Iraqi helicopter gunships destroyed entire villages. In less than a month, tens of thousands of people were killed and nearly two million displaced as the Kurds tried to establish an autonomous republic in Iraqi Kurdistan under the leadership of Jalal Talabani and Masoud Barzani.

Kurdish civilians were trying to escape through the mountains to Iran and Turkey. Iran opened its borders, but Turkey had initially allowed some refugees in and then shut the rest out. Three hundred thousand Kurdish men, women and children gathered at the border where Turkish soldiers physically pushed them back. Behind them, Iraqi helicopter gunships and tanks continued to do their worst, killing indiscriminately.

I had been covering the story from London before we were sent to cover it properly. From the Turkish capital, Ankara, we chartered a Cessna and flew to Diyarbakir in south-east Turkey, an ethnically Kurdish city. As soon as we arrived, cameraman Pete Blanchard, our Paris based producer Barbara Gray, and picture editor Roger Pitman, we began working on a piece for *News at Ten* with our own material and some very good pictures from French TV TF1. We cut two minutes forty-five for *News at Ten*. It led the bulletin.

We had to get to the border. Barbara organised a minibus and we spent a sleepless night travelling dangerous, muddy mountain roads. Next morning, we stopped in Gevaş on Lake Van to do a live phono into ITN. The satellite phone at the time came in a small suitcase which opened into an umbrella-shaped disc. We were in a farmyard, surrounded by chickens, on the shore of Lake Van with snow-capped mountains reflected in its waters, next to a cherry orchard lapped by the waters of the lake. The villagers gathered around in amazement. Who were these strange people with their even stranger technology? It felt like we had just landed from Mars.

We also met some of the famous Lake Van cats, large, white and with different coloured eyes, one amber the other blue. Known as the swimming cats they frequently (and presumably uniquely among cats) took to the waters of the lake.

We stopped in the town of Hakkâri for a breakfast of omelettes and bread before a further three-hour drive to a small mountain town, Çukurca, right on the border. Senior Reporter Michael Nicholson was already there, working with cameraman Alan Downes, cutting a package for ITN and being rather grumpy about it. Barbara found us somewhere to stay, the living room of a Kurdish family's apartment. There were four of us. Producers Barbara Gray and Mary Amthor had beds, Pete and I had the floor.

At first light, such a desolate scene. These proud people covered in mud, cold and hungry, reduced to relying on foreign aid. Pete Blanchard, Mary Amthor and I spent much of the day with a Kurdish doctor, Assam A'Ahmed. We helped him erect a tent for his family. The tiny local hospital was completely overwhelmed.

Nicholson tried and failed to poach Mary! He already had Barbara working with him, not to mention one of ITN's most experienced cameramen, Alan Downes, picture editor Roger Pitman and not one but two interpreters. We cut two minutes for *News at Ten* on why aid wasn't getting to where it was needed. We fed from a TRT (Turkish TV) satellite dish. The Turks were denying access to starving, freezing refugees, but were happy enough to help us and to take ITN's money.

We had a wide array of pronunciations for the town of Çukurca. Nicholson's was particularly bizarre. We would be sending two packages, one by Mike the other by me, with the same location sign off but wildly different pronunciations. No one back at base seemed to notice, or care.

Day two and Michael Nicholson and Alan Downes marched up the mountain to get to where the Turkish soldiers were holding back the refugees. Pete and I filmed around the town. There was almost a riot at the food distribution centre, shocking scenes. These people were desperate.

Then it was our turn to go to the top of the hill. Pete, our interpreter Ayad, who was himself a Kurdish refugee, and I hitched a ride in ABC's Land Rover, but we didn't get far. The road, such as it was, was blocked by an aid truck which had been ambushed by hungry refugees. There were also ambulances and doctors who couldn't get through. We had to climb the rest of the way.

It was a sunny day in the mountains, blue skies over the scene that looked almost festive, like a Kurdish Woodstock, until we got close. Then the horror revealed itself. Babies severely dehydrated, old people dangerously weak and dying. It was still very muddy, even after several hot days, in the rain it must have been Hell. At night it was freezing cold.

We filmed medical tents and the line of extremely hostile Turkish soldiers before crossing into Iraq and the main refugee camp. The Kurds are very photogenic. The children with their ready smiles and giggles, the men striking and handsome, the young women very beautiful. I was surprised that many were blond until I was told that they were the descendants of the army of Alexander the Great.

We filmed a parachute drop of aid from an RAF Hercules straight onto an area sown with landmines.

As night was falling, we headed back down to Çukurca. Michael Nicholson and Alan Downes had some very good material of refugees being forced out of the town by Turkish police and troops. WTN had harrowing shots of a mass grave for babies. There were no words.

But words had to be found. We sent a package for *News at Ten* which was very well received back in London. I felt almost guilty to be eating dinner in 'The Ritz', bread, cheese and tomatoes, all sent from Hâkkari, and red wine! Local and rough but very welcome.

Eurovision's satellite dish arrived in Hâkkari. Eurovision is a TV satellite service, part of the European Broadcasting Union, jointly owned by several leading European broadcasters. The Turks withdrew their satellite dish from Çukurca. So, Eurovision had arrived late and they were three hours away. Great! As ever, though, their operation was smooth and very professional.

Another day and another climb up the mountain, this time with Alan Downes and our Kurdish fixer/interpreters Ayad and Faisal. Once again, aid trucks had been ambushed by desperate refugees who were literally fighting for food. Just awful.

Alan Downes was the cameraman who, with sound recordist Tom Phillips, had filmed the unforgettable images during the Vietnam War of nine-year-old Kim Phuc running towards the camera her body on fire after south Vietnamese warplanes had dropped napalm on her village. I was very conscious that I was working with a legend! We had worked together before, including in Czechoslovakia covering the Velvet Revolution. But that had been urban and with a lot of politics. Now, were we out in the open in a war zone which felt much closer to Alan's natural habitat.

The Turkish army was, at last, imposing some order and method to food distribution. At the top of the hill, refugees were forming queues. We filmed the efforts of Médicins Sans Frontières and heard from the Kurds horror stories of what had been happening in the city of Duhok. We cut a two-minute package for the five forty news and a longer version for *News at Ten*. These beautiful people living in such indescribable squalor, with babies and the elderly literally dying all around us. In one tent, we had come across an old man sitting on the floor and cradling a woman in his arms. In English, he repeated over and over: "My wife is dead."

We left Çukurca after just over a week. The plan was to move further along the border when news came from London that the coalition allies were planning to send troops to bring the Kurds back down from the mountains. I did a live two-way with *News at One* and got reaction from the nearby Isikli refugee camp. We drove as fast as possible through the mud and potholes to Hâkkari, where Barbara also had some good material she had shot with WTN at an RAF Chinook base. We cut and fed a package for both the five forty and *News at Ten*.

We stayed the night at a very grotty hotel an hour away in Yüksekova. Apparently, it was the best hotel in the area. I'd hate to see the worst! But we had a bed and our own rooms, although there was no food and no running water. Compared to what we had just seen, we were in the lap of luxury.

On the road again early the next morning, we stopped for breakfast in a mountain village, Başkale. Bread, eggs, cheese, honey and tea, most acceptable. We stopped at Hoşap with its amazing castle for emergency repairs to our increasingly battered car. We drove through stunning landscapes. Lake Van, snow-capped mountains, green valleys and villages where everyone still wore traditional dress. We came upon a Kurdish wedding in a field. There was dancing and music in front of large nomad tents. We were invited to share in and film the celebrations. It was very photogenic, set in the most spectacular scenery.

Our next stop was Batman, where I phoned ITN for a planning update. Batman was disappointing, a very boring town. I was desperate to do a piece for ITN with a Batman sign off but the foreign desk wasn't having it! Another three hours took us to our hotel for the night near Nusaybin. My own room and a hot shower. Luxury!

Throughout this time, just two mountains away, fellow ITN reporter, Andrew Simmons, was covering the same story. Peter Sharp was in Sulaymaniyah. I didn't see any of Peter's no doubt excellent work, but Andy and I were saying the same thing. In my words: "These people need help, and they need it NOW."

Finally, the American and British governments acted, declaring a 'safe haven' in Iraqi Kurdistan and banning the Iraqis from using helicopters.

The tide began to turn on April 19th. At Silopi, we filmed a thousand US marines with a lot of American helicopters. It looked like a scene from the Vietnam War. Alan Downes was in his element and got some great footage. After much searching we found a British officer, one of just a handful who had so far arrived. In the Haj resting area, twenty thousand Kurdish refugees were being protected. They were all members of the same clan. We interviewed the clan chief, a magnificent fellow who looked like a mountain bandit straight out of central casting, with huge white whiskers, a colourful waistcoat and wearing a ceremonial dagger. He liked the British because they had supplied guns to his father! After feeding what, in all modesty, I thought was an excellent package for *News at Ten*, we headed back to our hotel in Nusaybin, a long drive but a half-decent hotel. I wanted to stay in a fleapit much closer to the story, but I was outvoted.

Next day we drove past fields full of newly landed US marines. Towards the end I ordered us to stop as I had spotted what looked like British troops. It was 45 Commando Royal Marines. We strode across the field to greet them. Their senior officers were gathered around a map table, the bonnet of a Land Rover. They had come directly from Arctic training in Norway and weren't yet sure of the lie of the land. In fact, I think it would be fair to say they barely had a clue where they were! I was in my element showing them where we were, where the refugees were and where the Iraqi forces were believed to be.

We had a huge row with the BBC. There was a pool arrangement for one crew to fly on a US marines' helicopter into northern Iraq and share the pictures with everyone else. We were the assigned crew, but the BBC made such a bloody fuss annoying the Americans that we were all in danger of not being taken anywhere. Eventually, I found a compromise. The BBC reporter would go with Alan Downes. The pictures were all that mattered. As a reporter on a pool facility, the rules are simple: you cannot do a piece to camera or use first person lines like 'I flew into northern Iraq with US forces'. You are really only there to take notes, get information (which you are supposed to share) and help the cameraman.

While Alan was in the air, I was gathering information to talk around his pictures. Barbara Gray organised copies of his pictures for the other broadcasters, and we cut two minutes thirty for the late evening news. Tremendous pictures, and quite rightly, we were the lead story. Word came back from Mike Nolan on the Foreign Desk. "Great piece and much better than the BBC's." Even though they had had access to precisely the same pictures.

Next day, we were with 45 Commando of the Royal Marines. Their commanding officer, Colonel Jonathan Thomson, was taking a helicopter to the Iraqi town of Zakho and would take a small handful of journalists. The BBC were ahead of us, but Alan and I busked our way on. If we hadn't, we would have been well and truly scooped.

We filmed the Royal Marines setting up their field headquarters, a school in the village of Darhawzan, followed a foot patrol for a while, filmed a coordination meeting with the US marines and talked to the local Kurds, who were very happy to see the allied forces.

It was hot and dusty, the hills covered in red poppies. A walk in the hills with Alan was like a nature ramble. He loved filming the birds and lizards, and seemed to know the name of every plant.

At the US marines headquarters, we chatted to General Jay Garner, who lent us his personal Blackhawk to fly back in!

The EBU satellite dish was now up and working in Cesri just on the Turkish side of the border. We edited and fed our package for the five forty with a longer version for *News at Ten*. The verdict from Nolan on the foreign desk: "Another cracker."

Cameraman Bernie Glancy arrived that evening, so the next day I had two cameramen. The Americans were laying on pool facilities. The BBC were to go to the refugee camp at Işikveren. There was also a pool facility to go to the town of Zakho. I tried to get Bernie onto that one but it was Sky's turn. I returned a short time later to discover that the list had been torn up, pool places were suddenly up for grabs and that German ZDF had grabbed our place. Outrageous! I managed to get myself onto the helicopter, but not Alan or Bernie.

ZDF were hopeless! An incredibly pompous and self-important reporter and a cameraman who needed constant directing. Obviously, I'd been spoilt by working with some of the best camera crews in the world. When we returned, ninety per cent of the footage was unusable due to some technical problem. ZDF dubbed the little that was salvageable for us, although we had to provide our own machine (a BW35 for anyone who cares), but they were unable to do so for anyone else, leaving the BBC, Reuters, Sky News et al very angry. This was not how a pool facility was supposed to work. Fortunately, BBC cameraman Albie Charlton had some very good pictures from the camp at Işikveren which saved the day, and we cut those with the usable ZDF pictures to package a very good looking piece for *News at Ten*.

There were no Western military media facilities the next day, so Alan and I simply walked into northern Iraq. The Turkish soldiers were indifferent. On the Iraqi side, dejected revolutionary guards glared at us but we passed unmolested. We hitched a ride in an American Humvee into Zakho, where we discovered the US marines were pulling out under the watchful eyes of heavily armed Ba'ath Party militia. We didn't understand why until we were told that the Brits were taking over. Shortly afterwards, three companies of Royal Marine commandos arrived, giving us a great story. We also filmed at Zakho's hospital, where we found an Iraqi militia man who had managed to shoot himself in the leg (intentionally?) with his AK-47.

That evening, after talks in Baghdad, Saddam Hussein promised the Kurds an 'autonomous region' within Iraq. There are thirty million Kurds scattered across Iraq, Turkey, Iran and Syria. They really should have their own country, but an autonomous region in northern Iraq was at least a start.

There was a pause for diplomatic efforts. Next morning, Alan and I walked across the border again and got a lift in a pickup truck to Zakho. Very little was happening. The marines were not going out on patrol, ordered to keep a low profile and wait to see if the talks in Baghdad would resolve the situation in the north. But we did come across some Kurdish Peshmerga fighters, great pictures, and interviewed their leader. We got some shots around town and assorted interviews. ITN Defence correspondent Geoffrey Archer had arrived two days earlier. It was his turn to do the package for *News at Ten*, but he and Bernie Glancy were stranded on a mountain top. The weather had closed in and their helicopter couldn't fly, so we packaged for the five forty and *News at Ten*.

We spent the evening conspiring with various Fleet Street journos to take a Land Rover into Iraq and tried to get to Dohuk, which was still under the control of the Iraqi army. No one had yet got that far.

Early the next morning, we met up with Stewart Paine of the *Evening Standard,* who kindly lent us his Land Rover. We persuaded a British officer to drive the Land Rover across the border at the head of his convoy. We did some shots around Zakho: the Royal Marines, the hospital, the police station with its horrific blood-stained walls. Jed Evans of the *Today* newspaper drove Alan and me to Dohuk. No one else wanted to come, it was deemed 'too dangerous'.

We collected a very frightened policeman, Mardi, in a village en route. He was willing to guide us but was scared and spent most of the time crouching down on the backseat. We drove past Iraqi tanks and troops without incident. In Dohuk, we filmed destroyed Kurdish homes, looted shops, and the blackened ruins of the Ba'ath Party headquarters. I did a very quick piece to camera, we didn't want any of the Iraqi soldiers to become curious.

In Zakho, there were rumours of refugees coming down from the mountains. The rumours were unfounded. We drove a few miles up the road they would have to take, but there was no sign of them.

Back safely in Cesri, we had to argue our case to ITN. Robin Staniforth on the foreign desk didn't understand the significance of what we'd done (risking life and limb!). He had never heard of Dohuk. Mary Amthor, with her charm on full beam, sold the story to *News at Ten*. We sent a two-minute-thirty package. The pictures were fantastic. I was so lucky to have Alan Downes on camera. Our piece got an 'exclusive' tag and we received a lot of praise from ITN in London. Robin, ever the gentleman, had the good grace to admit he had been wrong.

By now, the British and American military had begun holding morning off-camera briefings. The day after our little Dohuk escapade, they were offering another facility to the Işikveren refugee camp. I put Bernie Glancy and Roger Pitman on that (picture editors like to get out once in a while to actually see some action), while Alan and I drove across to northern Iraq with the Americans and then hired a local driver. We interviewed people at a 'safe enclave' camp that had been set up. There was still no sign of the refugees coming down from the mountains.

Royal Marine commandos were patrolling the town and menacingly asking local people and uniformed policemen: "Where are the secret police?" The question was peppered with the strongest expletives.

We drove back across the border in an American army truck, and cut a package for ITN using our material and pooled pictures from ABC, WTN and TF1.

ITN, it seemed, was broke! We were restricted to one satellite feed per day. The next day was a Sunday, and senior foreign editor Mike Nolan insisted we feed track and rushes (that is, raw footage with a voice track from me to be edited together in London for the lunchtime news). I disagreed, thinking we should keep our powder dry for later, but orders are orders. In the afternoon, we got some great material: Peshmerga roadblocks, British Royal Marines pushing east, French Paras distributing food and so on. We rushed back to discover we couldn't feed to London. Only one feed a day was allowed. I was angry and had a row with Nolan, which was unusual as I not only liked him very much but also respected him as the best in the business. Later, we both apologised and made up, and they simply ran my lunchtime piece in the late news bulletin.

Fred Hickey arrived. He said our coverage had been fantastic and had made him 'proud'. Praise indeed from one of the ITN Greats.

ITN had discovered a large hole in its budget, millions of pounds, much of it due to expenses paid out but not yet receipted or accounted for. All ITN teams abroad had been called back to London. We were the last team standing. Something of a catastrophe, and hence the restriction to one feed a day.

ITN's new editor-in-chief Stewart Purvis was imposing much-needed discipline back at ITN HQ. There was also a new sobriety. The bar in the ITN building was closed. ITN's maverick, cavalier attitude was changing. There would be no more extravagant and usually fairly riotous celebrations of a story success. Management was imposing a more disciplined and cash-conscious system.

One of the first casualties was the head of news input, the hugely talented Nigel Hancock, who had to resign after 'irregularities' were discovered in his expenses claims. Nigel was certainly extravagant in spending ITN's money rewarding reporters and camera crews for their hard work, often in arduous and sometimes dangerous conditions, with expensive dinners and drinking sessions. Although he admitted to spending ITN's money freely, he couldn't accurately account for where it had all gone, other than to say none of it had gone into his own pocket. This was clearly true. But Nigel was old school and his style of management was now out of fashion and severely frowned upon.

Nigel was an inspirational leader, and a heroic drinker. He could be very demanding, and so he should have been, and would have ten ideas, eight of which were completely mad and impractical but two of which would be pure genius. He could also be immensely infuriating. At one particularly drunken affair he had said something that had so annoyed cameraman Nigel Thompson that he had punched him hard enough to knock him to the ground. As he fell, Hancock held his glass of wine aloft and hit the floor without spilling a drop!

Anyway, back in Iraqi Kurdistan, BBC correspondent Kate Adie turned up and immediately began demanding that the British military provide her with an excusive helicopter facility. The ego had landed! We soon put a stop to that. Helicopter facilities were pooled, we shared them.

That day, Mary and Bernie went on a military facility to Zakho, while Alan and I drove across the border. We took Phil Reeves of the *Independent* and the *Guardian*'s David Hearst with us. The plan was to go to Saddam's summer palace but, after advice from Colonel Thompson of 45 Commando, we headed instead for Kani Masi, the marines' most easterly advanced position. The village had been raised to the ground by Saddam's forces. People were living in tents next to the ruins of their homes. A Royal Marines doctor was doing his best to help. We came across one dehydrated baby who was probably beyond saving. It was gut-wrenching.

The next day, April 30th was The Big Day: the refugees began to return home. In Zakho we filmed at the UN's new camp, which was basically one tent and a flag. Further up the mountainside, we filmed great shots of a huge convoy of refugees coming down. The Peshmerga, helped by the Royal Marines, were loading the refugees onto military trucks. For us, it felt like we had seen the story through. The Kurds, some of them at least, were coming home. Jim Ackhurst on the foreign desk said we'd probably come home at the end of the week. It felt like the story was more or less over.

Two days later, we got to Saddam Hussein's summer palace at Sirsenk. After a briefing and interview with Brigadier Andrew Keeling we drove to the airstrip at the summer palace. Royal Marines were arriving in convoy by road, while others landed in helicopters and jumped off going through their drills, crouching in a circle, rifles pointing outwards. We were the only television crew there.

There was an army PR officer there, a major.

"Where are you from?" he asked.

"ITN."

He turned to his colleague. "Oh shit, what will Kate Adie say?"

Although the summer palace at Sirsenk was surrounded by armed Iraqi revolutionary guards, they put up no resistance and we were free to roam and film at will. To say the palace was opulent would be a massive understatement.

We drove back along difficult mud tracks and through some of the most beautiful countryside any of us had ever seen, and fed our exclusive to ITN.

Next morning, the Turkish soldiers at the border had once again become hostile. They delayed us for three hours. Robert Fisk of the *Independent* had written a brilliant article about their dreadful behaviour, physically abusing the refugees and stealing their food. Fisk was to be expelled from the country and they were making life difficult for the rest of us.

We returned to Batufa which had been the staging post for the move east to Saddam's summer palace. It was now virtually deserted. In Zakho we got shots of more refugees coming down from the mountains and the inadequate and rather pitiful UN camp, and fed for *News at Ten*.

There was one fantastic piece of news that day, the little dehydrated baby girl we had filmed three days earlier close to death in Kani Masi had pulled through and was regaining her strength. Wonderful news.

It was finally time to go home.

We were supposed to get a US military helicopter to Diyarbakir, but that didn't happen, so four of us piled into a car. Our route took us along the Syrian border, and more breathtaking scenery.

Plan B was to hitch a ride back to the UK with the RAF, but that too failed. There were no RAF flights back to the UK that day, so getting home took a while, although in some comfort. A passable hotel in Diyarbakir, a night at the Hilton in Ankara, from where our flight to Frankfurt was delayed and we missed our connection to Heathrow so we stayed overnight at the airport Sheraton. A bit of a tortuous journey, not unpleasant, but all we really wanted to do was get home. We left Iraq on a Saturday and finally arrived home in the afternoon of the following Tuesday.

Next on the agenda was some serious leave, and another Caribbean cruise courtesy of my sister. It was great to see old friends and drinking buddies still working onboard. As well as visiting Jamaica, Puerto Rico, St Thomas, the Dominican Republic, Grand Cayman, Cozumel and once again, the Mayan Ruins at Chichen Itza and Tulum, we spent some time in Miami and New Orleans.

Back at work in London in June, big news was afoot at ITN. Alastair Burnet and Sir David Nicholas were retiring, a great loss, the beating heart of ITN. The newspapers were full of bad news from ITN. For the first time in the company's history, there were to be compulsory redundancies. An absolute disaster. No one was being sent to cover stories abroad thanks to the financial meltdown. In fact, our team in Kurdistan had been the very last to be recalled. Needless to say, morale was dreadful. There were to be one hundred and thirty-seven redundancies, a substantial proportion of our ITN family. We got the number, one hundred and thirty-seven, before we were told who was on the list so we were all worried, even though I had been assured that I had absolutely nothing to be worried about. All this at the time when we had moved from Wells Street to our shiny new building in Gray's Inn Road because (oh the irony!) we needed more space. It was heart-breaking to see friends and colleagues losing their jobs in this way.

I spent eight hours ostensibly working that day in late June. Most of it was spent commiserating, reassuring and encouraging, accompanied by some heavy drinking.

The news did not stop, of course, and needed to be covered. The very next day, I interviewed anti-apartheid chairman, Archbishop Trevor Huddleston, who was returning to South Africa for the first time in thirty-five years, and various MPs on various political stories.

A week later, I was deep under the English Channel with camera crew Chris Squires and Roger Dove. We were covering the breakthrough of the Channel Tunnel, the moment when British and French excavators with their huge tunnel-boring machines (TBMs) finally met.

In hard hats and overalls we were taken down a deep shaft before a seventy-five-minute train ride on a narrow gauge track in semi-darkness. The breakthrough, when it came, was spectacular, with warm handshakes when the French climbed through their huge TBM to greet their British counterparts and open the champagne.

Other stories I covered that summer included two IRA men who shot their way out of Brixton prison, the launch of the largest and most expensive European Space Agency satellite, a G7 summit, cuts in the armed forces (*plus ça change*) and an interview with Defence Secretary Tom King, Romanian orphans being put up for adoption, cricket (about which I know very little), and a ten-year plan to revitalize British Rail.

In Moscow that August, newly-elected President Boris Yeltsin sat astride a tank outside the Russian parliament building to defy an attempted coup by hardliners opposed to Mikhail Gorbachev's reforms. Troops and tanks were on the streets of Moscow. It looked like the end of glasnost and perestroika. There was a standoff for three days before the soldiers and tanks returned to barracks. The dye was cast. On Saturday August 24th, Mikhail Gorbachev resigned from the Communist Party of the Soviet Union, and advised it to wind itself up. It was the end of the Soviet Communist Party. It seemed almost inconceivable.

By December, the Soviet Union had been dissolved.

All this time, colleagues were being made redundant. Among them, cameraman Steve Harrow, who had been one of the stars of ITN's coverage of the first Gulf War just a few months previously. "From hero to zero," as he put it. Another was cameraman Frank Harding, the reluctant tripod-user. He was clearly upset but bearing up well. Several of us took him for a drink and a lot of teasing about tripods.

It was time for my second spectacular holiday of the year, three weeks in Kenya staying with friends near Mombasa and visiting several game parks. On one trip, I took the train from Mombasa to Nairobi along the old British Imperial route through stations with rusty old enamel signs showing the name of the place, the population and the altitude. Children ran screaming and laughing up to the train, whose arrival was the highlight of their day. Arriving in Nairobi, I wanted to get a taxi to Lake Nakuru to see the flamingos. A charming taxi driver, who was from Nakuru, said he would take me.

"My car is a lion," he assured me.

In fact, his rust-bucket had no floor on the passenger side, so I had to spend the journey with my feet up on the dashboard. When we arrived, he took me to see his mother. On Kenya's liberation in 1963, President Kenyatta had settled the Mau Mau fighters by giving them one cow and a small plot of land each. My driver Patrick's mother still had one cow and a small garden of maize crops. He also took me to a bar full of former Mau Mau fighters, complete with impressive dreadlocks. I walked in, first provoking absolute silence, but they relaxed when they saw who I was with and told me stories about their fight for liberation from the British Empire.

I was excited to be going to the Croatian capital, Zagreb, at the end of September, but also slightly wary. Two journalists had already been killed there.

The journey to Zagreb was slightly strange. A flight via Frankfurt to Graz in Austria, then an airline coach to Zagreb. An airline bus to a war zone! Bizarre.

There were a few Croatian roadblocks to negotiate, and Zagreb itself was under blackout with almost every window taped up and basement entrances blocked with sandbags. They were preparing for the worst.

Our hotel, the InterContinental, was also under blackout but otherwise functioning normally. I joined the ITN team already there for a late supper. My colleagues, Terry Lloyd, Angela Frier, Phil Bye, Patrick O'Ryan-Roerder and Mike Lawrence were all in good form and already had plenty of Zagreb stories to share.

The fighting between the Croatian army and the Federal Republic of Yugoslavia (FRY) military had already begun in the east of the country. The majority of Croats wanted Croatia to leave the FRY and become a separate sovereign country, but ethnic Serbs in the east opposed the secession and fought to become part of Serbia together with those parts of Bosnia-Herzegovina which also had majority ethnic-Serb populations.

Croatia had declared independence in late June. The FRY/Serbian response had been to try to occupy Croatia to force the Croats to remain part of Yugoslavia. They failed. So they implemented a plan B, the creation within Croatia of a separate Serbian Republic. Hence the fighting. It would take another four years for Croatia to finally establish its independence and the integrity of its borders.

The fighting had not yet reached Zagreb, but the citizens of the Croatian capital were braced for conflict. Air raid sirens disturbed the peace day and night in this pretty city with its beautiful national theatre/opera house, gothic cathedral and streets of eighteenth and nineteenth century Austro-Hungarian architecture. It felt like the lull before the storm.

On my first full day in Zagreb, reporter Terry Lloyd and camera crew Phil Bye and Mike Lawrence headed for the coast while I covered the politics using a CNN crew. A press conference at the Foreign Ministry followed by a very good interview with the Croatian foreign minister in which he revealed that Belgrade had rejected Croatia's latest peace offer. That was the lunchtime news sorted. In the afternoon, a good interview with the Croatian defence minister and some very strong pictures of the fighting from a local TV source. That was the later bulletins fed.

We were woken early the next morning by yet another air raid siren, another false alarm. WTN got some very good pictures of the fighting, and I packaged them with updates for all ITN bulletins but without actually leaving Zagreb. Terry and co returned from the coast with some good material for the next day.

We tried over subsequent days to get the other side of the story, with several trips to the military district HQ of the federal army. Each time, we were denied access to the barracks. They did not want to talk to the Western media.

This was to become the pattern of the Yugoslav war. The Serbs treated us as the enemy. For the first time, Western journalists were actively targeted. The Serbs did not recognise, let alone respect, our neutrality.

John Schofield, who was just twenty-nine, was a keen young reporter at the start of his career. John had been an ITN trainee before joining the BBC, for whom he was covering the war in Croatia. He and his crew had got out of their car to film when they were targeted by small arms fire. The killers were Croatian soldiers rather than Serbs, but bullets have no nationality.

We finally got into the federal army military district HQ, and I interviewed General Raketa and was given the full tour of the barracks at Boragai. Despite our efforts, ITN had lost interest in the story and we were to be recalled home the next day. The main team in Belgrade was also heading home. It was a reduction rather than a full pull-out. Terry Lloyd was to stay for a little while longer. There had been a lull in hostilities ahead of peace talks which, in my view, were certain to fail. The Yugoslav air force had bombed two towns in Croatia that same day. Some ceasefire!

The money men had struck again. ITN was counting the pennies. I was withdrawn from Croatia, Michael Nicholson and his team in Belgrade were also to return to London. The conflict in Yugoslavia was by now barely featuring, if at all, on the BBC World Service, CNN or Sky News. The newspapers had also largely lost interest. I was to return later to Croatia, but on that last day of this first job in that country we went to Sisak as the Yugoslav air force bombed two nearby towns.

Before we left, Patrick O'Ryan-Roerder and I went to watch the changing of the guard at the Presidential Palace in Zagreb which was hilarious and positively Ruritanian.

On my return to London, the Zagreb team was moved to Bucharest where coal miners had stormed the parliament building leading to the overthrow of the post-Ceauşescu government of Petre Roman, the country's first non-communist government since 1945. Interest in the story in Zagreb and more widely in Croatia had evaporated.

By early October, it was back to doing rather run-of-the-mill stories in the UK. There was a Paul Gascoigne story, one of so many as he was so frequently getting into all sorts of trouble. Help the Aged launched a new Home Safety campaign with Home Secretary Kenneth Baker. I interviewed him with Nigel Thompson on camera. As ever with Ken Baker, it was a good interview, but both Nigel and I longed to be somewhere more interesting.

In early November, there were cases to cover at the High Court and I got to interview the England football manager Graham Taylor and coach Laure McMenemy when Bryan Robson announced his retirement from international football. Laurie remembered me from my Metro Radio days in Newcastle, which was nice of him and typical of the man.

I covered the Gulf War investitures at Buckingham Palace, including two of ITN's own: reporter, Michael Nicholson, and cameraman, Eugene Campbell, an OBE and an MBE respectively. No such awards for me, sadly, just two hours of standing around in the freezing cold!

I was expecting to stay with that story for the rest of the day when news came in that Robert Maxwell was missing and feared drowned. Our newsroom, like others no doubt, went into full-on headless chicken overdrive. I live-voiced a package for the five forty news, and dubbed my piece for *News at Ten* at the last possible moment to make sure we included the very latest information on what had become a very fast-moving story.

Maxwell's death remains a mystery. His body was discovered floating in the sea hours after he was reported missing from his luxury yacht. For months, his business empire had been on the brink of collapse. He had stolen hundreds of millions of pounds from his companies' pension funds to stay afloat (pun intended) and pay for his lavish lifestyle. Thousands of his employees lost their pensions.

There have been many theories about how and why Robert Maxwell died. One that gained traction for years was that he was working for Israel's Mossad and was about to go public with damaging information about the activities of the Israeli secret service, and therefore had to be eliminated. Or he was depressed over his business empire failing, expected his theft of the pension funds to be discovered and took his own life. The truth is probably more prosaic, that he slipped or possibly had a heart attack, fell into the sea, and drowned.

Cameraman, Nigel Thompson, meanwhile, had got himself to somewhere far more exciting. With reporter Paul Davies, he was sending back award-winning pictures from the siege of Dubrovnik as artillery shells pounded the medieval Croatian town, a UNESCO World Heritage site. Dubrovnik was rebuilt in the mid-1990s, and with memories of that awful war fading, is probably best known these days as the location for King's Landing in *Game of Thrones*.

By now, mid-November, I was desperate to get back to Croatia, or Belgrade, or anywhere in Yugoslavia to cover the war. I was almost assigned, but Michael Nicholson was sent instead. A fair decision, as he was far senior to me, far more experienced, and had just been awarded an OBE. A fair decision, entirely justified, but still disappointing.

It was Remembrance Sunday, so I focused on my package from the Cenotaph and stopped worrying about Yugoslavia.

Another story that month was the naming of the two Libyan intelligence officers suspected of masterminding the Lockerbie bombing, a story I had covered three years earlier. Our Scotland correspondent, my friend David Chater, had been sent to Yugoslavia, so I covered the biggest Scottish story for some time.

On November 15th, it emerged that the former assistant general secretary of the British Communist Party, Reuben Falber, admitted to being funded from Moscow for more than twenty years. Hardly surprising to anyone except, apparently, Communist Party members. *News at Ten* wanted a slightly tongue-in-cheek treatment.

We were filming various set-up shots including a KGB dead-letter box (a loose stone beside Coram's Fields) when we heard that David Chater had been shot and badly wounded in Vukovar. He was with camera crew John Martin and John Boyce, taking shelter from sniper fire in a church. They should have been safe enough. He was caught by a bullet in the back which travelled out through his stomach even though he was wearing body armour. Everyone at ITN was deeply shocked. Editor-in-chief Stewart Purvis took command, while Nigel Hancock and David Mannion flew with David's wife and his parents to Belgrade, to where he had been flown by an army helicopter for surgery.

I interviewed Reuben Falber, who was not the world's greatest interviewee and my heart wasn't in it. We'd seen absolutely appalling images of David being carried away on a stretcher. We were all deeply shocked.

My Communist Party story made an amusing 'And Finally' for *News at Ten*, and gave everyone in the newsroom a good chuckle, which was desperately needed. Chater had undergone a five-hour operation and was 'serious but stable' in intensive care. By some divine grace, the bullet had missed his spine but he was to lose a kidney.

Once *News at Ten* was finished, news came in of an IRA bomb in St Albans, and I was sent to cover it. Cameraman Steve Harrow, who lived there, had already got all the shots available and even interviewed two eyewitnesses.

IRA bombers, Patricia Black, who as just eighteen, and Frankie Ryan killed themselves when the bomb that they were carrying exploded prematurely in the doorway of a former bank.

I did a piece to camera just as the local nightclubs were closing and people were emerging. A few minutes later and the bomb would have caused many deaths. I had to shout at drunken revellers to, "SHUT UP! People have died here", so that we could work. They did. At two a.m. the head of anti-terrorism squad, George Churchill-Coleman, held a press conference, and we sneaked some good shots of the anti-terrorist squad investigating and clearing up.

It was an all-nighter as we headed back to ITN to cut the lead story for the morning news bulletins on ITV and Channel 4.

Four days later, we witnessed the return of the Archbishop of Canterbury's special envoy Terry Waite who had finally been released from captivity in Beirut and had arrived at RAF Lyneham. He delivered a moving, memorable speech and managed to be both profound and funny. It was a tour de force from someone who had just been released after more than four years in captivity.

David Chater was recovering well in hospital in Belgrade. Just five days after he was shot, he was on the five forty news being interviewed from his hospital bed, joking and looking in relatively good shape. He needed another week before he would be well enough to fly home. It was a huge relief to see him.

My other stories in November included a Dutch trawler rammed by a hit-and-run Cypriot cargo ship in the Channel with the loss of all six lives, covering the annual CND conference, and the return home of businessman Ian Richter from Baghdad where he had been in prison for more than five years on trumped-up charges. He flew back on the private plane of the Aga Khan who had negotiated his freedom.

Senior producer, Angela Frier, was to return to Yugoslavia. Frustratingly, I wasn't going, not yet at least. I was packaging pictures from Yugoslavia at ITN HQ. Bizarrely, but not untypically, my local corner shopkeeper said, "I thought you were in Yugoslavia." I had to explain how it worked. If there was no PTC or no sign off, it meant we weren't there, just slaving away at the picture factory back at base.

At the end of the month, a particularly grisly story. An eleven-year-old boy who had been kept by his mother in a house of ultimate squalor with ninety animals, half of them dead. We talked to some neighbours, the director of Surrey social services, and the head of the local RSPCA animal sanctuary to see which animals had survived.

The next day was also grim, footballer Gary Lineker's eight-week-old son was being treated for a rare form of leukaemia at Great Ormond Street children's hospital. His chances of survival were not good. We were at the hospital, trying to be as supportive and unobtrusive as possible while telling the story. This one, at least, had a happy ending. Baby George pulled through, and as I write, is alive and thriving.

I seemed to be getting all the gruesome stories that November. The day after the Gary Lineker story, came the tale of the Edinburgh man whose wife had died on honeymoon climbing in the Himalayas. He had to bury her, then walk for days to Kathmandu. How dreadful.

The next day we were in Chingford where a police officer, Sergeant Allan King, had been stabbed to death.

In December, I was in Scheveningen in The Hague for a meeting of European finance ministers. Most of my colleagues hated having to cover such events. As something of a political nerd, even back then, I loved it. Next day, we were in Brussels for meetings of European foreign and finance ministers. I interviewed Chancellor of the Exchequer Normal Lamont and Foreign Secretary Douglas Hurd after each held a press conference.

This was all part of the long process leading up to the signing of the Maastricht Treaty which, once signed by the member states of the EEC, would be the Foundation Treaty of the European Union. As far as I was concerned, this was history in the making and we were there to witness it and share the experience with our viewers.

The contrast, incidentally, between the way Lamont and Hurd handled their press conferences could hardly have been greater. Before almost every answer, Norman Lamont would consult with his civil servants. Douglas Hurd, on the other hand, seemed far more on top of his brief and answered each question fluently and in depth. Perhaps it was simply that Lamont was being more cautious, and wanted to ensure that he didn't say anything that might adversely affect the UK economy and the value of the pound. Or maybe it was because Hurd was the more competent minister.

The story was becoming somewhat esoteric. There was, for example, a flurry of excitement (if you could call it that) one evening when the French suggested that the world 'Federal' (known back then as the F word) had been removed from the proposed treaty. An hour later, Dutch Foreign Minister Hans Van den Broek confirmed that this was not the case.

It was a busy news day. American hostage Allan Steen had been released in Beirut after being held hostage for more than five years and Kevin Maxwell had resigned from the board of Maxwell Communications, so we just squeezed onto the ITN bulletins. I was more than a little surprised when the BBC *Nine O'Clock News* led with the Brussels, the F word, story. Strange decision.

Those few days in Brussels were packed with politicians coming and going. As well as Douglas Hurd and Norman Lamont, I interviewed Michael Howard, Leon Brittan, Paddy Ashdown, Neil Kinnock (who greeted me, as always, with a cheery, "Hello Glen",) and many others. The story wasn't really going anywhere, not yet. It would be some time before the Maastricht Treaty would be signed and the European Union would be established.

They did produce what was billed as a 'final draft' of the treaty and commission President Jacques Delors gave a press conference which was rich in provocative soundbites. Delors was something of a bete noire in Britain. One of he *Sun*'s most famous front page headlines was the marvellous: Up yours, Delors.

That day, though, I got Brunsonned. There had been a lot of Maastricht Treaty related activity in Parliament, and ITN's political editor Michael Brunson packaged for *News at Ten*, taking in our material from Brussels. Our argument that a Brussels story should be done from Brussels fell on deaf ears. There simply wasn't room for two packages on the same story. The BBC, however, managed to do just that. For once, a sound BBC decision in my humble opinion, an opinion clearly entirely without any self-interest whatsoever!

One day in early December, Kevin Maxwell appealed to the High Court to have his passport returned to him. He wanted to go to New York on business. Camera crew Ted Henley, Dave Prime and I were tasked with doorstepping the High Court judge who was to decide the fate of Kevin Maxwell's travel plans. Lord Justice Harman emerged from his home clutching a briefcase to cover his face. He kicked a photographer and aimed another kick at the cab driver who had come to collect him, presumably mistaking him for some sort of impertinent journalist. Surely this could not be a High Court judge? Our dispatch rider followed the taxi to the High Court, where the mystery man let himself into the judge's chambers using his own key.

Kevin Maxwell got his passport and was off to New York. I was booked on the same flight and was due to fly with cameraman Mike Inglis on

Concord! Disappointingly, the decision to send us was overturned. Too expensive.

Lord Justice Harman had, the previous year, claimed to have no idea who Paul Gascoigne was when the highly-gifted footballer was constantly in the media for the right reason, his performances at the 1990 World Cup. 'What is a Gazza?' entered the language to exemplify someone completely out of touch with contemporary life.

He really was from another era and reminded me of the famous Lord Kitchener quote from the Boer War when he was confronted by a gaggle of journalists. He strode past them, snarling, "Out of my way you drunken swabs." This is apparently true. It is not from an episode of *Blackadder*!

More High Court drama in that last month in 1991 when TV presenter, Esther Rantzen, sued he *People* newspaper for libel. That kept us entertained for several days. Esther won her case. The jury decided what I had regarded as a highly complex case with finely-balanced arguments incredibly quickly. We interviewed Esther on the steps of the High Court and packaged the story for all ITN bulletins.

In Clapham south London, I interviewed a wife who had killed her brute of a husband after a vicious beating, and interviewed Jack Ashley MP who was campaigning to change the law to reduce the charges against such women so that they could no longer be convicted of murder.

December 22nd began as a slow, sleepy pre-Christmas Sunday, but soon erupted into one of those newsroom frenzies. Terry Waite had been seen out and about and the game was afoot, to get an interview with him. Cameraman Mike Garner arrived at Waite's house in Blackheath before me and got some shots of him leaving. We had been assured by our bosses at ITN that Terry Waite definitely would not be doing interviews and that if I did see him, I shouldn't ask anything controversial for fear of jeopardising our pitch for a full-scale sit-down interview in due course.

Fair enough, until we heard Terry Waite give a long interview on BBC Radio Four. Worse, they carried a trailer for a BBC TV special that evening, a half hour interview with the BBC's Michael Buerk. It emerged that Terry Waite loved the BBC World Service and had agreed to do the interview with someone from the BBC's Religious Affairs Department. Producer Nigel Dacre was sent to bid for an interview on behalf of presenter Trevor McDonald (who was sent to sit in a car nearby!). I managed to doorstep

Terry Waite and asked a lot of questions. Dacre, meanwhile, got a negative response to our formal interview bid. My interview made a three-and-a-half-minute piece for ITN and included a terrifying account of a mock execution.

On Christmas Eve, a hardy perennial story, Christmas shopping, doing live two-ways from Brent Cross shopping centre, my local shopping centre in north London. As ever, this was a story designed to fill air time during what is often, but by no means always, a quiet time of the year for news. Surprisingly, it was actually quite entertaining. Helping me, I had a young ITN trainee, Lauren Taylor, who I noted at the time was very bright, speaking four languages and with an MA from Oxford, very charming, and who I thought at the time would go far. She went on to become a political correspondent for ITN before jumping ship to anchor for Al Jazeera.

For once, Christmas was spent at home with the family, but only for two days. Stories before the year ended included foreign aid for Russia (which seems very odd in retrospect), a new drug to treat AIDS, and Stella, a very sweet ten-year-old pit bull terrier from Bristol whose family was petitioning Prime Minister John Major after she was condemned to death by a magistrate sticking strictly to the letter of the law in the new Dangerous Dogs Act. The offence was that her owner had removed her muzzle.

There was also an interview with the actor Sir Brian Rix, elevated to the peerage for his work with the mental health charity MENCAP (I had been friends in school with his son, Jamie, so we had much to catch up on), and a truly gruesome story of a seventy-year old widow who had been raped in her home in Crawley on Christmas Day. I shudder at the memory of it.

At the risk of sounding like Bridget Jones, I ended 1991 still single and childless, and still relentlessly optimistic.

My first TV interview, at university with Terry Jones of Monty Python, 1982

The sea wall breached at Towyn. February 1990

Berlin, November 10th 1989

Reporting from the TV station scaffolding! Bratislava, November 1989, John Boyce on camera

Literally The Iron Curtain. River Danube, Slovakia, November 1989

Christmas Day lunch on the road to Sibiu, Romania. Bread and cheese

CHAPTER 7

1992: General Election. Laura Davies. The Galloping Major. Euro Disney. Rostock neo-Nazi riots. Black Wednesday. Sochi and the START 2 Treaty

For us, 1992 was dominated by the general election.

After thirteen years of Conservative government, Neil Kinnock's Labour Party was widely expected to win. John Major was (wrongly) seen as lacking charisma and the leadership qualities needed to be prime minister.

It didn't pan out that way.

John Major had been crucified by the press and by Spitting Image as 'the grey man'. In fact, he was (and is) nothing of the sort. For a start, he is taller than most people imagine, and he does have that charisma thing. When he enters a room, you can feel it. Not on the same scale as Tony Blair, let alone Bill Clinton. Nelson Mandela is on a different level entirely. But he did have some of the X factor. It simply didn't come across on television. Years later, Gordon Brown suffered from the same problem. The cameras simply didn't like them, and their warmth and humour didn't travel through the lens. John Major is also one of the nicest and most decent people in politics. So too is Neil Kinnock, who was also pilloried in the press. The Sheffield rally didn't help, nor did that slip on Brighton beach.

The year began, as they often do, with a massive hangover. Slumped in front of the TV, I watched my old university friend Iain Glen in the title role of *Adam Bede* opposite Patsy Kensit who, in a dark curly wig, looked disturbingly like the woman I was currently obsessed with!

Next day it was back to work and that hardy perennial, drink-driving at Christmas. The FT 100 Index had risen sharply, so I interviewed Michael Hughes at BZW (Barclays De Zoete Wedd merchant bank) who explained to me and our audience what was happening on the stock markets. The 'me' is important here as my grasp of economics has always been sketchy to say the least. Other interviewees (the chairman of ICI and the governor of the Bank of England, Robin Leigh-Pemberton) gave me enough to make a coherent package that even I understood!

I ended that first day back at work racing to an armed siege in Peckham. It was all over by the time we got there. The gunman had given himself up.

The following day was equally varied, one of those days when, as a reporter, you need to be an instant expert on a range of subjects. First up that day, reports that the United States, Britain and France would not be imposing sanctions on Libya for the bombing on PanAm 101 over Lockerbie. I was on my way to the Foreign Office when I was diverted to another story, the Palestinian delegation had postponed or possibly cancelled their attendance at peace talks in Washington because the Israelis had, once again, deported yet more Palestinian people from the occupied West Bank. *Plus ça change*.

Once we'd packaged the Palestinian story for the early evening news there was another one to cover, on the Polisario Front's fight with Morocco in the former Spanish Sahara, and then a complete change, a package for *News at Ten* on the legendary racehorse Red Rum, who was twenty-seven and very ill. My knowledge of and interest in horseracing was and remains as limited as my knowledge and interest in Formula One motor racing. Fortunately, Channel 4 racing presenter, John McCririck, was more than happy to be interviewed and filled me in on everything you could ever want to know about Red Rum and much more.

The big foreign story that January was the tension building between Russia and its neighbour Georgia. Reporter Peter Sharp had been sent to Moscow, Paul Davies and cameraman John Martin had deployed to Tbilisi. I was not assigned, not this time, but I was visa-ed up for Moscow by the foreign desk, ready to go if needed. I was happy enough covering a wide variety of stories and, of course, the politics.

There had to be an election in 1992. Whereas Margaret Thatcher (and later Tony Blair) opted to go to the country every four years, John Major had chosen to keep the Conservative government in office for the maximum-permitted full five years. The Tories were behind in the opinion polls and no doubt hoping that, as one cabinet minister put it to me, "something will turn up."

My other stories that first week of January included covering the self-styled Muslim parliament and the supposed death of the LP record. WH Smith announced that its shops would no longer be selling LPs as they accounted for only three per cent of music sales. In future, the chain of high street shops would only be selling CDs and cassettes. Thirty years later, vinyl made a comeback. I got rid of mine years ago.

There was another hardy perennial story when *Holiday Which?* magazine published its list of the worst holiday destinations, a mid-bulletin fodder story. I flew to Paris to cover the GATT (General Agreement on Tariffs and Trade) talks on farming. A very dry subject, but we made it more colourful with a pleasant drive to Chartres and Orleans to talk to some French farmers. This also included a very rustic and very cheap lunch en route. ITN also had some interviews with American farmers in Iowa which gave our piece another interesting dimension. Our package led *News at Ten* part two, after the commercial break, always a good slot.

Back in London, I had to cover another horseracing story about which I knew nothing, a plan to introduce horseracing on Sundays at a time when Sundays still saw most shops and everything else closed. Football and horseracing happened on Saturdays. At the Jockey Club, I interviewed horseracing presenter Brough Scott. It seems absurd now, but there was a lot of opposition to the plan at the time, Sundays were supposed to be sacrosanct. Although my interest in The Sport of Kings was virtually nil, with Brough's help I became knowledgeable enough on the subject to sound reasonably authoritative. Needless to say, my knowledge was only skin deep.

I was soon back in my comfort zone, covering a report for *News at Ten* on Iraq's nuclear weapons capability. German firms had sold Saddam Hussein so many uranium-enriching gas centrifuges that he could be on the verge of mass-producing nuclear weapons, and might already have done so. Saddam Hussein and WMD, a story ahead of its time! This was a running story throughout the 1990s which would eventually lead to 'dodgy dossiers', Gulf War Two and the overthrow and death of the Iraqi dictator. Back then, we interviewed Dr John Hassard of Imperial College and UN weapons inspector Dr David Kay who had recently returned from Baghdad.

The following day, it was more Iraq and Saddam Hussein's so-called 'Supergun'. Dr Christopher Cowley, one of the gun's designers, was giving evidence to the House of Commons Trade and Industry select committee. The project had begun in 1988 and had been part of Saddam Hussein's efforts to portray himself as the leader of the Arab World. The 'Babylon Supergun' was huge, with a barrel length of forty-six metres. It was set up on a hillside at a forty-five-degree angle and had a range of nearly five hundred miles. Israel and Iran were within range. Iraqi Scud missiles could already reach both countries, but this was a new threat.

The gun's original designer, Canadian artillery expert Gerald Bull, had been assassinated two years earlier. At the time, it was widely believed that the Israeli intelligence service, Mossad, had killed him to stop the Babylon Supergun project.

At the end of the first Gulf War in 1991, Iraq had admitted that project Babylon was in progress. UN inspectors destroyed much of the hardware in Iraq as part of the disarmament process but, as with so much else, the suspicion persisted that Saddam was hiding weapons, including the Babylon Supergun. Such was the level of interest and depth of that suspicion that day in mid-January that my piece led *News at Ten*. Saddam Hussein's military capacity was already under intense scrutiny, years ahead of the second Gulf War.

There was an air crash in France later that month. A nine-year-old boy had survived, a bit of better news for once. On another late January day, we interviewed Diana Lamplugh, the mother of Suzy Lamplugh, the estate agent who had disappeared in 1986 after showing a man around a house for sale in Fulham, south-west London. She was never found. It was to be another two years, 1994, before she was officially declared dead, presumably murdered. Suzy's parents, Diana and Paul, had set up the Suzy Lamplugh Trust to raise awareness of personal safety and offer support to the families of missing people. That day, we also interviewed female estate agents to gauge how safe or otherwise they felt doing their jobs and what, if any, precautions they were taking. This remains, of course, an issue to this day.

That same day, in Birmingham, estate agent Stephanie Slater was released after nine days in captivity. Her kidnapper, Michael Samms, initially escaped with a large ransom but was later caught and imprisoned for kidnapping Stephanie and for the kidnapping and murder of teenager Julie Dart the previous July.

The Robert Maxwell pensions scandal continued to resurface occasionally. ITN had acquired a video of Maxwell, back in 1988, urging his employees to continue paying into their company pension funds, the very funds he was raiding. The video caused a flurry of excitement, and we cut a package for the five forty news and *News at Ten*.

Next day, another change of gear covering a story about the alleged sexual misdemeanours of a certain governor from Arkansas. He was a contender for the Democrats' presidential nomination at the time and the story was creating uproar in the United States and beyond. This was years before the Monica Lewinsky scandal and Bill Clinton's subsequent impeachment.

January ended with a terribly familiar story of a man in Cornwall who had appealed on TV for his missing wife to come home before confessing to the police that he had buried her in their back garden.

Oleg Gordievsky was the KGB's bureau chief in London. He was also a British double-agent, MI6's most highly placed and valuable asset. He had been betrayed by a CIA double-agent and ordered back to Moscow. After an elaborate and dangerous escape plan, itself worthy of a Hollywood movie, Gordievsky was smuggled out of Russia into Finland and flown to the UK via Norway.

I interviewed Gordievsky for the second time. The first occasion, some years earlier, had been pure John Le Carré. We were taken blindfolded by James Bond types to a safe house in the countryside outside London. Gordievsky was wearing a rather absurd disguise, a false beard, dark glasses and a deerstalker hat. Now, he was undisguised. He was writing a memoir, which was said to include allegations against a former Labour Party leader. Three years later, Michael Foot successfully sued *The Sunday Times* when it claimed he was a KGB agent. The newspaper had used extracts from the original manuscript of Gordievsky's book which were not included in the published version. Michael Foot won substantial damages. This time, Gordievsky was far more relaxed than when I first interviewed him, and seemed settled in his new life in exile in Britain. I was thrilled to be once again entering the John Le Carré-esque world of Cold War spies. I'm not sure if camera crew Ted Henley and Dave Prime shared my enthusiasm.

There was speculation that the French Foreign Minister Roland Dumas would be forced to resign after the leader of the PFLP (Popular Front for the Liberation of Palestine), George Habash, had received medical treatment in Paris the previous week. At the time, Habash had been labelled one of the world's most wanted terrorists. Although Habash was known in Arabic as Al Hakim (the wise one) he had masterminded several hijackings, including the Dawson's Field hijacking of four airliners in 1970 and advocated all-out 'military and psychological warfare'. Several top officials had already been fired, but so far at least, there had been no ministerial resignations.

Sometimes covering the news leaves you empty handed but can still be enjoyable. So it was that the day after the Gordievsky interview I was up at an ungodly hour to catch a six o'clock flight from Heathrow to Charles de Gaulle airport for yet another daytrip to the French capital. Hooking up with ITN's Paris producer Barbara Gray and cameraman Raymond Grosjon, this involved standing on doorsteps in the cold and rain. Friends were envious that we were once again in the City of Light. They needn't have been. In February it is more like the City of Dull Grey.

We doorstepped interior minister Philippe Marchand as he left a meeting with Prime Minister Edith Cresson, who was herself under pressure to resign. After a fine lunch in a nearby brasserie (what is it with the French and lunch?) we filmed a Foreign Ministry meeting at the National Assembly before more 'hurry up and wait' hanging around for nearly three hours before a six p.m. press conference at the Quai d'Orsay at which Dumas made it crystal clear that neither he nor anyone else would be resigning.

Not much of a story then, and *News at Ten* editor Nick Pollard agreed, so I caught the nine fifty p.m. flight back to London. All that effort for no reward, but that's inevitable from time to time in the news business.

We rehearsed how we would cover the death of the Queen Mother. This may sound ghoulish, but it was something that every news organisation has to do. Obits are often written/recorded well in advance. In this case it was a full rehearsal. It included Jon Snow in Petticoat Lane, hamming it up talking about how she and the King had been, "With us in the Blitz. She was one of us", in a terrible mockney accent, and Lawrence McGinty poetically describing a piper outside Balmoral Castle playing a lament, a lone tear falling slowly down his cheek. We were discovering our inner actors!

I was at Buckingham Palace where astonished American tourists were asking me if it was really true that the Queen Mother had died. I had to reassure them that this was a rehearsal. In Adelaide, Australia, it was the middle of the night. A half-asleep television engineer in our sister station was moments away from switching us out live across Australia, believing the news of the Queen Mother's death to be real. The next time we did this kind of full-scale rehearsal, we had to use the Queen Mother's secret service codename, 'Mrs Robinson' (an alternative was 'Taybridge'), and hold up a card with the word 'Rehearsal' written on it. Very high tech!

That week, we had our own political scandal when it was revealed that Liberal Democrat leader, Paddy Ashdown, had had an affair with his secretary five years earlier. The party's MPs and his wife publicly forgave him and the story blew over, but the tabloid nickname 'Paddy Pantsdown' stuck. Personally, I found the entire story intrusive, absurd and politically motivated. Three days later, opinion polls showed that Paddy was more popular than ever.

We were standing on another cold, wet pavement, this time at the City of London magistrates' court. Not part of our usual beat of the High Court or the Old Bailey (the Central Criminal Court). It was just a burglary case, but Brighton burglar Simon Bekovik and his ex-wife Maria Watson had stolen money and documents from the office of Paddy Ashdown's solicitor. It was a straightforward enough remand hearing, but the plot thickened when the chairman of the Hove Conservative Association revealed that Bekovik was a fully paid-up member. We jumped up the running-order to story two for the five forty news, and led *News at Ten* after news editor Peter Wallace set up an exclusive interview with Bekovik in Brighton.

The following Sunday, when the opinion polls favouring Paddy Ashdown were published (and this in an election year), I got paid to watch the New Zealand vs England test match and package it for all ITN bulletins. This sounds like a cushy number, and it was, but there are great perils in covering sport. Get one thing wrong, one name, one fact, and you get jumped on. Fortunately, I didn't!

I spent Valentine's Day with coal miners in Yorkshire! British Coal had announced plans to halve the number of the country's miners within four years. We spent the afternoon in the miners' welfare club beside Sharlston colliery interviewing miners, an NUM official, and in the village, a shopkeeper and a local council employment officer. I had covered the miners' strike back in 1984/85, so I understood what was at stake. Unless you've been to a pit village, you won't realise just how important the coal mine is. Not only is it the main employer, generating all the money in the local economy, it is also the heart of the community, representing a tradition and a sense of pride that runs very deep. Close the mine and the village dies.

Back from Yorkshire, and it emerged that Albanian police and soldiers were stealing British charities' relief supplies. We had six hours of video to wade through! Buried in that six hours were some 'money shots' which, together with an interview with the ICRC (Red Cross) and an aid convoy driver, Jan Van Weenan, made a respectable package and a strong story.

At the end of February, I was once again in a small town in Germany. This time it was Verden in Lower Saxony for a court martial. Mrs Christine Dryland, wife of a British army major, Antony Dryland, was accused of murdering her husband's mistress, Marika Sharfeld, by running her over with a car and then driving over her body three times. She was also accused of the attempted murder of her husband.

The British press, newspapers, TV and radio were there in force. We were allowed into the makeshift courtroom to film before the proceedings began. I did a PTC, no one else bothered to do so which was strange given this unique access. Christine Dryland was expected to plead not guilty but instead entered a qualified plea. Not guilty of murder but guilty of manslaughter on the grounds of diminished responsibility. The attempted murder charge was dropped.

The game now was to try to talk to Major Dryland. We drove to the equestrian centre at Solton, the riding club where the killing had happened, and had a fantastic stroke of luck, the major appeared mounted on his horse. The money shot! He refused to speak to us, of course, but that didn't matter. We had the shot no one else had, of a man who would henceforth be known as 'the Galloping Major'.

Over dinner that evening, a colossal German affair of eggs, herrings, gherkins and beetroot all on a huge bed of mince, the Fleet Street hacks were envious of our good fortune. BBC correspondent Mike Sullivan kept us entertained with his own 'When I' stories over far too many bottles of wine.

Next day, we filmed the Galloping Major leaving home and refusing to speak to us, Marika's grave and at the riding club where no one would do an interview. But we got lucky again, the club president turned up and we interviewed him. Rather, my cameraman Patrick did, in German. He said what I'd hoped he would say. Another mini-scoop.

The court martial adjourned that afternoon to await the arrival of a psychiatrist the next morning, so we went to Bergen-Belsen. I had been before. It was as eerie and chilling as I remembered it. The deafening silence. A place of pure evil.

I hadn't said much about the excessive consumption of alcohol during those years on the road. Just to give you a flavour, that evening we demolished several bottles of wine over dinner, way too much Mai Tai, beers and schnapps in two bars before whisky night caps back at the hotel. This was not unusual. Looking back, we must have qualified as functioning alcoholics. Some of my friends, colleagues and comrades-in-arms during those years were serious drinkers. Singing and dancing on the tables were de rigueur!

One cameraman was especially fond of getting naked in restaurants. In one Chinese restaurant there was an aquarium filling most of one wall. The rest of the team noticed that the cameraman, who had a shock of ginger hair, was missing. They looked up to find him swimming naked in the aquarium and making kissing gestures so that he looked like some sort of oversized human goldfish.

The psychiatric evidence the next day revealed that Christine Dryland had a long history of clinical depression. We had to wait another twenty-four hours for the verdict and sentence: Twelve months' psychiatric in-patient care. A wise decision.

It was a Friday. The foreign desk, very pleased with our efforts and especially the shot of the Galloping Major asked us to stay in Germany to do another story. The first British jobcentre outside the UK was to be opened at an army barracks to help soldiers who were to return to civilian life as the BAOR (British Army of the Rhine) was being wound down.

I was perfectly happy with this. As far as I was concerned, the object of the exercise was to get on the road covering stories and to stay as far away from the newsroom as possible for as long as possible. I was young, single, hungry and full of enthusiasm. Often though, I'd be with colleagues who wanted to get home in time for the weekend. They were usually the ones with young children or unsympathetic and uncomprehending wives.

Our business was riddled with divorce, but this could cut both ways. For some married couples, a return from a long job abroad was like a second honeymoon. After a while, once they were getting under each other's feet, a new story would break and the pattern would be repeated.

The jobcentre was to be located at Herford in North Rhine Westphalia. We had booked a hotel in Bielefeld. After Osnabruck, the autobahn was closed so we drove the last twenty-five miles through wooded countryside and villages, one of which was called Hitler! I was trying to get hold of the army PR officers who had been very helpful but appeared to have disappeared for the weekend.

On Monday morning we were diverted from the Herford jobcentre story and sent to Brussels for yet another foreign ministers meeting. This had obviously been scheduled for some time, but the editor had only just decided that morning that he wanted it covered. A budget row was brewing. I drove the four-hour trip with my producer, Mary Amthor.

At the Charlemagne building, we got up to speed on what seemed to be a very boring non-story. Douglas Hurd gave a press conference, which was not overly exciting, but Jacques Delors did one at which he was splendidly and typically bellicose. The British hacks jumped on this, conjured up some controversy, and we had a story. It was a very busy news day, but we persuaded *News at Ten* to take a piece from us. We cut one minute thirty and I literally ran to RTBF in Brussels to make the feed.

Next morning, the foreign desk wanted us to return to Herford to cover the jobcentre story. We set it up and filmed in a hurry, reasonable but hardly spectacular work. As we were driving back to Brussels yet again, to edit the feed, we were re-assigned. If there was any hooligan trouble at a football match in Rotterdam the next day, when Spurs were to play Feyenoord, we were to film it.

Before the match, in Brussels, we edited the Herford jobcentre piece so that it was ready when needed before driving to Rotterdam. In the event, there was no crowd trouble. We arrived two hours before kick-off. There were only about two thousand Spurs fans protected by almost as many riot police, or so it seemed. A Eurovision producer, Elsa, acquired us some passes for the match, so we got paid to watch the Cup Winners' Cup quarter-final first leg. It was a boring game which Spurs, playing for a draw, lost 1–0 through a ridiculous defensive mistake. Arsenal fans, I am not smirking as a write this!

We saw the Spurs fans safely onto their coaches after the game and headed back to Brussels. We arrived at one a.m. The Café des Artistes, where we had had lunch earlier that day, was still open so we joined Belgian cameraman Eric and producer Mary for a couple of well-earned beers.

Finally, on the Friday, a week after we were assigned to the story, our Herford job centre piece ran on the lunchtime news. A little disappointingly but not surprisingly, our pictures were absorbed into a more general package on defence cuts by ITN's defence correspondent Geoffrey Archer for *News at Ten*.

Back in London, I interviewed Richard Branson, who had just sold Virgin Record to Thorn-EMI for a cool five hundred million pounds. With him was his head of PR, my old university friend Will Whitehorn. A pretty easy job, working for such a great communicator.

That same day, David Chater was in the newsroom. It was great to see him back. He had lost a lot of weight and was still on morphine but getting better by the day.

Other good news that Friday in March, I was to be seconded to the political unit to cover the general election, working mostly on the road. I had no doubt that much of my work would be absorbed into other reporter packages (Brunsonned!) but was very happy to be so closely involved.

My personal election coverage began, perhaps ominously, on Friday 13th, a photo-op with Chris Patten and Michael Heseltine launching the country's biggest ever poster campaign, followed by a press conference at Labour Party HQ.

On the Saturday, I interviewed Des Wilson at the National Liberal Club. My crew, Ted Henley and Dave Prime, were sent to cover an earthquake in Turkey, but for me the day was dominated by a Labour Party rally with speeches by Jack Straw, Harriet Harman, John Prescott, Brian Gould and a star turn by John Smith. The lead story, followed by a John Major speech in Torquay. ITN was switching into full general election mode.

I found myself on 'Royals duty' the following week, ahead of an expected announcement from Buckingham Palace that the Duke and

Duchess of York ('Andy and Fergie') were to separate. On a day that I was supposed to be on the late shift, starting at two p.m., I was called in at seven a.m. to do a package on the rumoured break-up. With a huge pile of tapes and only an hour to cut them, we edited a three-minute package for ITV's *This Morning*. Two days later, it was live two-ways from the Palace on the official announcement.

This was all sandwiched by the continuing election coverage. My main story that week was the appearance of ex-Prime Minister Margaret Thatcher at a Conservative rally, with interviews with Norman Tebbit (who was all for it), Neil Kinnock, Paddy Ashdown and Labour deputy leader Roy Hattersley. The question was, is Mrs Thatcher a potential vote winner for the Conservatives or a liability?

I covered Labour Party rallies in Gravesend, Nottingham and so on, and interviewed Dr David Owen after he delivered a speech on Europe which was billed as his only speech of the election campaign. I interviewed him afterwards, a wise and perceptive interview, but David Owen wasn't wanted by *News at Ten*. A former foreign secretary and founding member of the SDP, just a few years earlier David Owen had been at the very epicentre of British politics. His opinions had mattered. Not, it seemed, any more.

At the end of the month, Labour was still slightly ahead in the opinion polls but within the margin of error of plus or minus three per cent. Ipswich was interesting (I mean politically!) so we spent a day in Suffolk's county town with Conservative, Labour and Liberal Democrat activists all hard at work. Douglas Hurd did a walkabout, which gave our piece some national significance.

The parties were producing very glossy and expensive PEBs (Party Election Broadcasts), which terrestrial broadcasters were obliged to run at peak time. There was a huge row over one, which became known as 'The war of Jennifer's ear', a reference to an actual war, known as the War of Jenkin's ear, an eighteenth century conflict between Britain and Spain.

Labour had run a PEB about a five-year-old girl, Jennifer, who had glue ear and had waited a year for a simple operation. Her case was contrasted with private patients who could pay to get treatment quickly, and was used to illustrate how those Nasty Tories were deliberately mismanaging and underfunding the NHS.

Neil Kinnock went into full throttle, telling the electorate that if they voted Tory, "Don't get old, and don't get ill", but the tactic backfired. The story as told in the Labour PEB was inaccurate. Labour's central point, about NHS funding, was lost in the row over using a young girl as a political pawn and which side had revealed her identity.

There were doorsteps in the freezing cold opposite 10 Downing Street, something which would become a regular task when I later joined Sky News as a political correspondent. Often our questions were ignored, or we might simply get a, "Good evening", from Prime Minister John Major as he got into his waiting car. But they had to be done, not only to get the latest shots of the prime minister and other cabinet ministers but also for those rare occasions when they actually deigned to talk to us.

There were lighter moments. On Neil Kinnock's birthday at the end of March we went to Clapham to interview an astrologer, Babs Kirby. John Major's birthday was the following day. She predicted that Neil Kinnock was going to be elected prime minister and that John Major would be spending 'less time in the public eye'. Astrology!

And then there was the Natural Law Party, whose members claimed they could levitate by meditating, something they called Yogic Flying. They were followers of the Maharishi Yogi of Beatles fame. They were filming their PEB. Their headquarters was a magnificent Rothschild family pile, Mentmore Towers in Buckinghamshire, which was owned by the time by the Maharishi foundation. The Yogic Flying turned out to be bouncing up and down in the lotus position, as if on a trampoline. We were so hoping to see someone actually levitate, but left disappointed! The Natural Law Party's only input on the 1992 general election was to make a funny 'And Finally' for *News at Ten*.

I did another 'And Finally' at the end of March when Anthony Hopkins won the best actor Oscar for his spellbinding performance in *The Silence of the Lambs*. Sadly, I covered this from London rather than Los Angeles, but we had some lovely reaction form the great actor's mother in south Wales so it made a warm, feel-good piece to end the news that night.

David Owen did make the news in early April, with less than a week to go to the election, when he decided to support John Major and blasted Neil Kinnock. Needless to say, his Labour Party critics, who had always accused him of being a traitor, claimed that we were now seeing the real

David Owen who'd been a closet Tory all along. I drove to his beautiful house, an old rectory in Wiltshire, but without success (he was out), so we had to base my package on the incendiary article he had written for the following day's *Mail on Sunday*. I did get to interview him that Sunday morning, which made another strong political package.

We got to film a George Harrison concert at the Royal Albert Hall. The former Beatle was fundraising for the Natural Law Party! We had no access to film the concert but the Natural Law Party people were so happy that our *News at Ten* package the previous week had been seen by their friends (and fundraisers!) in the States when it ran on CNN that they let us in.

We watched him going through some of his classics, including 'My Sweet Lord', 'Here comes the Sun', 'While my Guitar Gently Weeps', etc. Ringo Starr was on drums, so half a Beatles concert, sort of. It made another 'And Finally' item for *News at Ten* and certainly beat working for a living!

On that Monday, just three days before the election, Neil Kinnock's opinion poll ratings shot up while John Major's plummeted. Labour was getting celebrity endorsements while John Major was campaigning standing on a soapbox.

On the Tuesday, the Conservatives (specifically John Major, 'The boy from Brixton') produced a very effective PEB. The polls tightened. They had got it right, at last, but was it too little too late?

Thursday, April 9th: the Big Day at last.

My role was relatively minor. My place was Stockton-on-Tees, so I flew up to Teesside to link up with a local cameraman to do lives all evening. Stockton South was a three-way marginal. The sitting Conservative MP hung onto his slim majority as the Liberal Democrat vote collapsed, and that was the picture throughout the country as the night wore on. ITN's exit poll gave the Conservatives forty-one per cent, Labour thirty-seven per cent and the LibDems eighteen per cent. We were firmly in hung Parliament territory. In fact, it turned out to be Conservatives forty-two per cent, Labour just thirty-four per cent and LibDems eighteen per cent. Astonishingly, John Major's Conservatives had won a majority of twenty-one, the first time since the Napoleonic era that a party had won four consecutive elections. The opinion polls leading up to the election had been completely wrong, which was surprising back then, a lot less so these days.

The smaller parties suffered. The last two SDP MPs, John Cartwright and Rosie Barnes, lost. So too did Jim Sillars, the SNP deputy leader, in Glasgow Govan. The SNP were reduced from five seats to just three, even though they had been confidently expecting thirty or more. The Liberal Democrats were also expecting great things under their charismatic leader, but they were reduced from twenty-two seats to twenty.

The glamour candidates, Glenda Jackson in Hampstead and Highgate and Seb Coe in Falmouth and Camborne, both sailed home.

Labour was in crisis. How could they ever win if not in the depth of a recession against an exhausted-looking Conservative government which had already been in office for so many years?

As dawn broke, there were still a few seats left to declare. We drove to Berwick-on-Tweed where Alan Beith, as expected, held onto his seat. I interviewed him a couple of times during the morning. He went on a victory parade through Alnwick with about a dozen people and the Monty Python theme music!

On the news that day, Paddy Ashdown looked shocked, Glenys Kinnock was tearful, Neil Kinnock devastated. A sad sight for Labour supporters but it felt like time for a root and branch change if the party was ever again to enjoy electoral success. Prime Minister John Major, of course, was looking very chipper.

The IRA responded by detonating a bomb in the City of London.

From John Major to Mickey Mouse! On Saturday morning, I was off to Paris for the opening of Euro Disney. It seemed like an almost exact replica of Florida's Magic Kingdom which, presumably, was the idea.

Despite the previous night's IRA bomb, John Major's cabinet reshuffle, and the fact that the main ITN bulletin was sandwiched within a live ITV programme on the opening of Euro Disney, ITN wanted a package from us. I teamed up with Paris producer Barbara Gray and a French crew, Raymond and Julian. We spent a pleasant afternoon filming the attractions helped by a charming Disney PR woman, Vanessa Aves. One of the senior editors back at ITN was obsessed by the price of hamburgers, believing the entire enterprise to be a colossal rip-off, so we checked out the price of food and soft drinks to keep him happy.

The main event was a concert starring Tina Turner, the Gypsy Kings and others, but we had to pull out before it began to edit our package. One that got away.

We continued with the story on Sunday, messing about on the rides, filming a PTC on the back of a fake fire engine, driving up 'Main Street USA' and generally having fun. We sent a package for lunchtime, but the evening edit was anything but fun. Not one but two edit packs had a nervous breakdown and simply stopped working. Somehow, Julian got my package dubbed, edited, and fed to London. After a nine thirty evening flight from Paris, I was home for a proper post-election sleep.

Peter Hillmore wrote a scathing piece for the *Observer* newspaper that day on the opening of Euro Disney. He complained about the miserable hotels, computers going down, and said he longed for an easier assignment, for example, "The fall of Mogadishu". This was bizarre, to say the least, although I suspected that some of my bosses at ITN would have liked my piece to be more hard-hitting. But that had not been my/our experience. If you liked that sort of thing, the Euro Disney theme park seemed great fun.

We flew to Guernsey where a wanted IRA man's girlfriend had been arrested. She appeared for just two minutes at Guernsey Magistrates' Court, and cameraman Alan Thompson got a shot of her arriving, her face covered by a blanket. And that was it, which meant that Alan and I passed a pleasant afternoon admiring the fabulous views of Herm, Sark and across to Jersey. Back at ITN that evening, my colleagues were treated to some Guernsey fudge.

There was another concert to cover but mostly miss that April, a Freddie Mercury AIDS benefit concert at Wembley. We filmed the sound checks, including Elton John (in what looked suspiciously like a new hairpiece) and Liza Minnelli, chatted to Bob Geldof, but missed the best bits of the concert (David Bowie, Annie Lennox, George Michael, Paul Young, etc. etc.) because as ever, we had to cut and run to edit for *News at Ten*. We had to rely on a WTN highlights tape for our edit which we had to finish in less than half an hour. A mad scramble.

There was also an armed police siege at a house in Darlington and a Frank Bruno comeback fight to cover. I have bumped into Frank Bruno several times over the years (not literally, that would probably hurt!), and am always greeted with that huge, unique guffaw of the friendly giant.

After a ten-day break in Luxor, staying at King Farouk's former Winter Palace and visiting the Valley of the Kings, the Valley of the Queens, Karnak, Dendera Temple and generally exploring the wonders of the Nile, it was back to work.

May began fairly unexceptionally in a hotel near St Albans, I interviewed several members of the Liverpool team before they headed off the Wembley to beat Sunderland 2–0 in the FA Cup Final. I also interviewed several junior doctors when the new health secretary, Virginia Bottomley, announced that she planned to introduce a new law restricting their working hours to eighty-three hours a week (eighty-three hours a week!). Some said they were currently working more than a hundred hours per week. There were a couple of gruesome murder trials. And then, the story that would keep me busy, and emotionally engaged, for several weeks.

Laura Davies was a very cute four-year-old from Eccles, Greater Manchester. She was very bright and full of mischief. She had been born with a perished small bowel and developed liver failure. She needed pioneering surgery which was only available in Pittsburgh, Pennsylvania and would cost at least three hundred and fifty thousand pounds.

I flew to Manchester to team up with cameraman John Boyce and visited the Davies family. Laura's parents, Fran and Les, were very welcoming. Laura was absolutely delightful. She had to spend twelve hours a day on an IV drip, something she seemed to accept as simply a fact of life. We sent a two-minute package for the lunchtime news. The feedback from the news desk was that 'there wasn't a dry eye in the house'.

In the afternoon we were at the Royal Manchester Children's Hospital, where we interviewed Laura's surgeon, Adrian Bianchi, and sent a package for the five forty news followed by a live two-way with Laura sitting beside me on her bed, as good as gold and melting the hearts of our viewers. For *News at Ten*, we interviewed Laura's parents again at their home, and I did a PTC on Laura's bed as she slept. ITN's switchboard was overwhelmed with offers of money to pay for her operation.

Next morning, we went by coach with Laura's dad Les and supporters for a disappointing meeting with the government's chief medical officer. Les wanted a second opinion, from Addenbrooke's Hospital, Cambridge. It was a Thursday. At Addenbrooke's, Professor Roy Calne, a pioneer in organ transplants, said he would see Laura the following Monday.

When we went to Addenbrooke's that Monday, Fran and Les held a press conference. Professor Calne, at the very top of his field, did not enjoy being questioned by impertinent journalists. Not at all. He walked out.

On Wednesday, King Fahd of Saudi Arabia announced that he had donated one hundred and fifty thousand pounds to Laura's fund, bringing the total to the three hundred and fifty thousand pounds needed to have the operation in Pittsburgh. Fantastic news. We led the five forty news and packaged the story for *News at Ten*. The next day, Laura was back at Addenbrooke's for tests, and on the Friday, cameraman Alan Florence flew back to Manchester with the family to get shots of them during the flight. The family now had to decide whether or not to go to Pittsburgh.

As you might have gathered by now, we were following Laura's story very closely. We had made it our own. When her parents decided to take the plunge and fly Laura to Pittsburgh, we made sure we got that news first ahead of their press conference. Three days later, with cameraman Keith Edwards, we filmed little Laura packing her suitcase and got shots of her at Pendlebury Hospital where we interviewed her nurse, Christine Kenny, and consultant Adrian Bianchi. All this material was exclusive.

We flew to Pittsburgh via New York the next day. British Airways upgraded Laura, her parents and nurse Christine Kenny to first class. They were very excited. BA PR man, David Tattershall, upgraded me and Jill Burdett of the *Manchester Evening News* to business class, which was a pleasant surprise. We had a three-hour stopover at JFK Airport before the flight to Pittsburgh. American cameraman Geoff Dills took shots of the family on the plane, then followed Laura's ambulance to the children's hospital while Jill and I helped Laura's dad Les with the luggage (!) before following in a taxi.

And so we were in Pittsburgh for a potentially lifesaving operation. We were up very early the next morning to film at the children's hospital. We cut and fed from the Pittsburgh Teleport, a piece for the lunchtime news at seven thirty a.m. (twelve thirty BST) before tucking in to a hearty American breakfast. Laura was fine and in very good spirits, but the family needed some space. We had a stroke of luck when we were doing a fresh PTC at the hospital. A press officer came looking for the BBC, who were nowhere to be seen. Hearing my accent, she gave me a tape about the drug FK506, the anti-rejection drug with which doctors would be treating Laura. It was excellent new material and Geoff and I headed to WTAE, the local ABC affiliate, to cut a package for the late news.

Next day, and a press conference with Fran and Les, the Pittsburgh surgeons and Laura, who was in sparkling form. By sheer good luck, we bumped into an American mother who had been waiting at the hospital for seven weeks for a similar operation for her child. Without a hint of bitterness, she wished Laura and her family the very best of luck with what was pioneering (some critics said 'experimental') surgery. She gave our package another very moving element.

Outside that evening, Pittsburgh was going completely bonkers. People were waving flags, tooting their car horns, whooping and getting very drunk. The police had sealed off the downtown area. The Pittsburgh Penguins had won the Stanley Cup (that's ice hockey, I didn't know either!).

On June 2nd, I flew back to London. The plan was, hopefully, to return to Pittsburgh once a donor was found and Laura could have her liver-bowel operation.

It would only take a week, but it felt like a week of treading water, waiting to get back to a story I felt very involved in. There were a couple of other stories to cover. The Press Complaints Commission was highly critical of some newspapers' treatment of Prince Charles and Diana, Princess of Wales, describing it as 'odious', 'prurient' and so on, and a sad story of the death of a British mountaineer, Peter Boardman, on the north-east ridge of Mount Everest. But my thoughts were focused on Pittsburgh.

In the early hours of Wednesday 10th June, Fran Davis phoned to tell me that Laura was in the operating theatre. I was scrambled to Heathrow to catch the first available flight to New York. American Airlines offered me six hundred dollars to take the next flight instead. When I declined, they upgraded me to first class. Result!

Michael Nicholson was holding the fort for ITN in Pittsburgh until I arrived and would package for *News at Ten*. I caught an American Eagle thirty-seater twin-engine turboprop (a Saab 340 for anyone who cares) to Pittsburgh and arrived in time to join Nicholson and cameraman Jon Steele for dinner. Jill Burdett from the *Manchester Evening News* had arrived slightly ahead of me. I did a phono (a forty-five-second phone report) for the next morning and tracked down a WTAE copy of a hospital press conference, which we had somehow missed.

The operation was being hailed as a great success. Early the next morning, I was editing with Jon Steele in a WTAE truck at the hospital, a package followed by a live two-way into the lunchtime news. Fran and Les were exhausted but elated. At a press conference, the surgeons said that Laura had made 'the most remarkable recovery' from her fifteen-hour operation, was already off her ventilator, breathing well and "giving her nurses hell"!

The press conference was at one p.m., six p.m. in London, which gave editor Millie and I plenty of time to cut for *News at Ten*. Generally, US-based British correspondents don't send packages for the lunchtime news but focus instead on the flagship evening bulletins, which allows them an almost normal working day.

Within twenty-four hours, Laura was out of intensive care and back on the ward. The foreign desk wanted to know if we could get a camera inside, to Laura's bed! Of course, the hospital was not going to allow that, but Fran offered to do the filming for us. We hired a camera which, it turned out, was the same model which Gail, Fran's newly-arrived friend from Manchester, had at home so she knew how to use it.

We could do nothing but wait and hope for the best. In the event, it was the best. Jill Burdett arrived from the hospital with the tape, which was as good as we'd hoped. Laura sitting up, reading a book with her mum, chatting away cheerfully.

Our scoop was followed by another twenty-four hours later. After seemingly endless phone calls and a lot of hanging around, we decided to stake out the hospital's multistorey car park. We got fabulous shots of Laura outside in the fresh air for the first time since her operation. We edited the pictures under part of an exclusive interview with Fran thanking the doctors for 'giving Laura the chance of life'. It made a very moving piece which was very well received back home at ITN and, I hope, by all the people who had donated to the fund to get Laura to Pittsburgh.

Another little exclusive the next day. Laura was well but tired. Jill Burdett, with whom I'd been working very closely, had set up a meeting between Fran and the mother of the first ever liver-bowel transplant girl, Tracey Gonzales, who had returned to the children's hospital for a routine check-up. We collected Fran Davies and Pamela Gonzales from the hospital, took them to an ice cream parlour, wired them up, and recorded the conversation between the two mothers. Magic stuff! Back at the hospital, we met the delightful Tracey, who was due to start school in September. More lovely shots.

We got verbal herograms from Vicky Knighton and Mike Nolan on the foreign desk. They loved the 'Fran and Pam show'!

By the next day, Laura was walking, just a few steps but it was a major breakthrough. To celebrate, we went to Toys 'R' Us and bought her a new doll and buggy. That evening we drove around Pittsburgh with Springsteen's 'Human Touch' blasting from the car speakers. Not sure why, but it felt appropriate. It was our last night in Pittsburgh.

Before leaving the next day, we went to see Laura. She was in sparkling form and seemed to be getting back to her normal self, very talkative, positively bubbly. She was tired, of course, and had to sleep after half an hour of showing off! She loved her new doll and buggy.

I went back to Pittsburgh five months later to bring Laura home. I should say to film Laura coming home, but I was that close to the story. Happily, Jill Burdett of the *Manchester Evening News* also got assigned to return to Pittsburgh with her photographer, John Featherstone.

We checked into the Holiday Inn where Fran, Les and Laura were also staying. So too were Laura's consultant in Manchester, Adrian Bianchi, and nurse Christine Kenny. We joined them all for a celebration dinner.

My cameraman Sam King was American and very child friendly. He kept Laura (and Fran!) entertained and in fits of giggles with his party tricks and funny voices.

Sam got some great shots of Laura stuffing her face with pizza. She really had made "the most remarkable recovery" as the doctors had said five months earlier. Afterwards, we took shots of Laura trying on her new school uniform. Jill, in a tabloid moment, had brought the uniform with her from Manchester. Laura, such a born actress, giggled away as she posed in front of a mirror.

The hospital PR department was being obstructive and utterly useless. We phoned them at eight thirty the next morning, as arranged, only to be told they were 'in a meeting'. Two hours later, they told us that no doctors or nurses were available and there would be no facility for filming Laura saying goodbye and thank you. With Jill, I called Fran and Les and organised a few unilateral activities.

Back at the hospital that afternoon, we bumped into Pamela Gonzales, the mother of liver-bowel transplant girl, Tracey. Our first bit of luck. A few minutes later, we spotted Dr Andrew Tzakis who we hoped to interview but the PR people had told us was "out of the country"! He was very pleased to see us, though not as pleased as we were to see him, and was perfectly happy to give us an interview and pose for a few shots playing with Laura. Sam said he heard one of the PR people say, "Oh shit, they've found him."

I had no idea what their problem was, but I was angry and read them the riot act: Denial of access, deliberate obstruction. Didn't they realise what a good PR opportunity this was for them? Were they incompetent, malicious, stupid, or all three? I may as well have saved my breath, but it felt good to vent my spleen.

Anyway, we got some lovely shots of Laura and Tracey hugging goodbye to the further irritation of the PR people, Heaven knows why. Laura's departure from Pittsburgh children's hospital made a really good piece for all ITN bulletins. Verbal herograms from the *News at Ten* team.

On our penultimate night in Pittsburgh, Jill, Jim Taylor from Granada TV and I went to the Democrats' party at the Sheraton Hotel. Bill Clinton had won the presidential election, comfortably unseating George Bush, the first Democrat in the White House in twelve years. It was great to be in the States on election night, even though I hadn't been covering the election. It would have been fantastic to have been in Washington, New York or Little Rock, Arkansas, but Pittsburgh Democrats also knew how to celebrate.

We filmed Laura and her parents leaving Pittsburgh. At the airport, British Airways insisted on a photo-op with the family. Everyone, it seemed, wanted a piece of the story. When we stopped, briefly, at Philadelphia, Sam got some very amusing shots of Laura in the cockpit with the pilot and co-pilot and singing 'Show me the Way to go Home'. No one prompted her to do it, she just started singing.

I so wish Laura's story had a happy ending. I'm afraid it didn't. A year later, her health had deteriorated to the point where she needed another multiple organ transplant which she underwent in September 1993. Six weeks later, she passed away. Fran and Les were at her bedside. She was just five years old. It was gut-wrenching. I can still see her lovely, funny little face and her cheeky smile.

But that was all in the heart-breaking future.

Back from Pittsburgh, in June 1992, I visited friends in Newcastle to decompress, and there was another friend's wedding in London. A few days after returning, Laura was back in hospital in Pittsburgh. We were worried. The foreign desk wondered if I should get back to Pittsburgh. I spoke to Laura's doctors and spent an hour on the phone to Fran. Laura was stable and sedated, it was nothing serious. What a relief.

We spent a day in Madrid in late June chasing South African President F W de Klerk, who was there for a bilateral meeting with the Spanish.

After a night at the splendid Palace Hotel, I met up with a local camera crew the next morning to doorstep de Klerk at the Ritz Hotel. He had released Nelson Mandela from prison two years earlier, and the two leaders were negotiating an end to apartheid, which would eventually lead to Mandela's election as president of South Africa in 1994. As a member of the anti-apartheid campaign in my student days, it was very satisfying to see the endgame being played out.

It was a long doorstep, de Klerk didn't turn up until twelve fifteen. We were the only crew there and were rewarded with an interview before a photo-op with Spanish Prime Minister Filipe González. At a press conference later, de Klerk made some very promising remarks pointing the way forward to democratic elections, strong enough to make a piece for *News at Ten*.

In Pittsburgh, meanwhile, little Laura Davies was in intensive care but stable. The doctors had told Fran she was fine and "pulling through strongly".

There was another IRA bomb in the City of London to cover, fortunately a small car bomb which hurt no one. I managed to track down the security guard who had raised the alarm and persuaded him to come to ITN to be interviewed live off the back of my lunchtime package. The news tiger was satiated.

There was another raucous leaving party at the end of June. Owen Smith, news editor and resident newsroom scouse comedian, was off to pastures new. A great loss to ITN. For some reason, someone ordered a 'strip-o-gram' (do people still do this? I doubt it). Owen's face was bright red, I had never seen him so embarrassed. The drinking continued, after a lock-in, until ridiculous o'clock. I took a very 'tired and emotional' (and for once very quiet) Mr Smith home to north London in a taxi at four a.m.

More good people left ITN that summer, and we feared for the company's future. Among them were studio director, Derek Guthrie, and news editor, Nigel Baker, who was off to join Nigel Hancock who had already been lured away by GMTV. Nigel Baker was a superb news editor, is a great human being and was another great loss. Needless to say, drink was taken and 'When I' stories were in good supply.

July 1st, and another day trip to France. Only Calais this time. French lorry drivers and farmers were blocking the roads. *Plus ça change*!

I met cameraman Paul Keating in Dover for the hovercraft to Calais. We had just three hours on the ground, talking to the lorry drivers and farmers, getting GVs (general shots for the story), doing a quick PTC and then it was back to the hovercraft. At which point, the five forty news decided they wanted me to do a live phono over French TV pictures for their lead story. I did it in the hovercraft's toilet, with a Calais sign-off! The first but not the last time I would go live into the news from the toilet of a plane, train, ship or, in this case, a hovercraft! We cut a more conventional package back at base for *News at Ten*.

Interest in the Calais story peaked the next day. It seemed no one in the newsroom understood why I wasn't still there. They moved a team from Brussels to Paris, and sent a reporter and crew to Calais from London.

I couldn't go because I was already committed to another story. I had the great privilege of interviewing Professor Steven Hawking, whose book, *A Brief History of Time*, had entered the *Guinness Book of Records* as the longest-ever on the bestselling lists. By the way, I can't recommend this book strongly enough. It is so simply explained and clearly written that even a scientific ignoramus like me can understand it. Having said that, critic Bernard Levin claimed he, "Couldn't get past page twenty-nine". His loss.

From Pittsburgh, the news that Laura was still in intensive care but off her ventilator, breathing well and very cheerful.

More stories in July. Barbara Ashworth, Granada TV presenter and the former girlfriend of an ITN colleague, had been receiving obscene phone calls. BT held a press conference and gave us a tape, a reconstruction of the obscene calls, good pictures for my packages for the five forty news and *News at Ten*, along with an interview with the local chief constable and Barbara herself. The offender was caught and prosecuted.

There was a day trip to Amsterdam to cover a fire at a chemical plant in Uithoorn. Fortunately, no one was hurt, but the pictures were spectacular.

We spent a day at Crystal Palace where decathlete Daley Thompson was taking part in a specially convened decathlon, his last chance to qualify for the Barcelona Olympics. He had already won Olympic gold twice, and had broken the decathlon world record several times. Cameraman Paul Dickie got some excellent shots of the great Olympian limbering up, etc. The first event was the hundred metres, but Daley pulled up with a torn hamstring. That was it, the end of his illustrious career. I had the immense pleasure of interviewing the greatest all-round athlete of his generation.

There was another proper, old-fashioned ITN thrash that July, the leaving party for the head of news input, Nigel Hancock, one of the very best in the business who had always been very kind and encouraging to me. We drank ridiculous amounts of alcohol, a lot of food (bread and fish heads!) was thrown around, and there was some mildly obscene singing. It was very childish and tremendous fun. Hancock delivered a very amusing speech, as did head of lunchtime news, Andy Tilley, *News at Ten*, editor Nick Pollard (a poem, no less!) and reporter Terry Lloyd. There was a lot of heckling. I went to bed at some ungodly hour, convinced I had alcohol poisoning.

I just about made it through my friend Alison's wedding the next day when she married Radio One DJ, Johnny Walker. The bridal car, a Cadillac convertible, was escorted by friends of the groom on fantastic, gleaming Harley-Davidsons. Sadly, the marriage was not to last.

The day after, a Sunday, was a friend's stag party. It was a summer of weddings. My friend, Brian Milligan, had arranged a 'stag do' with a difference, the only time I had been paintballing (although I've taken my children several times since). We were given a boiler suit, a face mask and a pump-action paint gun. We played as a team, a bunch of novices, against another team who were experienced and seemed to be taking it terribly seriously. We, on the other hand were just messing about, but we wiped them out! They were deeply pissed off, slamming their face masks to the floor and kicking the furniture, which was very funny.

After such a mad weekend, I was on the early Monday morning flight to Frankfurt and then onto the beautiful Slovenian capital Ljubljana, where I met up with a local freelance crew, Tom and Vanya (who I immediately nicknamed 'uncle'. I had to explain this to them!). We waited for an Italian air force transport plane bringing seven-week-old Zeneida Agic from Sarajevo for a lifesaving heart operation. We got good shots of the aircraft, the ambulance and the baby and at the hospital were given complete access. We interviewed doctors, nurses and Zeneida's mother, and did a PTC beside the baby's cot. So far, so very good.

At the feed point, we discovered that the camera had malfunctioned, not a single frame was usable. What a nightmare! Luckily, time was on our side for once. We hired a camera and went back to the hospital to reshoot everything. It was OK and made a good piece for *News at Ten*, but it wasn't as good as what we'd lost. I went to bed that night fuming but also stoical: Machine faults are simply beyond our control.

We were following up Zeneida's story the next day when there was a change of plan. The foreign desk wanted us to go to Zagreb to cover the story of Croatia's refusal to take any more refugees from Bosnia. This had become a huge refugee crisis, the worst in Europe since the Second World War. Cameraman Tom drove like a lunatic to Zagreb where we got shots of the Bosnian refugees at the city mosque and a sports hall, a temporary refugee centre, and interviews with the Red Cross and Croatia's bureau for refugees. We rushed to the edit point only to discover it had been moved to another location but no one had told us! Fortunately, the freelance editor was fast. Tom drove like a lunatic, again, to the TV station and we just made the feed in time for the five forty news. We rewarded ourselves with coffees at the splendid Esplanade Hotel (of Orient Express fame).

The story, though, was in Sarajevo, which was under siege by the Yugoslav army and the Bosnian Serbs. Senior reporter Michael Nicholson was being replaced by Terry Lloyd, flying from London. I could have got onto a transport plane in Zagreb and got to Sarajevo, or simply tried driving there. It was frustrating, but they were both senior to me and ITN was holding on strongly to the purse strings.

The siege of Sarajevo was to last nearly four years, the longest in modern times, and a year longer than the siege of Leningrad in the Second World War. The city was being bombarded by artillery shells. It would soon be impossible to get in, or out.

We were in Pale, the administrative capital of the self-styled Bosnian Serb 'government'. Our mission was to find and interview Radovan

Karadžić, president of the so-called Republika Serbska. Pale was on the front line. We succeeded in getting there, but there were hair-raising moments. When you have to walk along a road and have been told that the fields either side have been sown with landmines, you do as you are told and stick to the road. And being mortared isn't a lot of fun either!

Karadžić was horribly plausible. This man, who had been largely responsible for the 'ethnic cleansing' of Muslims, tried to come across as the academic that he had once been, an educated man only interested in independence for Bosnia's Serbs. But I knew he was a monster, a psychopath, a mass murderer. He also wasn't in Pale, but we did find his most senior adviser, Jovan Zametica, an equally obnoxious zealot, and interviewed him.

After spending more than a decade in hiding, Karadžić was finally captured in 2008 and subsequently convicted at The Hague of genocide, war crimes and crimes against humanity.

Much later, we would be in Banja Luka and Gornji Vakuf with British troops. Their job was to try to protect convoys as part of the UNPROFOR (UN Protection Force). They were supposedly 'peacekeepers', but here was no peace to keep. The Royal Anglians were particularly adept at urban patrolling and making contacts with the locals, but it wasn't easy. They had plenty of experience from Northern Ireland, but this was very different. They were in the middle of a full-scale civil war, a war within a war as neighbours within Bosnia turned on each other.

Dealing with the local leaders usually involved drinking ridiculous amounts of slivovitz, the very strong local plum brandy. The locals took great delight in trying to drink British officers under the table! They came unstuck, however, when they met General Sir Mike Jackson, a legendary drinker. It was the local mayor and his cronies who found themselves unable to walk (or talk!), while the general was demanding a refill!

Fran Davies called from Pittsburgh to tell me that Laura was doing well and was being allowed outside to play.

That month, the QE2 ran aground off the US coast. I packaged the story for all ITN bulletins, including interviews with the US coastguard and Tynemouth MP Neville Trotter, who I'd interviewed so many times in my Metro Radio days. He'd been a passenger. Small world. And how the other half lives!

British weightlifters were sent home in disgrace form the Barcelona Olympics, accused of drug abuse. This was controversial, to say the least. I interviewed the IOC (International Olympic Committee) medical commissioner, Professor Arnold Beckett, who said they been treated unfairly and should sue, and packaged the story for *News at Ten*.

The trial of Simon Berkowitz (the Paddy Ashdown burglary) at the Old Bailey kept us out of mischief for a few days in mid-August, despite several liquid lunches in the nearby Harry's Bar. The jury found him not guilty of burglary but guilty of handling stolen goods.

There were live two-ways and packages from Scotland Yard and an unattributable briefing with George Churchill-Coleman, head of the Anti-terrorism Squad, after police raided several IRA 'safe houses' in London, and then it was back to Amman.

That was the last time I got drunk on an aircraft.

At Heathrow, our flight to Amman was delayed for more than two hours so we (camera crew John Martin and John Hunt, picture editor Fred Hickey and I) demolished several Bloody Marys while we were waiting. On the plane, John Martin and I got through several bottles of wine and some Johnny Walker Whisky also disappeared. I don't remember arriving in Amman or going through customs and passport control at all. Our wonderful fixer, Afnan, somehow got us through. The first thing I remember was helping to load our tons of kit onto a flatbed truck. Never again!

We were supposed to be going to Baghdad and getting Iraqi visas in Amman, but the Iraqis were playing silly buggers as usual. The InterContinental hotel felt like a home from home, a lot of familiar faces, but despite our best efforts and the best efforts of the British Embassy, we spent a very frustrating week not getting Iraqi visas. Afnan even went to Baghdad to argue our case, carrying with her a suitably grovelling letter from me. She had endless meetings in the Iraqi capital, but to no avail. In London, senior foreign editor Mike Nolan was talking to the Iraqi Embassy, again without success. The Iraqis were extremely suspicious of British and all Western media. Each day, they told us we would have our visas 'tomorrow'. Each day the Iraqi Embassy in Amman told me the same thing. We were 'top of the list'. Tomorrow never came.

By the following Monday, day five of this nonsense, we were told our visas would be issued that evening. Tuesday was the same story. 'Definitely today' according to the head of the visa section at the Iraqi Embassy in Amman and my new best friend!

Nolan was being incredibly patient. I wasn't. He said it was still worth waiting, as there were several very good stories to be covered in Baghdad. That evening, our drinking companions were the crew from CBS who had just been thrown out of Baghdad after CBS anchor, Dan Rather, made some disparaging remarks about not trusting Arabs. This did not help our cause.

Wednesday was simply ridiculous, my new best friend in the Iraqi Embassy in Amman, Ali, told us our visas would be ready 'in 10 minutes'.

Afnan, who had been working her socks off on our behalf in Baghdad, phoned to say it should take 'no more than half an hour'. Six hours later, 'there has been a change of heart'. There would be no visas for ITN, our application had been rejected. We should apply again in ten days' time!

Had there really been a last minute change of heart after all the promises of imminent visas, or had the whole episode been some perverse Iraqi game, a charade? We will never know. What we did know was that we had wasted a week and thousands of pounds. Afnan was told that the Iraqi information minister, Hamid Yusuf Hammadi, had decided he did not want any British or American networks in Baghdad. Needless to say, we felt deflated and very disappointed.

We flew home the next morning, but were almost immediately reassigned to go to Rostock in Germany and possibly on to Belgrade. Afnan, meanwhile, was re-applying for Iraqi visas in our names, so there was still some hope. Futile as it turned out.

Rostock in August 1992 was the scene of nationalist riots and the worst mob attacks against migrants in post-war Germany. There were attacking a temporary migrant shelter where several hundred asylum seekers were camping without access to even the most basic facilities. Thousands of right-wing neo-Nazi extremists were rioting and fighting the police. Incredibly, thousands of local people stood by applauding them as the rioters threw rocks and petrol bombs at men, women and children.

I was working with a freelance crew, Eric Fux and Patrick Geraarts, and we filmed the appalling scenes. I drove with Eric to the feed point, a ZDF (German TV) satellite truck. The autobahn was at a standstill, not helped by convoys of police vehicles, so we took back roads through a spectacular thunderstorm. We arrived with just half an hour to edit a package for *News at Ten*, but with no sign of Patrick, our editor, who had driven separately. A ZDF editor, Thomas, came to my rescue and we very quickly edited a two-minute-forty-package for *News at Ten*. We made it, but only just. Verbal herograms from the *News at Ten* team and the foreign desk.

Next day, we cut a package and did a live two-way for the early evening news, which was very well received. I was working with Patrick and this time it was Eric who got separated from us. When we found him, after darkness fell, he had got some tremendous shots of the neo-Nazi violence. We had the lead story, another package and another live two-way.

There was more violence, and then the aftermath. On the last Sunday in August, we filmed the cleaning up operation, explained the underlying causes as best I could, filmed the weapons haul (including several guns) at police headquarters and drove to Hinrichshagen where families of Romanian gypsies who'd been the victims of fire-bomb attacks had been re-housed in a former army barracks. They were not pleased to see us, to say the very least. We were shouted at, spat at and threatened. Nice! All of which made a good two-minute piece for ITN.

Over beer and schnapps in a bar that evening, I got talking to a builder, his wife and their friends. They felt they were better off in the GDR (the old East Germany) and had lost their national identity. However, they grudgingly recognised the long-term benefits of Germany's reunification.

That August, ITN continued to haemorrhage talent, more good people were leaving, among them some of the very best including *News at Ten* editor, Nick Pollard, who would later go on to become head of news at Sky News. Vicky Knighton on the foreign desk, someone for whom we would always go the extra mile, was another great loss. ITN was losing too many.

We flew home the next day from Berlin, we were not going to Belgrade after all and, of course, the Iraqi visas had not materialised.

One Sunday that September, I managed to get two packages on two different stories on air in the same ITN bulletin. A quiet Sunday had started at the Farnborough Air Show, great fun filming fighter aircraft, including Russian MIGs. We cut a package for ITN and headed back to London. As we arrived, a small bomb exploded outside the Hilton Hotel, Park Lane.

Fortunately, there were no injuries, and by the time I got there, cameraman Ted Henley had got all the pictures we needed. I interviewed the top cop at the scene, did a PTC, and headed back to ITN to edit for the late news. And so it was that I had TWO packages in the late ITN bulletin, with two PTCs! One from Farnborough the other from Park Lane. I was in two places at once! This was daft. Apart from anything else, it made ITN look like it was short of reporters. I don't think this had ever happened before, or since. But I certainly wasn't complaining.

In Baghdad, our mythical Iraqi visas were still being processed! But CNN, ABC and NBC had all been thrown out of Iraq so the signs were not exactly promising.

On Black Wednesday, 16th September 1992, the UK was forced to withdraw from the ERM (European Exchange Rate Mechanism) as the value of the pound plummeted. The government had made the Bank of England raise interest rates by an unprecedented five per cent, in an unsuccessful attempt to reverse the collapse of Sterling. This was still several years before the Blair government granted the Bank of England its independence to set interest rates. In retrospect you can easily see a direct line from Black Wednesday to Brexit.

In the background, the French were to vote in a referendum on the Maastricht Treaty. If the French approved it, economic catastrophe might be averted. If not, more chaos was likely. In September 1992, our economic fate was being decided in Paris, Brussels and Berlin.

Chancellor Norman Lamont was forced to back down. Interest rates were to rise by only two per cent as Britain crashed out of the ERM. The pound remained in freefall as currency speculators grew ever richer. Lamont looked exhausted and utterly wretched as he appeared in front of the cameras. Lurking behind the hapless chancellor and seeming to want to keep out of the camera shots was his young special adviser, a certain David Cameron.

And so it was that, the following Sunday, I was back in Brussels. The French had voted 'Yes' to the Maastricht Treaty. Only by the narrowest of margins, but it was enough. We interviewed various politicians and European commissioners, including Sir Leon Brittan, and packaged for the late news.

We spent the next two days covering the aftermath of the French vote, the fallout. On the Tuesday, I had to cover a European trade ministers meeting in the Charlemagne building, a tedious prospect even for a political enthusiast like me. In the event, it was spectacularly dull. It was chaired not by Trade Minister Peter Lilley (Britain held the European Commission presidency at the time) but by Minister of State Richard Needham. There was no story.

Back in London, I was in Putney (my parents' constituency). John Major's government had been hit by yet another scandal. The former mistress of heritage minister and Putney MP David Mellor, Antonia de Sancha, had sold her kiss-and-tell story to a tabloid newspaper in a deal brokered by publicist Max Clifford. The so-called Minister for Fun was making a speech, but for some inexplicable reason, did not want to talk to us! David Mellor resigned from the government the next day.

The story was not pleasant, as de Sancha claimed Mellor liked to make love in a Chelsea FC shirt, enjoyed spanking and 'toe-sucking', a truly revolting image. She later admitted that this wasn't true. Years later, in 2011, David Mellor would tell the Leveson Inquiry that the *Sun* newspaper story contained, "A lot of cynically invented trash about Chelsea shirts. The story was cooked up for cash by Max Clifford and *Sun* executives and given front page publicity even though they all knew it to be totally false".

Many months later, I had to interview Max Clifford in his office on an entirely different story. Sitting in his waiting room was a woman he introduced briefly to me as "This is Doris", as if I didn't recognise Antonia de Sancha!

In early October, a British tourist, Keith Thompson, was shot dead in Orlando, Florida. I pulled together the story from London. Central TV found and interviewed a nurse who had seen him shot and given him CPR to try to save his life. Junior reporter Jonathan Munro was covering the Washington bureau and sending back pictures, while senior reporter Peter Sharp was doing my leg work in Essex, which felt a little *Through The Looking Glass*. Or maybe ITN was simply trying to bring on the new generation of reporter talent. I included myself in that category, I was still in my early thirties.

There was another of those two-stories-in-one-day days. The first was about rail privatisation, and a live two-way from King's Cross station. The programme editor of the five forty news, Phil Moger, expressed his happiness in his inimitable way, "The perfect two-way. Fucking Excellent." For *News at Ten*, I packaged pictures from Cairo where there had been a devastating earthquake. At least three hundred people had been killed and more than four thousand injured. My colleague David Chater was on his way there.

There were more stories to cover from the Old Bailey, including an attempted kidnap and robbery at a KLM warehouse at Heathrow and a 'supergrass' giving evidence against Chinese Triad criminal gangs.

ITN still felt like a company in deep trouble. It was owned by all the ITV companies. Now, a consortium of Carlton, LWT Central and Reuters was, apparently, trying to buy eighty per cent of ITN. This takeover was being described to us as 'a restructuring opportunity'. ITN chief executive, Bob Phillis, gave us a very upbeat briefing, but editor-in-chief Stewart Purvis' face told a different story. Maybe he was just tired. As mere foot soldiers, we couldn't decide if this proposed acquisition was a good move or not. We simply didn't have enough information. What we did know was that it would not redeem the redundancies already announced. But it might save us from any more.

We already knew the names of most of the journalists being laid off. At the end of the month, we got the list for the camera department. Some of my favourite cameramen and sound recordists were losing their jobs. To say morale was low would be a massive understatement.

But the news never stops. We had to knuckle down and get on with it. I covered a sit-in by the UDM (the Union of Democratic Mineworkers, who had broken away from the NUM) inside a Nottinghamshire pit to protest against the thirty thousand redundancies just announced. Thirty thousand!

Still on the subject of miners, I had a fun story to cover, for once, meeting the famous Grimethorpe Colliery Band at the National Brass Band Championship final at the Royal Albert Hall. They won! It was the only possible result. Cue shots of the band with their huge trophy and a lot of drinking and singing.

When the Lord Chancellor, Lord McKay, announced a cutback in legal aid, I did my first (of so many) interview with Tony Blair, then Labour's shadow Home Secretary. He was very good, of course, but did not look like a future party leader, let alone a prime minister. For one thing, he seemed far too young. But fate was to intervene two years later.

On a quiet Sunday in late October, a terrorist bomb exploded in Victoria. I scrambled there with camera crew Tom Phillips and Geoff Moyes and VT editor Gordon Hickey. The links engineers got us up and running in a matter of minutes, and we were live into the evening news. The police moved us on three times, and were trying to move us again as I was live on air!

There was another of those two-story days, a piece about the illegal trade in exotic birds, and for *News at Ten*, live from Henley for a speech by Norman Tebbit. There were more cases at the Old Bailey and the High Court, including boxing promoter Frank Warren suing pugilist Tony Marsh for libel. The Aga Khan had a High Court dispute with the Jockey Club. Sadly but not surprisingly, the Aga Khan was not in court, he was in India. We spent two days waiting for a verdict on a drug smuggling gang. When the jury finally found them guilty, four of them promptly burst into tears. And more IRA attacks, one of them a car bomb in Whitehall, at the very heart of government.

I had kept in touch with the Davies family in Pittsburgh. There had been a scare two weeks earlier, a suspected brain virus, but Laura had recovered well and was ready to come home. So, on November 2nd, I was back in Pittsburgh for dinner with Laura and her family and flew home with them three days later.

That same month, I interviewed Labour leader, John Smith, for the first time. The subject was 'Iraqgate', a mythical conspiracy worthy of an Oliver Stone movie, and doorstepped Margaret Thatcher on the same subject.

There were more riots and racist attacks in Germany at the end of the month, first in Leipzig and then in Eberswalde, about thirty miles north of Berlin.

I was excited when I was assigned to cover the ITN Moscow bureau for three weeks at the end of December, seeing the churches of the Kremlin and Red Square for the changing of the guard at Lenin's tomb. But I wouldn't be in Red Square for New Year's Eve, not that time.

US President George Bush was to meet with Russian President Boris Yeltsin at a summit in Sochi on the Black Sea to sign The START 2 Treaty (Strategic Arms Reduction Treaty) limiting the nuclear weapons arsenals on both sides. The EBU (European Broadcasting Union) chartered a plane for the flight from Moscow to take all the broadcasters to Sochi. There was a six-hour delay because the runway at Sochi was fog-bound and icy. When we finally arrived at what had formally been a resort for Communist Party bosses, we were taken by coach to the magnificent Zhemchuzhina Grand Hotel. We had just unloaded a mountain of kit, including the EBU satellite dish, when an American Embassy official told us that the summit would be held in er, Moscow! The president's secret service detail had taken one look at Sochi airport and that was enough. They were slightly concerned about the weather, but mostly about the airport being vulnerable to attack from the hills of Abkhazia, which Russia was annexing from Georgia and meeting fierce resistance.

The EBU charter was booked to return to Moscow the next morning, January 1st, weather permitting. There was nothing for it but to enjoy New Year's Eve in Sochi, which we did in style in the hotel's cavernous basement restaurant. There was a stage show (a Georgian sword dancer, singers, Father and Mother Christmas, and er, a stripper!), dozens of local people, and indoor fireworks. They weren't actually indoor fireworks, but they were letting them off indoors anyway and every so often a rocket would be sent whizzing around the room and we'd have to duck! The people from the US Embassy were behaving obnoxiously, making disparaging remarks about 'Russian peasants', and the secret service were all over it, men in dark suits talking into their cufflinks. Subtle it was not. There was also, of course, a lot of local champagne, but for once, we didn't drink too much. Tomorrow was going to be very busy.

CHAPTER 8

1993: More Moscow. Sefton. It's grim 'oop North'. Croatia

And so it was that, early the next morning, we returned to Moscow after an insane twenty-four hours. It was minus twenty-five degrees, a bit chilly. One thing Moscow did well was central heating in the winter and air conditioning in the summer. Step outside, though, and it was a different story, icicles formed on your eyebrows and the cold took your breath away.

The START 2 summit finally happened on January 2nd. The EBU had set up on an entire floor of the Rossiya Hotel with striking views over Red Square, the perfect position for live two-ways. And we had instant access to all the pool pictures. For the late news we had Bush and Yeltsin at a state banquet in the Kremlin. Cameraman Jon Steele sent back some superb shots of the sunset over Red Square which apparently prompted spontaneous applause back in the ITN newsroom in London. They also provided the opportunity for me to speculate that the Cold War just might be entering its final days.

That night, I watched our ITN package run on CNN, who had three correspondents covering the summit. I expect they may have been pissed off.

We led the news all the next day as well, our opening shots of the Kremlin churches ringing their bells, beautifully shot by Jon, who also got pictures of a Communist Party anti-Yeltsin demo in Red Square where I did the obligatory PTC once I'd stopped shivering. I was wearing thermals, which helped but not enough.

We floated several story ideas to the foreign desk including going to Armenia to cover the Nagorno-Karabakh war with Azerbaijan (still going on as I write all these years later) and had a few hours to be tourists.

Moscow bureau producer Bridget took me to see the notorious Lubyanka, KGB HQ, and to the Arbat market to buy some souvenirs.

We also went to Detski Mir, apparently the world's largest toy shop. There were very few toys, and the entire ground floor had been transformed into a giant car showroom full of Western cars. It was disturbing to watch Moscovites gawping at the Mercedes and other luxury cars they would never be able to afford.

The gap between rich and poor was extreme. There were two economies, the dollar economy and the rouble economy. So, while some wealthy Russians (many of them undoubtedly gangsters) were driving around in expensive cars, baboushkas were standing on street corners in the freezing cold selling a jar of pickled onions or a pair of socks to get a few roubles to buy some food. One young woman I'd met, Natasha, had a reasonably good job. She earned four thousand roubles a month, less than ten dollars.

It was a fascinating time to be in Moscow. It felt pre-revolutionary. Bread riots had preceded the 1917 revolution. The total disconnect between rich and poor and the obscene gap between them felt like the Tsarist Russia I had read about in the history books.

The BBC had covered Armenia a few weeks earlier (though not particularly well), so the foreign desk became far more interested in another story we had suggested, the trouble in Tajikistan which would explode into a civil war four months later, a civil war which would last for five years and claim tens of thousands of lives.

We made a lot of phone calls to set up the story and our Moscow producer worked her contacts in the Tajik capital, Dushanbe. We needed to be there to properly set up and tell the story, but ITN's interest was waning. Senior foreign editor Mike Nolan was keen for us to go, others were more interested in a story about the Russians being unable to afford to bury their dead.

A Russian cameraman, Vitaly, who'd been in Dushanbe and was now back in Moscow, had been trying to get through to his contacts in the Tajik capital without success. He was going to fly there the next day and would keep us informed.

January 6th was Christmas Eve in Moscow. After a superb dinner with Jon, Bridget, *Channel 4 News* cameraman Eugene Campbell and his wife

Karin, we walked through the heavy snow to St Nicholas church for midnight mass, an unforgettable experience.

There was a time-travelling opportunity one evening when we went to see Tchaikovsky's Yevgeny Onegin at the Bolshoi. With its huge stage, massive chandeliers, portraits of Lenin, hammer and sickle carvings, it was all too easy to imagine generations of Tsars and Soviet leaders enjoying the same experience from the 'Royal Box'.

We did the cost of dying story. First I had to go to see Moscow's director for Forensic Sciences and spend an hour with him and his two deputies before he allowed us to film in Moscow's model mortuary. ITN wanted us to tell the story without showing any dead bodies, which was challenging. Jon was limited to filming the closed drawers containing the recently deceased. Our driver, Nicholas, introduced us to his sister who had lost her husband two months earlier and couldn't afford to bury him. We paid for the funeral and filmed her at his graveside where she told us her story on camera.

We filmed in a second morgue, and at Moscow's largest cemetery at Domodedovo to film a funeral. We got a lot of grief from the grave diggers, and even more from the gangsters who ran the place. They demanded money with menaces, wouldn't let us leave, and threatened to break our legs. Nice people! There were six of them, very large and very drunk. Our Polish cameraman, Romek, handled it brilliantly. He eventually got us out of there by suggesting that he wouldn't be working for a foreign TV company unless he had been approved by the KGB. The not very subtle implication was that he was actually working for the KGB. We still had to hand over some dollars.

After nearly a month in Moscow I was home for a few days to pick up my private life (my long-suffering girlfriend Kate, family and friends) before heading to Tel Aviv. The job can take a heavy toll on one's social life. Invited to a dinner party, I'd have to decline because I'd be working in Birmingham, Berlin or Bangkok. Sometimes this would be interpreted as 'I can't be bothered'.

The RAF were conducting an air lift operation to help Palestinian deportees stranded in the Israel/Lebanon no man's land. We had the lead story all day with additional pictures from WTN and ABC camera crews.

Every time I go to Palestine, I'm amused by the welcome text from the telecomms company: *Welcome to Palestine. Smell the jasmine, taste the olives*. We had our own version of this, along the lines of smell the cordite, dodge the bullets, hit the dirt!

ITN had run out of money, again, having invested heavily in the speculation of further military action against Iraq, which had been violating the UN-imposed 'no fly zone' in the south of the country, and coverage of the Braer oil spill disaster in Shetland. Oddly, there was no instruction to return home from Israel but nor did they want to spend any money. As Mike Nolan put it in his inimitable way, "I don't want to hear from you unless forty-five people are gunned down in central Tel Aviv. And I don't mean forty-four." Click!

The arguments over whether or not the deportation of the Palestinians was legal or not was to rumble on in Israel all week without resolution. Israel's attorney-general came up with a plan which allowed the deportees to appeal to Israel's Supreme Court, knowing full well that the court would not declare the deportations unlawful. It wasn't much of a story, it wasn't going anywhere. Nolan agreed. It was time to go home.

Back in London, and another of those three-stories-in-one-day days. The IRA detonated a bomb on a train in Beckenham, Kent. No one was hurt. The IRA had sent a thirty-minute coded warning. Then to Greenwich for an education story and finally an interview with Prime Minister John Major on the plummeting value of the pound.

I did a profile piece on Lord King, who had resigned as British Airways chairman, and a pleasant 'And Finally' on the restoration of the gardens at Hampton Court Palace. I covered the story of a couple arrested in Bangkok for smuggling heroin, and the funeral of American tennis star, Arthur Ashe, who had died at the age of just forty-nine.

And then, a story which still mortifies me to this day.

The England football team had a new strip. Cameraman Nigel Thompson persuaded me, against my better judgement, to do the PTC wearing the new kit. It seemed like the right thing to do at the time. I looked ridiculous! It provoked a huge roar of laughter back in the newsroom, and a lot of unflattering comments about my knees! ITN editor, David Mannion, did not approve and I don't blame him at all although, as my friend in the newsroom Kate Brian observed, "It certainly woke them up".

Michael Jackson gave his first TV interview for fourteen years. It was an Oprah Winfrey special. The BBC had bought the interview, but Robin Staniforth on the ITN foreign desk somehow persuaded the Beeb to allow us 'news access'. I packaged a long piece for the 5:40pm news. It was riveting stuff. The newsroom ground to a halt. Someone told me, "You could have heard a pin drop".

There was also a story about fox hunting (*plus ça change*, yet again), and I got to cover the Brit Awards, a nice, easy assignment made infinitely better by meeting and chatting with the exquisite Kylie Minogue.

Then there was the day I simply could not pronounce the word Mujahideen.

I had finished work at six p.m. and spent the evening in the wine bar opposite the ITN building in Wells Street, gossiping and drinking far too much. At nine forty-five p.m., a news editor appeared. They needed a reporter to voice some pictures from Afghanistan for *News at Ten*. I had a beer in one hand and a whisky in the other, but he zeroed in on me. In an edit room, I looked through the pictures. There had been a breakthrough in the Afghan peace talks although Ahmad Shah Massoud appeared to have been carved out. 'The Lion of the Panjshir', Massoud had led the resistance to the Soviet occupation in northern Afghanistan and remains a national hero to this day. If you fly into the airport at Masar-i-Sharif, as I have done in recent years, you will be welcomed by a huge portrait of the heroic resistance leader. He would later become the country's defence minister and fight against the Taliban. Just two days before the 9/11 attack on the United States, he was killed by al-Qaeda suicide bombers poising as a television news crew.

On that evening in March 1993, I was not entirely sober. With just two minutes to go 'on air', I attempted to voice my package. I simply could not say the word Mujahideen. Try it after a few pints and whisky chasers! With the clock ticking I opted for 'Afghan freedom fighters' instead. This phrase was hugely politically charged, but I got away with it. I was expecting a call from upstairs and a lot of viewers' complaints. Somehow, no one seemed to have noticed or objected.

It was time for another Caribbean cruise, and to visit my sister on her ship which was based in Miami. Ocean Drive is one of my favourite places.

We visited Jamaica, Grand Cayman, the Bahamas, the Dominican Republic, Puerto Rico, St John and St Thomas and the Yucatan peninsula.

There were many memorable moments, but two stand out. One evening, there was a party on the rope deck, the crew's private deck. My sister's friend, Tam, was raised in the Southern Gospel tradition. She treated us to an unaccompanied rendition of 'I will always love you'. It was gorgeous beyond words, every bit as good as Whitney. We all had goosebumps. A crew member, a Geordie girl, leaned across, and said, "Eeh Glen, me nipples 'ave gone all 'ard." She was sitting next to her boyfriend.

I thought, 'Tell him not me!'

And then there was a day of horse riding through the rainforest in the Dominican Republic. The ship's maître d' owned a stables. I was a very inexperienced rider and had some trepidation, so I chose the oldest horse available, a sweet creature with a gentle temperament. The scenery was breathtaking, but the keys to success were the little shacks our host knew where we would stop for rum. After a lunch of chicken stew and a lot more rum, we were properly fuelled and full of Dutch courage. We emerged from the rainforest for an exhilarating gallop along the deserted beach, any fear long forgotten.

I had a couple of days in Miami before flying home, lunching at the News Café (where else!), and chatted to the foreign desk to catch up on the gossip. There were a couple of stories where I was. British World Champion, Nigel Mansell, had crashed and was recovering in his Florida home, and a German tourist had been killed by robbers sparking tourist safety fears, a hardy perennial Miami story.

In the event, I covered neither which was fine as I was more than ready to be back home, but by coincidence, my first story back in London was the arrest of two men for the attack on the German tourists. The next day, I covered the arrest of four members of the Pakistan cricket team for possession of marijuana. In Grenada. I should have stayed in the Caribbean.

The next day, I covered a shooting in Baltimore, and the day after, a piece on US tourism. How safe is it? This was weird. I really should have stayed in the States.

I had the pleasure of interviewing Vinnie Jones the 'hard man' of Wimbledon FC who was to go on to have a successful career as a film actor.

He thought the game had gone soft, and said, "I watched the Chelsea Man United game last night, I didn't see a single tackle!"

A couple of days later, I covered the story of Manchester City being fined for a pitch invasion. At least the fans were still showing some passion but, post-Hillsborough, this was totally unacceptable and unforgiveable.

On April 24th a large bomb exploded in Bishopsgate in the City of London. I heard it from my flat in Highgate and looked out of the window to see a huge cloud of smoke rising from the scene. I was on a day off, but called the news desk, who were already all over it, of course. I went in and packaged the lead story all day. From one angle, with St Paul's Cathedral in the background, it looked like an image from the Blitz.

That month was busy with stories which were not going to have much lasting impact. An auction of Beatles memorabilia was fun, less so yet another teachers' dispute. I did a live two-way from Buckingham Palace, which was to open its doors to the public for the first time. Oh, and Arsenal beat Sheffield Wednesday 2-1 to win the League Cup!

There were several Bosnia stories to cover, including interviews with SACEUR (NATO's Supreme Allied Commander, Europe) and American Secretary of State Warren Christopher. I was due to go to Bosnia, but it didn't happen, not that time. I was also assigned to go to Belgrade, but that didn't happen either, disappointing.

We covered the fiftieth anniversary of the Dam Busters raid, complete with scenes from the movie and the famous *Dam Busters* theme music. Five forty programme editor, Phil Moger, was in raptures! There was a spat between Terry Venables and Alan Sugar, a Spurs power struggle. They weren't going public and we got nothing when we went to White Hart Lane (the Spurs stadium) but Alan Sugar agreed to break his silence. At first, we thought we had an exclusive but he had decided to go on the record to all media. We interviewed the business tycoon at his mansion in Chigwell, Essex. Terry Venables remained silent.

Rebecca Stephens became the first British woman to climb Mount Everest. We covered the story on the day of her triumph, and the day after, and the day after that we interviewed her by phone from Nepal. A week later, I had the pleasure of interviewing her at the Royal Geographical Society when she came home.

And Arsenal won the FA Cup in a replay after the first game ended one all. Once again Sheffield Wednesday were the losing finalists. We had earlier beaten them in the League Cup final. Arsenal became the first team to win both domestic cups in the same season.

At the end of May John Major re-shuffled his cabinet. The headline news was Norman Lamont being replaced as chancellor by Ken Clarke, a move long overdue in my humble opinion.

I applied for the position of ITN's Moscow correspondent, which had become vacant. There was an interview board. I got across most of the points I wanted to. I didn't get the posting. My friend and colleague David Chater also went for the job. He was told by the suits that he would get 'bored by Moscow within six months. Not long after, he joined Sky News as Moscow correspondent. ITN's loss. Again.

My disappointment was ameliorated by a pep talk from ITN editor David Mannion who told me I was, "Very talented, very gifted". Just the sort of massage my battered ego needed! Of course he was laying it on with a trowel but, as well as being a great journalist, man-management was one of Dave's many talents.

More domestic stories in June. I passed a very pleasant few days in Manchester covering a test cricket match at Old Trafford. The popular comedian Les Dawson passed away, I packaged his obituary for the five forty and *News at Ten*. There was a 'weather wrap', more damaging floods in Wales, and a package on Prince Charles injuring his back playing polo. There was another day of the Sugar vs Venables saga.

In mid-June, a serial killer was targeting gay men in London. When Scotland Yard revealed details of his fifth murder victim, I had the lead story for all ITN bulletins. Buckingham Palace opened to the public. Not surprisingly, advance ticket sales were through the roof.

In July, the police set up anti-terrorist chicanes in Bishopsgate, those concrete blocks with which we are now so familiar. After meeting up with them at a secret location we filmed them setting up a chicane. All a bit cloak and dagger, but the nation's press was out in force. We had the pictures exclusively to ourselves.

I did a rather strange obit, for a horse. Sefton had been severely injured in 1982 when the IRA planted a vicious nail bomb in Hyde Park as the Blues and Royals were on their way to the Changing of the Guard. Eleven people had been killed. Seven horses had also died. Sefton's recovery had been almost miraculous and had grabbed the nation's hearts. The public donated more than six hundred thousand pounds towards a new surgical wing at the Royal Veterinary Clinic which was named in his honour. He was thirty when he died, and the nation mourned.

The rest of that summer involved covering stories around Britain. Two very careless IRA men were arrested carrying a bomb in Neasden, north-west London. At Didcott barracks, Colonel Clive Elderton went to a lot of trouble to give us a demo of army bomb disposal. I had met him before, on operations, and he was incredibly helpful, allowing us to film in his operations room and laying on a demonstration of how they deal with devices including those using Semtex. The soldiers were fascinated by our story of discovering the Semtex factory in Czechoslovakia.

In Leeds for another gruesome murder, Warrington to interview a woman who had given birth to twins at the age of forty-six, and I got to interview Chapman Pincher (author of *Their Trade is Treachery* among many others), which was a thrill as I was fascinated by the world of spies. And yes, like many others, I have been approached a few times over the years.

At the end of July, we covered an awful story in Slough where a nine-year-old boy had been murdered. His naked body was discovered in a park. The story led the news, on and off, for four days, culminating in the arrest and brief court appearance of a fifteen year old accused of the murder.

In Sheffield, we filmed and interviewed twenty-two-year-old Sarah Smith who had spent three days in prison in Crete for 'dirty dancing'. The lunchtime news treated it as a serious story, but *News at 10* wanted it as an 'And Finally', the quirky/funny slot, which took a major re-think and a total re-write.

Workington coroner's court recorded an open verdict after an elderly man died when a kids' prank went horribly wrong. They blocked the chimney of his bungalow and he choked to death on the smoke that filled his home. They had been persecuting him for months. I interviewed one of the little yobs, who was just twelve years old. The youngest was nine. We filmed inside the poor man's home in Maryport and set up to do a live two-way outside. The neighbours were getting very restless, very nasty and threatening us with rocks. I tried to calm them down, but also called on the help of the local constabulary, a friendly and rather elderly bobby who defused the situation. It was the only time I have called for police protection, but I didn't want rocks flying at us as we went live. Or at all, for that matter!

This was ITN's lead story that day and the next.

At Hull Crown Court we covered the conviction of a paedophile priest. Unspeakable. By way of total contrast, we filmed the steam engine, the Duchess of Hamilton, on the spectacular Settle-Carlisle railway, the first scheduled steam service for twenty-five years. One of the 'great train journeys of the world'. We hung out of a window to film, interviewed the train driver beside the hot furnace (hard, dirty work), and cameraman Alan Haridan got some superb lipstick camera shots, for example with a tiny camera tied to the fireman's shovel as he loaded coal into the furnace. We had planned to do a live two-way, but in time-honoured British Rail fashion, the train was running thirty minutes late so we had to abandon that idea! We all got very wet and sooty, had great fun, and fed a fine picture-led package for the 5:40 and *New at Ten*.

After a few days off, in Aberdeen for the wedding of my university friends Bob Smith and Fiona Cormack, and Edinburgh to see several friends performing at the festival fringe, I received a severe jolt. Laura Davies was back in intensive care and rejecting her donated organs. Oh dear God! Her father, Les, said he believed she was dying. ITN did not want me to return to Pittsburgh. There was nothing I could do.

At Bilsthorpe colliery in Nottinghamshire, three miners were killed when the roof of a tunnel caved in. Amazingly, another three survived despite being trapped by seven thousand tons of collapsed rock more than two thousand feet underground. Everyone in the village was in shock. It was fraught. We spent several days there. At the end of the first day, Dave Mannion phoned to say, "Excellent work all day, excellently scripted and packaged", which is precisely what any reporter wants to hear from the boss.

I stayed in the north of England bureau for all of September. There was an 'And Finally' about flying pigs (really!) and a piece to camera on the beach at Scarborough in the freezing rain. There was another potential mining disaster, at a potash mine in Boulby, Cleveland. This time, three miners were rescued uninjured. We were lucky. After a two-hour drive, we arrived just as the mines inspector emerged to talk to the cameras.

In Pittsburgh, Laura had recovered but was back on the donor list. She would need to have everything transplanted all over again, another multiple-organ transplant. Poor baby.

In Leeds city centre we covered the self-styled 'Juggling Olympics', tailor-made for an 'And Finally'. I did a PTC attempting to juggle and failing miserably. It was edited out back in London, which was probably just as well. There was another prison riot, at Wymott jail in Leyland, Lancashire, the lead story all day. Updated versions (how and why the riot began, life in Wymott prison and so on) ran all the next day. To Halifax, with its magnificent town hall, for the inquest into the Sowerby bridge lorry disaster. A truck had ploughed into a post office killing six people, including a two-year-old baby girl. The lorry's brakes were condemned as "unserviceable". ITN wanted us to cover the funeral the next day, but the families didn't want any press to show up. I persuaded Peter Wallace on the news desk that we really should steer clear. He agreed. A small victory for decency.

In Hull, we covered another grim story, the murder of a fourteen-year-old girl. Her father spoke to us on camera. We sent a package for the lunchtime news and the five forty but it wasn't wanted for *News at Ten*, hardly surprising as on the day that Rabin, Peres and Arafat went to the White House to sign a peace accord. I wished I was in Washington or The Middle East.

The remains of Polish Second World War leader, General Władysław Sikorski, were returned to Poland after being buried for fifty years at Newark cemetery. He had died when his plane crashed in Gibraltar seconds after take-off. Many Poles remain convinced to this day that he had been assassinated. With cameraman Nigel Thompson, I filmed at the cemetery and edited with north of England cameraman Ray Queally for the 5:40 and *News at Ten*. Given my father's Polish heritage, this was a story I felt invested in.

When British tourists were murdered in Florida (again!), we got coverage of a families' press conference filmed by YTV (Yorkshire TV) and pictures from the ITN team in Florida, and cut a package for the five forty and *News at Ten*. The lead story with minimal effort. Had I been ITN editor, I would have preferred the package to have come from Florida.

The next day, little Laura Davies was back in theatre for a multiple organ transplant which was expected to take twenty hours. Apparently, ITN were five minutes away from sending me when it was decided to send our Washington team to Pittsburgh. Quicker, and of course, cheaper. I called the children's hospital and left supportive messages for Fran and Les. Twenty-four hours later, Laura was 'pulling through'. Everyone was 'hoping and praying'. On the Sunday, two days later, Granada TV ran a debate programme on the ethics of keeping Laura alive. Fran was live from Pittsburgh and did very well. Laura was up and about, singing and being her normal bossy self. But it was still very much one day at a time.

There was a coals to Newcastle story, a car dealer in Hull selling Ladas to Russian sailors, and some spectacular underwater shots of the Titanic which made a piece for the 5:40 (programme editor Phil Moger was fairly obsessed with the Titanic and very keen) and another 'And Finally' for *News at Ten*.

In Moscow that day, Boris Yeltsin illegally (or at least unconstitutionally) dissolved the Russian parliament. I was having fun and covering a lot of good stories in the north of England, but I knew where I really wanted to be. Two weeks later, Moscow erupted. Tanks were shelling the White House. The political standoff between Yeltsin and the parliament was being resolved by force, in Yeltsin's favour. Hundreds of people were killed or wounded in ten days of street fighting, the worst in Moscow since the Russian Revolution. It felt like the country was on the brink of civil war.

Senior foreign editor, Mike Nolan, was off to join Sky News International. Several senior correspondents had also been approached. The rumour mill went into overdrive. In the event, Jeremy Thompson, Peter Sharp, David Chater and others were all tempted to leave ITN for Sky News. Chater was to be one of two Moscow correspondents. He wanted me to be the other. He was on the phone to me constantly urging me to move. Mike Nolan said I should phone the head of news for the new channel, Ian Frickberg, choose a foreign bureau and name my price! My father said I should go to Sky for the money, but I am always loyal to the people I work for and work with. I was loyal to ITN. It would be more than another three years before I too jumped ship, but such was the exodus of talent from ITN that some at Sky News rechristened it SkyTN!

In October, another interview with miner's leader Arthur Scargill who, off camera, mostly talked about dogs. Apparently, he used to breed Airedale terriers. I grew up with an Airedale, our family dog, so at least we had that if little else in common. The next day I was up to my waist in freezing flood water in Market Rasen, Lincolnshire, doing a live for the lunchtime news.

At the end of the month, a long chat on the phone with Fran Davies. Laura was back in intensive care, on a ventilator. She was 'stable', but it didn't sound good. Not good at all.

In early November, I covered a Manchester United story and walked out to the centre circle at Old Trafford, which was a thrill, before heading to Belfast. At the Rising Sun pub in Greysteel, UDA gunmen had murdered eight people. It became known as the Greysteel massacre. Four men were later jailed for life. It was ITN's lead story, of course.

We stayed in Belfast to cover a speech by the Irish Taoiseach (Prime Minister) Albert Reynolds in Dublin. We would have gone to the Fianna Fáil conference, but given the Greysteel massacre and the Shankhill Road killings a few days before, it felt too risky to leave Belfast. We cut a package from RTE (Irish television) pictures, including some great black and white archive of Éamon de Valera. Reynolds, by the way, was at school with my future mother-in-law and remained a family friend.

I was doing a 'hostile environment' course (basically, former Royal Marines teaching us how to treat gunshot and other wounds) when the awful news came from Pittsburgh. Laura had passed away. Not entirely unexpected but still so very heart-breaking. Reporter Bill Neely was in Washington and would be sent to Pittsburgh from there. I would cover the funeral a week later. I phoned Alan Cooper, Laura's grandfather, but decided to leave Fran and Les alone to grieve. They gave Bill Neely a very moving interview the next day.

Over the next week I prepared the coverage of Laura's funeral. I was back in Leeds, covering stories in the north (a hit and run killing in Newcastle, a postman murdered in Sheffield). The streets were lined with mourners and well-wishers for little Laura's funeral in Eccles. She was taken from home in a horse-drawn glass hearse. The service was incredibly emotional. I cried, of course. I talked briefly to Les, but Fran was completely surrounded by family and friends sharing her grief.

Sometimes as a reporter you had to argue your case with the producers back at ITN. So it was that, two days after Laura's funeral I was in Leeds Crown Court. A seven-year-old girl, Nikki Allan, had been murdered. A man who lived a few doors away was on trial. The jury found him not guilty. The judge had refused to allow an alleged confession by the defendant, George Heron, to be admitted in evidence, accusing the police of being 'oppressive' during his interview with them. It had been a six-week trial and had got a lot of newspaper coverage. When the not guilty verdict was delivered, Nikki's family reacted. Her mother sobbed, other women were screaming, the men were shouting and threatening to kill Heron. There were uniformed police in court, which was just as well.

I got the family's traumatised reaction afterwards. I had to argue with not one, not two, but three senior producers and the news editor of the day back at ITN. They had decided they didn't want a package from us but would only run a ten-second written story. I told them they could not be more wrong. Not only did it need telling properly in a news package, but it should be their lead story. And so it transpired. It led all ITN's bulletins, and the newspaper front pages the next morning.

More gruesome murders. In Stockport, the double murder of two MOT inspectors. At Teesport, police seized a big shipment of arms (explosives, AK47s) bound for Belfast. In Liverpool two boys, Robert Thompson and John Venables, were found guilty of the murder of two-year-old Jamie Bulger. The murder of Jamie Bulger caught the country's attention. It was an awful story and very difficult to report on.

Back to Stockport for the trial of the two brothers accused of the double murder of the MOT inspectors. On the way there I was diverted to Hull by the news desk for another story then redirected back to Stockport. As a result, cameraman Keith Edwards had sat in court for me and took copious notes, it was clear that he (and not only Keith, most cameramen photo-journalists) could pretty much do my job. I sure as hell couldn't do his!

I had spent the summer and autumn of 1993 working out of ITN's north of England bureau which, at the time, covered pretty much everything north of Watford. Regional bureaux were still in their infancy. Finally, in December, I was back in Berlin. I was working not for ITN but for the

British army, something I'd been doing for several years and still do to this day.

The highlight of the trip, away from the work, was a tour of the 1936 Olympic games complex, still complete with Nazi insignia and statues. We dined in Hermann Göring's private dining room, the so-called whispering room, complete with a large swastika on the domed ceiling, now covered by a curtain. Nazi statues were everywhere. The fencing auditorium was particularly impressive.

The Berlin authorities were grappling with a dilemma. They were afraid that allowing the public into the Olympic complex or putting the Nazis statues on display would attract neo-Nazis. They were leaning toward putting them somewhere out of sight, locked in a museum basement. The counter argument ran that they were part of Germany's history and that this period of history, unspeakably awful as it was, had to be faced and not hidden away.

Other stories I covered that December included Bosnian children being rescued and sent to the UK. In Baghdad, Iraq released three British men who'd been arrested for crossing the border illegally. Ted Heath flew to Baghdad to bring them home.

Finally, a foreign assignment. I was to cover the Washington bureau for Christmas and the New Year. I was young and single and always happy to do this to relieve colleagues who wanted to be at home with their wives/husbands/partners and children. It also provided me with more fantastic Christmas and New Year experiences. The previous year it had been Moscow, this year the States.

Our first story in Washington was to cover President Bill Clinton at a memorial service for the victims of the Lockerbie bombings, five years precisely to the day. Five years! Where had they gone?

The next day Michael Jackson issued a televised statement from his home, Neverland, denying a claim of sexual abuse of a thirteen-year-old boy. I packaged that for the 5:40. *News at Ten* were more interested in Bill Clinton's sexual indiscretions during his time as governor of Arkansas. This was years before anyone had heard of Monica Lewinsky. We cut a delicate and self-censored piece for *News at Ten*, omitting some of the more graphic details.

We worked on that story for all ITN bulletins the next day, and again on Christmas Day. ITN also wanted a piece for Boxing Day. We were short of material, so I had to disturb people (from the Brookings Institute etc.) to get the necessary interviews. We cut and sent a reasonable package. It didn't run! The foreign desk had commissioned a piece, made us work and disturb people over Christmas, but we didn't get on air. In the Middle East, reporter Robert Moore and his team had the same experience. They worked Christmas Day on a piece commissioned for Boxing Day which also didn't run. Someone, it seemed, had panicked and over-commissioned stories. It happens. Our piece eventually ran on December 28th.

It snowed. Washington ground to a halt!

Other early morning calls from the foreign desk resulted in us covering several more, late December stories. Among them, a New York businessman was offering Toys 'R' Us gift vouchers to anyone handing in guns to the police. Then, as now, gun control was a huge issue in the States. The lunchtime news wanted a piece on the (in my view utterly ridiculous) claim that the American government had deliberately poisoned some of its citizens with radiation in the 1950s to study the effects. Our package ran just once, which was more than enough. And a story about Detoxahol, a Californian wonder drug that supposedly breaks down alcohol in the blood stream, reinforcing the work of the liver, and sobers you up in just a few minutes. If only!

CHAPTER 9

1994: Washington. Lorena and John Wayne Bobbitt. Nancy Kerrigan and Tonya Harding. Gazza again! John Smith. Scotland

Recovering from the New Year's Eve celebrations and nursing the obligatory hangover, I ventured to the top of the Washington Monument for the first time for the fabulous views, well worth the forty-minute queue in the freezing cold. For once there was no work to do, so I spent a pleasant day being a tourist with my Japanese friend, Yuki, who lived in Santa Fe which sounded like the Wild West of Mexican drug gangs, years before *Breaking Bad*.

The rest of January in Washington was busy, we were on air almost every day.

On January the 3rd we covered an armed guerrilla insurgency in the south of Mexico (from Washington!), sent a piece previewing Clinton's first visit to Europe as US President, and had the pleasure of dining with Pierre Salinger, former press secretary to JFK, who entertained us with 'Camelot' stories.

I was woken at three a.m. the next morning by a junior foreign desk bod who had heard that a British man had been shot dead in North Carolina. I phoned the local police and ABC affiliate. They knew nothing about it. Very strange. After a lot more phone calls, I eventually tracked down the origin of the story to a news agency in Bristol and the dead man's American stepfather, and discovered that the shooting had indeed happened. Four months earlier! I went back to sleep for an hour at six a.m.

Later that day, I interviewed Jeane Kirkpatrick at her beautiful home in Bethesda. A former policy advisor to Ronald Reagan and the first female US Ambassador to the UN, she was best known for the so-called 'Kirkpatrick Doctrine', which advocated supporting authoritarian regimes if they advanced American global interests. Most notoriously, from a British point of view, she had supported the Argentine regime during the Falklands conflict even though her boss, the president, supported the British. I disagreed with almost everything she said, which made for a very interesting and combative interview which we both enjoyed (or so she said!).

The next day, I interviewed someone else I profoundly disagreed with, another 'hawk', Caspar Weinberger, who had been Reagan's defence secretary and had also served in Richard Nixon's cabinet. We sent the best three minutes for *News at Ten* as a stand-alone interview. He was, of course, very 'hawkish' on defence and the Middle East.

Michael Jackson spoke at an awards ceremony in Los Angeles the next day, again professing his innocence. That made a package for the lunchtime and 5:40 news. Vice President Al Gore made a foreign policy speech in place of Bill Clinton, whose mother had died overnight. Clinton was about to leave for his first trip as president to Europe for a NATO summit and then on to Moscow. Gore, never the greatest of orators, nevertheless had plenty of new content, enough for a piece for *News at Ten*.

On the Friday, the next day, I did three different into-cameras for three different stories. One was a preview to the bizarre Bobbitt court case due to start the following week in Manassas, then one on a story about Gulf War babies which was overtaken by the news that a British man had been shot dead in Houston. A third PTC on that, which was the story that made *News at Ten* as a peg for my package about gun violence in the States spiralling out of control.

And that was just the first week of January in the Washington bureau. Very busy, very varied, and I was loving every minute of it.

Lorena Bobbitt claimed she had been repeatedly sexually, physically and emotionally abused by her husband Wayne. So, one night when he was asleep, she cut off his penis! The trial was an international sensation. We covered it for three days and returned at the end of the month for the verdict. On the first night, I was allowed to use the word 'penis' on *News at Ten*, but only once! On day two, the court was shown horrific images of the severed member. I was absolutely forbidden to include them in my *News at Ten* package.

We left the Bobbitt trial as they revealed lurid details of their hideous marriage to go to NASA HQ where they had received the first images from the newly-repaired camera on the Hubble telescope. That made a fabulous picture package for the 5:40. I was also beavering away on a long piece on Clinton's trip to Europe when another sensational story broke. The US national figure skating champion and Olympic silver medallist, Nancy Kerrigan, had been attacked, allegedly by the bodyguard of her rival, Tonya Harding. The immediate aftermath of the attack was captured on camera and was soon being shown around the world. I had been trying to sell the story to *News at Ten* all day. When they finally decided they wanted it, we had to scramble together pictures from ABC and CBS to make a package which we had to edit in a mad rush.

Tonya Harding denied any involvement, but was found guilty of conspiracy to hinder the prosecution of her husband, Jeff Gillooly. It was the end of her figure skating career.

The story was made into a Hollywood movie, *I, Tonya*, in 2017, starring Margot Robbie in the title role.

We dipped back into the Bobbitt trial when Lorena gave her tearful testimony on January 14th and cut a piece for *News at Ten*.

There was a terrible earthquake in Los Angles that January. It struck in the San Fernando Valley area. It was felt more than two hundred miles away. Fifty-seven people died and more than eight thousand were injured. It happened very early in the morning. If not, the loss of life would have been far greater.

We had a team en route to LA, but on that first day we covered the disaster from Washington.

The American networks were providing a constant flow of pictures. Not only damaged buildings, including several hospitals, but also major interstate freeways which had been destroyed. The Golden State Freeway collapsed completely, one of the most memorable images of that day.

Cameraman/editor, Ed Castner, and I cut a long piece to lead the 5:40 news, and an even longer piece to lead *News at Ten*. We edited up to the wire for both, with astonishing new pictures arriving by the minute into our Washington hub. That night's verbal herograms from ITN were well merited.

While our team of Bill Neely, Dave Sampy and Tony Hemmings mopped up the aftermath in LA, we moved on to the Iran-Contra report. It had taken seven years to write. It was unequivocal, accusing Presidents

Reagan and George Bush of lying. The US government had sold arms to the Khomeini regime in Iran, breaking an international arms embargo and hoping to use the proceeds to fund contra rebels in Nicaragua. Such funding had been banned by Congress. It was a huge political scandal.

Judge Lawrence Walsh held a press conference during which he pulled no punches. We got hold of the three-thousand-page report just in time for me to brandish it in my PTC outside the White House. It was freezing. I was sure that icicles were forming on my ears which I was equally certain must be turning blue. Our packages for the 5:40 and *News at Ten* began with a sound bite of Ronald Reagan, during his time in office, claiming to know absolutely nothing about either illegal arms sales to Iran or illegally funding the contras.

The next day, we were back to the ice skaters. Tonya Harding's husband had been arrested for the attack on Nancy Kerrigan. In the American media, Harding was being portrayed as some kind of pantomime villain, while Kerrigan was little short of a saint.

We did more on the bizarre ice skaters' spat the next day, as well as a piece on the anniversary of Bill Clinton's first year in office. At one point, it looked like the Bobbitt trial might end live during *News at Ten*, but the jury adjourned for the night.

The jurors returned their verdict the next day. Lorena Bobbitt was found not guilty due to temporary insanity. This weird story was to become even stranger. Wayne's member was surgically re-attached, and he subsequently sought to cash in on his fifteen minutes of fame by forming a band, The Severed Parts, and starring in what was described as an 'adult movie 'entitled *John Wayne Bobbitt — Uncut*.

We had cut (excuse the pun!) most of our package for *News at Ten* in advance, which was just as well as the verdict came less than half an hour before *News at Ten* went on air. I had already done a PTC in Manassas which worked for either a guilty or not guilty verdict.

Before I left Washington, an Australian, David Kong, had fired two blank shots from a starting pistol at Prince Charles, who was on tour in Oz. It was a protest against the treatment of Cambodian asylum seekers being held in detention camps in Australia. Prince Charles hadn't flinched. In fact, he hadn't so much as moved a muscle. He didn't appear to realise what was happening, or so it seemed. The Australian networks put it down to British reserve, the famous stiff upper lip, describing the prince as being as 'cool as a cucumber'. In the United States, NBC ran it as their quirky final item. Quite rightly, ITN treated it far more seriously.

On my final day, we learnt that a junior government minister had been found dead, gagged and wearing silk stockings! Apparently, this was some bizarre form of auto-eroticism. "Who was it?" I asked. Stephen Milligan. What a shock! I knew his brother well. Poor Brian.

ITN colleagues Bill Neely, Terry Lloyd and Tony Hemmings joined me for a last evening before leaving Washington. The Tabbard Inn and Old Glory in Georgetown had become favourite haunts. Terry was in one of his maudlin moods. Happily, Hemmings was on hand to help (that is, half carry) him back to his hotel. Tony was also there bright and early the next morning to accompany me to the airport. He was off to Little Rock, Arkansas, Clinton country. I was off on holiday, onboard my sister's ship in the Caribbean.

Two days into my fortnight of sunbathing and debauchery in the Caribbean, the foreign desk called. Two Brits and two Americans had been murdered in their yacht near Antigua. My sister arranged my disembarkation papers from the ship. The cost of chartering a flight to Antigua was fifteen hundred dollars. Foreign editor Robin Staniforth said, "Go for it". I should have headed straight to the airport, but I discovered that we couldn't feed from Antigua, there were no satellite facilities available. I would have to fly on to St Lucia (another three thousand dollars), where ITN put a local facilities house on standby. Time was ticking away. By now, good material from the murder scene was available in London. ITN went off the whole idea because I would have had less than two hours on the ground in Antigua. Actually, that would have been plenty of time. The real reason, no doubt, was that it was all getting too complicated and the cost was spiralling out of all proportion.

I had spent three stressful but nevertheless exciting hours on the phone anticipating the prospect of island-hopping to cover an intriguing story, all for nothing. Perhaps the foreign desk should have got me moving and worked out the satellite feeds, cost and logistical problems once I was in the air? But there would have been such an inquest afterwards into why so much of the foreign news budget had been spent so recklessly. When I first joined ITN, I was told: "Never worry about the money. If you need to hire a helicopter then hire a helicopter. Just make sure you get the story." How times had changed.

After that little adrenalin rush and return to work mode, it was back to soaking up the magic of the Caribbean.

On the way home, I flew from Fort Lauderdale back to Washington to catch up on the gossip. I dragged Tony Hemmings (hardly protesting!) to a few of my favourite bars, ending up in Café Lautrec for some thrashing jazz with several Washington lobbyists, including my good friend Jenny Ley.

Back in London, and a fairly slow start. I voiced the shooting down of four Serbian aircraft by NATO jets in the no-fly zone over Bosnia, and covered the Grammy awards from an edit suite at ITN. I did a *News at Ten* special report on small businesses which took several days to set up and film. I learnt a lot about SMEs (Small and Medium-sized Enterprises), but it hardly got the juices flowing.

The IRA launched five mortar bombs at Heathrow airport. Fortunately, there were no casualties and surprisingly little damage.

Then there was the curious case of the Hatton Garden bullion dealer who had unwittingly bought Prince Charles' stolen cufflinks. I went, with cameraman Richard Burridge, to his seedy office where we were greeted by two huge but friendly heavies, his minders, straight out of central casting. We interviewed one of them (the other was camera shy for some reason!) and their boss, which made an entertaining package for the lunchtime and 5:40 news, and the 'And Finally' for *News at Ten*.

Vicky Knighton on the foreign desk asked me to go to Bosnia for a month. It was dependent on other reporters being shuffled around and being available. It was the usual process of moving the pieces around the chess board. First, I had to do a week covering the north of England bureau again, which was always busy, varied and enjoyable.

The jokers on the foreign desk used to refer to 'global news warriors or domestic distributors'! I interviewed Pete Waterman at The Hit Factory for a *News at Ten* special on the validity or otherwise of the UK pop charts. There was a piece for all bulletins on the Child Support Agency.

I had always thrown fairly lavish parties. On the Saturday before heading 'oop North' (and after that to Bosnia), the excuse for a party was the visit to London of cameramen Dave Sampy and Jon Steele from Washington. By happy coincidence, my friend Caroline Robb's boyfriend,

Julius, was also in town, visiting from the Gambia. It was a very successful mix of ITN friends and colleagues and non-work friends. More than a hundred people ate every morsel of a mountain of food and drank epically.

In Leeds, we covered a row about sex education in primary schools. In York, we interviewed the family of one of the British soldiers who'd been found alive and reasonably well after going missing in Borneo for three weeks. The story led all ITN bulletins. Story two was an unintentionally funny piece by an ITN reporter on jungle survival. We concluded that he had spent far too much time reading the *SAS Survival Handbook*!

Bosnia was on hold, for now, so I largely continued being a 'domestic distributor'! There was a lucky escape in the skies over Colchester when a pilot had somehow managed to eject unintentionally (how do you do that?) at three thousand feet. His parachute had only half opened, but he had suffered only minor neck injuries. With cameraman John Martin, I interviewed this very lucky pilot in hospital and cut a piece with picture editor, Gordon Hickey. There was another Child Support Agency story to cover. Then, as now, mothers were fighting for more child support, fathers were demanding greater access.

After four years and two Parliamentary inquiries, the House of Commons Public Accounts Committee condemned the Thatcher government for wasting millions of pounds of British aid to fund the Pergau dam in Malaysia, a project described by a very senior Foreign Office official as 'unambiguously bad' because Malaysia could have produced electricity far more cheaply from other sources. The aid had been given to secure a major arms deal. *Plus ça change*, yet again.

The biggest star in English football, Paul Gascoigne, broke his leg during training in Rome. Cameraman Ted Henley and I just made the evening flight to Rome, along with half of Fleet Street. Dinner and drinks with the hacks that evening brought me up to speed on everything you could ever want to know about Paul Gascoigne and far more.

Rome was cold and wet, which was disappointing. We doorstepped the clinic where 'Gazza' had stayed overnight. We actually chased his ambulance to the airport! Leaving our Rome fixer to feed our package to ITN, Ted and I followed Gazza onto the BA flight to London.

Gascoigne was very reluctant to be filmed, let alone interviewed, which was odd as he had had the option of taking an air ambulance and avoiding the press pack. He threw wine over two snappers. Somehow, I persuaded him to do an interview, though I had to share the interview with the BBC and Sky News, and I let the newspaper reporters sit in and take notes. It was an excellent interview, the life and times of Gazza. Afterwards, one of the newspaper sports reporters said, "Glen, you're a diamond". And handed me an entire book of blank receipts from the restaurant in Rome where we'd eaten the previous evening! I was not at all sure what I was supposed to do with them but I suppose it was a nice gesture.

For the 5:40 we sent a package and did a live two-way from outside the Princess Grace Hospital where Gazza was being treated. We cut a fresh piece for *News at Ten*. It had been a mad twenty-four hours. The praise from our bosses at ITN was well earned.

Back in London and two stories in one day again. Liverpool MP David Alton, best known for his views on abortion, was steering a Bill through the Commons banning so-called 'video nasties'. The story aired and I was just thinking of going home when I was set to cover a double murder in Hounslow, west London, just a very short live two-way in the pouring rain. The glamour of television news!

That evening, the mighty Arsenal beat PSG 1–0 (2–1 on aggregate) to squeeze into the European Cup Winners Cup final.

NATO launched air strikes against Serb positions around Goražde. Bosnia was getting interesting again. I was due to go, but defence correspondent Geoffrey Archer had already been assigned. Meanwhile, I'd heard rumours that I might be asked to go to Glasgow instead, as ITN's acting Scotland correspondent.

The rumours were well-founded. I was asked to go to Glasgow for three months. I stayed for two years.

I was blessed with a fantastic team in Glasgow, producer Sandy MacIntyre, cameramen/editors John Boyce and Alan Dickinson, and later cameraman David Brain. First task was a handover from my predecessor Hugh Pym, and to transfer the correspondent's long wheel based Mitsubishi Shogun, a magnificent beast equipped with very intimidating bull bars.

Our first assignment was an oil rig story in Aberdeen, home of my alma mater. Filming GVs (general view shots) of Aberdeen allowed me a stroll down memory lane. At the heart of the ancient university (founded in 1495), the splendid King's library had been turned into a rather impressive visitors' centre.

Senior cabinet minister and future deputy prime minister Michael Heseltine was visiting the Scott Field so we headed off in a helicopter. We got some fabulous pictures and a good interview with 'Hezza', who was also known as 'Tarzan' after his stunt of swinging the mace in the House of Commons. We were the pool crew, so we took our pictures to the BBC before editing at Grampian TV and feeding our package to *News at Ten*.

John and Alan were keen amateur pilots. They flew out of Cumbernauld, where their pilot buddies included stunt pilots who flew Tiger Moth biplanes at air shows, usually upside down! They became our mad eating and drinking companions, as did Tom Kydd, not only an ace press photographer but also a helicopter pilot. Tom saved my bacon more than once. For my wedding in 1996, we'd hired a wedding photographer whose pictures were disappointing to say the least. Tom took some superb and atmospheric black and white photos which I treasure to this day. On another occasion, we were drinking in a Glasgow pub when a drunk became outraged by my English accent and began offering violence. Tom, in broad Glaswegian, told him to "Get tae fuck", or words to that effect, and he buggered off!

Back to April 1994. Prince Charles' favourite dog had disappeared from Balmoral. That didn't overly excite me, not least because we were scheduled that day to go up in a Tornado jet fighter. But the *News at Ten* team was very excited, so we cut an 'And Finally' for *News at Ten* while Alan Dickinson had all the fun going up in a Tornado and getting some superb shots once he'd recovered from the G force. The Tornado pilot performed outrageous stunts, for example, standing the aircraft upright then falling away at five hundred mph right next to the fighter Alan was filming from. Very *Top Gun*, and it made a fantastic picture piece for *News at Ten* the next day. There was a point to it all, a story about noise disturbance but really it was all about the pictures. We later set them to music and sent a copy to RAF Leuchars.

I interviewed the combative and very clever SNP Alex Salmond for the first of many times. Ditto the ever charming future Lib Dem leader Menzies Campbell at his home in Edinburgh.

Boyce's flying occasionally ended without us arriving at our destination. So it was, at the end of April, we set off for Orkney in a Cessna 172. The weather was appalling, there were instrument problems and the plane was being buffeted by strong winds. We were all over the place. We had to turn back. John messaged the tower at Edinburgh: *Pan! Pan! Pan!* They closed the main runway for us to land. Fire engines were on standby.

On another equally less than glorious occasion, it was the turn of Glasgow airport. We were circling above Erskine Bridge. John was doing something involving the throttle while the Cessna's engine (its single engine!) coughed and spluttered. He was laughing maniacally! In the back, normally fearless cameraman Chris Squires had his eyes tightly shut. He didn't like flying at the best of times. He assured our mad laughing pilot that, "If we get out of this alive I'm going to fucking kill you."

Having closed the airport and landed safely, I found us a cheap Loganair flight to Orkney, which is probably what we should have done in the first place. Definitely, not probably. It was insane to take a little Cessna up in such weather conditions. It was trebles all round in the bar at our hotel in Kirkwall that evening.

The story was about a seal cull, and we took the relevant and very gruesome pictures as well as plenty of shots of very cute baby seals. I did a PTC with seals behind me. I referred to them by turning towards them and holding out my hand, palm facing the camera. For the next week, my colleagues took great delight in playing it repeatedly and accompanying it with loud seal noises.

Actually, getting the seal shot wasn't easy. At first, we went out with Ross Flett of Orkney Seal Rescue. He took us to a place where there had been a large colony of seals the day before. There were none. "You should have been here yesterday", became the refrain of the day and was repeated by the local fishermen's leader, Jeff Temple. It was high tide which apparently explained why the seals were not visible on the rocks. But there were plenty in the water, the fishermen assured us, and they were "stealing their fish". And no, they weren't French or Spanish seals.

We finally found our seals by flying in another Cessna (not piloted by John!). We had just an hour to get to them on the ground at Bu Sands. As soon as they spotted us, they slid back into the water, but we got them eventually by sliding and slithering slowly and stealthily over the wet rocks until we were close enough. We got a lot of very good shots, mission accomplished. John, a diver as well as a pilot, was keen to get some underwater shots (and go diving with the seals), but we were out of time. We had to get back to Glasgow to work on another story.

The seals package was very well received by the lunchtime news, with re-cuts for the five forty and *News at Ten*, so our exertions had been worthwhile. They had also been tremendously enjoyable.

Over the next two years I was in Scotland, one or two of the suits back at ITN in London were critical because they felt we spent too much time covering stories in the Highlands and Islands and not enough focusing on 'the central belt'. Guilty as charged! But we spent more than enough time on the M8 between Glasgow and Edinburgh, and I felt we should be covering the whole country not just the two largest and most dominant cities. And of course, what we were doing was far more fun.

Our producer Sandy Mac was assigned to the story in Rwanda, where the Hutu genocide of the Tutsis had been making headlines around the world. The brutality of atrocity after atrocity beggared belief. Meanwhile, we covered local election results in Strathclyde.

We did the first of many stories on the crippling drugs problem in Scotland. The peg was a House of Commons select committee report. One element of our piece was to film a football match featuring Carlton Athletic, a team of recovering junkies. It was a cup tie, the Rangers cup for amateur teams sponsored by Rangers FC. After twenty minutes Carlton Athletic scored. As the scorer of the goal turned back to celebrate with his team mates, he was punched very hard in the stomach by the opposing centre half. Cue total mayhem! A massive brawl erupted between the two teams and their dozens of supporters. The referee fled and the match was abandoned. Later, the Carlton Athletic people pleaded with me not to use the punch up which we had filmed. I didn't. It added nothing to our story, and wasn't a fair reflection on the excellent work they were doing rehabilitating heroin addicts.

On May the 12th came the shocking news that Labour leader John Smith had died of a heart attack. I had interviewed him only the previous day before he'd flown to London to deliver a speech and he had seemed absolutely fine, in very good form. It really was a shock, and a great loss not only to the Labour Party but to British politics in general. John Boyce and I drove to Airdrie to get reaction, and in Glasgow, interviewed the principal of his alma mater, Sir William Kerr Fraser. Alan, meanwhile, was getting material shot by STV (Scottish Television). We packaged for the five forty and *News at Ten*, both of which were extended as were the BBC's news bulletins.

The following Sunday, camera crew Alan Dickinson, Rob Dukes and I were in Ardrishaig, John Smith's birthplace and childhood home, to cover a church service and talk to local people. We had to battle with the news desk to run our piece, a battle we won.

The day before John Smith's funeral, we flew to the island of Iona in a seaplane piloted by one of Boyce's pilot mates, the first time I had landed on water. We filmed what would be John Smith's final resting place among the graves of ancient Scottish kings.

The funeral itself, in Edinburgh, was covered by ITN political editor, Mike Brunson. The burial on Iona was a private, family service, which is why we had filmed there the day before.

I took a week off in London, being a tour guide for my American girlfriend who was visiting and going to see my old university friend Iain Glen's outstanding performance as *Henry V* at Stratford. I was still at home in London when a huge story broke in Scotland: the RAF Chinook helicopter crash on the Mull of Kintyre.

All twenty-five passengers and four crew were killed in what was a devastating blow to intelligence gathering in Northern Ireland. Among the passengers were almost all of the UK's senior Northern Ireland intelligence experts. The flight was carrying British intelligence officers from MI5, the RUC (Royal Ulster Constabulary) and the British army. Although terrorism was initially suspected, there was dense fog that evening and it was later established that the weather conditions were to blame, although the special forces pilots may simply have been flying too low. They flew into a hillside.

It was the RAF's worse peacetime disaster.

ITN scrambled. Had I been in the Scotland bureau at the time, I might well have been braving the ferocious elements with my colleagues who were doing everything possible to reach the site by land and in small boats. Too many reporters had already been sent, so I pulled together the lead story for *News at Ten* from the comfort of an edit suite in London.

We reported another 'And Finally' story for *News at Ten* that June. An American girl, Vicky Van Meter, was the youngest ever pilot to fly across the Atlantic. She was just twelve years old. She touched down at Glasgow Airport. We had exclusive cockpit shots. Boyce was up in his Cessna again, with cameraman Nick Edwards, to get air to air shots.

On a more sombre note, we covered the funeral of actor Mark McManus, who had died at the age of just fifty-nine. He was nationally famous for playing the Scottish TV detective *Taggart*.

In the European elections that month, Labour predictably triumphed. We covered the count at the SECC (the Scottish Exhibition and Conference Centre) all night, then immediately drove up to Aberdeen. Although the major SNP electoral triumphs were still years away, there was a glimpse of the future: the Nationalists had won north-east Scotland. Alex Salmond was basking in the glory and was even more effusive and ebullient than usual.

A long day had begun with a package for the five thirty a.m. early morning news from the Glasgow count, and via a live two-way at lunchtime, had ended with a *News at Ten* package from Aberdeen. We were grateful for our beds that night in the splendour of Leslie Castle after dinner in the magnificent banqueting hall.

We went deer stalking near Inverness, to film not to kill. It was for a piece on a red deer cull. We interviewed two representatives from the red deer commission, and were royally entertained by Sir John Lister-Kaye at the Aigas Estate, Beauly.

We spent two days working on the story. It was scheduled to run that Friday, but was deemed 'eminently holdable'. The verdict back at ITN was that it was a very good package, but could run over the weekend. I don't think it ever made it to air.

Lou Macari was sacked as Celtic manager, big news in Scotland. On another day we interviewed Sir Magnus Magnusson of *Mastermind* fame and met his fat Labrador, Lucy. I was missing my own black Labbie, Purdey.

A Strathclyde police officer was murdered the next day. We packaged for *News at Ten* story two.

When I first left university, I went to see a few senior broadcasters in London seeking advice. George Carey, former editor of both *Newsnight* and *Panorama*, was one. So too was Melvin Bragg, who was very helpful and encouraging. George Carey asked me which would be the lead story: a police officer killed in Birmingham, two dead in Paris or six hundred people killed in a ferry disaster in the South China sea. In my naivety, I opted for the six hundred people dead in China. Six hundred people dead! Of course, the right answer was one police office in Birmingham (or in this case Strathclyde), and I learnt the lesson that all news is basically parochial in the sense that what makes the news it what directly affects us.

As a bureau correspondent, you learn that there are busy times and lean times. Sometimes the stories come thick and fast, but at others days can go by without getting on air. From Scotland, we spent a lot of our time suggesting stories to the news desk in London and getting them knocked back. This was normal and we learnt to live with it and make the most of our down time. My friend and former colleague, Robert Moore, was covering the Middle East and not getting on air enough. I told him to relax, play tennis and keep his powder dry, the stories will come. A week later, he produced absolutely first rate coverage of the assassination of Israeli prime minister, Yitzhak Rabin. I once reminded another colleague that we were in 'a marathon not a sprint'.

So it was that we spent a week in June eating, drinking too much, and going to Loch Lomond, Glencoe and other stunningly beautiful and evocative places easily accessible from Glasgow. We had a rude awakening, though, on June 25th. A train had crashed in Greenock, at least two people had died. So far so bad, but the really shocking aspect was that vandals had deliberated placed concrete blocks on the railway line. The train hit the concrete block and smashed into a bridge.

We covered the story for two days for all ITN bulletins. The police later arrested two seventeen year olds from Greenock, Gary Dougan and Craig Houston, who were sentenced to fifteen years for culpable homicide.

That evening, *News at Ten* ran the story that Prince Charles had admitted, at least implicitly, that he had had an affair, presumably with Camilla Parker Bowles. I couldn't really care less, but he was in Edinburgh and we were to film him. The prince was due to visit the island of Islay the next day so, early that morning, we set off from Cumbernauld in a Cessna 170 Skyhawk with John Boyce at the controls. The weather was atrocious, the experience terrifying. We had to turn back. We hopped aboard a Cessna 310. This was a totally different proposition. For a start, it had two engines not one! It was a smooth enough flight, but when we got to Islay we had to circle for forty minutes. There had been an 'incident' and the runway was closed. Air traffic control assured us that the Royal flight was not involved. We were considering admitting defeat and turning back when we were finally cleared to land, just as we learnt that it had, in fact, been Prince Charles' plane that had caused the problem. It had overshot the runway and the prince was at the controls at the time. John Boyce was in good company!

Once we'd landed and hired a car, a policeman told us that no one had got pictures of the crash, all the press were elsewhere. Huge sigh of relief! A local man had shot some video and was looking for the press. The friendly cop described his car, including the registration number! We passed him on the road. Screeching U-turn and, with Chris Squires driving like a lunatic, we caught him. He had given the tape to our colleagues at Grampian TV, part of our ITV family. Another huge sigh of relief.

I called Simon Cole, on the news desk, who already knew most of it. The STV/ITN helicopter was on its way to get our material to Glasgow. Leaving Chris Squires to get more shots, I jumped on the chopper with Ian Smith of Grampian TV, who had possession of the exclusive tape. Back in Glasgow, we cut the lead story for both the five forty and *News at Ten*, including an exclusive Prince Charles sound bite. An excellent day, after such an appalling start. We had had several lucky breaks and scooped the opposition.

Helen Liddell held John Smith's Monklands East seat for Labour, but only just. A majority of sixteen thousand was reduced to just sixteen hundred. The SNP was breathing uncomfortably down Labour's neck.

That June, OJ Simpson was arrested, charged with the murder of his ex-wife Nicole Brown Simpson and her friend Ron Goldman. The American media were calling it 'The Trial of The Century'. For me, its significance was that Sky News was covering the court proceedings live for the entire trial. It was the story that put Sky News on the map and showed just what a twenty-four-hour news channel could do.

We had another go at the deer culling story in early July. Cameraman Alan Dickinson and I were in Abernethy forest near Aviemore with a professional deer stalker. We spent five hours looking for a red deer. We could not find even one. It seemed to me that they needed re-populating rather than culling. We called the Red Deer Commission people in

Inverness and went out with them for another two hours. Still no red deer! We told our rather strange story in a package for *News at Ten*, but our piece got dropped. No great surprise, and I had no complaints. No use flogging a dead deer!

We spent several days at Rosyth naval base which Defence Secretary Malcolm Rifkind had announced was to close as part of the latest round of defence spending cuts. The local MP leading the campaign to save the base was none other than Gordon Brown. Some Conservative MPs expressed their concern that such a blow to the local economy and the loss of jobs might threaten their eleven Scottish seats and would benefit the SNP which, at the time, had only three MPs. The base was reprieved a week later when the MOD awarded it a vital refitting order.

Despite that U-turn, three years later, in 1997, the Tories were wiped out in Scotland.

There was the bizarre story which we dubbed,a drug crazed granny bowler! It was an 'And Finally' for News at Ten. In Edinburgh, a bowls player, a grandmother, had been banned for taking performance enhancing drugs! In fact, they were her vital medication. The lady in question absolutely refused to speak to us but we interviewed a member of the Scottish Sports Council, filmed some pensioners playing bowls who also made entertaining interviewees, and sent a fairly amusing piece for *News at Ten*.

The foreign desk wanted to send me back to Moscow, but the order came from above that I should 'concentrate on Scotland'. Fair enough, and I was assured it did not mean that I wouldn't be assigned to cover foreign stories. In fact, while based in Scotland, I covered stories as far afield as Moscow and New Zealand but it was clear that foreign assignments would be fewer and farther between.

I ventured south of the border that month to do a live two-way from Trindon Labour club, Sedgefield, where Tony Blair was celebrating his elevation to Labour Party leader. Twenty-three years later, I would be back to cover his valedictory speech at the end of his premiership. But this was still the young, ridiculously boyish Blair, the fresh face of New Labour.

This was also an excuse to stay overnight with old friends in Newcastle before driving to Liverpool the next morning. Home Secretary Michael Howard was recommending that Venables and Thompson, the killers of

Jamie Bulger, to serve at least fifteen years in prison, twice the trial judge's recommendation. Back in Glasgow, we sent a piece for the lunchtime news on bull bars on the front of vehicles. Apparently, they are dangerous, especially to children. This was easy for us to do as we had massive and rather menacing bull bars on my ITN vehicle, the Shogun.

I liked Shetland, its wildness, its remoteness. It is unique, and often feels more Scandi than Scottish. So I was delighted when the news desk agreed to let us go there to film, underwater, the wreck of the Braer oil tanker which had run aground the previous year spilling eighty-five thousand tons of crude oil. This was for a *News at Ten* 'Special Report'.

John Boyce got hold of an underwater camera and dived with two professional salvage divers. We were operating from the Ocean Defender. I didn't get to dive, but I did get to swim with dolphins. Magical and unforgettable.

We also took the opportunity to visit the Isle of Ness, with its fabulous bird colonies of puffins, kittiwakes, shags, gannets, guillemots and so on, and sailed past a colony of basking seals. We also buzzed past the Eastern European 'Klondyke' fish factory ships, which were massively over fishing in these waters.

We had a very cocky (and cockney) producer who'd been sent up from London to help. On our first evening, we were in the Fisherman's Arms in Scalloway. The door to the packed bar opened and in strolled our producer.

"So this is Shetland. Shitland more like."

For a moment you could hear a pin drop. I thought we were about to be murdered! But then a couple of people laughed and everyone got on with whatever they were doing. A future as a diplomat? Possibly not. Although he did go on to become head of communications at a huge, international NGO.

Getting out of Shetland proved harder than getting in. We spent our last night in a truly dreadful disco. Boyce was furiously attempting (and failing!) to chat up a pretty young actress from Hampstead, Paris Jefferson, who was in Lerwick for a cousin's wedding. I have just Googled her. She went on to have a very successful acting career. The next morning, all a bit the worse for wear, we headed to the airport despite the dense fog. All flights were cancelled. We were supposed to be packaging the story for that evening's *News at Ten* but programme editor Chris Shaw assured us it could wait, so we booked ourselves on the overnight ferry to Aberdeen. There were no cabins available, so it was a night on a chair and very little sleep followed by the train down to Glasgow.

Our producer, Sandy MacIntyre, was being sent to Sarajevo. NATO planes had bombed Serb targets in retaliation for the theft of weapons which had been confiscated by the UN. It was a Friday. Our *News at Ten* special on the Braer was postponed until the following Monday because the programme was running several pieces on Bosnia. Just a few days earlier, I had been offered a free facility to fly with the RAF patrolling the skies over Bosnia. One of the ITN suits, Michael Jermey, had turned it down, most unfortunate.

Our Braer *News at Ten* special did run the following Monday and was heavily trailed, which was very gratifying.

Next, on August 9th, it was trains. To be specific, the one hundredth anniversary of the West Highland line. We drove up to Fort William to take the splendid steam train to Mallaig. Cameramen David Brain and Alan Dickinson got some fabulous shots. I did my PTC driving the train. Well, pretending to anyway! It was another picture-led, picture-rich piece, not exactly hard news, but such fun and another fine experience. I considered myself very lucky.

Just a few days later a far more serious train story when a runaway locomotive crashed head on with an Intercity express in Edinburgh. Although fifty-nine people were injured, most suffered only minor cuts and bruises. Amazingly, no one was killed. Cameramen John Boyce and David Brain worked all night and we fed for all ITN bulletins.

We were back in Rosyth the next day. Gordon Brown had obtained a leaked MOD document which, he said, revealed that the naval base was to be used for storing de-commissioned nuclear submarines. He held a press conference in Inverkeithing. It made a piece for the lunchtime news. *News at Ten* had stronger stories that day. The BBC *Nine O'clock News* ran a Rosyth package, but the *News at Ten* decision was the correct one. It's not often that I agree with a decision to drop one of my stories!

Gordon Brown still owes me a Parker jotter biro by the way. After one of the first times I interviewed him, at his home in Queensferry, I gave him a lift into Edinburgh. He asked to borrow a pen. After scribbling some notes in the margins of a speech he was to deliver, my pen disappeared into his pocket. Gordon was in absent-minded professor mode. I was far too polite, of course, to say anything but I was amused by the idea that the shadow chancellor would later be using my pen and wondering where it came from. I had a car full of pens, so it wasn't missed.

A national survey was published that August about the weapons that shopkeepers, especially newsagents, kept close to hand in case they were robbed. We knew exactly where to go. In Easterhouse, it seemed almost every shopkeeper was armed to the teeth. Not only bats of all shapes and sizes, but a frightening array of knives. One newsagent sported a lethal looking machete, which made the perfect prop for my PTC. The story made all ITN bulletins and produced predictable, "Oglaza: armed and dangerous", "do not approach this man" comments back in the news room in London.

We were back in Shetland for the second time in a month at the end of August for a story about the UK's last A-B push button payphone (younger readers will have to Google this!). It sat in its iconic red phone box on the island of Papa Stour, population fewer than twenty.

As always, getting there was an adventure in itself. Cameraman Rob Dukes and I flew to Aberdeen and from there to Sumburgh. After a helicopter to Papa Stour, the final leg of the journey found us on a flatbed trailer being towed by a tractor to the phone box. We filmed it from every conceivable angle, including aerials from the chopper on the way back. The piece made another picture-led 'And Finally' for the five forty and *News at Ten*.

After a couple of days at the Edinburgh Festival Fringe supporting friends' performances, it was a week in Crete with my future wife Marion and our friend Alison who lived there and showed us some of the most beautiful places way off the beaten track. One evening, Marion and I were having dinner by the harbour in Agios Nikalaos. An orchestra was playing on a temporary stage for a Greek TV special. I joked that, "Any minute now, Demis Roussos will appear". Suddenly, a large man in a black kaftan appeared in a boat being rowed by four strapping young men naked to the waist. It was! It was bloody Demis Roussos! He was rowed to the stage, it was his TV special, and we had dinner serenaded by Greece's most internationally famous singer. You could not make it up!

We often strayed south of the border to cover stories in the north of England while setting up more interesting fare in Scotland. So one day in mid-September we were in Newcastle where a six-year-old boy had been waiting far too long for an operation. We interviewed the parents, the medics, did a PTC at the Royal Victoria Infirmary and sent a package for all ITN bulletins. But what I was really focussed on was an archaeological dig of the ethnic cleansing of a village during the eighteenth and early nineteenth century Highland clearances at Aoineadh Mòr on Scotland's west coast.

Opinion back at ITN was divided. The forward planning desk shared my enthusiasm for the story, some others were less convinced. One or two managers thought we were having too much fun and should stay in Glasgow. We eventually won the argument, but only at the very last minute once we were in Oban preparing to board the ferry to Mull.

From there we took a smaller ferry to Lochaline on the Morvern peninsula. At first sight, the remains of the village were difficult to discern from the surrounding greenery, the tiny cottages covered in moss in a clearing in the forest. On closer inspection, the partially-excavated were clear to see and very telegenic. We interviewed the archaeologists and a shepherd, 'Chubby' Ives, who was seventy-three and full of marvellous stories. We also had Mary Wilson, a direct descendant of one of the evicted families, who read eyewitness accounts of what had happened there. With the pictures of the ruined village playing under her words this made an emotive piece of television.

Two ferries and a two-hour drive later we were back in Glasgow. It had been a fascinating day out and would make a colourful and interesting package which Alan Dickinson and I edited the next day. It ran two days later, although it was cut back in London from one minute fifty to just one minute ten, a terrible shame. I would rather it had been held over for a quieter news day. It did at least appear at full length on ITNs *World News*.

That night, a bus full of girl guides crashed in Glasgow. Several had died. It was back to harsh, present day reality. At the scene, cameraman David Brain captured the shocking and awful images and I did the obligatory PTC for our package.

We re-visited the scene, got local community reaction, interviewed a former bus driver and so on the next day and sent packages for all ITN bulletins. They would have remained the lead story, but the Americans invaded Haiti to re-instate the ousted but democratically elected president, Jean-Bertrand Aristide.

In Belfast, Prime Minister John Major announced a referendum on the Northern Ireland peace process (the Good Friday agreement was still some years away) and lifted the broadcasting ban on Sinn Féin after six years. We were finally able to hear the voices of Gerry Adams and Martin McGuinness which, by law, had previously been dubbed by actors. In Gerry Adams' case, most people thought he would have been better off keeping the actor's voice!

At the end of the month we were in Inverness for the annual SNP conference. We interviewed the main players, party leader Alex Salmond, Margaret Ewing MP and so on, and got some fine shots of the capital of the Highlands from the top of Inverness castle (a caretaker kindly let us in). But what was memorable was my PTC. At cameraman Alan Dickinson's prompting, I got up onto the side of the stage as Alex Salmond was taking a standing ovation after his keynote speech. Very cheeky! This stunt has been done by others since, but this was the first time a reporter had had such temerity. Alex Salmond's face when he saw what I was doing wore an expression of utter astonishment.

My friend, Simon Cole, resigned from ITN and joined Sky News. He was beyond irritated by one of the ITN managers in particular, a jumped-up little twerp who I also found annoying and had, apparently, taken a dislike to me too. He was the one who had been trying to insist that we stay in Glasgow all the time. Simon had been a good reporter who had gone on to become a superb news editor. With his departure, ITN had lost three top news editors in as many months. In any other company, the manager responsible would be questioned if not dismissed.

In early October, Saddam Hussein moved two divisions and three hundred tanks south of Basra towards the Kuwaiti border. It looked like more sabre rattling, gesturing, playing to the 'Arab Street', but the Americans were taking it very seriously and moving military assets accordingly. Bill Clinton went on television to warn Saddam to back off. I phoned the foreign desk. "My Middle East bag is packed!" In the event, it came to nothing.

Meanwhile, we were covering some 'hard news' and very Glasgow stories. A boy died after being chased by a gang onto a railway track where he was hit by a train. There was yet another drugs trial, and a doctor was murdered in Airdrie. All staple Central Belt stories.

That October, I was back in Germany not with ITN but working for the British army. I'd been helping the army for some time. This relationship with them began when ITN's defence editor who had helped the army with 'media interview training' was asked to recommend someone and recommended me. The work has become much more sophisticated over the years, first under Major Ken Molyneux-Carter and then under Major Andy Reeds, of whom much more later. Back in 1994, it was something of a one-man operation, run by Major Tony Gaite, who recruited journalists to help.

On this occasion, we were preparing a brigade HQ for deployment to Bosnia, Operation Grapple, led by Brigadier Robert Gordon. We worked out of the Normandy barracks in Sennelager. The dining hall was Rommel's map room, and it was easy to imagine the scene during the Second World War.

The job was pretty full on, interviewing officers all day long, holding mock press conferences and editing 'news packages' to reflect back to them how what they had said would have been reported. Such jobs with the military also allowed me the opportunity to think carefully about the way we report the news, how we select what to use and what to leave out, and so on, something there is rarely time for when you're in the thick of it and relying on your news instinct and experience.

Tony had a rather belligerent attitude to the press. He instilled in army officers the notion that we should be treated as an enemy, and urged us to grill them with interviews as hard as possible. In this he was wrong, but he was trying to prepare them for the worst. It is true that, in some circumstances, military officers may get a tough interview, but generally people, our audience, respect the uniform and support our troops. The interviews needed to be informative (within the bounds of operational security), colourful and interesting. They did not need to be hostile. It took years to change this mindset to the point where the press is now regarded in military doctrine as a 'non-lethal weapon system', a tool to be used rather than an opponent to be attacked. We now live in far more sophisticated and media-savvy times.

In later October, we spent a day at Gordonstoun school for a piece for *News at Ten*. His old school had been described by Prince Charles as 'absolute hell'. And I thought my school days were insufferable!

We covered the de-commissioning of HMS Resolution, Britain's first Polaris submarine. The Queen Mother had launched her in 1966 and was supposed to attend the de-commissioning but was fog-bound at Balmoral, so Prince Andrew took her place. We spent a pleasant morning at the Scottish Canal Centre at Ratho near Edinburgh, taking pretty pictures on a sunny autumn day, interviewing British Waterways chairman Bernard Henderson, and doing the ubiquitous PTC, this time on a canal boat. This made the soft picture story on a busy news day, but to my surprise, it ran. We filmed what was basically another picture story the next day on the 'menace' of low flying. The package ran at lunchtime and on the five forty but, although it was slotted to lead part two, got squeezed out of *News at Ten*.

I ended October covering a most bizarre story: Kermit the frog speaking at the Oxford Union. ITN loved it, and for weeks afterwards, friends and people in general would say, "I saw you interviewing Kermit the frog"! Never mind all the other stories, this was the one people remembered!

My former colleague John Suchet told of how, when he returned from covering the fall of President Marcos in the Philippines (a huge story at the time), he had to interview a talking parrot and suffered a similar fate. Never mind Marcos, for weeks afterwards he would be greeted by a chorus of 'pieces of eight'!

In early November, we covered the construction of the Skye Bridge which was controversial because it was the first major project funded by PFI (the Private Finance Initiative) and would be charging a toll.

On a beautiful autumn day, we took the ferry to Skye as people had done for hundreds of years. But the huge new structure was already towering above Lochalsh. It was impressive, but far from romantic (Carry the lad who's born to be King over the sea to Skye etc.). We got up in a helicopter to get fantastic aerial shots, interviewed the project manager and some local objectors. For once, we had both a hard news story because of the PFI political angle and a very colourful picture package.

The journey back to Glasgow was spectacular. The drive to Portree was stunningly pretty, as were Kyleakin and the Kyle of Lochalsh. We took some shots of Eilean Donan castle and the majestic Glen Shiel. What a country!

We cut the Skye package two days later, having been diverted to Edinburgh to cover the appeal of George Beattie, apparently wrongly convicted of murder twenty-one years earlier. It ran on the lunchtime news, looked really good, and was very well received, but we were scrambled to go to Sunderland (er, definitely not in Scotland!) where a man had been arrested for murder. After a long drive, we got the shots, did a PTC outside the police station and sent a package for the five forty from Tyne Tees TV in Newcastle. Despite the disappointment that our Skye package had run only once and we'd been sent instead to cover what was basically a hack story, it was great to be back among friends in Newcastle not least because that very day Colleen, the wife of my former Metro Radio boss Tony Cartledge, had given birth to a ten pound, one ounce baby boy.

Back in Scotland that November, we covered the government go-ahead for the development of the Foinaven oil field over one hundred miles west of Shetland, the first development out beyond the UK continental shelf, and the financial collapse of a private hospital. The concept of private hospitals was still very new. This had been one of the first, and it had failed.

We also covered one of those stories that make our job so much better than having to actually work for a living, the twenty-fifth anniversary of the Nimrod maritime reconnaissance aircraft, which had first entered service in 1969. The huge planes were modified with air-to-air side winder missiles for self-defence during the Falklands conflict in 1982. Inside, they were packed with state-of-the-art technology, some of which we were not allowed to film. But we did get to fly in one! Cameraman Alan Dickinson got some great air to air shots while I interviewed the crew and did a PTC onboard.

The Nimrod continued in service until 2010 when its successor, the Nimrod MRA4, was cancelled, a victim of the Strategic Defence and Security Review. At that point, it was nine years late and almost eight hundred million pounds over budget. It was finally replaced by the Poseidon MRA Mk1, but not until 2020.

1994 was a very good year for holidays! I was owed a lot of leave. I spent the last two weeks of November in beautiful Thailand, and a week in December in Israel with my future wife Marion who I took diving, her first time, when we went to the Red Sea.

Back in Glasgow there was serious flooding. We packaged the story all day. Prince Charles came to sympathise. I shouted a question and got a very good reply. Scoop! We are absolutely not supposed to doorstep members of the Royal Family, but fortune favours the brave.

I was only back in Scotland for a few days before heading off to Moscow to cover the bureau for two weeks. I took with me forty-five thousand dollars of ITN's money in cash for future bureau expenses. Moscow's Sheremetyevo airport was as chaotic as ever. The customs officers' eyes almost popped out of their heads when they looked into my bag of cash, and several were soon gathered around in utter astonishment.

Sheremetyevo airport at that time was a shambles. We were once stuck there for a couple of hours. It was lunchtime. We found the only restaurant at the airport, the only one, where we were told that it was closed because the staff were having their lunch.

A few dollars usually did the trick. If you wanted a taxi in Moscow, you simply held up a few dollars or a packet of Marlboro Red cigarettes. A dozen cars would screech to a halt offering to take you wherever you wanted to go.

War was raging in Chechnya. Our cunning plan was to try to get to Grozny from the west, from Vladikavkaz, before the Russians cut the road from the east. We tried, but couldn't get anywhere near the Chechen capital which the Russians were in the process of pounding into the ground.

Moscow that December was like the Wild West, or maybe that should be the Wild East. Every night, you could hear gunfire as the Russian and Chechen mafias fought for control. One evening, we went to a nightclub called Nightflight. When we tried to return the next evening, the door was guarded by militia men carrying machine guns, with grenades hanging from their belts and generally bristling with weapons. Some gangster (or war lord) had taken over the entire club for the evening. We were shoved and told to go away (or words to that effect!).

Christmas Day in Moscow. Red Square, the Kremlin, a winter wonderland, and a Russian Orthodox church service with marvellous chanting, pure theatre. Dinner at the Metropol Hotel with some of the ITN team and David Chater and his wife Mel. Chater was now working for Sky News and had just been given a small fortune in share options on top of his very generous salary. Maybe I should have left ITN too. Maybe I was working for the wrong company. Maybe I should have listened to my father! It wasn't the first or last time I had ignored his sound advice.

Chater had just returned from Chechnya. The words coming out of his mouth told us that it had been 'hell', but his swivelling eyes told a different story. He had obviously loved every second of it.

On Boxing Day, we heard from Chechnya that ITN sound recordist Paul Reilly, was very ill with an infection and in great pain. He needed to be brought back to Moscow, if not London. I spent six hours at Vankuva airport (much smaller than Sheremetyevo) trying to charter a flight, but to no avail despite the best efforts of the charter company. Our destination airport in Dagestan wasn't operating. There was simply no one there.

Early the next morning we were back at the airport. The deputy mayor of Makhachkala, the capital of Dagestan, was there with an entourage and several cases of Dagestani cognac (not recommended!). After endless toasts to Dagestan, Anglo-Dagestani friendship and world peace, he agreed to give us a lift! We also blagged seats for ABC and correspondents from the *Los Angeles* and the *New York Times*. The drinking continued until we arrived at Makhachkala airport where we were met by our lovely Moscow bureau producer, Bridget Else. Paul had improved since the day before and was full of painkillers.

We were only on the ground for two hours. The airport was technically closed. In fact, we were the only flight going in or out. We were taking another group of American journalists back to Moscow with us. Two Chechens, very dodgy looking characters, had clearly bribed some airport officials to get on to our flight. The Americans, convinced we were going to be hijacked, insisted they leave. I tried to mediate. The stand-off was resolved by the aircraft's captain who offered a lift to a group of Russian army officers, thus instantly transforming us into a top priority military flight!

We stopped to re-fuel in Voronezh in a snow blizzard and finally arrived back in Moscow at one a.m. We took Paul to the American Medical Centre where he was diagnosed with epididymitis (very painful) and given antibiotics and more painkillers. I finally got to bed in my hotel, the Penta, at four a.m. I had a throbbing headache caused by the after effects of drinking all that Dagestani firewater.

Meanwhile ITN's Moscow correspondent, the rather bombastic Julian Manyon, was relentlessly attempting to persuade ITN in London to allow him to 'bigfoot' reporter Andrew Simmons who was doing sterling (and dangerous) work in Chechnya. This was not how ITN comrades in arms treated one another. Whenever I had been bigfooted or sent to bigfoot another reporter, it was always done with great regret and reluctance on both sides.

New Year's Eve was another memorable one. We basically ate and drank all day, went to a wonderful performance of the *Nutcracker* at the Bolshoi, and then on to Red Square for midnight. The square was packed and very, very raucous. The favourite activity appeared to be draining a bottle of vodka and then lobbing the empty bottle into the air. Hard hats were not provided! Our Scottish producer Sandy MacIntyre had a section of the crowd singing 'Auld Lang Syne'. Then it was clubbing until sometime after dawn. It rained that night. Apparently, if it rains in Moscow on New Year's Eve it means the coming year will be a good one. I don't know if this refers to harvest, vodka production, or includes television news reporters.

CHAPTER 10

1995 and 1996: Bonnie Scotland. New Zealand. Moscow. Dunblane.
Bible John. Dolly the Sheep. Mad Cow Disease

Having gone to bed at six a.m., I woke on January 1st with a terrible vodka-induced headache.

My Moscow sojourn was over. At Sheremetyevo airport, we spent a tedious two hours on the tarmac while our aircraft was de-iced. I was always wary of flying with Aeroflot (or Aeroflop, as we called it). On one internal flight, rivets had been popping out of the fuselage into the cabin, not very reassuring. In Yerevan, a BBC crew who I knew had got off the flight and walked to the terminal building. As they entered, the aircraft they had flown in exploded. I could well believe it. More than once, I had seen planes being refuelled by men happily smoking cigarettes, unconcerned by the fuel and fumes all around them.

Except for trips to cover stories in Germany, Greece and New Zealand, 1995 was a Scottish year, running the ITN bureau in Glasgow.

Footballer, Duncan Ferguson (aka Duncan Disorderly), was on trial, but his case was postponed twice, the second time until May, very conveniently after the end of the football season. You could not, of course, speculate as to which team the judge supported!

On the subject of football, Newcastle United sold striker Andy Cole to Man. United for seven million pounds, a new record. How times have changed.

That January, as we were working away in Scotland on devolution stories, the Russians were closing in on the centre of Grozny.

We were doing a story on the threat to fishing vessels from submarines. We sailed onboard a trawler from Largs, near Arran, and found HMS Trenchant, the very submarine that had accidentally sunk the trawler Antares in Bute Sound four years earlier. The fifty-foot trawler's nets had become tangled with the hunter-killer sub which was passing stealthily sixty metres beneath her. All four crew members drowned. The incident led to a tightening of the rules for Royal Navy submarines operating in the vicinity of civilian vessels, which is why we were there, talking to local fishermen. Finding HMS Trenchant was a great stroke of good luck.

Our piece ran two days later, but was dropped from *News at Ten*. There had been a catastrophic earthquake in Japan which had killed more than five thousand people and injured more than forty thousand.

A helicopter ditched in the North Sea with eighteen people onboard. We were scrambled to Aberdeen. On the way, it emerged that all were alive and well. The helicopter had landed on the water in very rough seas after being struck by lightning. Talk about a miracle escape! We did a belt and braces edit for the 5:40 and, for *News at Ten*, a much more polished effort which included some fantastic video from the RAF. The next day we interviewed the 'hero' pilots who described their experience in vivid detail.

A two-year-old baby girl, Christina Murtagh, was found dead in a toilet cubicle after going missing from her bed at the Royal Children's Hospital in Yorkhill. We cut a package for *News at Ten* with predictable ingredients, interviews with the hospital's medical director and police, a PTC and so on. The next day, we went to see her grandparents in Drumoyne, not the most salubrious area of Glasgow, and incidentally, the birthplace of Sir Alex Ferguson. To my surprise, little Christine's grandparents were willing to be interviewed. It was heart-breaking, at times they were sobbing uncontrollably. I felt wretched, like a vulture. But this was a big story, and they gave us some family video of the baby girl. No one else had it, so this was something of a scoop and the centre piece of our packages for all ITN bulletins that sad Tuesday in January. I still felt awful about the intrusion though. I have always absolutely hated so-called 'death knocking'.

A week later, we had a much happier baby story, thank God, when the life of a baby born very prematurely was saved at the same hospital in Yorkhill.

In February, poisoner Paul Agutter was jailed for twelve years for the attempted murder of his wife. He had spiked her gin and tonic with atropin, otherwise known as deadly nightshade. He had also poisoned at least eight other people after he spiked bottles of tonic water in a supermarket and returned them to the shelves. The press dubbed him 'the Safeway poisoner'.

There were several political stories, for example, the resignation of Scottish office minister Allen Stewart after he'd brandished a pickaxe at demonstrators opposed to the construction of the M77 motorway. Arch-Thatcherite Sir Nicholas Fairbairn died at the age of sixty-one. John Major visited Edinburgh and Glasgow and delivered a two-hour speech which I can most kindly describe as entirely unmemorable.

Jo Salter became the first female 'combat ready' Tornado jet pilot. We interviewed her at RAF Lossiemouth and got great shots of the Tornados. She was articulate and inspirational. The fact that she was also very telegenic helped our piece to get on air for the 5:40 and *News at Ten*.

American former two-times World middleweight boxing champion Gerald McClellan was fighting for his life following an operation to remove a blood clot from his brain after he had been knocked out by Nigel Benn. We interviewed Glasgow Labour MP Sam Galbraith, who was also a renowned neurosurgeon and had strong views on the dangers of boxing. Happily, McClellan recovered but his boxing career was, of course, at an end.

With so many recent mountain rescues, we cut a special on the Mountain Rescue Services, how they are funded and the volunteers who work for them, who are nothing short of heroic.

One story, about epilepsy, ran on CNN and NBC as well as ITN, and I had to do a sign-off for Channel 9 Australia. No extra money of course.

There were weather stories commissioned by ITN in London (it snowed in Scotland! Shock horror!), a story about a high security housing scheme for 'problem families' in Dundee, and the *Scotsman* changing its masthead to the *Scotswoman* to mark International Women's Day. We covered a cot death story, every parent's nightmare. We reported on an apparent outbreak of listeria in cheese, and another protest against the construction of the M77.

The Scottish international footballer, Davie Cooper, died of a brain haemorrhage. He was just thirty-nine. It was a big story in Scotland, the front page of every newspaper and the lead story of all TV and radio news bulletins. In London, ITN's interest was lukewarm. The 5:40 ran our piece, *News at Ten* didn't.

Sometimes as a bureau correspondent you feed material to be included in another reporter's package. Among these, that March, were interviews with a ship building expert, nurses on a demonstration for more pay, the Bank of England Governor, Eddie George, at a conference in Edinburgh, and yet another interview with Alex Salmond. We also frequently interviewed other leading Scottish politicians, such as Donald Dewar and Robin Cook, for use by one of ITN's political correspondents. For our health correspondent, I interviewed a surgeon who was the cousin of the Kurdish leader, Jalal Talabani. Off camera, we discussed Kurdistan at length, which was a lot more interesting than the interview on the medical story.

After another week with the army in Germany, trying to train army officers to speak fluent human, we covered a story from Glasgow's Kelvingrove Museum where a delegation of Native Americans was demanding the return of a shirt taken from Wounded Knee.

In May, we filmed at Glasgow Cathedral and at the rally in George Square for the anniversary of VE Day and sent a package for an ITN special programme, *The Nation Remembers*. We were in Edinburgh the next day with Princess Anne for a service at St Giles Cathedral for more special VE Day programmes.

Duncan Ferguson's case finally came to court in Glasgow. We spent two days covering it, and another day two weeks later when he was sentenced to three months in Barlinnie prison for headbutting another player, John McStay of Raith Rovers. He was the first British international player to be jailed for assaulting a fellow professional during a match. His lawyers immediately appealed, and he walked free from the court into a huge scrum of us lot, the media. He lost his appeal at the High Court in Edinburgh five months later, but soon returned to his highly successful football career first as a player and later as a coach at Everton FC.

My favourite story about Duncan Disorderly was when two burglars broke into his home in 2001. Big mistake! He caught one of them, who subsequently spent three days in hospital. In 2003, another burglar was foolish enough to make the same mistake. He attacked Ferguson, who retaliated. This unfortunate burglar met the same fate as his predecessor and was hospitalised.

We went to Ben Nevis in May to interview mountaineer, Alison Hargreaves, who had climbed Mount Everest alone and without oxygen or any Sherpa help, an outstanding achievement. Three months later, we had to cover the awful story of her death in a violent storm as she was descending from the summit of K2. I had liked Alison a lot, but she had told me she knew her sport was dangerous.

A Nimrod went down in the Moray Firth. Fortunately, all seven crew members were rescued. We drove up to Aberdeen rather than Inverness as the RAF had flown the rescue video there. Fantastic pictures, and our package led the news at 5:40, but only just. The timings were so tight that we only just finished editing a two-minute-forty-package with less than two minutes to go to on air, so we had to live-roll it into the top of the programme, which is always exciting and not a little nerve-wracking. Some fine ten-year-old Macallan whisky was taken before we re-cut two minutes thirty for *News at Ten*. For once, very unusually, the 5:40 piece was longer than the *News at Ten* version.

The next day, our mission was to find the Nimrod's crew and get them to talk to us. We headed towards RAF Kinloss but were diverted to Edinburgh. The bishop of the Scottish capital had apparently condoned adultery as 'the normal human condition'. Turns out he was mis-quoted. Surprise, surprise! We got as far as far as Grantown-on-Spey before diverting back to RAF Kinloss where the RAF pilots were not only happy to talk but were holding a lunchtime press conference. We covered that, cut a package and sent it in a taxi to Grampian TV's studio in Inverness to be fed to London while we headed to Edinburgh because *News at Ten* wanted the bishop story. No sooner had we got there and met up with cameraman David Brain, who had been dogging the poor bishop's footsteps all day, than there was a change of mind. Now, *News at Ten* wanted the Nimrod story after all. We re-cut that for *News at Ten*, and sent some shots of the bishop as requested. We deserved our very late Italian dinner. I headed for our hotel, the Royal Terrace, leaving cameramen Alan and David to stagger off into the night in search of more beer!

We stayed in Edinburgh the next day to do a piece about saunas (i.e. brothels) before taking in some Greenpeace video. The environmentalists had occupied the Brent Spar, an oil storage facility in the North Sea operated by Shell. The pictures were good. The storage facility had become redundant following the opening of the pipeline to the terminal at Sullom Voe in Shetland. Now, Shell was planning to dump the large structure in the North Sea. The Greenpeace campaign and action attracted international media attention. ITN was always reluctant to use video originating from pressure groups or political campaigns. Our story ran, but only once.

Greenpeace won that battle, by the way, when Shell abandoned its plan to dispose of the Brent Spar at sea, despite the support of the government, and agreed to dispose of it onshore as Greenpeace had demanded. In the event, the Brent Spar was given a temporary mooring in a Norwegian fjord. Three years later, it was cut into pieces and the steel from its hull was used to build a new harbour facility near Stavanger.

On the day Harold Wilson died, at the end of May, we gathered tributes from senior Scottish Labour politicians. That same day, David Mannion resigned from ITN. He was off to run GMTV. It was another great loss to ITN. Dave was one of the best man-managers they had, always ready with a sympathetic ear and sound advice. Meanwhile, we were sent on a wild goose chase to Aberdeen. Twelve people had died in a plane crash near Harrogate. The aircraft was bound for Aberdeen. After a three-hour drive through torrential rain, the police confirmed that none of the passengers was actually from Aberdeen. The news desk had wanted us there just in case. A complete waste of time, not least because we had to return to Glasgow very early the next morning to cover Duncan Ferguson's conviction, three months for assault.

It was football again the next day, but without the violence! We went to Hampden Park for a piece previewing the Scottish Cup Final. I did my PTC on the hallowed turf.

Cameraman Chris Squires and I were supposed to spend five days with the US Navy on exercise in the Baltic Sea. To no one's great surprise, the job was cancelled. ITN was generally over stretched and short of reporters, so there was no one to cover Scotland in my absence.

June began with two military aircraft stories. A Harrier ditched in Solway Firth. There were no pictures and the pilot had ejected safely. The same day, we did have pictures of the Nimrod which had ditched in the Moray Firth two weeks earlier. It had been salvaged and taken to Rosyth. That made a short package for the 5:40.

The next day, June 2nd, and again a military theme: a memorial service on the Mull Kintyre for the victims of the Chinook crash one year earlier. Sky News provided excellent pool pictures. We sent a package for the lunchtime and 5:40 news. *News at Ten* wanted a longer piece which we cut and sent only for it to be reduced to fifteen seconds of underlay.

My friend, ITN foreign editor Angela Frier, was awarded an OBE in July. Fantastic. Later that month, Paul Gascoigne (him again) signed for Rangers and we interviewed him at Ibrox.

A train crashed into the railway station at Largs. No one was seriously hurt, just a few minor injuries, which was incredibly fortunate as the train had destroyed the station and ploughed on into the road beyond. We cut packages for the 5:40 and *News at Ten*. We were also lined up to do a live two-way from the scene for the 5:40, but instead they took a live from Los Angeles, where Hugh Grant had been misbehaving!

We filmed the final link in the Skye Bridge. Skye was no longer accessible only by ferry. The evening before, we had been in the Royal Hotel in Portree, the only place in town with live music. We wanted the 'Skye Boat Song' for our package the next day. The folk band was happy to play it but didn't know the words. No one did! Eventually at twelve forty-five, we found two young women who did know the words, and they sang it perfectly. But it had taken several hours to find anyone who knew the words to the most famous song about their island home.

Kyle of Lochalsh felt like an oil town, except with construction rather than oil workers. Drinking in the Islander pub one evening, we got collared by one of the foremen who, drunk, insisted on buying us a drink and banging on about what a fantastic achievement the bridge was and how this amazing feat of engineering was constantly being "slagged off by the media". This was because of the PFI angle. It was all our fault, as usual.

That evening, we saw the heart-breaking images, mostly shot by ITN's Dave Prime, of Bosnian refugees who had escaped from the little mountain town of Srebrenica, which had finally been taken by Ratko Mladić and his Serb killers. Very soon, the full story emerged. More than eight thousand Bosniak Muslim men and boys had been massacred on the orders of Mladić. It was the worst genocide in Europe since the Second World War.

We did a story on the start of a Tall Ships' race. I had offered it as a story idea the previous week (there were both weekly and daily forward-planning meetings at ITN), but it had been rejected. I had tried again the evening before it began, with the same result. But on the day, the 5:40 wanted a package. We were too late to get a good spot in Leith but STV had planned better and we used their pictures. This is not unusual in the news business, and is often simply due to how many or how few good stories there are on the day. Forward-planning is one of the most thankless tasks. If the planners got it right and coverage went smoothly, their efforts went largely unnoticed. But if they got it wrong there would be a major inquest.

I took a week's leave visiting the island of Mull with my future wife, Marion. We were lucky, there was a heatwave. Mull's sandy beaches and turquoise sea could have been in the Caribbean, except for the Highland cattle strolling around on the sand. We took boat trips to Lunga, largest of the Treshnish Isles, where we walked among the colonies of puffins and Staffa, where we lingered in Fingal's cave. Mendelssohn's *Hebrides Overture* became the soundtrack to our little holiday, and still brings back happy memories to this day. We also took a ferry to Iona, the enchanted isle. It was lovely to be there and have time to linger without the pressure of work. The last time I had been there was following the death of John Smith.

Straight back to work on August 1st, and a story about midges, the Scottish menace! We had seen none on our little Mull/Iona trip. We were out on the moors to film the Glorious Twelfth, the day the game shooting season starts, and innumerable people take to the hills to slaughter the grouse. Two hardy perennial Scottish stories. And there was another, a coastguard drill in the Firth of Clyde at Largs and later on the Isle of Bute with the coastguard, the RNLI and the helicopter from HMS Garnet going through their paces. This was part of a four-minute special for *News at Ten*.

We were in Arbroath interviewing the survivor of a boat disaster for a *News at Ten* special when we were sent to Bradford for a story on water shortages. Bradford! Also not in Scotland! It was a schlep to get there, but at least I had tried Arbroath Smokies for the first time. Delicious! Bradford was in the grip of a drought. We filmed standpipes being installed and tested and interviewed local residents, many of whom were angry that action hadn't been taken sooner.

We had interviewed Alison Hargreaves again in mid-June as she was preparing to climb K2. We had had lunch together halfway up Aonach Mòr, two thousand feet up, nothing to her. The views were spectacular.

In mid-August, came the awful and very upsetting news that Alison had been killed in an avalanche on K2. Her husband, Jim Ballard, held a press conference. That same day saw the funeral of reporter John Schofield who had been shot dead in Croatia. He was only twenty-nine, a very bright and very keen young reporter. Just terrible. The following Sunday, we were two thousand feet up Aonach Mòr again. Alison's death had been officially confirmed. We talked to Jim Ballard and Alison's parents but not, of course, to her children, Tom and Kate.

The furthest I've ever travelled for a story was to New Zealand that August, which is about as far from the UK as you can get. This involved getting the early morning shuttle from Glasgow to London, an eleven-hour flight to Los Angeles for a four-hour stopover before the twelve-hour flight to Auckland. From there, another short flight to Napier on New Zealand's North Island. The town of Napier was destroyed in an earthquake in 1931 and re-built in the Art Deco style. I had an Art Deco flat at the time and was heavily into all things Art Deco. ITN had sent me to the only Art Deco town in the Southern Hemisphere.

Before I left, the duty editor on the foreign desk, asked me, "Do you care more about ITN or your own personal comfort old chap?"

To which the obvious reply was, "My own personal comfort of course!" He told me how much ITN could save if I flew economy class. I suggested that if I flew economy I would probably need to sleep when I arrived and could hardly hit the ground running. They paid for business class, which is what they should have done in the first place without any quibbling. The rule of thumb was that anything over three hours, or maybe four, should be business class. This journey would take more than thirty hours.

The story: Two Scotland Yard detectives were flying to New Zealand to interview a suspect (one of many) in the Rachel Nickell murder case. Rachel had been murdered on Wimbledon Common three years earlier. She was just twenty-three and was stabbed to death in a frenzied knife attack in front of her young son. The police had wrongfully charged a suspect, Colin Stagg, who had been acquitted in September 1994. Now, they flew to the other side of the world to interview another suspect, John Gallagher, who it turned out was also completely innocent of the murder. My mission was to find him and interview him.

The British press had descended on Napier in force. I worked with a TV3 cameraman, Mack Seymour, who was Māori and as wide as he was tall, and it was all muscle! We spent a fruitless twenty-four hours staking out Gallagher's home, his lawyer's office, and two police stations in Napier and Hastings, ten miles away. We got an informal, off the record, steer from the Scotland Yard detectives. They had interviewed John Gallagher for two hours and believed that he was not the killer. We sent a package which ran on all ITN bulletins. I was also feeding voice pieces for IRN (Independent Radio News).

The next day, the Scotland Yard cops gave a formal briefing. They had interviewed John Gallagher's girlfriend for three hours, far longer than expected, and would resume the interview the following day. The plot thickened.

The police did interview both John Gallagher and his girlfriend again. They told us, off the record, that the prospects of an arrest were basically zero. They were making plans to return to London.

On our last day, Mack got exclusive pictures of John Gallagher, I persuaded his lawyer, Steve Manning, to do a statement to camera, and finally got an on-camera interview with the lead Scotland Yard detective, DCI Alan Jude. This aired on all ITN bulletins, even though it had become something of a non-story. What was wanted, of course, was a suspect in handcuffs or preferably in chains being taken onto the plane and flown back to London to face trial.

After a last dinner with assorted amusing and entertaining Fleet Street hacks, a few of us adjourned to an Irish bar, O'Flaherty's, where there was live music. Even later, Mack, took me to a club, the Blackmarket, which had an almost entirely Māori clientele. It was another of those moments when I walked in and the place went quiet, but everyone relaxed once they saw who I was with. If you've seen the film, *Once were Warriors*, you will understand the Māori predicament. Unemployment among these people was sky high. So too were alcoholism and drug use. It was tragic to hear their stories.

Before flying home, I had a chance to get out of Napier and visit Lake Taupō and Huka Falls. New Zealand reminded me so much of Scotland. The journey home was another thirty-hour-long epic, again via LA. I got into Heathrow at eleven twenty a.m., very early morning in LA, and God only knew what time in New Zealand.

The murderer of Rachel Nickell was finally caught and convicted in 2008. Robert Napper had murdered twice before. He was sent to Broadmoor Prison indefinitely.

It was time for another holiday with Marion, a week in Greece. At the ancient theatre of Epidaurus, and after a great deal of persuasion from me, Marion sang 'Musetta's Waltz' from *La Bohème*. On her very first note, all conversation and activity ceased, she had the complete and undivided attention of several hundred tourists. She sang beautifully (of course!) and received prolonged applause for her efforts. It's a great loss to the opera world that Marion has never sung at Covent Garden or La Scala.

Back in the saddle in Glasgow, we covered the curious case of the bogus schoolboy. A thirty-two-year-old man went back to school, passing himself off as a seventeen year old, to take his Highers. Brian MacKinnon, or 'Brandon Lee', got five A grades and won a place at university to study medicine, which is pretty good at any age.

We interviewed Labour MP and future NATO secretary-general George Robertson in Edinburgh's Princes Street. He was rubbishing the SNP. In Scotland, George Galloway was known as 'Gorgeous George', either because of his splendid head of hair and sartorial style, or because he was regarded as something of a narcissist. Scottish humour dictated that the other famous MP called George should therefore be known as 'Ugly George'. Halfway through the interview, a passer-by shouted, deadpan and in a broad Portobello accent, "Hey, George, keep taking the ugly tablets!"

Robertson didn't bat an eyelid, but as soon as we'd finished, rolled up his sleeves, and wearing a broad grin, said, "Right, where's that bastard?" Pure pantomime.

Our next job was in Leicester, which really is a long way from Scotland. At Leicester Crown Court, a lottery winner got eighteen months for car theft. He had won six million pounds, bought a mansion, luxury cars, even a helicopter. And yet, he was stealing cars, presumably for the thrill not the money. Now, he would pay for it.

Gerry Adams came to speak in Glasgow on October 1st. Outside Govan Town Hall, rowdy loyalists gathered and threw a few bottles. But there were fewer than two hundred of them, Gerry Adams' speech was conciliatory, and although it had looked as if both sides were spoiling for a fight (think a Celtic-Rangers match day), the protestors drifted away peacefully enough.

We covered a story about the wonderful twelfth-century Lewis chess men. Apparently they are cursed! Our piece (excuse the pun) ran all day. The Queen visited Gordonstoun school. How ITN loved a 'Royal story'.

I flew to Münster in Germany with Major Ken Molyneux-Carter for a week training army officers in the subtle art of excelling as a television interviewee. We were supposed to be met by a corporal to drive us to Sennelager, two hours away. There was no sign of him. There was a bank of pay phones at the airport. Ken was going to phone the Normandy barracks in Sennelager to find out what had happened when we overheard a man with a crew cut and wearing a pork pie hat on the phone.

"I don't fucking know. I'm supposed to meet two fucking majors or something, but there's no fucking sign of them."

Ken tapped him gently on the shoulder.

"I think you mean us."

"Oh, yes, sir. Sorry, sir."

I spent my fortieth birthday working in Sennelager. Although Champagne was taken, it wasn't my best birthday celebration by a long way. On the other hand, unlike the officers I was training, I wasn't about to embark on a six-month tour of Bosnia.

That autumn, we were in Dundee where Stephen Fry spoke for the first time about why he had fled from his leading role in a West End play and gone into hiding after poor reviews the previous February. He had disappeared for months. He was there ostensibly to talk about being re-installed as Rector of Dundee University. STV had had the only TV camera at his press conference, during which he opened up about his depression, going so far as to say he had considered suicide.

After a break to conduct more army media training at Sandhurst and deliver a talk in Germany on the relationship between the military and the media, it was back to the Scottish devolution story. Prime Minister John Major was offering a rather watered down version of devolution which was, nevertheless, something of a political U-turn. We got the expected reactions when I interviewed Alex Salmond, Jim Wallace, George Robertson and Michael Forsyth, all four parties getting their views across in our packages for the 5:40 and *New at Ten*. Devolution politics kept us busy for much of that autumn.

Diana, Princess of Wales, gave her now famous (or infamous) interview to *Panorama*. ("There were three of us in the marriage, so it was a bit crowded.") It was dynamite. She revealed her bulimia, her unfaithfulness to Prince Charles, his involvement with Camilla Parker-Bowles, and her doubts over his suitability to be King. Like everyone else, we watched open-mouthed and slack-jawed. Our tiny role in the fallout was to get reaction in Scotland, which was mixed. She had her supporters but most people thought she should have kept her thoughts to herself.

Among the other news that November, stories about banning cigarette advertising (how times have changed!), a postal strike in Edinburgh, the police in Scotland calling for the drink-driving limit to be halved, and Paul Gascoigne was in trouble again, up before a Scottish Football Association disciplinary hearing. He escaped with just a one match ban.

I went to see Mel Gibson's *Braveheart* at a cinema in Glasgow. The audience cheered and yelled, hollered and whooped in a nationalistic frenzy. I felt it wisest, and safest, to keep my mouth shut and my English accent to myself!

We reported on a boom in venison sales which involved us going to a deer farm near Auchtermuchty. ITN was so obsessed with weather stories that I had once got a spoof message from a news editor with a sense of humour: *Snow flake alert in Auchtermuchty. Urgent. Go now!* I had finally got to Auchtermuchty, and yes, it was snowing!

Talmine in Sutherland was the furthest north I've been on the Scottish mainland. We were there to do a piece about crofters and how they still lived and somehow made a living in a traditional way that hadn't changed in centuries. Once the dense fog lifted, we were treated to stunning views across Tongue Bay. There was a Labour party internal row in Govan, there had been riots in Brixton the night before, and the Bosnian peace deal was being signed in Paris. But to my surprise, *News at Ten* wanted a piece from us and ran it.

'Urgent' was a favourite word of news editors sending bleeps (on pagers.) This was in the days before we all had mobile phones, a concept my children simply cannot grasp! Sandy Mac was fond of sending: *Phone Sandy. Urgent*. To the point where he became known simply as "Sandy Urgent"!

Legendary ITN programme editor Derek Dowsett retired in 1995. Derek was a giant among British broadcast journalists. Always calm, unflappable, quiet and incredibly modest, he was always at hand to offer sound advice. Sue Carpenter organised his retirement party, in the Reptile House at London Zoo, a venue we all thought hilarious, reptiles in the Reptile House. Under Derek's stewardship, ITN's five forty-five news, which evolved into the five forty, had become the most successful news programme on British TV, with audiences regularly topping ten million. He had an unerring sense of what an early evening news audience would be interested in. He also made sure the programme was pacey by restricting reporter packages to one minute fifteen. A major political resignation, natural disaster or big foreign story might merit one minute thirty. The outbreak of World War Three might have got one minute forty-five! Derek was also famously understated. Terry Lloyd used to call him "the man from Del Monte" because if Derek approved your package after viewing it, he would simply say "yes", and move on. That 'yes' was praise enough.

Before Christmas, we reported on a murder in Kilmarnock, the trial at Edinburgh High Court of three men who had been sentenced for smuggling guns to loyalist militias in Northern Ireland, Princess Anne's son, Peter Philips, making his international rugby debut for Scottish Schools at Murrayfield (they lost to France 18-12), and the final story of the year. Yes, you've guessed it, the weather! Snowflake alert in Auchtermuchty!

1996 began where 1995 had left off, running the ITN Scotland bureau in Glasgow. Many of the stories we covered are now largely forgotten, except for one. This was the year of the Dunblane massacre. It was also my last full year at ITN.

The fatal accident inquiry into the Mull of Kintyre Chinook helicopter crash began at Paisley Sheriff's Court. We cut a package for the lunchtime news, but had to argue quite strongly for it to run. In the previous month alone, more than four thousand five hundred Second World War incendiary bombs had washed up on beaches on the west coast of Scotland. These phosphorous bombs were designed to explode on contact with air. A four-year-old boy, Gordon Baillie, had picked up one near Campbelltown. It had burnt his hand and leg.

The BBC, *Channel 4 News* and Sky News ran both stories. The 5:40 ran neither, and *News at Ten* ran just fifteen seconds of underlay on each.

On a happier note, we had the story of a woman in Stranraer who had found a ring she had lost in 1974 in the park where she had last remembered having it. This made it on to the 5:40 and was a potential *News at Ten* 'And Finally' but was pipped at the post by cricket umpire Dickie Bird announcing his retirement.

Another potential *News at Ten* 'And Finally' also bit the dust, the launch of Walkers' Salt & Lineker crisps. It was fairly amusing but was rightly regarded by ITN as too much of a free puff for Walkers crisps. But I got to chat with Gary Lineker and, once again, Paul Gascoigne.

A fishing trawler hit the rocks in Orkney. We got helicopter shots and packaged for all ITN bulletins. A bill to change daylight saving hours was debated in the House of Commons, so we were out interviewing farmers near Loch Lomond. We covered a story from Yorkhill Children's Hospital, a possible breakthrough in the treatment of meningitis.

When I was a student at Aberdeen University, I had wound up a room full of Scottish Nationalists on Burns' night by making 'breastie' failed to rhyme with 'beastie'.

Wee sleekit, cow'ring, timorous beastie,
Oh, what a panic's in thy breastie!

By pronouncing it brestie rather than breestie, I sent a room full of Scot Nats into an apoplectic rage! Now, in 1996, we had a pleasant day out in Ayrshire. In Alloway, we interviewed John Strathers, director of the Burns' International Festival, filmed Burns' cottage of course, and sent an entertaining piece for all ITN bulletins to celebrate Burns' night. With no deliberate mispronunciations!

When six whales got stranded on the beach at Cruden Bay, I argued that this was a story we should be covering, but without success. It was not wanted for any ITN bulletins. Until, that is, the *News at Ten* team decided that they did want a package from us after all. By then, it was too late to get to Cruden Bay to film and, anyway, it was pitch black, so we relied on Grampian TV pictures. The package looked fine, though obviously not as good as it would have been had we got the go ahead earlier and filmed it ourselves, with the ubiquitous PTC.

Bible John was a serial killer who murdered three young women in Glasgow in 1968 and 1969. He met his victims at the Barrowland ballroom. They were raped and strangled. His nickname was coined after witnesses had seen him with one of his victims at Barrowland told police that he had repeatedly quoted from the Old Testament. Despite an extensive manhunt and years of investigation, Bible John was never found.

Now, at the end of January 1996, police were to exhume the body of a suspect, John Irvine McInnes, from his grave in the village of Stonehouse in Lanarkshire. They wanted to carry out DNA and fingerprint tests. The day before the exhumation, we filmed at Stonehouse cemetery and sent a package for all ITN bulletins.

Bizarrely, the news desk sent us to Inverness that same evening for some daft story about the Loch Ness monster the following day. For once, I was arguing that we should stay in the Central Belt to cover a story rather than heading for the Highlands. I was overruled.

Sure enough, the next morning, ITN wanted us on the Bible John story. Fortunately, I had sent cameraman David Brain to film the exhumation, which happened at dawn. David sent his pictures to London for the lunchtime news, while I sent a voice track from Inverness! The piece was edited in London, and we were told, looked good. We repeated the same trick for the 5:40. It was a very odd way to cover the story.

Meanwhile, cameraman Alan Dickinson and I were filming for the Loch Ness monster story. Various interviews on the shores of the loch, moody shots, an interview at the Nessie Exhibition Centre in Drumnadrochit and a PTC at Urquhart Castle. The light was superb, the water was absolutely calm, but no monsters! We packaged a piece for the lunchtime news the next day.

The identity of Bible John remains unknown to this day. The murders of Helen Puttock, Patricia Docker and Jemima McDonald are still unsolved.

On February 6th, it snowed heavily. Our packages led the lunchtime news, 5:40 and *News at Ten*. We led the news with the same story the next day too. It wasn't until the third day that ITN finally tired of our saturation coverage. How ITN loved a weather story, provided there were dramatic pictures.

After another week of training army officers at the appropriately named Battlesbury barracks in the even more appropriately named Warminster, we were in Aberdeen. Ken Clarke was visiting, provoking lively protests outside the old Town Hall on Union Street. Ken enjoyed winding up the mostly Scottish Nationalist protestors. The meeting of the Scottish Grand Committee inside was also very lively and made for a good knockabout piece for the 5:40.

Two days later, we were in Fort George after a glorious drive via Aviemore, all blue skies and glistening fresh snow. The roguish but charismatic 'Chief' Nicholas Gcaleka was searching for the skull of his Xhosa ancestor. In the Highlands of Scotland!

The Duke of Atholl had died, leaving his estate to a charitable trust. After a little persuasion, we were allowed the run of Blair Castle and its estate. It was the last castle in Britain to be besieged, during the Jacobite rising in 1746. But what made the duke's passing most interesting was that it threw into doubt the future of the Atholl Highlanders. The duke was the only person in the UK allowed to have his own private army. The regiment, originally raised in 1777, survived and continues to be the only private army in Europe.

We had two 'And Finally' stories in the frame in late February. It was a leap year and we'd found a barmaid who was planning to propose (on camera for us) to her unsuspecting boyfriend, and we had the story of Clyde the Burmese cat. Two families were disputing the ownership of Clyde. The cat's DNA had been taken. But Diana, Princess of Wales, announced that she would agree to a divorce, and *News at Ten* went completely divorce-tastic.

Our Clyde the DNA cat story did run a couple of days later, as we were setting off for Eigg. We had an amusing evening in Mallaig. The only event in town was an Irish Country and Western band featuring Paddie O'Brien, the Irish yodelling champion (I kid you not). Just too awful to recall! At the Central Bar, cameraman David Brain and I discovered a folk group (pipes, drums, guitars, bagpipes) and a hen night in full swing. At twelve thirty p.m. we couldn't resist going where everyone else was going, to 'the disco'. This was in a gym, with no bar! It was perfectly dreadful and very funny. When it closed at one thirty a.m., we did what everyone else did and hung around at the harbour. It was like a scene from the film *Local Hero*.

Getting to Eigg, where islanders were trying to buy the island as a Community Trust, was mildly tortuous. The ferry wasn't operating. At the

223

harbour, the fishermen told us they were doing very good business 'taking a thousand pounds a day', and the best price I could get for taking us across to Eigg was three hundred pounds, far too expensive. Eventually, by phoning from Arisaig, I got through to a fisherman on Eigg, Stewart Miller, who took us across for one hundred and fifty pounds.

It took an hour and a half in Stewart's small boat. At the other end, we were met by 'Davey's Taxi', as I'd arranged. Our transport for the day was his rather battered old Ford Transit van. We met around half of the population of sixty souls, interviewed several of them and took shots of their beautiful island.

It had been a lot of effort for a story that ran only once, on the lunchtime news, but another fantastic Scottish experience for us.

Dolly the sheep was an international sensation. Two scientists at Edinburgh University, Ian Wilmut and Keith Campbell, had cloned Dolly by somatic cell nuclear transfer. They believed that with this method that they could clone limitless numbers of mammals and genetically engineer superior breeds. Of course, this might also one day include humans. We interviewed the scientists, but they had given exclusive access to pictures of the sheep to the BBC's *Tomorrow's World* programme and therefore to BBC News. We simply wandered around the Roslin Institute at will, but outside. In an adjacent field, we found her! We filmed away, hoping that this was the correct sheep. Afterwards, it was confirmed to us that this was indeed Dolly. Our piece for the 5:40 and *News at Ten* also ran on CNN among others.

I was at home in London for three days leave when I was asked to cover for another reporter, Colin Baker, whose father was seriously ill. With camera crew Mike Inglis and Paul Robinson, we filmed the pigeons in Trafalgar Square. Someone, or so it was being claimed, was stealing the pigeons! I did a live two-way surrounded by squabbling pigeons for the 5:40, and packaged for *News at Ten*.

So, that was a cat (Clyde), a sheep (Dolly) and pigeons all in the space of one week. The David Attenborough of ITN!

We had to go to Easterhouse again to get some vox pops for a package being cut by our north of England bureau in Manchester. The area was a wasteland of deprivation. To be brought up here must have been so brutalising, de-humanising. When Prince Charles had visited Easterhouse not long before he had said that young people there, faced with little prospect of a job and readily-available drugs, stood little chance. Tell us something we don't know!

We had another snow blizzard in Glasgow, so we did yet another 'weather wrap' for the 5:40 and *News at Ten*, taking in pictures from Grampian TV in Aberdeen and from the ITN team in Leeds. The north of England was also under a blanket of snow.

Wednesday March13[th]. Cameraman Alan Dickinson and I were filming in a snow drift in Barrhead when news came through that a child had been shot dead at a school in Dunblane and others had been injured. Then, an unconfirmed report that as many as twelve children had been shot. We headed straight to Dunblane. An ITN cast of thousands was on its way from London.

We arrived to a scene of absolute horror. Sixteen children and their teacher, Gwen Mayor, had been shot dead by a gunman, Thomas Hamilton, who had burst into the school gym and opened fire.

Sixteen children.

All were only five or six years old. It was believed that another dozen children had been wounded. We were the first TV news crew to arrive. Outside the school, frantic parents were in a total panic, running up and down and screaming. No one knew if their child was among the victims.

I did a live two-way for the lunchtime news. ITN ran a newsflash at two o'clock. I asked the senior home news editor how long was wanted from me. I was told two minutes, so I talked, describing the awful and distraught scenes all around me for precisely two minutes. Great job, according to the news desk, but I got shouted at by Nigel Dacre, ITN editor, and someone who was normally very mellow, because I had run over time. Apparently, the whole newsflash was two minutes long, and I was only supposed to talk for one minute. So, when I had asked Malcolm Monroe on the news desk how long was wanted from me, he had told me the total length of the newsflash, not something I needed to know, nor the question I had asked. Dacre wasn't listening to my explanation. Apparently, I was in his 'little black book' from then on.

Dacre would quit a few years later and be replaced by Dave Mannion, the same man he had ousted to get the job, to everyone's immense relief.

We were working frantically, filming and talking to parents, police and paramedics. Imagine the impact of a bullet on a little five year old's body. It was just too terrible to contemplate.

Meanwhile, no fewer than six reporters were among the ITN horde that descended on Dunblane. We cut story two for the 5:40. Colin Baker did a superb job on the lead story, and again for *News at Ten*.

After a short sleep, we fed a package for the early morning news at five thirty a.m. followed by a live two-way and lives into *The Big Breakfast* at seven a.m. and eight a.m. It was difficult to convey the full horror. Impossible really. We had had school shootings in the States, but this was here, a quiet little town in Scotland.

We were still producing packages and lives on the Friday, including for *The Big Breakfast* at seven a.m. and eight a.m., but my piece for the lunchtime news took the theme that the people of Dunblane now needed to be left alone, to be given the time and space to grieve. The media were everywhere, hundreds of us from all over the world.

Prime Minister John Major and opposition leader Tony Blair visited the school. Major, especially, seemed best able to express the nation's shock and grief.

Producer Claire Donaldson found Tom Allan, who had played Father Christmas for the children of Dunblane primary school and knew them all. We interviewed him and sent a package for the 5:40 which programme editor, Phil Moger, described as, "Excellent. A very moving piece". It was, but that was entirely due to Tom Allan.

That evening, I drove back to Glasgow before flying to London the next day for wedding preparations. Mine! I told Marion I was feeling rather traumatised now that I had had time to pause, think and reflect. I was also very tired. It was so awful, those tiny, beautiful children. She said the entire country was traumatised, so it must be even worse for me. But it was far, far indescribably worse for those directly involved, those poor families. I wept uncontrollably watching the BBC *Nine O'Clock News*, and again watching *News at Ten*. God only knows how it must have been for them.

On the Sunday, a one minute's silence was held for Dunblane. Colin Baker was the reporter, and produced a very emotional piece for the lunchtime news. I doubt there was a dry eye in the country. That same day, the Queen went to Dunblane. She was red-eyed and seemed to sum up the nation's mourning.

On the Monday, cameraman Alan Dickinson returned from Dunblane. Like all of us, he was in pieces. I spoke to the duty senior home news editor back at ITN (who I won't name, but maybe I should) about the shock we were all experiencing. He said he was "shocked by the bill". Halfwit.

The reporters and crews covering Dunblane had been moved from hotel to hotel, sharing rooms in some cases, while covering the worst story of their lives. One reporter had a furious row with ITN manager, Michael Jermey, who had refused to let them stay at Gleneagles Hotel because it would cost ninety pounds per night, five pounds over company guidelines. Another example of appalling man-management. On the plus side, Jermey sent me a herogram for our coverage, which was very much appreciated.

We were all emotionally drained. It would take a while for our equilibrium to be restored, but Dunblane would live with us forever.

Two postscripts to Dunblane. As everyone probably knows, tennis stars Andy Murray and his brother Jamie were in the school at the time. Andy Murray was eight years old and heading towards the gym at the time. Jamie was ten. And ITN won the RTS (Royal Television Society) award for the best coverage of a news event, my third after the fall of the Berlin Wall and the plight of the Kurds in the wake of the first Gulf War.

And life, for us, did go on. Our next story, just a couple of days later, was covering the Fatal Accident Inquiry into the Mull of Kintyre Chinook crash at Paisley Sheriff's Court. Our package for *News at Ten* took in an interview with pilot Richard Cook's father in London, and a very moving press conference from Belfast with the widows of some of those who had died.

After that, we were at the High Court in Edinburgh for the judgement on the right-to-die of a woman, Janet Johnstone, who was in a Permanent Vegetative State. It was a complex and inconclusive holding judgement which I just about managed to make sense of, and packaged for all ITN bulletins. The final judgement would come a month later.

Britain was in deep trouble over BSE/CJD, the so-called Mad Cow Disease. There was a worldwide ban on British beef. The risk appeared to be very slight, so had the world lost all sense of proportion? We interviewed some angry Scottish farmers, and covered a Scottish NFU (National

Farmers Union) press conference at which they claimed the BSE threat was nonsense, a scare story that was threatening to destroy their industry. The government continued to insist that British beef was safe, and at the time, there was little if any evidence linking BSE to the human variant, CJD.

Ultimately, piles of British cows were incinerated, more than an a million in total, those unforgettable images of the mounds of dead cattle burning.

The BSE story kept us busy for much of that spring. There was also an armed siege in Glasgow which ended peacefully. A syndicate of nineteen Tax inspectors won four point two million pounds on the National Lottery, we interviewed them and packaged their story for the 5:40 and ITN *News at Ten*. An NAS/UWT teachers' conference in Glasgow was very boring until David Blunkett's inflammatory speech, which made a package for the lunchtime news on a slow news day.

On April 10th, the gym at Dunblane primary school was demolished. In order to be as unobtrusive as possible, we agreed to send just one camera crew on a pool basis. STV provided the pool camera, sharing their pictures with the other broadcasters. We cut a piece for the 5:40. Programme editor, Phil Moger, was keen to run it, but editor-in-chief Nigel Dacre got cold feet for some reason and pulled it. He very bravely gave it the green light for *News at Ten*, once STV, the BBC and everyone else had run the story first!

By way of total contrast, there was one more fun story before I left Scotland, the two hundredth anniversary of the Battle of Culloden. On Culloden Moor, we interviewed clan chiefs and cut a picture-rich package for the lunchtime news. Our story was squeezed out of the 5:40 by the official announcement that the Duke and Duchess of York ('Andy and Fergie') were to divorce. Monumentally uninteresting as far as I was concerned, but I was in a small minority. ITN loved a Royals story. Our piece did run on *News at Ten*. Somewhere at home I have a ridiculous photograph of me charging on Culloden Moor, wielding a Claymore sword.

In Edinburgh, Lord Cameron of Lochbroom issued his judgement in the case of Janet Johnstone. As expected, he decided that doctors were allowed to withdraw artificial feeding and permit her to die, as her family put it ,"with dignity". She had been in a Permanent Vegetative State for four years. She was fifty-three. We interviewed a BMA spokesperson and an anti-euthanasia campaigner, Mary Kearns, and packaged this landmark judgement for all ITN bulletins.

My last story in Scotland for ITN came when a fifteen-year-old girl died in Glasgow's Southern General Hospital of suspected CJD. It was believed that she was the world's youngest victim of the disease. We packaged the story of her death for all ITN bulletins.

And then it was all over. After two years as ITN Scotland Correspondent, I was returning to London. Among my parting gifts was a reflector, also called a bounce board, from the crews. Apparently, I have deep set eyes and am difficult to light. I had also never mastered the skill of folding a reflector, a kind of very fast figure of eight motion. Now, they said, I would have plenty of time to practice!

Before resuming ITN work, I spent another week in Germany training British army spokesmen. On our first evening, Paddy Ashdown was in the officers' mess, talking to General Roddy Cordy-Simpson. Plenty of drink was taken. It was a bit of a messy evening!

I was up early the next morning to give a lecture. I had to follow Colonel Gary Coward (of Sarajevo fame), who later rose to three-star general and was knighted. A hard act to follow. The rest of the week passed in seemingly endless interviews and debriefs. Armed Forces minister, Nicholas Soames, visited just as I was debriefing Lt. Colonel Paul Brook, who was to be the army spokesman in Bosnia for the following six months. Soames told some very funny, self-deprecating and rude stories which I can't repeat here. Too many of the very strongest expletives.

The first story back in London was packaging around an interview with the Director of Public Prosecutions Barbara Mills. She had refused the BBC who'd asked for an interview on changes to the defending yourself in your own home guidelines. There had been a few recent cases when homeowners had dealt with burglars a little over zealously. A couple of phone calls later and she agreed to my interview request. My first story back in London, and a bit of an exclusive for *News at Ten*.

Publicist Max Clifford lined up two female police officers who were complaining of sexual harassment. It was a *Sunday Express* story but we were being offered exclusive TV interviews. The news editor of the day was all for it, but Michael Jermey vetoed it. He was worried about being sued, and also about using 'someone else's exclusive'. Some newspapers were not renowned for their reliability or veracity, so this was a reasonable concern. Not for the first time, I had to tell Clifford thanks but no thanks. He wasn't overly impressed. Too bad.

I did a package on Israel's general election for ITN's *World News*, but my main focus was trying to get exclusive interviews, which is what I'd been asked by Nigel Dacre to do. I tried for General Sir Peter De La Billière, Salman Rushdie, who was still in hiding following the Iranian regime's issuing of a fatwa, a death sentence, and more realistically Sir Thomas Bingham, who was to become Lord Chief Justice the following week. Sir Peter Taylor, Lord Justice Taylor, had cancer, which was awful. He died the following year. He is best remembered now for his Hillsborough Stadium Disaster inquiry report, The Taylor Report.

None of these came to fruition. Neither did a bid for an interview with Yasser Arafat, who I had interviewed a few years earlier.

June and July were beyond frustrating. I had been given a mission. To get interviews but only exclusives with people who had previously refused to be interviewed. I tried very hard, but it was a tall order to say the least.

I tried for dozens of people, including disgraced Welsh office minister Rod Richards, who had resigned over an extra-marital affair, Hugh Grant to talk about his disgrace in Los Angeles (fat chance!), and many others.

I had a meeting with ITN editor, Nigel Dacre, at which I pointed out that spending my days trying to get interviews with people who did not want to be interviewed or had been bought up by a newspaper really wasn't working. He seemed to think I could do something else at ITN, though he had no idea what.

In a way, this was a blessing in disguise as it prompted me to think about what I wanted to be doing five or ten years down the road. There was little point arguing, Dacre's mind was made up, although I did go through my herograms of the past twelve months and my 'appraisal' from the previous year, which had been positively glowing. I had lost my top cover, that is senior management people who rated and valued me, and I was left with Nigel Dacre and Michael Jermey. Not a good place to be.

I had seen many colleagues treated this way over the years, with the same end result. Now, it seemed, it might be my turn. Cameraman Steve Harrow, who had been caught up in the compulsory redundancies in the year following the first Gulf War, summed up his experience: "From hero to zero in eighteen months".

Morale at ITN had at this point hit rock bottom. A lot of my colleagues were looking to get out, many if not most felt undervalued. Leadership comes from the top, and the mood had changed with the departure of the avuncular Sir David Nicholas and his replacement as editor-in-chief by Stewart Purvis. Stewart had lot on his plate. Away from his own superb journalism, there was ITN's new building in Gray's Inn Road, with very expensive office space standing empty, and the terrible financial mess that ITN was in. There was pressure, too, from those ITV companies who wanted to move *News at Ten* to a different time slot, a move that, when it came, slashed ITN's viewing figures and almost proved fatal. Nevertheless, whereas if you passed Sir David Nicholas in the corridor he would greet you by name, Stewart seemed pre-occupied and would walk straight past without any acknowledgement at all.

I secured an exclusive interview with Salman Rushdie. The news editor of the day was delighted, but then had to tell me that it wasn't wanted. Not his decision, it had come from "higher up".

ITN held its annual summer party. Almost no reporters, camera crews or VT editors bothered to turn up, in stark contrast to previous years. It felt funereal. I stayed for a couple of hours, ever the optimist.

My last piece for ITN, although I didn't know it at the time, came in early August when Britain's Olympians returned home from the games in Atlanta. I packaged the story for the twelve thirty lunchtime news.

I got married at the end of August, a perfect wedding in so many ways which had taken a lot of planning. We honeymooned in Kenya, staying at the famous Treetops Hotel, safari lodges and in a hotel in Mombasa. The early morning game drives were incredible, Marion's first experience of an African game reserve.

In the Maasai Mara, a village chief asked "This your wife?"

"Yes."

"Small one."

Yes, Marion was petite, but I didn't know in Kenya size mattered! Presumably he preferred wide child-bearing hips! At our hotel in Mombasa, the waiter would bring us breakfast in the morning and asked, in his broad Kenyan accent and with a twinkle in his eye, "How was the night?"

When I returned to work, I began planning my departure from ITN. This involved a lot of meetings during which I was assured that I would be found a fitting and fulfilling role and that I shouldn't even think about leaving. Sky News was largely run by my former colleagues at ITN. Nick Pollard was the head of news, Mike Nolan his deputy, and Simon Cole was the managing editor. I went to look around the newsroom, and for lunch with Simon and Mike.

At ITN, I was still doing bits and pieces but not much. One highlight was an interview with the actor Sir John Mills. I had another week training British army officers in Germany which included a dinner with Nicholas Soames and Brigadier David Leakey, who was the source of some very funny and indiscreet anecdotes. I also delivered a lecture to thirty Royal Navy officers in the magnificent Great Hall at Greenwich, followed by a very lively Q&A session.

A friend on the ITN news desk confirmed what cameraman Phil Bye had told me a few days earlier, that they had been told to set me 'impossible tasks', for example to get 'an interview with the Queen'. He also told me that a senior manager had said there would be several new jobs coming up, mostly in the regions, that I would be in the frame for one of those, and that when they announced them the following week they would be 'spreading happiness throughout the newsroom'. The fact that we had had a pay freeze (a cut in real terms) for five years and that many if not most of our best people had left didn't appear to register.

In the event, absolutely nothing happened the following week.

I spent a few days training army officers in Camberley, where I had the great pleasure of working for the first time with Alastair Bruce. He is directly descended from the Scottish King Robert the Bruce (de Brus), the hero of Bannockburn. We used to tease him. 'We have a little place in Scotland, we call it Ayrshire', although Sutherland would have been more accurate. Alastair would later become a Royal commentator for Sky News, historical consultant for films such as *The King's Speech* and the TV series *Downtown Abbey* and, as a reservist having served in the regular army for several years and seen action during the Falklands conflict, rose to the rank of major-general. In 2019, Alastair was appointed governor of Edinburgh castle.

Meanwhile, doing the rounds on the gossip mill at ITN was the notion that I was going to be offered a newly created position as crime producer. Sorry, but really not for me.

In the event, they offered me a new role as 'summaries presenter', based entirely in the newsroom, presenting hourly short news bulletins on ITV. It was a cushy number. The hours were eight a.m. until three thirty p.m., but it would be extremely boring. It was a dilemma though. Some advised that I should do it for six months to see how it went. Marion thought I should get out of ITN asap.

By the end of November, my mind was finally made up. I told ITN editor Nigel Dacre that I would prefer to leave, provided there was a generous redundancy package. I felt a huge sense of relief, a weight had been lifted from my shoulders. Friends in the newsroom told me I was being 'very brave', which was the last thing I wanted to be! But the dye was cast.

At a second lunch with Simon Cole in December, he told me there were no full-time staff vacancies at Sky News, though that might change in the new year. In the meantime, he could offer me "a living if not a job" as a freelance reporter. That suited me just fine as I had been in contact with several media training companies given my experience with the military, and was seriously considering setting up my own company to do media training and consultancy as well as news reporting and presenting. Voice-overs could also be an avenue to pursue.

Just before Christmas, veteran ITN reporter, Vernon Mann, had a leaving lunch which then continued into the ITN reporters' Christmas drinks, and via two more bars, leaving drinks for cameraman, Richard Gammons. I was sad that I too would soon be leaving ITN, but I was in good company.

Paul Carleton (left) and Tony Hemmings (right) abandoning the Volvo's undercarriage! Near Mineu, Romania December 1989

Rebel fighters at yet another roadblock, Romania December 1989

Interviewing Yasser Arafat February 1991

Kurdish children April 1991

Alan Downes with Kurdish leaders, April 1991

Cameraman Sam King with Laura Davies, Pittsburgh, June 1992

Interviewing Oleg Gordievsky, September 1991

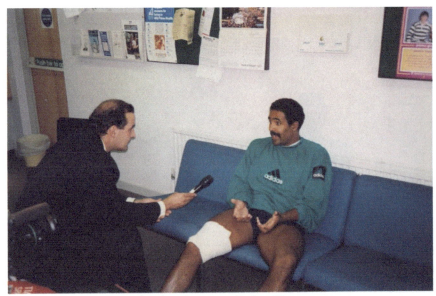

Interviewing the great Daley Thompson

CHAPTER 11

1997: Labour Landslide. Leaving ITN. Joining Sky News

There was yet another leaving party in early January, two ITN legends, Paul Carleton and Peter Read. It was, of course, a day of ridiculous alcohol consumption. Nearly forty serious drinkers boarded the nine thirty a.m. train to Dover and drank it dry. There was more serious drinking in a pub before we poured ourselves onto a ferry to Calais. A lot of fizz, and a very good lunch at which producer John Toker delivered a few words of 'ITN speak', but cameraman Mike Inglis delivered the proper tribute. There was an excellent turnout of ITN reporters and camera crews, several of whom were also about to leave ITN. Mervyn Hall, a colossus of the news desk who had already left ITN to join Reuters, was in top form. Another pub in Dover was almost drunk dry! There was singing, if you could call it that, on the train back to London and several whiskies in the Coal Hole pub in the Strand. I got the last tube home with cameraman Phil Bye. I still have no idea how we could possibly have still been standing.

I was offered several jobs, mostly through old ITN colleagues who had moved elsewhere. Some of them were quite interesting, but none was as enticing as the prospect of working for a twenty-four-hour news channel and linking up again with some of ITN's very best who were now at Sky News. One door closes, another opens.

Among many, many others at ITN, Phil Moger and Vicky Knighton told me how sad they were that I was leaving and how they couldn't understand why. But I had already set my mind to working for myself and as a freelance to see what that would bring. I had already started media training corporate clients, which was both lucrative and interesting as one got to see behind the scenes of a large enterprise, a company or organisation, in a way normally forbidden to a journalist. I had also discovered that I was rather good at it. A lot of journalists think they would make good trainers. Most don't.

At the end of January, there was a joint leaving party for sixteen people. Sixteen! Among them, some of ITN's best. It was beginning to feel like a mass exodus. Editor-in-chief Stewart Purvis actually gave an amusing speech based around the application forms to join ITN of some of those who were leaving, some of them from as long ago as twenty-five years earlier. There were several of the old faces there, ITN people who had already jumped ship. I received a lot of compliments, basically along the lines of what a top reporter I was and that ITN must be mad to let me go. Ego suitably massaged, but it felt like the end of an era, and in many ways, it was.

My turn came on January 31st. I had received a generous redundancy package, and while I felt some elation and a sense of relief that my situation had been resolved, I also felt betrayed. It had been a strange few months, negotiating with Nigel Dacre. As he had said, we went back a long way. When I had first joined ITN over ten years earlier to help launch ITN's *World News* programme, Nigel had been programme editor. He had been one of ITN's bright young things, a rising star. We had become friends, often going together to the Pizza Express in Soho on Tuesdays, live jazz night. Nigel was an accomplished jazz pianist. But something had changed when he became ITN editor, and it had not been a change for the better.

My leaving party was held in a wine bar near the ITN building in Gray's Inn Road. Reporters, Colin Baker and Mark Webster, made valedictory speeches, which was very sweet of them. Trevor McDonald was very supportive. Sometime after midnight, picture editor Bill Frost took a few of us to Quinn's Irish pub in Camden for a lock-in. Bill is Irish and knew the manager and, it seemed, the entire north London Irish diaspora.

We made the front page of the *Sun* the next morning! Somehow, cameraman Micky Laurence had fallen asleep in the loo and was locked in at the wine bar all night.

A new year, a new job, a new home (we were renovating a splendid Victorian house in Crouch End), a new (married) life. Onwards and upwards.

Very soon after I joined Sky News, John Major called the 1997 general election. With the Conservatives way behind in the polls, the prime minister had waited until the last possible moment, at the end of a full five-year term, hoping that something might turn up. By the time ITN political editor Mike Brunson had done his one live two-way into the ITN lunchtime news, his opposite number at Sky, Adam Boulton, had done about fifteen! I wondered what on earth I had let myself in for. But very soon I was in tune with nonstop news and could not imagine going back to terrestrial television news. By the time ITN or the BBC news went on air with a story, Sky News had already been all over it, often for several hours.

My first assignment for Sky News as an education story on the Assisted Places Scheme. I interviewed Education Secretary Gillian Shephard and her Labour shadow, Estelle Morris. It was also my first introduction to Sky's political unit at 4 Millbank. I was impressed by the people who worked there, and by how fast and good my picture editor was when we cut the package for Sky's lunchtime news. I soon discovered that the people working at Sky News were every bit as good and sometimes better than those who were still at ITN.

I had always preferred working in a semi-autonomous bureau, away from the clutches of HQ with its hideous office politics. Westminster suited me perfectly. But first I would have to earn my spurs at Sky News.

I also loved the fact that much of the work involved live two-ways, bringing the audience up to date on the very latest from the scene. And packages didn't have to wait for the next terrestrial news bulletin, they could run as soon as they were ready.

The flagship programme was *Live at Five*. The humourists in the newsroom referred to it as 'Live at Five, dead by five past'. It was in fact an excellent news programme, a fast moving mix of packages and live two-ways, with a high story count and presented by the legendary Bob Friend (who always called me 'your Grace' for some inexplicable reason) and a young Anna Botting, who Bob regularly reduced to fits of giggles live on air. It was serious, highly professional but also fun and very user- friendly.

That first day, after the education story, I had also interviewed a spokesman for the Gulf War Veterans Association and persuaded him to come in live for *Live at Five*. I re-cut a package for the programme, which was edited by John Ryley, who had been a rising star at ITN. I cut another package for the seven p.m. and the rest of the evening on the visit of Israeli President Ezer Weizman. It had been a busy first day. I had loved it.

Our ITN team won the RTS Home News award for the coverage of Dunblane. Cameraman, Alan Dickinson, phoned from Scotland. Almost all the pictures had been shot by him and David Brain, but no one at ITN bothered to tell him or David about the award, or to tell me for that matter. Alan had phoned Nigel Dacre to complain and had been shouted at. I was so glad to be out of there.

In March, I did some more British army training in Germany before deployment to Bosnia, and was invited to 7th Armoured Brigade regimental dinner, which was a special honour. Brigadier Andrew Stewart was later, as a major general, to command the Multi-National Division (South East) in Iraq. I did more training that month in Camberley, and in May, it was back to Germany and a few days in Bosnia to reinforce the training.

I was set on doing other work as well as covering the news, and I did a few days, here and there, media training for various corporate clients and establishing a reputation in that field. But I got so busy at Sky News I barely had the time for anything else. Although I was freelance, I quickly became the first to be called. At times I was doing as many as twelve consecutive days of twelve-hour shifts. Sometimes it felt there was barely time to draw breath, but it was nice to be wanted and I was doing what I loved most, reporting the news.

In mid-March, I did my first shift at Sky News HQ in Osterley, a large hangar near Heathrow. They were a very friendly bunch, with so many people saying, "Welcome aboard". I soon discovered an *esprit de corps* which ITN had once had but had now largely lost. I regretted not jumping ship earlier, as the others had, for the generous salary and share options. I regretted my residual loyalty to ITN. I am, though, immensely grateful to ITN. In my ten years there, I had covered some huge stories, had had some unforgettable experiences and worked with some extremely talented people.

My story that day was to package the timetable for the 1997 general election. This mostly involved graphics. Sky's graphics were fairly basic back then and looked cheap. The graphics department needed more people and more investment. Both would be forthcoming, but not yet. I cut a package for twelve o'clock, with fresh re-cuts for one p.m., two p.m., three p.m., five p.m., seven p.m., eight p.m., and nine p.m. Phew! This place felt at times like something of a sweat shop, but it was great to be fully back in the swing of things.

It was the day that John Major finally called the general election, the day that Adam Boulton seemed to be attempting to break the world record for live two-ways from Downing Street. It was said of Adam that he spent more time on air than off it!

West Midlands Tories were calling for a limit on immigration. They were led by Nicholas Budgen MP who, incidentally, was one of the so-called 'Maastricht rebels who had so undermined John Major's premiership. He was also vociferous in arguing for the rights of gun owners in the wake of the Dunblane massacre. In my packages, I used some old Enoch Powell footage. Budgen was MP for Powell's old seat of Wolverhampton South West.

A mere five packages that day, the first at noon, the last at eight p.m. Oh, and Nicholas Budgen lost his seat in the Labour landslide on May 1st.

The next day, I packaged the latest employment figures which were down, a morsel of good news for the Major government. My piece, with several re-cuts to include assorted political interviewees, ran all day. I also packaged another story on cloning, which was based around an interview with the editor of the *Bulletin of Medical Ethics*, who I interviewed in Highbury (though not at the sacred stadium!), which also ran in the evening bulletins.

On March 27th, I actually had a day off, but it was still a busy day. We were converting the loft at our new home in north London. A team of mad scaffolders arrived at the ungodly hour of six forty-five.

Deep breath and back to work the next day to package a story on Easter travel with re-cuts at twelve p.m., three p.m. and seven p.m., and a piece for the following morning's *Sunrise*, Sky's breakfast show, on heart transplants.

I did an overnight shift at Sky, my first, at the end of March. This was something I needed to nip in the bud. I am not a vampire! I thought the poor producers and others who regularly worked overnight looked pale and unwell. *Sunrise* had the highest ratings of any Sky News programme in relative terms, as a percentage of the breakfast TV audience which was in itself comparatively small. In numbers terms *Live at Five* drew the largest audience. Viewing figures were small compared to ITN or BBC news, but I soon learnt that most of the movers and shakers in politics, business and in the investment banks had us on all the time. I cut a story on an NUT (National Union of Teachers) conference for *Sunrise*, but mostly just struggled to stay awake!

One plus, though, was that we got to see the Hale-Bopp comet, clear and bright in the night sky and later dubbed 'the great comet of 1997'. It was astounding. According to astronomers, it was the first time it had been visible to the naked eye for four thousand years. I wondered what our distant ancestors made of it. Armageddon? Or perhaps they worshipped it. Even now, in the late twentieth century, it affected some people in the strangest way. In California, thirty-nine members of the Heaven's Gate cult committed suicide apparently believing they would teleport to a spaceship which they were convinced was flying behind the comet.

I did another overnight shift which involved interviewing space experts about the moons of Jupiter. The space probe Galileo had discovered carbon and nitrogen on one of the moons. For once, overnight felt like the right time to be doing the story.

I spent a pleasant day at Wembley Stadium, for once covering a sport I understood! It was the Coca-Cola Cup final, Leicester 1 Middlesborough 1 (Leicester won the subsequent replay 1-0). We vox popped fans before and after the game, a very good atmosphere, a friendly rivalry. But we weren't really there primarily for the football. We were on IRA bomb alert. The previous day, the Grand National at Aintree had been postponed following an IRA bomb threat.

Veteran BBC reporter Martin Bell announced that he was standing in the general election as an anti-sleaze candidate against Conservative Neil Hamilton in Tatton, Cheshire. He was being backed by both Labour and the Liberal Democrats, who had both withdrawn their own candidates. I had begun the day rather bizarrely, packaging CBS pictures of snow blizzards in Minnesota, but switched to the Martin Bell story in the afternoon to package Sky's lead story. 'The man in the white suit' was front page news and, of course, he won Tatton in the general election.

From snow blizzards in Minnesota to floods in Russia, where the river Volga had burst its banks, and a story I had covered so much in Scotland, the National Trust held a press conference on banning deer hunting. Our package ran from six a.m. (a preview piece by our deer hunting correspondent!) until at least eight p.m.

It was a strange day because I had also been working on a story from Albania and another on cancer. At one point, my cancer package ran at eleven fifteen a.m., Albania at eleven forty-five a.m. and deer hunting at twelve fifteen p.m.! I wasn't confused, but our viewers may have been!

The same day, I also did a story on racism on the fashion industry, which model Naomi Campbell claimed was rife. This involved a few shots and interviews at the Select model agency in Covent Garden, very pleasant. The package ran in *Live at Five*.

I escaped for a day to Upavon in Wiltshire to help media train General Angus Ramsay, who was due to become GOC (General Officer Commanding) Scotland. He had had a remarkable career, in Oman during the Dhofar rebellion, in Northern Ireland and in Bosnia. The following year, when I was working in Cyprus and he was Commander, British Forces, he invited me to dinner at his splendid home, the former governor's residence.

We went to Lord's cricket ground for the Metropolitan Police Operation Bumblebee roadshow, their anti-burglary campaign. I had cameraman, Simon Oliver, but no producer or sound recordist. Simon did an excellent job. The lovely Jill Dando was there for the BBC's *Crimewatch* with about twenty people in her team. Now that, I thought, was the way to do it.

Later that afternoon, I interviewed Michael Howard, then the Secretary of State for employment. I was getting a bit of a look in on Sky's general election coverage though nothing, of course, compared to later years. From there we were sent to Trafalgar Square, where a riot was building up. Echoes of the poll tax riot of 1990. We blagged our way through the police cordon. There were scuffles and skirmishes, bricks and bottles were flying. Not nice at all. Hundreds of riot police, including mounted officers, cleared the square in a series of charges.

The next day, a Sunday, was far more pleasant, filming a vintage car meeting at Brooklands with cameraman Mark Williams. It looked great and was widely praised back at base. You couldn't really go wrong in such a picture-rich environment. A classic (excuse the pun) Sunday story.

I worked with Mark again two days later, doorstepping Conservative Party Deputy Chair Angela Rumbold MP, first at her home and then at her constituency office in Mitcham. It was a long doorstep but we were eventually rewarded for our patience with an interview. The BBC had a crew there, ITN didn't. On the 5:40 news that day ITN reported that, "Rumbold wasn't speaking today". Really? They would get a shock when they watched the BBC's *Six O'clock News* or bothered to watch Sky News.

A week before the general election, Labour accused the Tories of planning to abolish the state pension. The Tories retaliated and accused Labour of lying. In fact, there was a plan floating around to reduce the State Pension but not until 2040, which would affect today's teenagers. It was extremely unlikely ever to come to fruition, but it was the main political row of that day in late April. We went to a lunch at a pensioners' club, talked to a group of sixth formers sitting around a table in their school library, and cut three minutes for *Live at Five*.

In the evening, Claire Short delivered a classic political foot-in-mouth story by claiming that Labour's policy was in favour of a united Ireland. It wasn't. I interviewed her and cut a package.

The next day, a Saturday, I was sent to the London Toy & Model museum. To mark the centenary of Enid Blyton's birth, the museum was mounting a Noddy exhibition. Six days before a general election and I was doing a story about Noddy!

It was quite fun, though, and a bit of light relief from all the politics. I interviewed the museum curator and Enid Blyton's daughter, and did a PTC holding the original and very spooky if not downright sinister 1951 Noddy doll. I cut a three-minute package. *Live at Five* loved it, and ran teasers all afternoon featuring me with Noddy!

The piece was still running and still being trailed between its runs when I went to bed at midnight. Like my interview with Kermit the frog at the Oxford Union, these are the stories that people remember and mention for weeks afterwards.

On the Sunday, a package on which newspapers were backing which party, and whether or not it mattered or significantly affected how people were planning to vote. In the evening, a piece on young Russian students who were in London to study our general election. How times have changed.

Tuesday, two days before the election, and I had two stories running. Firefighters were on strike in Essex, and an 'election issue' package on unemployment. I was also working up a piece on election workers and the mechanics of how polling stations operate, to be broadcast on the Thursday, once the polls were open.

Thursday, election day, and as ever it was quiet in the Westminster newsroom, the lull before the storm. With the polls open, we were restricted by law not to report on any actual politics. So, I did a piece on where the election night parties were due to be held. The Marquis of Granby pub, Conservative Central Office, Pizza on the Park (the Liberal Democrats), The Ritz (exterior shots only, and even then we got some grief from the pompous and ill-informed head of security), and the Royal Festival Hall (Labour). The package ran all evening until the polls closed at ten p.m.

We all know what happened that Thursday in 1997, but to watch the result unfolding was incredibly exciting. It was a stunning result, a huge Labour landslide and yet, as we quickly calculated, on roughly the same vote that the Conservatives had got in 1992. Labour was heading for a majority of around one hundred and seventy (in fact, it was one hundred and seventy-six). Echoes of 1945. It was the worst election result for the Conservatives since 1906, although some said since the 1830s.

There had been massive tactical voting. The Liberal Democrats increased their seats from twenty-eight to forty-six. The Referendum Party took fewer than one million votes but cost the Tories a few seats.

Labour had been expected to win, but not by such an astonishing margin. They gained one hundred and forty-five seats, the Tories lost one hundred and seventy-eight. With the exception of the decent and honourable John Major and a few others, the Conservatives had been widely perceived as drowning in incompetence, complacency and sleaze and 'time for change' reflected the mood of the country. Labour had run a very good, though not excellent, campaign, while the Conservative campaign had been an almost unmitigated disaster.

Three ministers, Michael Forsyth, Ian Lang and, unfortunately, Malcolm Rifkind lost their seats. The Tories were completed wiped out in Scotland and Wales. They were now an English party. David Mellor was out in Putney, Sir James Goldsmith was heckled at his count, Martin Bell won in Tatton (on paper at least, the fifth safest Tory seat in the country), and Norman Lamont failed to win Harrogate and Knaresborough, supposedly a safe Tory seat, which was won by Liberal Democrat Phil Willis. Most amazingly of all, Michael Portillo lost his seat in Enfield

Southgate. And yes, we were all still up and working for what became known as the Portillo moment.

A footnote on Norman Lamont. At a press conference in 1993 Lamont had been asked if he regretted claiming to see 'the green shoots of recovery' or talking about 'singing in the bath'. He had replied by quoting the Edith Piaf song, 'Je ne regrette rien'. The newspapers and the satirists had had a field day. *Spitting Image* had been merciless.

Tony Blair, the shiny, new, young prime minister made a speech in Trimdon, and later, at the Royal Festival Hall ('a new dawn has broken has it not?'). He seemed to exemplify a new national spirit of optimism and renewal.

After just two hours sleep, Friday morning confirmed the new political reality. We had a new government with a huge majority. Labour had four hundred and eighteen seats, the Conservatives a mere one hundred and sixty-five. I spent the day packaging Conservative leader speculation and Blair cabinet appointments. By the end of the evening, Tony Blair had named seven cabinet ministers (Prescott, Brown, Cook, Straw, Blunkett, Beckett and Lord Derry Irvine as Lord Chancellor), with more to come the following morning.

Sunday was another of those rather surreal days. In the wake of Thursday night's incredible election results, my task was to cover the Eurovision Song Contest! Britain had won (how times have changed, it was a lot less political back then) with a song by Katrina and the Waves, who I'd never heard of before (or since). The newspapers were having a field day, labelling the victory another British landslide, with Britain at last 'calling the tune in Europe'!

The next day Michael Heseltine was taken to hospital with angina pain. Although it was nothing too serious, he ruled himself out of the Conservative leadership race. Having covered that, I also did a piece on the Blair children and how their world would now be turned upside down, living in Downing Street, the pressure of fame and living in the spotlight, security and so on.

I was still determined to pursue a parallel career away from the news. The following week, I spent two days media training at Hillside Studios in Bushey, Hertfordshire, only half an hour's drive from my home in north London.

Hillside was a large country house once owned by J Arthur Rank. It was operated mostly by former BBC production staff and made films and TV shows. Media training was a relatively small but highly lucrative part of the operation. The gardens were sublime and run by two full-time gardeners, and there was a lovely black Labrador called Austin. It was an extremely pleasant working environment. Sadly, the house has now been converted into apartments.

We went to North Weald airfield in Essex for 'Fighter Meet '97'. It had been an important base during the Battle of Britain and its museum was now home to a unique collection of aircraft including Spitfires, Mustangs and Dakotas as well as Hunters, Venoms and Vampires. To say it was picture-rich was an understatement. It was perfect for a Saturday feature piece. We sent a four-minute package, which went down very well. Apparently, there was applause in the gallery, something which really doesn't happen every day.

The next day, a Sunday, it was back to Brooklands for another feature piece. Brooklands opened in 1907 and was the world's first purpose-built banked motor racing circuit. It hosted its last race in 1939 and is now a museum. Part of the original concrete banked circuit is still intact. It must have been terrifying to drive it at speed. We were there to film an exhibition of large and rather magnificent Packards. We worked between heavy showers venturing outside to film before running for cover. The weekend programme editor was obsessed with vintage cars and aircraft so, for the second day running, we had made his day.

After a couple of days of army training in Germany we covered a story about Hospital Acquired Infections. It was an interesting and important subject, but a professor and his team had spent three years compiling a report and were determined to go through almost every page in minute detail! Their press conference was attended by health specialist journalists from the *British Medical Journal*, *The Nursing Times* and so on, and me. Happily, my fellow hacks were only too happy to explain the more esoteric aspects of this academic melange.

Then it was back to the politics. Stephen Dorrell announced his candidacy for the vacant Conservative Party leadership, Ann Widdecombe was merrily sticking the knife into her former boss at the Home Office, Michael Howard ("something of the night" about him), while William

Hague and Donald Dewar were enjoying some pantomimic jousting in the House of Commons.

For the first time, I went to the magnificent Carlton House, official residence of the foreign secretary, where Robin Cook was meeting his Japanese counterpart. Japan was under pressure to apologise for its treatment of prisoners of war during the Second World War. There was a First World War story two days later when I interviewed Andrew MacKinlay MP who was campaigning for pardons for 'deserters' who had been shot following a court martial. There were three hundred and seven of them who were clearly shell-shocked and suffering from what we now recognise as PTSD. Some had been heroes before they had cracked. A pardon was long overdue.

There was one of those mad days where I seemed to be covering every story under the sun. In a single day, I interviewed surrogate mother Kim Cotton and packaged a story about surrogacy, voiced some 'exciting' police car chase pictures from Australia, cut a package on the confidentiality of the medical history of hospital staff, and interviewed the chief medical officer, Dr Kenneth Calman and dermatologist Dr John Hawk for a piece on skin cancer. All that, before a breaking story. The directors of Camelot, which ran the National Lottery, had awarded themselves huge pay rises, averaging forty per cent. The boss got a fifty-three per cent pay rise, and the head of PR's pay went up by ninety per cent. Scandalous! I cut the lead story for *Live at Five* from Millbank with an update for seven p.m. to run all evening.

The next day was only marginally less mad. I packaged a story on the German government's attempt to de-value its gold reserves to meet the Maastricht criteria. The Bundesbank objected to what it called 'creative accounting'. These were the birth pangs of the single European currency, the Euro. Bill Clinton was visiting the UK and I would rather have been covering that, but my Euro piece was story two (Clinton was the lead), so not too shabby. Then a package on car pollution and traffic congestion, and how various countries were suggesting various solutions. This was years before London Mayor Ken Livingstone introduced the London Congestion Charge. I seem to remember 'Red Ken' promising that the charge of five pounds per day would never rise. As I write, it is fifteen pounds and has been extended to cover weekends. Kerching!

My day finished with a package for the following morning's *Sunrise* on the one hundred and fiftieth anniversary of the worst year of the Irish famine. From the Euro via car pollution to the Irish famine of 1847. It was certainly varied.

Stories in June included the conviction of the Oklahoma bomber, Terry McVeigh, yet another military coup in Sierra Leone (this was three years before the British army intervened, defeated the rebels of the Revolutionary United Front and the West Side Boys and ended the civil war), and the return home of teacher Sandra Gregory from a Thai prison. She had been jailed for four years for heroin smuggling. She was transferred to a British prison to serve the rest of her twenty-one-year sentence. After three years, she was pardoned by the King of Thailand and released in July 2000.

There was another of those mad multi-story days. From London, I packaged an election in Ireland, and yet another piece on deer hunting. An aircraft flying from Malta to Istanbul was hijacked to Cologne. I was packaging for the top of the hour. Ten minutes before deadline the hijack ended. We re-cut with just forty-five seconds to spare.

The stories continued to come thick and fast. I did another piece on surrogacy and interviewed surrogate mother Kim Cotton for the second time. I spent a couple of days in Birmingham when Tony Blair visited a council estate in Redditch and did the first of his meet-the-people televised PR walkabouts in Worcester. In Wolverhampton, we interviewed nursery nurse, Lisa Potts, who was to be awarded the George Medal for bravery. The previous year, when Lisa had been just twenty-one and working at a school in Blakenhall, Wolverhampton, she defended the school children from an attack by a maniac wielding a machete. She had suffered serious injuries. Four of the children who had been cowering in terror behind her, had also been injured. Their attacker, a paranoid schizophrenic, was jailed indefinitely in a secure mental hospital.

We stayed in Birmingham to interview rape victim and campaigner on sexual violence, Jill Saward,, and thank goodness, a more cheerful story about Father's Day.

Following Labour's landslide victory, the Tory leadership contest was in full swing. Ken Clarke, had won the second round of voting, but only just: Clarke sixty-four, Hague sixty, Redwood thirty-eight. It was assumed that John Redwood's supporters would switch to Hague. Astonishingly,

Redwood emerged from his campaign headquarters and declared for Ken Clarke. Even more astonishingly, Ken Clarke and John Redwood held a joint press conference urging William Hague to stand down. Europe, it seemed, had ceased to be an issue. We reckoned Redwood's lot loathed Hague even more than they despised Clarke. It felt as though Ken Clarke had it in the bag, but that evening, Margaret Thatcher endorsed William Hague. All bets were off.

The next day, I cut a John Major political obit which ran all afternoon before heading to the results of the third and final round of the Tory leadership contest. Something of a shock result: Hague ninety-two, Clarke seventy. Almost all of Redwood's supporters had switched to William Hague.

At Conservative Central Office, Ken Clarke was gracious in defeat. He had declined the offer of a position in William Hague's shadow cabinet and would be returning to the backbenches after nearly thirty years in government or on the front bench.

As John Major had been the Stop Heseltine candidate, it seemed that now William Hague had been the Stop Clarke candidate. I doorstepped Margaret Thatcher, who told me she thought the result was "marvellous". And Ken Clarke joined the list of the best prime ministers Britain never had.

Next day we were back at Conservative Central Office for William Hague's new appointments. William Hague emerged at midday with the new chairman of the Conversative Party. It was Cecil Parkinson! I have rarely seen so many political journalists' jaws drop in unison.

Brian Mawhinney was to be shadow home secretary. Michael Howard and Peter Lilley were appointed shadow foreign secretary and shadow chancellor. John Redwood got the job of shadowing the Department for Trade and Industry.

In between all this, I was packaging the forthcoming meeting of the G8 in Denver, Colorado. The most memorable image was of the new Prime Minister Tony Blair boarding Concorde.

In the evening, we went to Opera Holland Park to see *The Magic Flute* and a wonderful Queen of the Night, Jacqueline Parker. As anyone who has been to the open-air Opera Holland Park knows, the singers have to contend with the park's many peacocks, who like to join in, creating a constant cacophony!

In late June, Charlie Kray, older brother of the notorious twins, was sentenced to twelve years for his part in a multi-million-pound plot to supply cocaine. We were at Woolwich Crown Court to cover the sentencing and talk to Kray's supporters, a scary bunch.

Twelve-year-old Belfast schoolgirl, Margaret Gibney, had written to Tony Blair asking him to contribute a poem or a photograph for a 'peace wall' at her school. To her amazement, the prime minister went a lot further and invited her to visit him in Downing Street. We covered their meeting. Tony Blair said that her letter had strengthened his resolve to find a peaceful solution to the Northern Ireland Troubles. Yes, it was a great photo-op, but he seemed absolutely genuine.

That same day, I cut the regular PMQs package. It was William Hague's first Prime Minister's Questions as opposition leader. He would become very adroit across the dispatch box, but his debut was not overly impressive.

In late June, I covered a story close to my heart given my happy years spent in Newcastle working for Metro Radio, the one hundred million pound development of the Gateshead bank of the Tyne, centring on the iconic Baltic Mill building.

Somehow, throughout that summer, I was still fitting in other work, away from Sky News. Among others, I media trained senior lawyers from one of London's leading law firms, executives from British Airways and Shell, others from a regional health authority, the RNIB, and gave a talk to thirty British army colonels. I was told there would be up to two hundred officers attending, including several generals, so a mere thirty colonels was a breeze.

I had spent years talking into cameras, but the first few times I had found talking to a live audience disconcerting. They were all looking at me! And they were asking me questions! By 1997, I had learnt to love it. I still do. And I was beginning to specialise, primarily with the military but also with children's and cancer charities.

July began with a story on the banning of handguns, and the first of many interviews with Home Secretary Jack Straw. I covered a Gay Pride march in London led, rather oddly, by Barbara Windsor, and the TGWU (Transport and General Workers Union) annual conference in Brighton.

Lord Irvine, the new Lord Chancellor, had a pop at 'fat cat lawyers'. Several interviews on that, including the chairman of the Bar Council, for a package for *Live at Five*. Fashion designer, Gianni Versace, was shot dead outside his home in Miami. A flood of pictures was coming in from the American networks which needed logging and editing into a coherent news package. Closer to home, Philip English was released from prison after being given a life sentence four years earlier for the murder of police Sergeant Bob Forth in Gateshead. He didn't do it. Bob Forth had, in fact, been stabbed to death by twenty-five-year-old Paul Weddle. English, then just fifteen, had been a hundred yards away and was convicted under the joint enterprise law, a conviction now overturned by the Law Lords as a miscarriage of justice.

An IRA ceasefire announcement was imminent, so we went to Canary Wharf where, the previous year, the IRA had detonated a truck bomb. Although the IRA had sent a warning, there had not been enough time to fully evacuate the area. Two people had been killed and more than a hundred injured. Cameraman Adam Murch had covered the bombing and knew a block of flats where every window had been smashed. We got some tremendous interviews with some very colourful characters in their homes, and a moody end-shot of a Docklands Light Railway train against the backdrop of an almost full moon in the evening twilight.

On July 19th, three stories. Floods in Poland and Germany, Mohamed Al-Fayed being very rude about Camilla Parker-Bowles, and the restoration of Brunel's SS Great Britain. But they all seemed mundane, because Marion was pregnant! Everything else paled into insignificance.

Andy Carmichael was an MI5 agent who infiltrated the National Front in the West Midlands and then, ostensibly on behalf of the National Front, also infiltrated the Referendum Party. He had decided to go public, but had sold his story to *The Sunday Times*. The way to get to him was through espionage writer Nigel West (the Conservative MP Rupert Allason). It took more than twenty-four hours of phone calls, but eventually I went to *The Sunday Times* building in Wapping to meet the heroic spook. We took him to 4 Millbank for a two-camera shoot. Andy was a very good talker with a fascinating tale to tell. It made for a great three-minute piece for Sky News, and it was an exclusive. The BBC and ITN were nowhere in sight.

I interviewed Schools Minister Stephen Byers when he launched a 'literacy task force', a literacy programme for primary school children and, crucially, their parents.

In early August, an Australian ski instructor was found alive and virtually unhurt under an avalanche which had struck three days earlier. A miraculous escape story which kept me busy for two days as the pictures came into Sky from Australia. My first package was at seven thirty a.m., with updates every half hour. By ten a.m., rescuers had got him out onto a stretcher and into an ambulance. The story led Sky's bulletins. By day two, he was chatting away from his hospital bed. I updated packages all day.

In Portsmouth, we covered what was to be the final voyage of the Royal yacht Britannia. She had brought Prince Charles and the last governor of Hong Kong, Chris Patten, back from Hong Kong after its handover to China the previous month. This was a comparatively short journey, a cruise to Aberdeen for the Royal Family's annual retreat at Balmoral. We had two cameras, one on the ground with me and the other getting topshots as Britannia sailed into history. There had been a Royal yacht since King Charles the Second ascended to the throne in 1660. But no more.

The next day, I had two stories running. Liverpool goalkeeper, Bruce Grobbelaar, was found not guilty of match fixing after a saga that had rumbled on for three years since the *Sun* published the allegations. It was the third trial, the previous two juries having been unable to reach a verdict. The other story was far grimmer. In a gangland shooting, five-year-old Dillon Hill had been shot dead by a bullet intended for his stepfather, a small-time heroin dealer. His murderer, contract killer Paul Seddon, was jailed for life.

The day after, it was a Royal Family day. First, to Sotheby's to preview the sale of the possessions of the Duke and Duchess of Windsor. It was a huge sale, forty-four thousand items from their home in Paris which was expected to raise more than five million pounds for children's charities. I got to do a PTC holding the 1911 ceremonial Investiture sword. Then, a piece on Diana and Dodi along the lines of: who was Dodi? I cut that for seven p.m. The *Daily Mirror* had video of Diana and Dodi doing what can probably be best described as canoodling. A hasty re-cut to include the *Mirror*'s pictures.

Next, a story on cystic fibrosis and another on paedophiles. The government was to allow police to inform schools (but not the general public) if a known paedophile was living in the area. At one stage, at two p.m., I had both packages running in the first ten minutes of the programme. For the three p.m., another reporter re-voiced the cystic fibrosis package.

Occasionally, I would be seconded to the business unit at Sky News. So, I covered the takeover by the Royal Bank of Scotland of Birmingham Midshires, at the time Britain's fifth largest building society, and the potential poisoned chalice/banana skin of BSkyB's annual report. I survived! Rather strangely, I had to do the PTC outside Sky's main building with the company logo behind me. We were doing a story about ourselves.

I did a story about mosquitoes. Apparently there was a plague of the non-malarial variety in Britain. Among the elements was an interview at the Natural History Museum with mosquito expert Dr Ralph Harbach, who was American and very friendly. But I couldn't help wondering what would make anyone want to dedicate his life to the study of these flying pests.

We went to Ashfordby in Leicestershire, where the coal mine was closing. Echoes of the miners' strike of 1984. We interviewed the president of the UDM (the breakaway miners' union) and talked to local people about the devastating impact of the pit closure. We packaged all day and got the pit's managing director live into *Live at Five*.

The Australian cricket team wanted to take the Ashes home with them. They lost the final test that day (all out for 104!) but had won the series 3–2. The Ashes sit in pride of place in the museum at Lord's. We filmed there, and did some vox pops. The general consensus seemed to be 'bloody cheek!'.

A day of fun and a day of politics. Covering the Notting Hill Carnival was always entertaining, and so it was that August. Despite heavy showers, the revellers were out in force and the floats were as impressive as ever. Tony Blair visited a school in Whitechapel and chatted to us afterwards. But not about Northern Ireland. He was in 'education, education, education' mode. Later, in Downing Street, we interviewed David Trimble and the Ulster Unionists as they emerged from a meeting with the prime minister. We doorstepped Northern Ireland Secretary Mo Mowlam and Tony Blair too, but they refused to answer questions on Northern Ireland. The situation was clearly very delicate. An announcement was expected the next day, and it was expected to say that Sinn Féin would, after all, be allowed to participate in peace talks.

Before going on holiday, my last piece at the end of August was a near miss at Heathrow airport. We interviewed an air traffic controller. The picture he painted was bloody terrifying.

We holidayed in Northern Cyprus, a pariah state since the Turkish invasion of 1974. There are no direct flights from the UK, the only way to get there is via Turkey.

Northern Cyprus is unique. Where we were, the border was an iron fence at the end of the beach. The ghost town of Varosha lay just beyond, in the 'Forbidden Zone'. The Turks had taken the most beautiful part of the island. We wandered around Famagusta with its massive Venetian wall and where St Nicholas' Cathedral had been turned into a mosque. We had the Othello tower to ourselves. There were no other tourists. We also had the ancient Greek site of Salamis to ourselves. In ancient times the capital of Cyprus, Salamis was further developed by the Romans. Excavations had revealed a stadium, gymnasium, public baths and a magnificent amphitheatre. Much remains to be discovered, but the site was completely deserted. As with Jerash in Jordan a few years earlier, there were pieces of Roman pottery and statuary just lying around, unprotected.

This is not a travelogue, so I won't record the splendours of Northern Cyprus, the ancient Persian palace, Famagusta, Kyrenia, Salamis, the Roman mosaics, the Royal Tombs, the incredible monasteries, the other-worldly abbey at Bellapais, the house where Lawrence Durrell wrote *Bitter Lemons*, the Crusader castle at Kantara, the pretty fishing harbours, the vast, empty sandy beaches etc. etc. etc. However, one thing that struck me was that every Northern Cypriot we spoke to wanted their former Greek Cypriot neighbours back. Northern Cyprus was now home to thousands of Anatolian farmers and twenty-five thousand Turkish troops, and local people were not at all happy about it.

While we were on holiday in Northern Cyprus, the news broke that Diana, Princess of Wales, had died in a car crash in Paris. At first, we thought Mother Teresa of Calcutta had died. When it became clear that the breaking news was referring to Diana, it was almost impossible to believe.

It seemed utterly inconceivable. I called Sky News to see if I was needed. I wasn't. Like every other news organisation, Sky News had descended on Paris en masse.

I trained officers from the King's Own Royal Border Regiment at Catterick before their deployment to Bosnia, returning to Cyprus just over a week after returning home from holiday. After a flight in a VC10 from Brize Norton, facing backwards which always feels odd, Major Ken Molyneux-Carter and I were in Akrotiri, the British sovereign base. We spent ten days at Episkopi Garrison training army officers.

The Cyprus working day is perfect. Although you start very early, usually at about six thirty a.m., it's all over by three p.m., which meant we had time to enjoy the local area and sites, Kolossi castle and the ruins of the ancient city-state of Kourion. Our camera team were soldiers, so we had to get them back to base in time for their dinner at six p.m. Of course, I would rather have stayed out enjoying the villages and beaches, but this was work not a vacation,

There was what I dubbed a 'spooks conference' going on while we were there, characters in suits from the Ministry of Defence, the Foreign Office and GCHQ who were very reluctant to tell us what they were up to. We had dinner one evening with Mervyn Wynne-Jones, head of PR for British forces, Cyprus. He was later to become head of PR at GCHQ, which I thought must surely be the cushiest job ever since he could reveal so little, and I teased him about it accordingly.

In mid-October, it was back to the grindstone and back to Sky News. One of the train operators came up with the slightly mad idea of producing trains which were impenetrable to radio waves and therefore on which mobile phones could not be used. From the Sports Dome bar in Camden I covered a football international, England v Italy, shouting my live two-ways above the deafening cacophony of dozens of drunk England fans. We certainly captured the atmosphere.

With cameramen Martin Ayling and Tom Radburn I interviewed Rhône-Poulenc chairman Jean-Rene Fourto, a two-camera shoot for a stand-alone interview. I covered the Booker prize, won that year by Arundhati Roy for her fabulous novel *The God of Small Things*, and spent two entertaining days at Hillside talking about birds, training senior people from the RSPB. There was more training that month, including the WWF, who I supported and still do.

There was a roller coaster day on the markets. At one point, the FT100 index was down ten per cent, but it fully recovered by the end of the day. I had to do constant live updates. No one seemed to have any idea why the markets were acting so strangely. There hadn't been an event to trigger such a response. The markets were simply being skittish.

The Foreign Office asked Brazil to extradite the Great Train Robber Ronnie Biggs, there was yet another French lorry drivers' strike, and I also packaged BT's annual profits. But Sky News had become obsessed with the trial of Louise Woodward, which we were broadcasting live from Boston.

Woodward, a nineteen-year-old British au pair, was on trial for the manslaughter of eighteen-month-old baby, Matthew Eappen, who she had been looking after at his home in Massachusetts. Baby Matthew had died from injuries which included a fractured skull.

At the end of October, she had been found guilty of second-degree murder and sentenced to life in prison. I packaged the story all day. On appeal, two weeks later, that verdict was overturned and branded a miscarriage of justice, and Louise Woodward was freed after having spent two hundred and seventy-nine days in prison.

There was a huge gas explosion in Loughton, Essex, and I got scrambled to go there with cameraman, Mark Hamilton. We interviewed a fire officer during one of my live two-ways. At the end of one, we were moved on by the police just as I was finishing, very dramatic. A cloud of acrid smoke was heading our way and was almost upon us. There was utter devastation, it looked like the immediate aftermath of a massive bomb explosion. One person had died, two had been injured. It was amazing that the casualties weren't far worse.

I was doing lives using ITN's satellite truck. Camera crew John Martin and Micky Laurence, two of my favourites, were covering the story for ITN. It felt just like old times.

Later that November, I was back in Scotland. In Edinburgh, we covered the story of a boy who was having a total blood transfusion in an attempt to save the life of his twin brother, who had leukaemia.

In Peterhead, we filmed a huge Dutch crane barge salvaging a fishing boat. Peterhead fishermen were always a joy, with their almost impenetrable accents laced with Pictish words. People in Aberdeen struggle to understand anyone from Peterhead! There is a famous clip from the UK-Iceland Cod War of the 1970s when an America TV reporter tried to interview a Peterhead fisherman. His question got a reply that was completely incomprehensible. The TV reporter turns to his cameraman in total bewilderment and just says, "Oh shit!"

Back in Edinburgh, we interviewed veteran Labour MP Tam Dalyell who, as ever, had his own unique take on the main story of the day. Saddam Hussein had expelled UN weapons inspectors, provoking a threat of military intervention from the United States.

We also interviewed Bay City Rollers' manager, Tom Paton. The Spice Girls had been booed somewhere or other, and Head of News Nick Pollard had the idea to compare their experience with that of the Bay City Rollers. I knew nothing about the Bay City Rollers except that they wore tartan scarves, silly trousers, and were hugely popular, especially in Scotland. Tom Paton gave us an excellent interview. In his opinion (his, not mine!), the ex-Rollers were either mad or permanently drunk, or both!

The little sojourn to Scotland concluded with a story about the 'Beast of Cupar'. A wild animal was thought to be at large in Fife. There had been a 'Beast of Bodmin' story, this was the Scottish version. I interviewed the relevant police officer, and there was a still of the 'Beast', a blurry picture of what looked like a panther. I did my PTC in a field of sheep! We sent a package for Sky News. In the old days, it would have made a classic 'And Finally' for ITN's *News at Ten*. It was very well received at Sky News Centre.

Back in London, I packaged the shooting of sixty tourists in Egypt, in the Valley of the Queens at Luxor. This was a largely successful attempt by Islamic fundamentalists to destroy the country's tourist industry, damage the economy, and de-stabilise the government.

I love the Valley of the Kings and the Valley of the Queens. The next time I visited them, Egyptian police and soldiers were everywhere. There were almost no tourists. To drive from Luxor to Aswan, we had to travel in a heavily-armed police convoy and go through several police check points. But that is another story.

Rather more mundanely, we went to a school in Ramsgate which had come bottom of the government's latest league table of exam results. We interviewed the head teacher and got shots of the school kids. Our package also included interviews with Doug McAvoy of the NUT and schools minister Estelle Morris.

In Upavon, I trained three more army officers, a colonel and two brigadiers, one of whom was David Leakey, who was now director of Military Operations at the M.O.D. As amusing as ever, I had worked with him at the Higher Command and Staff Course at the UK Defence Academy in Shrivenham, where I had lectured and conducted media training. David had been the UK military representative at the peace talks which ended the Bosnian war and resulted in the Dayton Agreement. Much later, after his retirement having reached the exalted rank of Lt. General, he was appointed Gentleman Usher of the Black Rod in the House of Lords.

At the Home Office, I interviewed Home Secretary Jack Straw on the tagging of prisoners, and stayed with him while he did a live two-way off the back of my *Live at Five* package. And we filmed the Royal yacht Britannia for the final time when, having taken the Royal family up to Aberdeen, she returned for the last time to her home port of Portsmouth.

The Humanities Reading Room at the British Library was to be the successor to the Round Reading Room at the British Museum. On the day before it opened at the end of November, we filmed it and interviewed Chief Executive Bamber Gascoigne (of *University Challenge* fame). I also had the pleasure of interviewing David Attenborough, Tony Benn (not for the first time), Maureen Lipman and Fay Weldon. We cut a package, and topped and tailed the David Attenborough and Tony Benn contributions to run as stand-alone interviews.

To round off November, in Downing Street I interviewed Sports Minister Tony Banks, he of the acerbic wit, and a British Medical Association lobby campaign against the sponsorship of sport by tobacco companies, and reported from the Merrill Lynch offices in Farringdon Road where Gordon Brown delivered a pre-Budget speech. I also covered a press conference announcing a crackdown on illegal immigration. *Plus ça change*.

I spent much of December based in Manchester, covering stories in the north of England. On the first day, after leaving London at six a.m. to drive to Manchester, I packaged an IVF story at the Withington Hospital for *Live at Five* and babysat a live two-way with the hospital's medical director.

261

After a fairly full day's work, we were assigned to drive to Anglesey for a Welsh farmers' meeting ahead of their blockade of the port of Holyhead. We sent track and rushes for eleven p.m., midnight and one a.m., and a separate package for *Sunrise*. I finally got to bed at the Trearddur Bay Hotel in Anglesey at four a.m. It had been a twenty-two-hour day.

We covered the farmers' blockade from early the next day and all day, with live two-ways at ten p.m., midnight, and three a.m., and sent track and rushes for *Sunrise*. They went well. Shame there is almost no audience in the middle of the night. I got to bed at three thirty a.m., a slight improvement!

At Old Trafford, we interviewed Manchester United fans who were off to Turin for a match against Juventus and interviewed club secretary, Kenneth Merrett, who kept us waiting for over an hour. At Manchester University, a splendid story. They were re-building the 1948 first digital stored-memory computer.

In Haydon Bridge we had the amusing if somewhat eccentric story of a couple who had bought a sixty thousand pound fairground organ for their eleven-year-old son, cashing in their life insurance policy to do so. The ultimate Christmas present! Not only did we do a package and a live, but *Live at Five* ended the programme with thirty seconds of this marvellous instrument playing live.

A far more serious story the next day. Manchester had the highest suicide rate in the country among young people. We interviewed Parliamentary Under-Secretary for Health Paul Boateng MP and several counsellors and social workers, as well as talking to young Mancunians.

In Liverpool, we covered the curious case of two young boys who had taken the council to court to force them to repair their dilapidated primary school. They won!

We had fun at non-league football club Emley FC. They were the FA Cup giant-killers who had knocked out Lincoln City and had now been drawn against West Ham in the third round. We interviewed Emley's manager, Ronnie Glavin, and I did a PTC on the pitch, a far cry from Old Trafford or Highbury!

Back in London, just before Christmas, we were doing another fun story, an auction of toy trains at Christies, when news came in of a ship on fire in Falmouth. I had both packages running at five p.m. and six p.m. before another reporter was assigned to re-voice one of them.

I worked on Christmas Day, doing lives from the children's ward at the Royal Brompton hospital, and in the evening, cut a package on fox hunting to run the next day, Boxing Day, my day off. On the 27th, my last story of the year was that hardy perennial, the Christmas holidays getaway which we did from Manchester airport. Really very predictable.

CHAPTER 12

1998: Crime Stories and Politics. Stephen Lawrence. The Good Friday Agreement. And more Gazza!

1998 was my first full year as a freelance. This brings certain freedoms. You can do a variety of different jobs. But there are also disadvantages, including never quite belonging anywhere. It also means no paid holidays, so taking a vacation becomes a double whammy, you pay for the holiday with nothing, no salary, going into the bank. However, for the time being at least, I was content to see where freelancing would lead me.

Sky News was keeping me very busy, for which I was grateful. In the first week of January, I interviewed Home Secretary Jack Straw, a three-minute stand-alone interview which led the news, did a story on Chechnya, Hong Kong bird flu (they were slaughtering thousands of chickens in an effort to contain the outbreak), a package on the continuing peace talks in Northern Ireland, and the lead story on storms (Britain was getting battered).

The rest of the month was equally busy and varied. On January the 8th, we were in the town of Selsey in Sussex. Flooded at the weekend, it had now been hit by a tornado. A real tornado, in Sussex! Fortunately, no one was hurt but the damage was extensive. There was a day when I did three separate packages, first on a boy who had been rescued unharmed from a grain silo by firefighters, then a James Bond exhibition, and finally he seizure of thirty-two million pounds worth of cocaine.

There was a piece on Foreign Secretary Robin Cook's marital problems (why was this any business of ours?), a package on the Princess Diana Memorial Fund, Bill Gates was accused of anti-competitive practices and faced a possible multi-million dollar fine, a drop in the ocean as Microsoft's profits for the previous year were more than four billion dollars. We filmed Richard Branson's air balloon which was being tested before flying to

Morocco for another attempt to fly around the world. I was to meet and interview Richard Branson again just a few days later, a libel trial at the High Court. Oil prices took a tumble, so we were on the trading floor at the International Petroleum Exchange near Tower Bridge for shots, interviews and a PTC.

The Bill Clinton/Monica Lewinsky scandal broke. I spent two days working on that. There was plenty of material coming in from the American networks, but a deafening silence from the White House. Then came Bill Clinton's now famous denial ("I did not have sexual relations with that woman"). Eleven months later, in December, the president was impeached by the House of Representatives, though not by the Senate. He was only the second POTUS to be impeached, after Andrew Johnson in 1868. Donald Trump later joined this small club, but is in a league of his own: Impeached twice!

The Queen Mother was taken to hospital with a broken hip after she fell at Sandringham. At first it seemed very serious, she was ninety-seven. But doctors operated overnight, and she had a new right hip to match her left which had been replaced ten years earlier. It was our lead story and I cut fresh packages every hour for eleven hours.

Before the end of January, a bit more politics and more Jack Straw, this time delivering a speech to the NACRO (National Association for the Care and Resettlement of Offenders) conference, and an update on Foreign Secretary Robin Cook. And more media training for the British army.

February was just as busy. I packaged the Australian Constitutional conference (another attempt by Republicans to ditch the Queen as their Head of State), Richard Branson won his libel case at the High Court, and Peter Davis, the head of Oflot which regulated the National Lottery, was summoned to a meeting with Culture Secretary Chris Smith and subsequently resigned. He allowed us to film him clearing his desk and leaving his office.

Football giant-killers Stevenage Borough had drawn 1–1 with Newcastle United in the FA Cup at their home ground, Broadhall Way, capacity six thousand seven hundred. Now, they were off to St James' Park for the replay. We were in Stevenage to see them off, the team and their very excited fans. We did lives from the Pig and Whistle pub, which was packed full of noisy fans and very atmospheric. Sadly for them, Stevenage lost the replay 3–1, but it was the most famous day in the club's history.

By way of total contrast, we were at the Old Bailey the next day for a very grim trial. Three boys, aged ten and eleven, were accused of raping an eleven-year-old girl. They were found not guilty, but the evidence presented by the prosecution had been stomach-turning.

Before the end of the first week of February, I was also packaging the latest from Iraq and the standoff between Saddam Hussein and the United Nations over the issue of weapons' inspectors.

We went to Sainsbury's supermarket, in Forest Hill, London, where the so-called Mardi Gras Bomber had struck again. He had earnt his nickname by leaving a calling card that said, *Welcome to the Mardi Gras experience.* Edgar Pearce had conducted a three-year campaign of terror and blackmail using home-made bombs. At first, he had attacked banks before switching to supermarkets. In total, he planted thirty-six devices. He was eventually arrested the following April and was sentenced to twenty-one years in prison.

Thirteen-year-old schoolgirl, Caroline Dickinson, had been murdered in France in July, 1996. She had been sexually assaulted and suffocated. The French police had still not found her killer. Now, in February 1998, they released a photo-fit of their prime suspect. We had been following the story, and I packaged this latest development. Eventually, a Spanish waiter, Francisco Montes, was arrested. He was a serial abuser who had previously been convicted of sexual assault in several European countries. He was finally convicted in June 2004 and sentenced to thirty years in prison.

There was some much needed light relief the next day when we filmed twenty-six-year-old inventor Eddy China, who had built a sofa-car. You basically drove along, open air, sitting on a sofa! No prizes for guessing where I did my PTC.

Next day, we were in Chippenham where a Second World War UXB (unexploded bomb) was being detonated. I had spent the morning reporting on a row about Enoch Powell, who had died the previous week, being allowed to lie in state in Westminster Abbey. Apparently, it is an honour extended to anyone whose funeral is held in St Margaret's church. By the time I got to Chippenham, it was early evening. I took over from a fellow reporter, the great Alex Crawford, who had been covering the story since six a.m. I did several live two-ways, interviewed several people who were being allowed back into their homes and army co-ordinator, Captain Ed McMahon-Turner. This time, my PTC was in a bomb crater.

In Wolverhampton, I interviewed Schools Minister Estelle Morris (again) on new government guidelines on how much 'reasonable force' teachers were allowed to use (too late for me and my contemporaries, the victims of vicious thrashings at school), before heading off to Cyprus once more to work with the British army for a week.

There was another day of jumping through hoops back at Sky News. After a seven a.m. start, I began by packaging the latest on the Northern Ireland peace talks which had been threatened by a bombing by dissident Republicans in Moira, County Down, twenty miles from Belfast. Eleven people had been injured when a car bomb exploded outside the police station. From there, to interview Peter Mandelson on the proposed Millennium Dome, now a London landmark but very controversial at the time. Peter's attempts at doing the PR for the much-criticised project were not entirely convincing. Later came news from Baghdad with UN Secretary General Kofi Annan saying he was confident of a deal with Saddam Hussein. We couldn't feed from Baghdad, technical problems, so I hastily scrambled together a piece for *Live at Five*. My Millennium Dome package also ran all evening.

After a few days of corporate media training, I covered a Countryside Alliance demo in London, campaigning for 'the rural way of life', which basically seemed to mean field sports. Hunting, shooting and fishing. Fox hunting was a hot political issue. It still is.

Ford announced the end of production of the iconic Ford Escort after thirty years. Its replacement, the less than iconic Ford Focus, was unveiled at the Geneva Motor Show. My package was peppered with suitable library pictures.

I was pumping out the stories from an edit suite at Sky News in Osterley. A piece on Kosovo, another on the Northern Ireland peace talks resuming with Sinn Féin represented, a report that claimed that British children are selfish and spoilt (who'd have thought!), an interview with Norwich Union CEO Richard Harvey, another with the former British Lions rugby star, millionaire Tony O'Reilly, who was in the process of buying the *Independent* newspaper, and another hideous paedophile story.

Teenager Stephen Lawrence was murdered in April 1993 in a racially motivated attack in Eltham. He was stabbed to death by a gang of five white youths. Charges against two youths, Neil Acourt and Luke Knight, were dropped after the Crown Prosecution Service said there was insufficient evidence to convict. Three others had been found not guilty by a jury at the Old Bailey in 1996. Now, five years later, I was covering Sir William MacPherson's public inquiry. I interviewed Stephen's parents, Doreen and Neville, and would interview Doreen several times in the subsequent months and years as the Metropolitan Police were accused of institutionalised racism and corruption during the investigation of the murder. Jack Straw later said that ordering the inquiry was the most important decision of his four years as Home Secretary.

The inquiry concluded that the Metropolitan Police investigation had been incompetent. Officers had made fundamental errors including failing to give Stephen first aid at the scene, failure to follow transparently obvious leads, and failing to arrest suspects. Most damning of all, the inquiry concluded that the Metropolitan Police force was indeed institutionally racist, and proposed seventy reforms to both policing and criminal law, including the abolition of the rule of double jeopardy if new and vital evidence came to light.

Eventually, in 2012, Gary Dobson and David Norris were convicted of Stephen's murder.

For the rest of March I worked in London covering stories from all over the place, including the Pope visiting Nigeria, a tornado in Georgia (USA), more on the Northern Ireland peace talks, a stabbing in Fulham and another in Gillingham. The *News of the World* had a story about the salacious misbehaviour of senior board members of Newcastle United. On a Saturday evening, I was in the *News of the World* newsroom to cut a package and for a live with the newspaper's editor, Philip Hall.

On April the 2nd, our daughter, Maddie, was born. It was the best day of my life. It had been a long labour. Marion had been absolutely heroic. Maddie emerged, two weeks late, looking like a doll. She greeted the world with eyes like saucers, taking it all in.

Paternity leave was blissful, watching our baby daughter eat and eat and eat! She was a smiling, happy baby who rarely cried except, of course, at night! One of the highlights was her first day out, to Kenwood on

Hampstead Heath, with car seat, baby sling and that bag full of spare nappies etc. with which every parent is familiar in use for the first time. Maddie slept throughout this entire landmark experience.

On my first day back at work there were lots of congratulations from colleagues, which was lovely, and a gossip catch-up. I did a piece on drugs and another on Earl Spencer setting up a Princess Diana memorial museum, but mostly I just tried to stay awake and reasonably alert.

In Belfast, the signing of the Good Friday Agreement seemed to have ended The Troubles. This was history in the making. It had taken years of work to secure agreement. Several Northern Ireland secretaries had laboured to engineer it, most recently the feisty Mo Mowlam. So too had Tony Blair's Chief of Staff Jonathan Powell. John Major deserved a lot more credit than he generally got although Blair himself was quick to praise the groundwork of his predecessor.

There was that moment of levity when Tony Blair actually said, "This is no time for sound bites, but I feel the hand of history on our shoulders." Of course, 'the hand of history' was the front-page headline in just about every newspaper the next day. No doubt the prime minister knew he was delivering a sound bite even as he said it.

Like many others, I could barely believe my eyes when I saw the new First Minister Ian Paisley and his deputy Martin McGuinness together, all smiles and warm handshakes. They had been mortal enemies for years. Now, they were smiling and laughing together so much that, before long, they would become known as 'The Chuckle Brothers'.

Maddie was two weeks old and thriving. I was at work, covering the Neill Committee on standards in public life and George Galloway, who was in Baghdad and bringing back with him a four-year-old girl for leukaemia treatment in Glasgow.

The US Federal Aviation Administration wanted all Boeing 737s re-wired. Not great news for British Airways. I went to the company's splendid headquarters at Heathrow to interview senior executives and record a PTC for our package.

When JJB Sports published its annual report, we went to interview the chairman (and former Blackburn Rovers footballer) Dave Whelan, who had built a multi-million-pound empire from humble beginnings, a sports shop in Wigan. On the way, cameraman Simon Oliver's Volvo estate conked out.

This was unheard of. Like ITN, Sky News used Volvos as camera crew cars. In the ten years I had worked at ITN, not one of the company's fleet of Volvos had broken down. We pranged a few, but they performed in all weathers and all conditions. At one point, Volvo wanted to use ITN in its marketing. They were willing to pay a lot of money for the deal. ITN declined on the grounds that we might have to do a negative story about Volvo in the future. I disagreed. We would do whatever story was necessary, a deal with Volvo would not interfere in any way with our news coverage. Besides, ITN needed the money. The decision was taken, of course, at board level. Our opinions didn't come into it.

Not only was the Volvo estate immensely robust and totally reliable, it also had a fantastic turning circle. You could 'turn it on a sixpence'. I liked them so much I bought one. They were also very spacious. I sold mine, eventually, to a colleague who used it to transport his two Great Danes.

We resolved our Volvo breakdown problem by getting a Sky motorcycle despatch rider to wait by the car for the RAC to arrive while we took a taxi to do the interview. By the time we returned, it was fixed.

Despite BA's Boeing 737 problem, just a week later we were at Olympia in west Kensington for a BA recruitment fair. It was the largest ever mounted by a single company. BA was taking on seven thousand new staff over the next twelve months.

Very early the following Sunday, I was in Blackheath for the start of the London Marathon, about which I knew virtually nothing. The news desk sent some copy and cuttings with the camera crew so I was able to sound terribly knowledgeable and authoritative! We were live every thirty minutes all morning. Mostly it was colour, talking to people running to raise money for charity or wearing daft costumes, but at one point I had to do a serious sport live two-way, talking about the favourites to win the men's and women's races. I could not, of course, have done it without first reading the information the news desk had sent me. Yes, kids, there was life before Google!

In the afternoon I switched to covering a dreadful story from the States, where a six-year-old child had shot dead a four year old. He had used his father's gun, which was not locked away. The piece focused on American gun culture and why they would not abandon the second amendment, the right to bear arms. The amendment was introduced in 1791, when militias were still needed in the wake of the American War of Independence. From this side of the Atlantic, it seemed a dangerous anachronism which had no place in the late twentieth century. This remains the case now, in the twenty-first century, but it still appears politically impossible to change America's lethal gun culture.

Next day was another of those multi-story days, Sky News getting its pound of flesh! I was sent to the ongoing BSE inquiry. There were no new developments, no story, but the news editor of the day insisted on a package so we sent one. It never ran. But I did have a piece running on a government drugs White Paper. Later, I interviewed the nineteen-year-old girl who had managed to come last in the London Marathon, and the two winners, Abel Antón and Catherina McKiernan. It made a classic 'And Finally' package, but both ITN and the BBC missed it! Later still, the story of another nineteen-year-old girl who had died of a drug overdose in Bristol. Her father made an emotional appeal to teenagers and young people to stay away from class A drugs

We had a pleasant day in the village of Kinlet, Shropshire. We were there to interview Janet George of the Countryside Alliance which was selling its membership list to the Conservative Party! A far less pleasant day at the National Neurology Hospital where boxer Spencer Oliver, the European super-bantamweight champion, needed surgery to remove a blood clot from his brain after he was knocked out in a title fight at the Royal Albert Hall. He had been treated in the ring by paramedics for more than fifteen minutes, a shocking sight. Of course, the package included interviews with the BMA and others who wanted boxing banned. Happily, the surgery was successful and Spencer went on to become a pundit for Sky Sports.

In early May, I spent my first night away from baby Maddie when I went to Germany, again, to media train British army officers, a three-day job. And I missed her dreadfully.

When I had been younger and still single, working at ITN, the object of the exercise was to get as far away as possible from the newsroom and stay away for as long as possible. So, if we were sent to cover a story in Moscow, I would try to find us another either there, or in St Petersburg, or Kiev, or Vladivostok! Sometimes, one of the ITN team would want to get home for the weekend. They were the ones with young children. I never understood that attitude, I loved being on the road. Now, as a parent myself, I finally understood.

I was also doing corporate media training. One Disney executive was so busy that he had to leave after just two hours. We had been booked for and were paid for the full day. Working out the hourly rate made me very happy!

I was also covering plenty of politics. There was a story that May on drugs in prisons. I interviewed the director general of the prison service and Home Office minister George Howarth. The government wanted to do something about salt, we had far too much of it in our diets. I also regularly covered PMQs, always a very fast turnaround to get a package ready for the top of the next hour. There was a row over arms sales to Sierra Leone in breach of an international embargo. This surfaced at PMQs and again the next day when the head of the Diplomatic Service, the Foreign Office Permanent Under-Secretary Sir John Kerr, gave evidence to a House of Commons select committee. I also interviewed Michael Howard, who was shadow foreign secretary at the time and was sticking the boot into the Blair government's handling of the Sierra Leone affair.

After every election defeat the outgoing party of government looks inwards, their leader often having resigned. This was happening to the Conservatives in the wake of the Labour landslide of 1997. It would beset them again in 2001 and, to a lesser extent, in 2005. So it fell to us to be asking the questions, the ones trying to hold the government of the day to account. It wasn't exactly an opposition vacuum, but the Tories were not performing at all well.

That May, Arsenal won the FA Cup Final, beating Newcastle 2–0. I couldn't have gone to Wembley even if I'd had a ticket, which I didn't. I watched the game on TV before going to Heathrow to interview Brits returning from Jakarta. Indonesia was in the throes of very violent riots which would overthrow the government of President Suharto. At least one thousand were killed in the violence, nearly two hundred cases of rape were reported. Some of our returning compatriots had been stuck in the middle of the violent uprising.

We were busy for three days when two British nurses were released from prison in Saudi Arabia. They had been convicted of the murder of fellow nurse, Yvonne Guilford. They faced beheading. After pleas from their families, who had travelled to Saudi Arabia, and pressure from the British government, King Fahd issued a pardon. On the day this was announced, I interviewed the Saudi ambassador in London. Next day, the nurses returned home to Gatwick airport, where there was an enormous bunfight, at least one hundred press photographers and camera crews. We filmed Deborah Parry, her face hidden under a blanket, as she was bundled into a *Daily Express* Range Rover, but we didn't get so much as a glimpse of Lucy McLauchlan as she was spirited away by the *Daily Mirror* in a helicopter. So, I had no choice but to report on the *Express* and *Mirror* stories when they appeared. The BBC's *Panorama* programme got an interview with Deborah Parry which was frustrating for us but we had news access, so her interview made up much of my package on day three of the story.

The following Sunday, I did a story literally from home. Tesco had issued advice to the winners of a World Cup tickets competition on the best place to hide the valuable tickets at home in case of burglars. We needed a house to film in and our house, in Crouch End, fitted the bill perfectly. Cameraman Sid Bray met me at Tesco in Islington for some shots and interviews, then came home with me and filmed Marion hiding a lottery ticket inside a bible. I did a long PTC in our bedroom! Most bizarre.

I covered the visit to Britain of Japanese Emperor Akihito, cut a Ronald Reagan standby obit (he had been ill, but was to live for another six years), and covered a nuclear test by Pakistan.

On the last day of May, I was at Silverstone for a classic car rally. It was a Sunday, a feature piece. I got to drive the circuit, as a passenger, in a Lotus Elan with a professional driver at the wheel. We were only doing a top speed of one hundred and ten miles per hour, but it felt very fast. Formula One drivers must have nerves of steel, or no nerves left at all.

Paul Gascoigne was in the wars again, and I spent three days outside his home doing lives almost every hour. For three days! The press was camped on his doorstep en masse. There were two problems. The *Sun* had paid a lot of money for an exclusive, and nothing was moving, which is a struggle if you have to do a live 'update' every hour with nothing to update. We tried to do a deal with the *Sun* to get them to agree to let me interview Gascoigne. It would have been good publicity on television for them and their story, but they weren't biting. At one point, Gazza came out and gave us all small chocolate footballs! He couldn't say much, he'd taken the *Sun*'s cash, but he did tell me he'd liked my piece earlier. I had joked on air a couple of times that he might be watching Sky News. It turns out he was! A few weeks later, ITV broadcast a documentary about him. It included a shot from his window of me doing a live two-way outside his home with Gazza lying in bed watching it on his TV. He said, "What's he saying about us, like?" We all found this very amusing.

That evening (Gascoigne day three!), ITV ran a rather sordid documentary about conspiracy theories surrounding the death of Diana, Princess of Wales. The next day, I packaged a story questioning the pointless and insensitive media speculation about her death.

After a few days of corporate media training and a day of army media training in Upavon where my students included Brigadier Richard Holmes (already famous as a TV presenter of historical documentaries. He certainly didn't need much help from me!), it was off to Cyprus again for a week.

Once again, Major Ken Molyneux-Carter and I were hosted by Mervyn Wynne-Jones for a week of lectures and media training. Away from work, there were two highlights of the trip. Dinner at the home, the former governor's residence, of the Commander, British Forces Cyprus, General Angus Ramsay. We ate on the veranda, a warm summer's evening. For some reason, the waiters were Sudanese, all pressed whites and silver trays. The chef had worked at Chequers! Great company, excellent food, port and ten-year-old Macallan, and a perfect location to watch the sun go down. The next evening, we went to see a performance of *Othello* at the amphitheatre in ancient Kourion. Sadly, it was pretty bad as the actors playing Othello and Iago simply could not act. But it was still a magical experience to see Shakespeare performed (after a fashion) in such a location.

I had spent half of June working at Sky News and half doing other work, away from the news, but Sky News was gradually beginning to take over my working life, which was good. At the end of June, back to the serious and often grim business of reporting the news. My first two stories after my Cyprus jaunt were an IRA hit and run in Northern Ireland and a devastating earthquake in Turkey.

There was lighter fare to begin July, a preview of a contemporary art auction at Sotheby's. There were some fabulous works by Freud, Bacon, Warhol et al., but also some absolute rubbish at shocking prices. Most astonishing of all was some Italian artist's faeces, apparently sealed in a small tin. The guide price was more than ten thousand pounds!

I did a piece about homelessness in London, a growing problem which is still continuing. We filmed and spoke to people sleeping in doorways and Louise Casey, the head of Tony Blair's Social Exclusion Unit, who the tabloids had dubbed the 'Homelessness Tsar'. Sometime later, when Jeffrey Archer was hoping to run as a candidate in the London mayoral election, I interviewed him about London's homelessness problem, with so many people reduced to sleeping rough. "It's terrible," he began. Yes, I thought, he gets it. "What will tourists think seeing these people sleeping in doorways? We need to get these people out of the way as quickly as possible." I was speechless. Where did one even begin to counter that?

After a week of army Theatre War Games at Bracknell in Berkshire, I covered the story of the Post Office recording record profits and interviewed John Prescott for the first time. He was extolling the virtues of moving mail by rail rather than road. I would interview John Prescott several times in the following years, often with amusing consequences, but he managed to carry out this fairly straightforward assignment without incident.

I had to cover a daft story about Cherie Blair's crystal pendant which supposedly had 'magical powers' according to crystals 'experts', and another on garden safety. Summer stories, as was the return home of round the world micro-light pilot Brian Milton. I did a live commentary as he landed at Brooklands. I had done my research, and just for that moment, knew more about micro-lights than I care to remember. I interviewed Brian and his daughter live into *Live at Five*.

I went to the Public Records office at the National Archives in Kew where SOE (Special Operation Executive) files were being made public after fifty years of secrecy. They included some far-fetched if not utterly fantastical British plots to assassinate Hitler.

John Reid, the Armed Forces minister, made an announcement on First World War deserters who had been shot by firing squad. There were to be no pardons. Instead, an apology and recognition that they too were 'victims' of the Great War. John Reid, by the way, was a heavy smoker. I got to know him better later, when he joined the cabinet. He was terrible at tapping me up for cigarettes, his usual greeting being, "Glen, Glen, got a fag pal?"

There were other silly summer stories, including one on homeopathy and herbal remedies with a PTC at a complementary health clinic in Notting Hill, and another that meant doing a PTC at Tooting lido. In a suit and tie! Then, something altogether sadder.

Seven-year-old Raymond Southall had gone missing from a caravan park at Billing Aquadrome leisure park in Northampton. I was working with Pete Baker, an ex ITN cameraman. A former ITN team was on the case! More than one hundred police officers were searching for the little boy. It ended badly. His body was found two days later. He had drowned. Having become a parent myself, I shuddered at the thought and at what his family must have been going through. A coroner later recorded a verdict of accidental death.

On the first Saturday in August, four stories in a single day. Six IRA prisoners were released, a new weight-loss wonder drug (yeah, yeah!) was being sold for the first time. That was two packages. There was a coach crash on the M4. Fortunately, it was a small coach and almost empty. Four people had bumps and scratches. We scrambled to get there. I had three camera crews in case it was a bad one. They took plenty of good shots. It made just ten seconds of underlay for the news. Finally, that day, we took some pictures in from Cyprus of 19 Regiment RA shot by an army mobile news team. And very good they were too. I packaged them for the evening, with the appropriate picture credit.

Next day, a story I could walk to from home. Honey bees on Hampstead Heath had been infested by parasites. I risked life and limb (well, bee stings) doing lives besides the hives. The north London beekeepers were a jolly bunch, and their Highgate honey is delicious.

Our summer holiday that August was in a remote spot on the west coast of Ireland at Marion's family cottage overlooking Lough Gill, Yeats country, 'The lake Isle of Innisfree'. Maddie was four months old. The aunties all declared her 'a dote'. Maddie had her first solid food. In Ballymote, it seemed every other house was a pub. Marion and I went to one with her cousins, leaving the baby with one of the doting aunts. When we returned, the aunt was feeding a very happy baby mashed potato! Oh, and in the window of the small local supermarket was a handwritten sign which read: *Congratulations Michael. Potato Champion of all Ireland*. I kid you not.

In the Hazel Wood, on the shore of Lough Gill, I recited Yeats' 'Song of the Wandering Aengus', and we visited the neo-classical Lissadell House where Yeats fell in love with at least one of the daughters of Sir Robert Gore-Booth, and where Marion spontaneously sang in the music room to thunderous applause. The entire holiday was very Yeats-centric.

Early September was dominated by the publication of the Starr Report, Ken Starr's hotly-disputed report which would eventually lead to Bill Clinton's impeachment. My tiny role in this saga was to package a profile of Hilary Clinton, a piece on the relationship between Tony Blair and Bill Clinton, reaction from Americans in London, both Democrats and Republicans, and a week later, covering Tony Blair's visit to New York where the Clinton tapes, more than four hours of unedited testimony given by Bill Clinton to the Grand Jury, were released. Clinton was to give a major speech at the UN, which was ostensibly the reason why Tony Blair was in New York, but we knew it was also to support his friend.

The tapes were excruciating, an unbelievable humiliation for an American president to suffer, but there seemed to be few if any grounds for impeachment. That didn't prevent the impeachment, of course, even though Ken Starr later retracted some of his conclusions.

Former Prime Minister Edward Heath launched a verbal attack against new Conservative leader William Hague, not a particularly wise thing to do. It rebounded badly. I interviewed Chris Patten, who had been Conservative Party chairman before his appointment as the last governor of Hong Kong. He told me he had had Sky News on all the time while he had been writing a book in France. What we lacked in audience quantity we more than made up for in quality!

I cut two very different packages simultaneously one Thursday at the end of August, using two editors in separate edit suites at the same time. The South African army (officially the South African Defence Force) had 'intervened' in Lesotho. They had invaded. In the edit suite next door were pictures from a fashion show staged in prison by murderer Tracie Andrews, who was serving life for killing her fiancé by stabbing him more than forty times. That same day, I also cut a piece on a report on doctors' handwriting which concluded that it's often illegible. Shock! Horror! Who knew?!

At Gatwick airport the next day, we spoke to British holidaymakers who had flown home from the Dominican Republic. They had been caught up in a hurricane, Hurricane George. They shared their experiences. I had been in two hurricanes in the Caribbean, Fiona and Victor (why do we give them such innocent sounding names? I can think of a few that would be more appropriate), so I knew what they had been through. My sister was still working in the Caribbean at the time, but was well clear of Hurricane George.

On the last Sunday in September, I was back at Brooklands again (for the last time) and again working with cameraman Mark Williams, filming an exhibition of record breaking fastest cars, including Thrust SSC and Electric Bluebird. A pleasant day out. In the evening, I packaged the German election. Helmut Kohl, who I had covered so much back in 1989, had finally been defeated after sixteen years and four successful elections. The SPD was finally back in power. The new Chancellor, Gerhard Schroeder, was already being called Germany's Tony Blair. He wasn't.

Talking of Tony Blair, his premiership seemed to be going well although, that September, his speech to the Labour Party Conference in Blackpool was, in my view, somewhat platitudinous.

I went to Germany to help the army train spokesmen twice in October. I also gave a talk to a Premier League referee's conference in Birmingham. It was the first time the referees had allowed TV cameras into their conference, and a team was there from Sky News. They filmed my talk, and used part of it in their report. The referees were debating whether or not they should do media interviews after Premier League matches to explain their decisions. I passionately urged them to do so, to explain to fans why they had taken a particular decision. Even if people disagreed with their reasoning, they would at least appreciate an explanation. I went further, and advocated fitting referees with a microphone during games so we could hear what was being said. It works in rugby and American football but, as I write more than twenty years later, neither of these measures has been introduced and Premier League referees continue to be widely ridiculed and almost universally regarded as incompetent.

October also meant covering the BSE inquiry, a package on England football fans fighting the police in Luxembourg, and reporting on the Nobel Peace Prize, awarded jointly to John Hume and David Trimble.

Former Chilean dictator General Augusto Pinochet was arrested in London, the Spanish government was demanding his extradition. I covered the story for several days. Pinochet was placed under house arrest. In March 2000, Home Secretary Jack Straw released him on health grounds without facing trial, even though the House of Lords had decided to extradite him to Spain to face trial for mass murder. Pinochet had 'disappeared', that is murdered, thousands of political opponents and tortured tens of thousands more. He returned triumphantly to Chile where he died in 2006 without ever having been convicted for his terrible crimes.

I started October 23rd covering a daft story from Baltimore, where a schoolgirl was being accused of being a 'witch' (very Salem!) before switching to the Middle East peace talks. There had been a major breakthrough in the talks chaired by President Bill Clinton. Benjamin Netanyahu and Yasser Arafat signed the Wye River Memorandum which was to facilitate the Israeli withdrawal from parts of the West Bank in exchange for guarantees of security, implementing the Oslo Accords. Although the Wye River agreement was popular in Israel, with seventy-five per cent support in opinion polls, Netanyahu delayed implementation to appease opposition from within his Likud Party. The Israeli-Palestinian peace process stumbled on, and is still deadlocked more than twenty years later. The two-state solution seems as far away as ever.

I was back at Old Trafford again at the end of the month. Sky had been trying to buy Manchester United! Sky's bid had been referred to the Monopolies and Mergers Commission. While maintaining impartiality, it was one of those stories where you needed to be extra careful as Sky's most senior executives would be hanging on your every word.

November dawned with media training in Edinburgh and Wiltshire, and a *Question Time* at RAF Bracknell with James Cox of the BBC and David Fairhall of the *Guardian* on the relationship between the media and the military.

We went to the UCL Space Science Laboratory near Dorking for the spectacular Tempel-Tuttle comet and meteor shower, something only seen every thirty-three years. The Royal Navy test-fired its first cruise missile. The ITC (Independent Television Commission) ruled that ITV was indeed permitted to change the broadcast time of ITN's flagship bulletin. *News at Ten*'s days were numbered.

Kate Winslet got married. Hearts were broken. I packaged the pictures. The groom was someone called Jim Threapleton, a film director. She was married in her home town, Reading. I was in London. I never stood a chance!

It had been my fourth story of the day after BSE (speculation that Brussels would lift the EU ban on British beef the following week), a piece on Culture Secretary Chris Smith suggesting (or threatening?) that National Lottery company Camelot would probably lose its licence, and an interview at the British Museum with Angela Salt of the Millennium Commission. Many years later, Angela would become chief executive of the Tony Blair Faith Foundation.

On November the 26th, Britain's last manned lighthouse closed. At North Foreland in Kent, Prince Philip presided over the end of a tradition dating back hundreds of years. Packaging the story provided an opportunity to use some wonderful old black and white footage, a wallow in nostalgia, as lighthouse-keepers receded into our island nation's history.

The unions and management at Rover cars struck a deal after a long negotiation, and the Flying Squad (the Sweeney!) had some very good video of the arrest of two armed robbers. One of them was pointing a gun at police officers who were waiting in ambush as the men robbed a Securicor van outside a bank. The arrests were the conclusion of weeks of surveillance, code named Operation Purvis (unrelated to Stewart!). Described in court the following year as 'professional, ruthless criminals', David Adams and William Harding were found guilty of a string of armed robberies. In one, Harding had shot a security guard in the leg. They were sentenced to life.

In the splendour of the Royal Horticultural Hall, we covered the London Festival of Chocolate. I returned to the newsroom with a display slab of Cadbury's Dairy Milk so huge that we needed a hammer and chisel to break off pieces for my chocaholic colleagues!

Health Secretary Frank Dobson introduced a White Paper aimed at improving residential care homes for the elderly. In Southwark, we covered a meeting of Liberal Democrat dissidents who were concerned that Paddy Ashdown was getting too close to Labour. The FBI released papers alleging links between Frank Sinatra and the Mafia. Scenes from classic gangster movies featured prominently in my packages!

We went to Coventry where Rover workers voted to accept the deal agreed between unions and management two weeks earlier. In Bristol, we interviewed live a group of teenagers after the government said young people were eating too much junk food. *Plus çca change*.

In mid-December, American and British aircraft bombed Iraq for four days in Operation Desert Fox. The allies also launched cruise missiles aimed at Iraq's ability to produce and store weapons of mass destruction. Saddam Hussein had failed to comply with UN Security Council resolutions and was impeding UN weapons inspectors. Had I still been at ITN, I would have probably been sent to the Middle East. Now, as a mere freelancer at Sky, I had the more pedestrian tasks of reporting the effect on oil prices and getting political reaction to the bombing campaign.

The ice cream industry was referred to the Monopolies and Mergers Commission. We went to the Mars factory in Slough to interview the managing director, and returned with boxes of ice cream Mars bars for those newsroom chocoholics. We were very popular!

The final story of the year: Four people were killed in an avalanche on Aonach Mòr, Ben Nevis, with which I was very familiar. It was our lead story, but a very sad way to end the year.

CHAPTER 13

*1999: More Crime and more Politics. Mary Chipperfield. War in
Yugoslavia. Columbine. London Nail Bombs. The Welsh and Northern
Ireland Assemblies. The Beef War. Jeffrey Archer*

January began as December had left off, leading the news reporting a fatal
avalanche. This time, it had happened in Canada, so we relied on Canadian
TV for the pictures. I also reported on national treasure Ernie Wise, who
had been taken to hospital in Florida after two heart attacks in a week. He
survived, but sadly died from heart failure two months later. He was only
seventy-three. I also packaged atrocities in East Timor and the start of Bill
Clinton's impeachment trial in the Senate.

In Portsmouth, we filmed the departure of aircraft carrier MS
Invincible, heading for the Gulf. We covered the event in style. I had four
cameras, three on the ground and one in a helicopter. Back to Westminster
for a farmers' conference and to interview Agriculture Minister Nick
Brown. The farmers were, once again, demanding reform of the CAP (the
EU's Common Agriculture Policy). The big political story that Monday in
January was the potential damage to the career of Foreign Secretary Robin
Cook after his wife's book was serialised in *The Sunday Times*. She was
merciless in her accusations of heavy drinking and womanising.

I followed Home Secretary Jack Straw around a housing estate in
Southall. He was promoting his 'beat the burglar' campaign. British
servicemen who'd been abused in Japanese POW camps during the Second
World War were still campaigning for compensation. I heard their stories of
the atrocities and interviewed Foreign Office minister Derek Fatchett and
Shadow Foreign Secretary Michael Howard, among others. We sent a
package for *Live at Five* before we were sent to the High Court where
boxing promoter Frank Warren had paid seven million pounds to end his

partnership with Don King. I got lucky. We found Frank Warren in a wine bar across the road and he gave us an exclusive interview.

The government issued a damning report condemning conditions and the behaviour of staff at the Medway Secure Training Centre, in effect a prison for 'challenging' teenagers. As I write, the most recent Ofsted report on the centre, in December 2019, condemned pain-inflicting techniques used on children in the centre's care, saying: Children are at risk of harm. So, that report of twenty years earlier doesn't appear to have had much effect.

At the RAF staff college in Bracknell, I gave a lecture followed by a lively Q&A session with my fellow speakers, *Telegraph* defence correspondent, Tim Butcher, and senior BBC executive and former editor of *Newsnight* John Morrison. These sessions were always instructive as they gave me the opportunity to escape the treadmill of twenty-four-hour news and think more deeply about how we report the news.

Foreign Secretary Robin Cook delivered a speech in Swansea, he had survived his wife's revelations. In Kosovo, forty-five people were massacred by Serbs in the village of Račak. I cut a long package for midday with re-cuts every hour all afternoon with political reaction from Paddy Ashdown among others. I was working at Sky's Westminster bureau in Millbank. Sky's teams in Kosovo were doing an amazing job. Nick Pollard and head of operations, Jackie Faulkner, had positioned four satellite trucks in the war zone. By leapfrogging, they were able to keep up with, and sometimes ahead of, British KFOR troops. One of our correspondents would reach a truck, do a live two-way, then move on to the next live-spot at the next satellite truck which had already headed up the road. I would love to have been a part of that outstanding operation. We knocked the opposition for six. I never did get to go to Kosovo.

While Kosovo was suffering, I covered a pig farmers' march in Westminster with a rally in Trafalgar Square, and later the same Saturday, an Elvis Presley concert at Wembley Stadium. This involved a huge video screen showing Elvis in concert with a live band and backing singers. It was rather morbid and somewhat exploitative, but the fans loved it.

In Andover, I covered the trial of Mary Chipperfield of circus fame, or notoriety. We were shown hideous video of her viciously assaulting a young chimpanzee called Trudy, who she repeatedly kicked, kept for up to fourteen hours a day in a small box, and fed on scraps. There were heart-breaking images of Trudy sobbing. There was also video of her husband mercilessly beating an elephant. Chipperfield was convicted of twelve counts of cruelty to animals. Her punishment? A fine of eight thousand five hundred pounds. Personally, I would have sent her to prison for many years. Whenever I see or hear reports of cruelty to animals, I want to see the perpetrators whipped through the streets. I was incandescent. Of course, this was not reflected in my package that day, a dispassionate reporting of the facts. Very, very occasionally, I wished I had gone into politics or become a newspaper columnist rather than chosen broadcast journalism so that I could vent my spleen and say what I really thought. I would have been a hopeless politician, though, unable to dissemble.

Trudy was taken to an animal sanctuary in Dorset to live with a family of chimps, where she was adopted by an adult female.

I had just about calmed down by the next day when we went to interview twenty-six-year-old Scot, Elizabeth Hoff, who was planning to be the first woman to row solo across the Atlantic. Off camera, and in a very friendly way, I told her I thought she was barking mad. She laughed. She was certainly brave, but her attempt ended when she capsized in mid-Atlantic and had to be rescued.

Glenn Hoddle was sacked as England manager. I was at FA headquarters in Lancaster Gate the evening before as rumours spread of his imminent departure. He had been quoted in *The Times* talking about reincarnation and suggesting that disabled people are paying for sins in a previous life. There was a huge clamour for him to be removed. The axe fell the following evening. We were sent to White Hart Lane to vox pop Spurs fans. Hoddle had, in his time, been their most gifted player. I did not wear my Arsenal scarf!

In Belfast, the IRA said that dissidents, the so-called 'Real IRA', had stolen some of their weapons which were due to be surrendered as part of the peace process. In Grimsby I did a day's media training and was heading home when the news desk called to send me to the National Centre for Pop Music in Sheffield. At the West Yorkshire Playhouse, I had the privilege of interviewing live the great actor Ian McKellen once again. He had been nominated for an Oscar for best actor in the film *Gods and Monsters*. I spent half a day following Tony Blair around Newton Aycliffe in his Sedgefield constituency, and persuaded him to talk on camera about Kosovo. He didn't need much persuasion. This was liberal interventionism when it was still working, before the invasion of Iraq.

After days of speculation, including on air by yours truly, Kevin Keagan was appointed the new England manager two weeks after Glenn Hoddle's departure.

Kurdish activists seized and occupied the Greek Embassy in London. They were protesting over the arrest, two days earlier, of PKK leader Abdullah Öcalan by Turkish special forces in Nairobi, where he'd been taking refuge in the Greek Embassy. The Kurds weren't speaking to the media, but because of my experience with the Kurds after the first Gulf War, they spoke to us.

I was back with the Kurds two days later when thousands rallied at Trafalgar Square. This was not only about Öcalan. They felt they had been abandoned by the West. They had been, and are abandoned still despite their sacrifices as our allies in the war against ISIS.

In one day of media training in mid-February, at the Bush House headquarters of the BBC World Service, I did fifteen radio and twenty television interviews. I wondered just who was being exercised! It was my first time back at Bush House since, soon after leaving university, I had done book reviews for the World Service. This involved reading a book, writing a review and then going into Bush House to record it. I did several. They were paying me to read books. Perfect! I had an MA in English Literature and might easily have become a book or theatre critic, but my path was to lead in another direction.

I covered a Cancer Research campaign on children's cancer. At a press conference, the campaign produced parents and children with harrowing stories to tell. The next day, a very different and unrelated combination of cancer and children. First, a story about skin cancer. That morning, Radio Four's *Today* programme had found a seventy-five-year-old woman who had fostered seven hundred and thirty-two children. Seven hundred and thirty-two! I tracked her down and she came on live into Sky News *Live at Five*.

March 5th was spent jumping through hoops. First, an interview with Friends of the Earth on petrol prices as part of a package a week ahead of the Budget. Next, a different kind of war, and EU/US banana trade dispute which became known as 'The Banana War'. Then, a long interview with Lord Derry Irvine, the Lord Chancellor, about Lord Denning who had died at the age of one hundred, part of my obit package.

I sent a message to my former colleague, Trevor McDonald. It was the final night of ITN's *News at Ten* before ITV moved Britain's most popular and successful news programme to a new time slot. Sky News and the BBC were quick to take advantage, the former re-branding their ten p.m. bulletin as *Sky News at Ten*, and the latter moving their nine p.m. news to ten p.m. Two years later it returned, but had to be called ITV (rather than ITN) *News at Ten* before being shifted to ten thirty p.m. in 2004. The programme became known as 'News at When?' or 'news at sixes and sevens'. It was not until 2008 that *News at Ten* again returned to its rightful slot.

In a spectacular display of ineptitude, ITV had irreparably damaged its most successful brand (apart from *Coronation Street*!), and the rebranding from ITN to ITV News (which is what ITN stood for anyway) was, in my view, also a mistake. Apparently it was to reinforce the concept of the 'ITV family', but it further diluted the brand and the perception of quality. If every regional news programme was ITV news, what distinguished the national and international news and the vastly superior ITN programmes?

The Banana War was being waged relentlessly. First, I covered a WTO meeting in Geneva, and three days later, a meeting between Trade Union leader Bill Morris and Tony Blair. In between, Gordon Brown delivered his Budget. There were tax cuts, but also the abolition of MIRAS mortgage tax relief. My modest contribution to the coverage was a package on what the Budget meant for business.

Mid-March, media training English Heritage in the morning, very interesting, and two managers from a regional airport in the afternoon, not so much. Back at Sky, I packaged shots of an oil tanker in trouble off Dunnet Head, Caithness. It still felt odd not to be at the scene on the north coast of Scotland, once my news patch. We went to Wentworth, where anti-Pinochet protestors had gathered outside the house where the Chilean dictator was under house arrest. His fate was still very much in the balance.

The month ended with another week of training the military at RAF Bracknell, against the background of NATO continuing to bomb targets of the Milošević regime and with the Serbs continuing their slaughter in Kosovo.

I spent a week reporting on the NATO bombing of the city of Novigrad. NATO destroyed the city's bridges over the Danube and bombarded the oil refinery, causing widespread pollution. An unknown number of civilians were killed, others injured. The bombing of Novigrad was to continue for more than two months. Civilian areas were attacked. The people of Novigrad had no clean drinking water, electricity or communications. NATO was accused of committing war crimes. They had also hit the Ministry of Education and the local TV station. People in Novigrad could not understand why there were being singled out since the city was governed by the Democratic Opposition which was opposed to the Milošević regime in Belgrade.

A year later, NATO. Secretary General George Robertson claimed that the Yugoslav military had been using civilian buildings which had therefore become legitimate targets. Subsequently, NATO expressed 'deep regret at any civilian casualties'. After two years, the bridges and infrastructure (water, electricity and communications) were re-built and restored with funding partly from the British government. British war planes had contributed to the bombing of the city in 1999. It was not the most glorious chapter in NATO's history.

Teacher Blair Peach had been killed twenty years earlier, in April 1979, during an Anti-Nazi League demonstration in Southall where the National Front was holding an election meeting in the Town Hall. He was hit on the head, almost certainly by a member of the Metropolitan Police SPG (Special Patrol Group). The blow was fatal. There had been several calls for a public inquiry. Now, twenty years on, Home Secretary Jack Straw and Minister of State for Home Affairs Paul Boateng turned down the latest demands for a public inquiry even though they themselves had called for one when Labour was in opposition. Paul Boateng told us that Blair Peach's death had happened too long ago for a public inquiry to be of any benefit.

The previous year, I had covered the bombing campaign of Edgar Pearce, the so-called Mardi Gras bomber. Now, he was on trial at the Old Bailey, where he was found guilty and sentenced to twenty-one years in prison. The next day, I witnessed the unedifying spectacle of Gary Dobson, one of the five men accused of murdering Stephen Lawrence, hosting a phone-in on Talk Radio. It beggared belief. The Anti-Nazi League was demonstrating outside just two days after the Blair Peach decision, although the two events were unrelated, and we were the pool camera inside. After getting shots of the studio through the glass from the control room, I got an impromptu interview with this despicable character who would later be jailed for life for Stephen's murder. Sky ran the interview at full length and, as we were the pool news team, shared it with the other broadcasters. It left a very bad taste in the mouth.

That day also marked the tenth anniversary of the Hillsborough disaster. Ten years! It had flown by. The families of the ninety-seven were still demanding justice.

Although Dunblane had shocked us to our core, in the United States school shootings were becoming almost commonplace. To mark Hitler's birthday, two senior school students at Columbine High School in Colorado murdered twelve school children and one teacher. Eric Harris and Dylan Klebold then killed themselves. At the time it was the deadliest school shooting in US history. Columbine became a byword for school shootings. Bizarrely, some of the blame for the massacre was directed at the heavy metal rock band Marilyn Manson.

Like every other serious news organisation in the world, Sky News sent a large team to Columbine. My modest contribution was a package focussing on messianic, satanic and neo-Nazi cults in the United States. Three years later, Michael Moore's *Bowling for Columbine* won the Oscar for best documentary feature.

I spent three days in late April working solely on the war in Yugoslavia, but packaging from London. On the 26th, we were at Heathrow doing a story about a false alarm (someone had pressed a button which activated an emergency message on a flight from San Francisco, terrifying the passengers!) when we heard the unbelievable news that someone had shot dead the lovely Jill Dando. She had been murdered on the doorstep of her home in Fulham. At the BBC, I did live two-ways and live interviews with Tony Hall, Alan Yentob, Nick Ross and BBC Director General Sir John Birt. Everyone was in a state of shock.

Jill had been killed by a single shot to the back of her head. The following year, Barry George was convicted of Jill's murder, but once some of the forensic evidence had been discredited, he was found not guilty at re-trial in 2008. In the years following, there were many theories about the identity of the gunman, but despite a huge police investigation, Jill Dando's killer has never been found.

I interviewed Milošević at the end of April. Not the Serbian warmonger but a Serb journalist, Branislava Milošević, no relation, who had to live with her now notorious surname.

The April 1999 London nail bombings were particularly vicious. There were three, in Brixton, Brick Lane and at the Admiral Duncan pub in Soho. Each bomb contained more than one thousand four-inch nails in bags that were left in public places. The bombs killed three people, including a pregnant woman, and injured one hundred and forty others, some of whom lost limbs. Our friend Naomi's mother had been among those injured in Brixton and taken to hospital. Thankfully, her injuries were not too serious and she made a full recovery. But the psychological effects are not so easily remedied.

It very quickly became apparent that the bombs were aimed at ethnic minorities and gays. After the Admiral Duncan attack, Scotland Yard held a press conference at which senior officers warned London's 'ethnic communities' that they were at risk. We went to Brixton to talk to people there, and to Stamford Hill to talk to Orthodox Jews and film the high-profile policing. Although the three bombs had targeted black, Bengali and gay Londoners, the Jewish community feared they could be next. Two days later, police arrested a twenty-two-year-old neo-Nazi, David Copeland. The police response had been swift. The following year, Copeland was sentenced to six concurrent life sentences.

The next day, I was at St Thomas' hospital to interview a woman injured in the Admiral Duncan bombing, and also packaged CCTV images released by Scotland Yard, the last pictures of Jill Dando before she was murdered.

Early May saw three separate developments in the Yugoslav war. Britain agreed to take more refugees, Bill Clinton delivered a televised address justifying the NATO operation, and NATO accidentally bombed the Chinese Embassy in Belgrade, prompting anti-NATO demonstrations in China. In between, I put together another obit. Actor Dirk Bogarde had died at the age of seventy-eight.

We were in Edinburgh for the Scottish Parliamentary elections. As with most elections, this was an all-nighter. We managed to get an interview with

Scottish Labour leader Donald Dewar just as he was slipping away for a quick sleep. Everyone else missed him, so we had an exclusive even if only for a few hours. The SNP was making progress, so a PTC at Bannockburn the next day seemed appropriate, next to the statue of Robert the Bruce.

Julie Ward was just twenty-eight when she was killed while on safari in the Maasai Mara game reserve in Kenya. Julie had been in Kenya for seven months photographing the wildlife. Her father, John Ward, had to fight to persuade the Kenyan authorities that his daughter had in fact been murdered and to get them to track down her killers. The horror of this case was that her father found Julie's dismembered remains in the ashes of a fire. The Kenyan authorities had tried to claim that she had been eaten by lions and struck by lightning. I have been to Kenya many times both before 1999 and since, and can well imagine the Kenyan authorities coming up with such nonsense. As her father uncovered further evidence, the Kenyan authorities accepted the situation. They had been trying to cover up the murder to protect the country's vital tourist industry. A Kenyan coroner's report had been altered to say that Julie's body had been gnawed by lions when, in fact, she had been cut with a sharp blade.

John Ward made more than a hundred trips to Kenya. Three people were eventually charged with her murder but were later acquitted. The trial moved from Nairobi to London for two days to hear evidence from a pathologist who was too ill to travel. I covered his testimony at the Kenyan High Commission. He concluded that Julie Ward had been dismembered with a machete, doused in petrol and set alight.

Despite extensive investigations by the Kenyan police and by Scotland Yard over the following years, those guilty of this horrific murder have never been brought to justice.

That May, I spent another week packaging pictures from the war in Yugoslavia, often the lead story, without leaving an edit suite at Sky News Centre. My local chippie, Greek George, said he thought I was in Yugoslavia. I had to explain how it works. No PTC or no Yugoslavia location sign-off meant we were not there. I wished I was rather than slaving away in the picture factory.

Kenneth Noye, the 'road rage killer', was extradited from Spain to face trial in Britain. He was out on licence from prison after being convicted of handling stolen goods from the notorious Brink's-Mat robbery. He had fatally stabbed twenty-one-year-old motorist Stephen Cameron during a road rage incident near Swanley in Kent in 1996. After months of legal argument, he was finally being extradited from Spain. It was not only the police who were waiting for him. We, the media, were also out in force. Welcome home! The murder had captured the imagination of the tabloids. Noye pleaded self-defence, but was eventually convicted of murder and sentenced to life.

We covered a small moment in history when the Queen opened the Welsh Assembly. Dolly the (cloned) sheep was reported to be ageing prematurely. Manchester United paraded their three trophies through the city. As an Arsenal fan, I bit my tongue and reported this triumphant spectacle dispassionately! Two Australian oil workers were jailed in Belgrade for 'spying'. The stories in May were coming thick and fast. I reported on the latest from the Kashmir conflict (I had been there back in my ITN days), more from the Yugoslav war, the IRA revealed the location of unmarked graves of their victims, and we spent a wet and windy day filming an army training exercise on Salisbury Plain which made a filler piece for *Sunrise*.

The new Euro currency was plummeting in value. The Conservatives made hay. Party leader William Hague held a press conference to tell us 'I told you so'. My piece on the European elections that May focused on voter apathy.

The rest of June was spent on holiday in Crete, where baby Maddie was the centre of attention. We met up again with our friend Alison and her nine-month-old daughter, Artemis. We bumped into ITN picture editor Fred Hickey and his lovely wife Irene who were also, coincidentally, in Xania on holiday. We had dinner together which was highly entertaining but our waiter, Theo, plied us with far too much raki (raki rather than ouzo). I staggered back to our hotel blind drunk, which was extremely rare for me, helped by Marion. Next day, we learnt that Fred had been in a similar state.

Angela Frier and Phil Bye got married in the Crypt of St Paul's Cathedral, a privilege afforded those who held a suitable rank or award, in this case Angela's OBE. It was a grand reunion of ITN's finest, an unforgettable wedding, a very special day. It was good to catch up with my old ITN colleagues, almost entirely camera crews and VT editors, the people with whom I had formed such a close bond. Only two other reporters had been invited, Jeremy Thompson and James Mates, so it felt an honour to be there.

The Conservatives were not at all happy with the appointment of the BBC's new director general, Greg Dyke, who was a Labour party donor. As boss of TV-am, he had given the nation Roland Rat, a far worse offence! After a meeting at Conservative Central Office, Greg Dyke, Sir John Birt and BBC Board of Governors Chairman Sir Christopher Bland spoke to us, justifying the appointment. Tory party Chairman Michael Ancram issued a statement. Despite the BBC's assurances, they were still extremely concerned. I've always thought that if the BBC was getting it in the neck from the political left one day and from the right the next, they were probably getting it just about spot on.

After a couple of days of army training in Germany (20 Armoured Brigade, Brigadier Nick Parker and their Bosnian interpreters), a frankly unbelievable story: A hospital in Sheffield had accepted donor organs on condition that they only went to a white person! Racist organs! The story had been leaked to *Newsnight*. They should have kept it quiet until they went on air. We scooped them, as did ITN.

Marks and Spencer was in financial trouble, their share price had fallen sharply. I went to the company's AGM at the Grosvenor House hotel. Their food was popular but their clothing lacked identity and was only appealing to the elderly. Younger people were shopping elsewhere.

The first day of the new Northern Ireland Assembly, July the 15th, was boycotted by the Ulster Unionists. First Minister-elect, David Trimble, was the party's leader. They said they would not take their seats until the IRA de-commissioned all of its weapons. The Deputy First Minister, Seamus Mallon of the SDLP, resigned. The peace process was to be 'reviewed'. It seemed to be unravelling before our eyes.

A week later, the IRA issued a statement lamenting the lack of progress in the Northern Ireland peace process. It felt like a thinly-veiled threat. I was back in Downing Street as Tony Blair held talks with David Trimble and Gerry Adams to urge them to make greater efforts to get the peace process back on track.

Other stories that July included the launch of NHS walk-in health centres (interviews and a PTC at the Department of Health), a government plan to limit the pay of 'fat cat' company directors, and Secretary of State for Work and Pensions and future Chancellor Alistair Darling introduced a package of welfare reforms. I also packaged PMQs, Paddy Ashdown's last as Liberal Democrat leader.

The Tories scraped home in a by-election in Edinburgh, supposedly a safe Conservative seat. I interviewed William Hague and, for Labour, Home Office minister Mike O'Brien. You wouldn't have thought it listening to William, but the Tories were clearly in deep trouble in Scotland.

On the last Saturday in July, I had two packages running in the first ten minutes of the seven p.m. news, both simple voicing of pictures coming into Sky News Centre. CBS had a story that Osama bin Laden was threatening to blow up the FBI headquarters in Washington, and there was yet another atrocity in Kosovo.

I was in Downing Street when Tony Blair delivered a speech on Europe and again, two days later for a government re-shuffle. The cabinet remained unchanged, but we got a lot of new junior ministers. Tony Banks and Glenda Jackson were among the casualties, although Glenda intended to stand as Labour candidate for London mayor. I thought at the time that her chance of success was extremely remote. So it proved, but she remained an MP, my local MP, until 2015.

In August, the government announced plans to speed up the criminal justice system (interviews and a PTC at the Home Office) and there was an Ebola outbreak in Germany. It seemed someone had brought the virus home from the Ivory Coast. The Germans were also dragging their heels over the lifting of the ban on British beef. I also did my first package on the Millennium Bug, a story that would retain our attention until one second after midnight on New Year's Day. For reasons which I couldn't quite fathom, there were dire warnings that everything electronic or digital would return to zero as we entered the new millennium. It was going to be Year Zero. It wasn't.

As expected, Charles Kennedy won the Liberal Democrat leadership contest to succeed Paddy Ashdown. A popular character, Charles saw off four other candidates, with Simon Hughes coming second. It had been a campaign remarkably free of bitterness, rancour or hostility. The main bone of contention was Paddy Ashdown's close relationship with the Labour party. Simon Hughes wanted more distance, Charles Kennedy broadly supported Paddy's position. None of them could imagine for a moment going into coalition with the Conservatives as they did, of course, in 2010. Such a suggestion would have been universally ridiculed.

We watched the total eclipse of the sun from Waterlow Park in Highgate on August the 11th. It was, we were told, to be a once in a lifetime experience. It was a warm, sunny day. Then, eerily, it turned to twilight and then darkness. And it got very cold. For a few seconds, it felt like the apocalypse.

Petrol prices went up sharply. That was a very easy one to do. There was a Shell petrol station at the end of the road from Sky's Osterley headquarters, so a PTC there and some vox pops with motorists made up most of my package. Home Secretary Jack Straw said something about gypsies which was wrongly interpreted as all travellers are criminals. We went to the travellers' site under the Westway at White City. The travellers were suspicious of us at first and slightly hostile, but soon relaxed and we got some good shots, interviews, and a PTC.

On Monday the 23rd of August, Britain exported its first beef after a ban which had lasted for three years. I packaged that, and then George Robertson's elevation to the House of Lords. He was now Baron Robertson of Port Ellen. The same day, I also packaged Jack Straw announcing yet another crackdown on crime.

Into September, and a Mo Mowlam speech on Northern Ireland, followed by an interview with William Hague at Conservative Central Office. I got to go first, ahead of BBC political editor Robin Oakley and my erstwhile colleagues, ITN political editor Mike Brunson and Jon Snow of *Channel 4 News*. Most satisfactory, although in the back of my mind I harboured the suspicion that William might be using me as practice, the warm up act!

I packaged the creation of 16 Air Assault Brigade who, wearing my other hat, I was to media train sometime later. I spent another day with the Premier League referees, this time in the magnificent surroundings of Lilleshall, the National Sports Centre and former home of the Duke of Sutherland, and this time to give them some media training. They were a lively bunch and very friendly, but some were still camera shy. They were still debating whether or not to give interviews after matches to explain and justify their decisions. I positively encouraged them to bite the bullet and do so.

I also spent another two days media training at Upavon with Brigadier Geoff Sheldon, who was to be the next commander of the Falklands garrison, and Tricia Purves, the only female brigadier in the British army. The only one! Later in the month I would spend a week in Munster training the German-Dutch corps. I also spent a day in London training lawyers who were specialists in Internet law. It was as confusing then as it is now. A few days later, I was back in Germany training officers from the Royal Regiment of Wales.

Michael Portillo made two announcements on September the 9th. In the morning, he told us that he had, indeed, had gay relationships while at university but not, he insisted, since. As far as I was concerned, this was no business of mine or of anyone else, but try telling that to the tabloids. In the afternoon, he said he would be standing as Conservative candidate in Kensington and Chelsea, where they weigh the Tory vote (he didn't say that last bit!).

Pinochet was still a story. I interviewed a group of Chilean senators when they came to visit him on the twenty-sixth anniversary of his military coup. They went on the meet him at Wentworth, where he was still under house arrest. APTV provided the pool camera, but tried to claim the pictures as exclusive. After a massive row, the rest of us got their pictures.

Gordon Brown made some disparaging remarks about the 'work shy' which didn't go down well with Labour voters. I packaged that all day. Hull University economics lecturer, Dr Robin Pearson, was exposed as a spy. For twelve years he had been working for the East German Stasi, talent spotting potential British recruits. He had only stopped when the Berlin Wall fell in 1989. Dr Pearson kept me busy all day.

October found me media training, among many others, Premier League referees once again. They were still very reluctant to go on air after matches to explain themselves. We also moved house and began restoring and refurbishing another new home.

Back at Sky, I reported on the French continuing a now illegal ban on British beef. Some supermarkets were boycotting French imports. It emerged that some French farmers had been feeding their own cattle human waste. That did not sound at all credible, but was apparently true.

The next day, a Saturday, we were at McLaren headquarters in Woking waiting for decision on whether or not Ferrari would be disqualified from the previous grand prix, handing McLaren the world championship. Ferrari's disqualification was overturned at a meeting in Paris, so all rested on the last race of the season, the Japanese grand prix. McLaren boss, Ron Dennis, was standing by to hold a press conference. The reporters and cameras were all in position. I had warned the many McLaren press officers who were buzzing around that we would be switching to him live as soon as he walked into the room. He walked in and we switched to him live. Despite my warning to the press officers, he said that the decision from Paris was as he'd expected, reasonable, and no great surprise. I said, "You are live on Sky News."

Then he came out with, "Right, is everyone ready? Cameras rolling?" Before exploding in faux anger, expressing his shock at this appalling and unjustifiable decision from Paris!

After the press conference, I explained to him what had happened. He still had the good grace to hang around for a live interview.

That afternoon, we were in Gosport for the return home of round-Britain wind surfer Richard Cooper. On the way back, I listened to Chelsea 2 Arsenal 3. Chelsea had been 2-0 up with fifteen minutes to go. A Kanu hat trick and a game happily seared into the memories of Arsenal fans.

The *Observer* that Sunday had a story about a small accident at the Atomic Weapons Establishment at Aldermaston. According to the newspaper, there was the potential risk of some kind of nuclear contamination. So, off we went to Aldermaston, scene of the famous CND marches of the past, to get some GVs and do a piece to camera. This led to a row with the police officers and security men guarding the highly-sensitive establishment, but we were well within our rights to film it from the road. We sent a package, but in the end, the story amounted to very little.

We returned to the French farmers' story. With cameraman, Gary Blayer, I was in Calais talking to farmers and local shop keepers about the British supermarkets' boycott of French foods. The next day, the farmers blockaded the Port of Calais. We had ventured into the countryside at first light to get some shots of farms, and specifically, of French cows. When we got back to Calais, the satellite truck crew were set up and ready to go live. As I put in my earpiece, I heard, "Coming to you live in ten seconds". That was tight! One red traffic light on our way back through Calais and we would have missed our first live spot. We did lives for the rest of the day.

With help from a Reuters producer, we found a car park where dozens of tractors and hundreds of French farmers were gathering, along with a huge number of British and French reporters and cameras. We swapped notes with my old ITN pal Bill Neely and the BBC's Jon Sopel before we headed off to the blockade, which provided a lively backdrop for my lives for the rest of the day, burning tyres, lorries sounding their horns, farmers shouting their defiance.

In early November, I was back to covering foreign stories but from London. The Pope visited India. In Columbia a serial killer, Luis Garavito Cubillos, admitted to the rape, torture and murder of one hundred and thirty-eight children. He was continuing to admit to more, possibly as many as three hundred. He was sentenced to one thousand, eight hundred and fifty-three years in prison. I guess in Columbia a life sentence means life, and then some.

There was more media training, including a third session with Premier League referees at Premier League headquarters in Connaught Place, and another attempt to persuade them to do TV interviews after Premier League games. They were lively, funny and articulate, but still extremely reluctant to put themselves into what they saw as the firing line.

We spent a day at Millbank Tower when Labour held a selection board to choose the party's candidate for London mayor. I was live all day. There was supposed to be a press conference at five thirty p.m., but we were kept waiting and doing live two-ways trying to explain the delay. Finally, at eight thirty p.m., a very brief press conference to announce that the selection board would meet again two days later. The issue was whether or not Ken Livingstone would toe the party line and stick to Labour's manifesto. In the event, he wouldn't and stood as an Independent, winning the election the following year handsomely, beating Labour's Frank Dobson and Conservative Steve Norris. Susan Kramer had stood for the Liberal Democrats.

Steve Norris, who came second ahead of Labour and the Lib Dems, had replaced the Conservative's original candidate, Jeffrey Archer, who had dropped out of the race after being accused of committing perjury in a libel trial back in 1987. He was later convicted and imprisoned. In the very early days of the campaign, I had interviewed both Ken Livingstone and Jeffrey Archer in a central London park. What was astonishing was that so many people came up to Livingstone to meet him and tell him they would be voting for him. Not a single person spoke to Jeffrey Archer, even though he was a high-profile celebrity as a bestselling novelist. Not one. If I had doubted it before, which I hadn't, I was absolutely convinced from that moment that Ken Livingstone would become London's first elected mayor.

The Jeffrey Archer story broke two days after Labour had chosen Frank Dobson rather than Ken Livingstone as Labour's candidate. The *News of the World* had the story. It was political dynamite. Archer withdrew his candidacy. I spent the weekend doing packages of epic length and seemingly endless live two-ways. On the Sunday, we got exclusive shots of Andrina Colquhoun, the 'close female friend', Jeffrey Archer's former personal assistant and the subject of the lie during the libel trial which led to Archer's downfall. We also got an exclusive interview with Steve Norris, who was expected to replace Jeffrey Archer as the Conservative candidate. The Archers were at home in Grantchester. They were not going to emerge, let alone talk to the press. What a mess!

Cherie Blair was pregnant. The Blairs were expecting their fourth child. A rarity, a child born to a serving prime minister. It was bitterly cold doing lives in Downing Street. It often is. The street acts as a wind tunnel for the strong gusts coming from the river. We were live every hour and our efforts were rewarded when, during a live at six thirty p.m., the Blairs emerged from Number Ten. Perfect timing.

December was busy as I squeezed in some more media training before Christmas including another regional health authority, more with BG International, the British Library and the Human Genetics Commission chair Helena Kennedy QC, who was now Baroness Kennedy and a consummate media performer who certainly didn't need much help from me.

There was a football riot in Chile and floods in Venezuela to report, and I spent a pleasant evening with the parents of British astronaut, Michael Foale, Colin and Mary, as we waited for a Shuttle launch which was eventually postponed. Michael Foale was to become the second Briton in space and the first to perform a spacewalk, eight hours replacing components of the Hubble telescope.

My final story of the year was another small political explosion when Witney MP Shaun Woodward defected from the Conservatives to Labour.

We welcomed the new millennium from a friend's flat on the top floor of the Barbican's Shakespeare tower. We had fantastic views of the fireworks at first, but after a few minutes, everything was obscured by smoke. Soon, even St Paul's Cathedral became invisible. I hoped this wasn't an omen for the new century! It was still very dramatic, the loud bangs and flashes of colour in the smoke, which seemed an appropriate way to see off the twentieth century.

CHAPTER 14

2000: London Elects a Mayor. MI6 Building Attacked. Meeting Mandela,
in Brighton!

And breathe! The computers didn't crash, all the numbers on everything digital did not reset to zero-zero-zero-zero. Year Zero! The Millenium Bug crawled back to whence it had come. 2000 began like most years, with a stonking hangover. And yes, we did party like it was 1999. Because it was!

On my first day of the year/century/millennium back at work at Sky News, I reported on house prices. Very boring. Then, a company owned by the colourful (and very rich!) senior labour MP Geoffrey Robinson was being investigated for fraud. I had always got on very well with Geoffrey. We were both married to opera singers, so we empathised.

I spent several days at Stansted airport where hijackers were holding one hundred and fifty-seven passengers and crew hostage. I was packaging every hour, which was a slog but better than being tied to the live spot at the airport perimeter in the freezing cold. A succession of reporter colleagues shared that fate. The Afghan Airline plane had been hijacked on an internal flight and forced to fly first to Moscow, then Frankfurt and finally to Stansted. After four days of intense negotiations, the hostages were released. More than sixty of them claimed political asylum in the UK. Nine hijackers were jailed the following year, but in 2003 they were acquitted and they too were given political asylum.

When Frank Dobson was selected to be the Labour candidate for London mayor rather than Ken Livingstone in late February, I went to Wood Green Labour Club in north London to gauge reaction. The general consensus was that this had been a typical Labour Party 'stitch up' (their phrase) with MPs and the unions freezing out grass roots members. They were furious. Quite a few said they would be voting for Livingstone regardless. What really struck me was just how much they seemed to despise Tony Blair. Even at this early stage of his premiership, he clearly had a serious problem with the rank-and-file membership.

I spent another two days doing packages and lives on the London mayoral election, which was still five weeks off, and returned to it several more times over the following weeks.

Bob Ayling suddenly resigned as British Airways chief executive. This came as a surprise, it had not been expected. We had a package on air within the hour with updates all day as I got reaction and we tried to fathom the reasons for his decision to quit. Bob Ayling had been very close to New Labour and was thought to have the ear of the prime minister. In four years in the job he had survived a 'dirty tricks' scandal involving Virgin Atlantic, a bitter and protracted cabin crew strike, and had failed to secure a comprehensive partnership deal with an American airline. BA's share price had been plunging. It surged by twelve per cent on the news of his resignation. It emerged that the BA chairman and the company's board had decided weeks earlier that he had to go. His professional assassination had been plotted for weeks away from the public eye, all very cloak and dagger. The day after Bob Ayling opened his pet project, the London Eye, he tendered his resignation to the Board of Directors and took his family abroad to avoid talking to us lot, the media. It was a swift and rather cruel end to the career of a high-flying executive.

Education Secretary David Blunkett launched the government's city academies in March, private money for inner city schools, very New Labour. I spent another morning walking around a run-down housing estate with Home Secretary Jack Straw, this time in Brixton, and interviewed him again two days later about rural policing. The Lib Dems, meeting in Plymouth, were demanding more police officers in rural areas. And I interviewed him again the next day, this time on asylum seekers. I also interviewed Ann Widdecombe for that story. She and the Conservatives claimed that the Labour government was making a complete pig's ear of the issue.

I had two days packaging foreign stories without leaving the building, once again. Pope John Paul II visited Israel. The FBI sent a reconstruction of the Waco siege, when they had stormed the Texas compound of the Branch Davidians religious cult back in 1993. Seventy-six Branch Davidians had died in the ensuing massacre, including twenty-five children, two pregnant women and the cult's leader, David Koresh. Now, seven years on, a US Justice Department report concluded that the Davidians themselves had deliberately started the large fires which had led to so many deaths. The issue of who had opened fire first in the shoot-out that also claimed many lives remained unresolved, with each side blaming the other.

There were anti-Beijing demonstrations in Taiwan to cover, and Bill Clinton in India on the day of Gordon Brown's Budget, which held few surprises. Income tax was reduced by a penny, stamp duty was increased from three and a half per cent to four per cent but capital gains tax was cut from forty per cent to thirty-five per cent. That was good news for anyone selling a second property, and really not very Labour. The next day, I reported Tony Blair's post Budget statement in which he focused on the increase in spending on the NHS. David Blunkett was doing the rounds explaining how he planned to spend the increased money earmarked for education. The Blair government was living up to its 1997 promise in Labour's election slogan, 'Schools and Hospitals first'.

The *Independent* newspaper was campaigning for the legalisation of cannabis. I got their side of the argument, and spoke to the BMA, who were very much against. I also interviewed the lovely Sue Arnold, *Observer* and *Guardian* journalist, who was slowly going blind due to a hereditary condition, retinitis pigmentosa. Very, very sad.

Conservative party treasurer Michael Ashcroft was elevated to the House of Lords. He was a major Conservative party donor. This was particularly controversial because he lived in Belize as a tax exile. He had joint British and Belizean nationality. Although he was known as a philanthropist, giving millions of pounds to charitable causes, he became the focus of the debate about the transparency and accountability of political funding. Labour and the Lib Dems were up in arms. The Tories were keeping their heads down. The Cabinet Office told us that Lord Ashcroft would give up non-domiciled tax status and take up permanent residence in the UK for tax purposes. In 2017, the leaked 'Paradise Papers' claimed that he was still resident in Belize and not paying full U.K. tax.

I covered the auction for mobile phone franchises, with bids already topping twenty billion pounds. A windfall for Chancellor Gordon Brown. He decided it was most "prudent" (Gordon's favourite word at the time) to use it to pay off some of the national debt rather than spending it on health and education.

We previewed Lord Cullen's imminent inquiry into the previous October's Paddington rail crash. Railtrack and the train operators were, basically, blaming each other. There was a day trip to Southampton with cameraman, Martin Ayling, when the new telephone codes were launched, and a day at the Foreign Office for talks on Zimbabwe.

Then, it was back to the London mayoral election. Four days before the votes, there was some kerfuffle about Ken Livingstone's election expenses. I interviewed him about it. It was a storm in a teacup.

On May Day, 'anarchists' gathered in Parliament Square for their annual demo/punch up with the police. Of course, we were attacked for being 'agents of Murdoch'. Despite saying that they were working for Reuters, cameramen Neil Morris and Tom Radburn were assaulted as they filmed the yobs smashing the windows of the McDonald's in Whitehall. They weren't badly hurt, and got the best pictures of the day. As usual, the main action was in Trafalgar Square, which the police cordoned off. Their tactic of kettling appeared to have worked. A few cars and shops were damaged and the Cenotaph in Whitehall and Churchill's statue in Parliament Square were covered in graffiti, but on the whole, the damage was relatively minor.

Next morning, I did a piece on the clear up operation before switching to the Northern Ireland peace talks, yet again. I also had a background piece running on the London mayoral candidates.

On the night of the London election, which Ken Livingstone duly won, I had two packages running, profiles of Steve Norris and Frank Dobson, and interviewed William Hague and Charles Kennedy. Although some argued that this was only a city-wide election, it had national significance. The election for London's first elected mayor had national implications and resonance.

Secretary of State for Northern Ireland Peter Mandelson made a statement in the House the following Monday. The IRA had agreed to full weapons inspections, promising to hold nothing back. This was the major breakthrough in the talks which had been dragging on, stuck on this all-important issue.

That Saturday, and a story of two demonstrations. Brunel University student, twenty-year-old Ricky Reel, was killed after a night out in Kingston upon Thames. His family was convinced that he had been the victim of a racially motivated murder. Earlier on that evening in 1997, Ricky and his friends had been attacked by a group of white youths shouting, "Pakis go home". Ricky's body was found in the Thames a week later. The police were treating his death as an accident. Worse, the police appeared to be spying on the family who had launched a campaign demanding that the police find Ricky's killer or killers. Scotland Yard disputed this claim, saying they were conducting 'routine enquiries'. The Police Complaints Commission got involved, and there was an internal investigation conducted by the Derbyshire police force.

Now, on this Saturday in May 2000, the family and their supporters were mounting a picket line outside Scotland Yard. I interviewed them and packaged the story for Sky News. A coroner had recorded an open verdict. Scotland Yard's special undercover unit which had investigated the case has since been disbanded, and more than twenty years on, the cause of Ricky Reel's death is still unresolved. His family remains convinced beyond doubt that he was murdered by a racist.

The second protest of the day was an altogether more straightforward affair. People from Sierra Leone, opposed to the British army's (successful) intervention in their country, were demonstrating at the end of Downing Street. This was worth a quick live two-way, and I persuaded the chairman of the Sierra Leone People's Party to go live into *Live at Five*.

Other stories that May included going to the dome in Greenwich. Bob Ayling, who had been sacked as BA chief executive in March, had now also resigned from his position as chairman of the New Millennium Experience company. Foreign Secretary Geoff Hoon made a statement in the house on Sierra Leone, and the government planned to issue a questionnaire to the public asking for ideas for reforming the NHS. It felt like carte blanche for people to moan, a complainers' charter. While it might seem like a good idea, I suspected that people preferred governments that offered solutions rather than one which asked for solutions to be offered. Gordon Brown attacked Oxbridge 'elitism', a story which rumbled on for a week and provided me with more than one lead story. I was also at the Home Office when Jack Straw met his Dutch and Belgian opposite numbers to discuss security ahead of Euro 2000, the European Football Championship, due to be held that year in Belgium and the Netherlands.

I was also still busy media training various clients in London, Edinburgh and Newcastle, with several trips to RAF Bracknell and two days with 45 Commando at Warminster. My partner-in-crime media training the army, Major Ken Molyneux-Carter, was awarded an MBE. Fantastic news.

BA and KLM were in merger talks, Steven Byers tried to introduce a government scheme to limit the price of new cars (how was that anything to do with the government?) and, after Gordon Brown's Mansion House speech, the Conservatives were trying to stir up Labour divisions over joining the Euro. There was some division in the Labour party, but talk about the pot calling the kettle black.

On June the 19th, there was shocking news from Dover. Fifty-eight illegal Chinese immigrants had been found dead in the back of a lorry. My job was to package a political backgrounder, looking at the wider problem of illegal immigration and people trafficking. Twenty years later, this is a problem which is still with us and unlikely to go away any time in the near future. If anything, it is more likely to get a lot worse in the years ahead.

Malcolm Rifkind met Geoff Hoon to ask for the 'gross negligence' finding against the pilot of the Mull of Kintyre helicopter crash in 1994 be reviewed. I interviewed them both and packaged for lunchtime and *Live at Five*. I was covering the Mull of Kintyre disaster again, this time for Sky News rather than ITN.

I did a piece on the North-South economic divide in England (really, nothing changes). In Dundee, William Hague delivered a speech to the Scottish Tories on the same day as the Labour Women's conference in Southport. That made one package, with a PTC from Westminster seamlessly linking the two. Well, almost seamlessly!

A Sunday newspaper had a story that Lord Levy had only paid five thousand pounds in tax the previous year. Known as 'Lord cashpoint', Levy was Labour's most successful fundraiser for many years. He was very close to Tony Blair. In fact, Lord Levy had paid a lot more than the newspaper story claimed. He gave a pooled TV interview. It was abundantly clear that his tax affairs were completely above board and that the newspaper story was nonsense and, presumably, libellous.

Lord Levy was also, at the time, Tony Blair's personal envoy to the Middle East. He was praised by Palestinian President Mahmoud Abbas for always offering constructive suggestions. This was at a time when a two-state solution seemed more feasible than it does today. Now, there is a greater emphasis on a one-state solution, with Palestinians given the right to vote in national elections, freedom of movement and other basic human rights. The concept of a one-state solution is widely regarded as idealistic rather than realistic, but something very similar worked in South Africa and Northern Ireland, so why not in Israel-Palestine?

At the end of June, I went to my first lobby briefing, the meeting of Parliamentary lobby journalists to be briefed by the PMOS (the prime minister's official spokesman). Once I became a full member of the lobby, this was to become a daily routine for me, often very amusing and occasionally hostile (on both sides) as the political correspondents and the PMOS argued about spin. I dubbed them the Downing Street Follies, after the pack of lies of the Saigon Follies of the Vietnam War.

That weekend, Michael Cockerell presented a documentary on Alastair Campbell and his role in Downing Street. I had to package this for Sky News. It only seemed damaging to Alastair in its central proposition that he should be promoting not himself but Tony Blair, who didn't come out of it looking terribly clever. He appeared to be manipulated by his communications chief, which was basically the premise of the film. Entertainingly, they had Bernard Ingham, Margaret Thatcher's former press secretary, huffing and puffing in disapproval.

I covered a meeting of the Shadow Cabinet in July. They were thrashing out the details of their party manifesto for the next election. The Conservatives were already on war footing for the general election expected in 2001. Almost immediately afterwards, I spent two days previewing the government's Spending Review which had been widely leaked and which I covered on the day it was officially announced and, the day after, went to Millbank primary school behind the Tate Britain art gallery and a short walk from our Westminster bureau, to interview Education Secretary David Blunkett. Home Secretary Jack Straw made a statement in the commons, and I packaged how government spending would focus on education and fighting crime. John Prescott unveiled a ten-year transport plan.

Jack Straw's car was stopped doing one hundred and three miles per hour on the M5. His Special Branch driver was at the wheel. This was our lead story. I did a live two-way when the story broke, during which the presenter rather randomly decided to ask me about the G8 Summit happening in Tokyo. The summit seemed to me to be pretty pointless and achieving very little, and I said so. It emerged later that French President Jacques Chirac had been incredibly rude to the US Secretary of the Treasury Larry Summers, snoring loudly and theatrically while Summers was speaking.

Clause 28, or Section 28, was a law introduced by the Thatcher government to ban the 'promotion of homosexuality', specifically in schools. The Blair government was determined to repeal it, and eventually succeeded in doing so in 2003, but that July in 2000 the government was again defeated in the House of Lords, even though the law had just been repealed in the new Scottish Parliament. I covered the predictable fallout and reaction from the NUT, Stonewall and others, and packaged our lead story. It was also, incidentally, the main reason why Shaun Woodward had defected from the Conservatives to Labour the previous December.

The Neill committee on Standards in Public Life called for a limit on the number of government Spads (Special Advisors). I interviewed Lord Neill and Mo Mowlam, who said that the government would accept the committee's recommendations. That didn't last, there are now more of them than ever.

At the end of July, I was doing lives in Downing Street as Tony Blair had talks with Irish Prime Minister Bertie Ahern. The lives went well, but only because I had got my colleagues from the Irish press to fill me in on the very latest developments and on what Ahern would be saying.

August 1st, and another committee report, this time a House of Commons select committee condemning the spiralling cost of the dome at Greenwich. I packaged that story before being diverted to Downing Street to do lives because Tony Blair had decided to allow a photo-op of his family holiday in France, reversing the decision of the previous day. This didn't seem that interesting, but the media, including Sky News, got more excited (and excitable) as the evening wore on. Also that evening, millionaire Conservative and gay rights campaigner, Ivan Massow, defected from the Conservatives to Labour over the issue of Clause 28. He later returned to the Tory fold, saying he had known that his defection would make front page news and that he wanted the Conservatives to focus on repealing Section 28.

ITN launched its ill-fated twenty-four-hour news channel to rival Sky News and the BBC. It looked cheap, was irritatingly repetitive (it was deliberately designed to be watched for just twenty minutes before repeating the same stories) and was generally unconvincing. To me it seemed that ITN felt it needed to have a twenty-four-hour news channel to be in the game, but its heart wasn't really in it and it wouldn't or couldn't properly resource it.

The next day, and another select committee report, this time on pensions. Not very sexy, but I cut a package which ran all evening. This was somewhat overshadowed by the news that Gordon Brown was getting married. The very next morning! It was supposed to be a secret, but it had leaked, the matrimonial equivalent of a Budget leak. Gordon's wedding to Sarah Macaulay, a quiet, family affair at his home in Queensferry, witnessed the unedifying spectacle of a huge media scrum at the gate. Eventually, a photo-op was agreed, and a hundred reporters, photographers and camera crews poured up the gravel drive. The newly married couple were beaming, but this was probably the last thing they wanted. "A kiss, please," shouted the hacks.

"Is this the happiest day of your life?" shouted one. No response. There was a written statement later, saying that they had had 'a wonderful day'. They might have added 'except for you horrible lot turning up uninvited'. The joke doing the rounds was that Gordon had ditched Prudence and married Sarah.

I spent two days media training the National Union of Students, of which I had once been a leading member in Scotland. I was looking out for future political talent.

Just before going on holiday, I had a strange day which began at Buckingham Palace where there had been an intruder alert (it was a false alarm) and ended with an EU ban on the imports of British pigs and pork. There had been an outbreak of swine fever in East Anglia. Tens of thousands of pigs were subsequently slaughtered. At the time, it was feared that the outbreak could become as serious as BSE had been for British beef, but the swift if draconian response by the Ministry of Agriculture had the desired effect.

In late August, we moved home again, to a beautiful house, formerly the village doctor's home, in Stroud Green, north London. I was also very busy media training various clients to pay for the renovations we were planning.

We took our family holiday that summer in Tunisia, a mix of excellent hotel, fine beaches and culture. We did the tourist stuff like a horse and carriage to the oasis at Nefta, a paradise, and camel rides in the Sahara. Maddie, who was now two years old, fed milk from a bottle to a baby camel. Photo-op! In Tunis Medina, all three of us were enchanted by the heady mix of colours, sounds, scents and people. Other cultural highlights included the Bardo museum and the UNESCO World Heritage Centre at Dougga, with its Roman forum, capitol, temples, fabulous amphitheatre, baths, and er, brothels. There are still glimpses of the pre-Roman city of the Numidians. We visited the ruins of Carthage and the incredibly impressive colosseum at El Djem, the second largest after the colosseum in Rome and where the scenes in Ridley Scott's *Gladiator* were shot.

Maddie was proving to be an excellent traveller. Despite the heat, strange food, irregular sleep and constantly getting in and out of coaches and cars which might have reduced many two year olds to tantrums of indignant rage, she smiled and laughed her way through it all. The Tunisians loved her.

While we were away, we had missed the news, deliberately, but now I caught up. There had been strikes and blockades over petrol prices, the country had been virtually at a standstill, the government was in crisis. Friends described fights breaking out at petrol stations. Although as a journalist this would have been a great story to cover, it also felt like the perfect time to be out of the country.

Once back at work, I was covering the petrol shortages. Fights were still breaking out at petrol stations. The Tories were claiming they would cut petrol tax by three pence a litre. A rather extravagant claim, but I guess the job of the Opposition is to oppose. No sooner had we finished editing for *Sky News at Ten* than news came in of an explosion at MI6 headquarters in Vauxhall. I walked there as the police had closed Vauxhall Bridge to traffic. I did a long phono (a live on the phone, we didn't yet have a satellite truck nearby). There were no flames, no smoke, no immediately visible signs of any damage. I talked to eyewitnesses. There was nothing official from Scotland Yard, but we eventually saw and filmed the damage to the eighth floor of the south side of the building which is known, without any great affection, as 'The Lubyanka'. It slowly emerged that the building had been hit by an RPG (rocket-propelled grenade). No one had been injured. It was the work of the so called Real IRA.

The damage had been only superficial, the building was bullet proof and bomb proof (supposedly. I guess that depends on the size of the bomb!). What was most striking about this particular terrorist attack was not only the target but also that it had been the first time Irish terrorists had used a rocket launcher. At first, it was suspected that the dissidents had somehow got it from the IRA's arsenal, but it later emerged that the Russian-built launcher had come from former Yugoslavia.

To Brighton for the Labour party annual conference. I gave up my room in Brighton to a producer, Lizzie Downton, who was doing early shifts all week. I was working ten a.m. until ten p.m., so I stayed in nearby Worthing, which seemed only fair. The arrangement was really to my advantage as I stayed in a proper hotel in Worthing rather than a B&B in Brighton.

I previewed Gordon Brown's speech the evening before and doorstepped him the next morning for what became a kind of impromptu mini press conference, and was in the hall when he delivered it. It was passionate. Later that day, there was a bomb alert at Brighton station which came to nothing. We still had to rush there, hard on the heels of the police, just in case.

There was also a farmers' demonstration that day. I packaged all afternoon, and got the lead story for *Sky News at Ten*. It was a ridiculously late night. I got to bed at two thirty a.m. after far too much Guinness, Glenlivet and gossip, which is par for the course at party conferences.

I covered Tony Blair's speech the next day. A passage about his 'irreducible core' was very well received, although I thought it was a bit corny. Overall, it was an impressive performance, calm and authoritative. Less passion than Gordon Brown's, it nevertheless trumped it, as would become the pattern over the next few years. The tabloids, however, focused on how much Tony Blair was sweating!

We did the round of parties that evening. With Adam Boulton, I went to the ITN party (Adam was invited, I wasn't!) which was boring despite a few (but only a few) familiar faces. Bermuda next door (the Bermuda Tourist Authority party) was infinitely better. Tony Banks was somewhat the worse for wear! The British Airports Authority party was even more generous. Des Wilson, one of the founders of the homelessness charity Shelter, former President of the Liberal Party, and now my neighbour at our new house in Stroud Green was doing the PR. Excellently, of course.

In Belgrade, meanwhile, street protests against the Milošević regime were growing in numbers and intensity. Tony Blair was calling for Milošević to go, saying Britain would hold out the hand of friendship to the Serbs if they embraced democracy. It felt like the end for Milošević, and so it was. Just over a week later he was gone.

I spent the next day doorstepping Tony Blair, various trade union leaders, Labour NEC (National Executive Committee) members and so on, and interviewing Alistair Darling, Barbara Castle and others. The main debate was on pensions. The unions wanted earnings-related pensions, the government said we couldn't afford it. The unions won the vote, though the chances of it ever becoming government policy were zero. I packaged the story for *Sky News at Ten*

I finally met Nelson Mandela! He was the conference's guest speaker. I was in awe, and as excited as anyone. Now the ex-president of South Africa, all I could think of to say to him was to tell him he was an inspiration to the world. He thanked me politely and moved on. He must have heard it a thousand times before. I never had the opportunity to interview Mandela, but simply meeting him was a thrill. Undoubtedly, and by a huge margin, the highlight of the week.

I returned to Brighton the following Sunday, a warm and sunny day, this time for a family day out. First stop was lunch on the seafront, then the pier (rides for Maddie), then the Royal Pavilion, which Marion had never seen. It was such a different experience of Brighton without the politics or the pressure of deadlines.

Back in London, I covered the launch of the Human Rights Act, our lead story all day and all evening. Vojislav Koštunica succeeded Milošević as president of Yugoslavia. He was to be that country's last president, although he went on to serve two terms as prime minister of Serbia. I interviewed Foreign Secretary Robin Cook live from the Foreign Office, and put together a profile of Koštunica for *Sky News at Ten*. I was live again with Robin Cook the next day, this time at Chevening, the beautiful country retreat of the Foreign Secretary.

Seven Tory cabinet ministers admitted to smoking dope when they were young. No big deal except that Ann Widdecombe had just launched a policy of 'zero tolerance' which meant that if that policy had been law when they were young they would all quite possibly have criminal records. Along with half the country! I interviewed William Hague and packaged all day for our lead story.

Among the guests at Sky Millbank one Sunday in October was Russell Watson, the new 'opera sensation' who had sung at Wembley Stadium the day before and was selling a lot of albums. Always on the lookout for an opportunity for Marion, I chatted to his manager, Perry Hughes. After sending him a CD of Marion singing and some photos, she went to meet them and the upshot was that she was the support act and partner for duets for his first full UK tour, starting at the Bridgewater Hall in Manchester.

The much-admired and popular First Minister of Scotland Donald Dewar collapsed and died in Edinburgh. Although he had had a heart condition, he had suffered a massive brain haemorrhage. He was only sixty-three. I'd interviewed and chatted to him many times when I had been ITN Scotland correspondent, and most recently, at the Labour Party conference in Brighton just two weeks earlier. He was always warm and friendly, thoughtful, considerate and very knowledgeable. I interviewed Charles Kennedy, William Hague live at Conversative Central Office and Tony Blair live in Downing Street. It was my first time ascending the famous staircase with the photographs on the wall of past prime ministers. It was also a good opportunity to compare the performances of the three party leaders. Blair and Kennedy had known Donald Dewar for many years. I thought at the time that Tony Blair was just about spot on if slightly hammy, Charles was sincere and delivered very good soundbites, but William was all over the place.

In 2000, we had already also lost Sir Stanley Matthews, Ian Dury, Robert Runcie, Sir Alec Guinness, and the indomitable Sir Robin Day. Gangster Reggie Kray had died ten days before Donald Dewar.

The next day, the Israeli military attacked a Palestinian police station in Ramallah after claims that Israeli soldiers had been 'lynched' by a mob. Former Israeli Prime Minister Simon Peres, one of the handful of Israeli politicians I admired, came into Sky News Millbank to do a live interview. The BBC, who lived on the floor below Sky News at 4 Millbank, were desperate to get him on air first, before us, tried to intercept and poach him on his way in. They failed. With Israel in a state of some turmoil, we also got the Israeli ambassador to come in for a live. The BBC tried it on again and, I'm happy to say, failed again.

The second half of October was busy. Geoffrey Robinson accused Peter Mandelson of lying about the home loan affair in his memoirs, which were being serialised in the *Mail*. Back in 1998, both had resigned from the cabinet after Robinson gave Mandelson an interest free loan of three hundred and seventy-three thousand pounds to buy a house in Notting Hill even though Robinson's business affairs were, at the time, being investigated by Mandelson's department. Peter Mandelson said he had deliberately NOT got involved in his department's inquiry. However, he had failed to declare the loan in the Register of Members' Interest. Peter Mandelson had bounced back after ten months out of the cabinet, replacing Mo Mowlam as Northern Ireland Secretary.

Now, the issue was back. I interviewed Geoffrey Robinson, who was indignant. Although he weathered the storm, Peter Mandelson had to resign from the cabinet for a second time just three months later, in January 2001, after accusations that he used his position to influence a passport application for an Indian businessman, Srichand Hinduja.

Prince William visited Chile. There were good pictures, so I packaged them with a PTC at Buckingham Palace for eleven a.m., midday and one p.m. I tried to get sponsors Raleigh International for an interview, but the people there were reluctant. Apparently, the pictures had not been 'sanctioned'. They had been grabbed by Chilean TV. The Raleigh International people thought they might get into trouble with the Palace if they were seen to condone the use of the pictures. It emerged that we were in breach of a voluntary media agreement not to film what was supposed to be a private visit. A memo from Sky Head of News Nick Pollard instructed all of us not to use the pictures again.

By then, our focus had shifted to Hatfield where a train had derailed killing four people and injuring more than seventy others. We were live on that accident for the rest of the day. It very quickly became a political row with claims that Railtrack, the privatised national railway infrastructure company, had not been maintaining the tracks properly. The tracks were cracked due to something called 'rolling contact fatigue'. Replacement rails had been made available the year before the accident but were never installed. Railtrack was subsequently replaced by Network Rail, and five years later, was found guilty of breaking health and safety laws.

All of the UK's hunter-killer submarines were recalled for tests after HMS Tireless developed a leak in its nuclear reactor primary cooling circuit. It was basically a cracked pipe somewhere where you really do not want a pipe to crack. I spent all afternoon doing lives outside the Ministry of Defence, where we were repeatedly assured that the recall was purely precautionary and 'nothing serious'. It seemed bloody serious to me!

The government agreed a multi-million-pound compensation package for people who had suffered from CJD, the human variant of BSE, and for the families of those who had died from the disease. Two days later, a three-day stint covering Lord Phillips' report on the BSE crisis. The Blair government said paying compensation was a moral responsibility regardless of whether or not the report would find the government liable for the BSE crisis.

Lord Phillips' report on the BSE crisis concluded that it had been too complex and too prolonged to blame anyone or any particular decision. However, it was critical of a succession of Conservative agriculture ministers. More than anyone, John Gummer had played down safety concerns when, in May 1990, he was filmed feeding a beef burger to his four-year-old daughter to illustrate that beef was safe to eat.

As an aside, when Britain won gold at the Olympics for shooting in the 'small bore prone position', one of the newspapers had a front-page headline, Small Bore Prone Position, next to a picture of John Gummer and a totally unrelated story. This was simply too good not to stick up on the newsroom wall.

It was one of my favourite front-page headlines, along with the *Sun*'s 'Up yours Delors'. So too was the clever play on words back in 1992 when President George Bush senior was sick during a banquet hosted by the

Japanese prime minister. He had fainted after vomiting all over Prime Minister Miyazawa's lap! His vice-president at the time was the not overly bright Dan Quayle. The *Independent*'s headline: Bush sick, America quayles. Best of all, though, was the *Sun* splash in February 2000 when Celtic suffered a shock 3–1 defeat at the hands of Inverness Caledonian Thistle, a team, according to the *Sun* that 'no one had heard of or could even spell'. Sun sub-editor Paul Hickson came up with this genius headline: Super Cally go ballistic Celtic are atrocious!

Gummer's successor at agriculture, Douglas Hogg, who had been the public face of the BSE crisis in John Major's government was criticised for being too slow to act but emerged largely unscathed despite our frustration at all those times that he'd refused to talk to us and seemed to be hiding his face under his wide-brimmed hat.

Stephen Dorrell, health secretary from 1995 until the 1997 general election, was criticised for insisting that beef was safe to eat just months before the link between BSE and the human variant CJD was officially confirmed, and his Department of Health was accused of 'inertia'.

I reported on all this, and we got exclusive figures from the National Farmers' Union on the economic cost of the crisis and the number of jobs they claimed had been lost. Overall, the inquiry concluded that there had been a degree of incompetence and a culture of secrecy at the Agriculture Ministry (MAFF, the Ministry of Agriculture, Fisheries and Food), but there were no 'villains or scapegoats', much to the disappointment of the assembled press.

Betty Boothroyd became something of a legend as speaker of the House of Commons. When she retired, MPs elected her successor. The new speaker, Michael Martin, was elected on October 22nd. He won easily. There were twelve candidates. This involved eleven rounds of voting, with speeches every time from the candidates, their proposers and seconders. Many backbenchers were also determined to have their moment of glory. The standard of debate was feeble. A ballot followed by a runoff between the two leading candidates would have been so much quicker, but eighty-four-year-old Father of the House Edward Heath was determined to conduct the election by the traditional method, despite the number of candidates. It would have been very difficult to change the rules at the last minute, but MPs had had all summer to work something out. I packaged from three p.m.

until ten p.m., then had a short break before the ceremonial nonsense (Black Rod presenting the new speaker of the Commons to the House of Lords) at eleven thirty p.m. I was live and with a hot-rolled package from Millbank into the midnight news. It had been a tiring and at times tiresome day, but also amusing if just a little Ruritanian.

Gordon Brown announced new funding for inner-city regeneration. He did it in Canning Town, and I travelled on the new Jubilee line, all steel and concrete, very modern, though I thought it looked unfinished. Not to miss out on a photo-op, William Hague and several shadow cabinet ministers toured an inner-city housing estate. Useful pictures for my package, though they really did look like fish out of water.

Ofsted reported that black children were under performing at school. For my package, I interviewed the report's author, Nigel de Gruchy, of the NAS/UWT, Trevor Phillips and Baroness Blackstone. The arguments then, twenty years ago, were precisely the same as they are now.

Fuel protesters were planning a slow-moving lorry convoy from Jarrow to London, aping the Jarrow Crusade. I found this ridiculous, and something of an insult to the Jarrow marchers of 1936 who had suffered genuine hardship and extreme poverty. Gordon Brown and Michael Portillo clashed over tax and spend. The Tories were claiming they could both cut eight billion pounds from public spending and yet spend more on public services. I thought at the time that this did not sound credible and that the voters would not believe it. I wasn't wrong.

In November, a pensioners' protest with a rally at Westminster Hall. Tony Blair and Gordon Brown posed for pictures with assorted pensioners, while Tony Booth (Blair's father-in-law) gave a marvellous ranting speech. There was an attempted diamond heist at the dome. Diamonds worth three hundred and fifty million pounds. It would have been the world's biggest robbery, but Flying Squad officers were lying in wait for the villains. It was like an episode of *The Sweeney*, only better. "Put the diamonds down, son, you're nicked!"

On the same day, George W Bush won the 'hanging chads' presidential election in the United States, beating Al Gore who had won the popular vote. It was one of the closest presidential elections ever. I would love to have been in Washington. As it was, I was glued to Sky News and CNN all night. The BBC called it wrongly. The 'results' the BBC announced were, in fact, exit polls from the US networks who had got it totally wrong. It all hinged on Florida which was 'too close to call' (the phrase of that election), and there would need to be a recount.

John Prescott held a 'rail summit' in Downing Street. This involved the usual, standing in the gutter (we know our place!) opposite Number Ten for hours in the freezing cold before Prescott emerged and took some questions. He was in the invidious position of defending the privatisation of the under-performing rail companies. A few days later, Railtrack's Chief Executive Gerald Corbett resigned. Little changes. As I write, a few months ago my local rail company had a partial strike. My local platform was packed. There was a station announcement saying that, due to the strike, first class was suspended for the day. Excellent, I thought, more space for people in what was clearly going to be an overcrowded train. It arrived. They had simply locked the empty first class carriages. We were packed in like the proverbial sardines. I thought the company, already generally providing a poor and unreliable service, should have lost its franchise for that piece of stupidity alone. It didn't, and it still hasn't.

The creation of the European Rapid Reaction Corps was controversial because it was seen by some as the precursor to a European Army, a debate still raging today. France admitted to having cases of BSE, and the next day, Germany admitted it had two cases of infected cows. There were strident calls for a ban on French imports. KFC was planning to create ten thousand new jobs, and Domino's Pizza was also creating thousands of new jobs. I went to Domino's Pizza in West India Dock to interview the company's chief executive. He turned up an hour and a half late and was greeted by a grumpy and hungry reporter and crew. We hadn't been offered even so much as a slice.

There was more BSE to cover, the Queen's speech, and further arguments over the future of Britain's rail network. I previewed a speech by William Hague on proposed Conservative tax cuts the evening before he delivered it, interviewing Oliver Letwin and Alistair Darling for my package. The next day, I covered the Hague speech and a Gordon Brown speech on tax policy which was clearly designed to upstage the Tories.

The House of Commons Transport select committee slammed Railtrack's incompetence (tell us something we don't know!), which made a package. So too did an argument over fish quotas, with interviews with Fisheries Minister Elliot Morley and shadow agriculture minister Tim Yeo.

On the day my fishing quota story was running, Al Gore conceded the US election. George W was President-Elect. The reaction of the left in Britain varied from 'farce' to 'corruption'. William Hague gave a speech on crime and police morale, which he claimed was suffering under Labour, and I attended the lobby briefing again for some fairly low-key Alastair Campbell spin.

At the Home Office, I interviewed minister Charles Clarke on a crackdown on motoring crimes, and had to chase Culture Secretary Chris Smith on the announcement that Richard Branson had failed in his attempt to win the franchise to run the National Lottery. It had been re-awarded to Camelot which, at the time, seemed incredible given their recent track record.

Fox hunting was a political hot potato. I packaged pictures and interviews from the Fernie Hunt in Leicestershire, and a pro-hunting demo. which marched on Parliament. This was a demo the like of which I had never seen. They sang the national anthem and gave three rousing cheers for the police!

I also packaged the last PMQs of the year, and just before Christmas, did a one-to-one interview with Tony Blair at Coram's Fields which was a pooled interview shared with ITN and the BBC. Right before Christmas, Labour held on in a by-election in Falkirk West, but only just. Labour's Eric Joyce won with a majority of just seven hundred over the SNP, down from the thirteen thousand majority enjoyed by his predecessor Dennis Canavan who had resigned from Westminster to become an MSP at Holyrood. Canavan had been very popular in his constituency, but the real story was the onward march of the SNP, a taste of things to come.

I finished the year doing a piece on the markets, a year-end performance review (they were all down compared to the previous year), and the failure of various dot com companies. At the time, dot com was a relatively new phrase, a new concept, at least to me. My final story was to report on Tony Blair's New Year message, which was overshadowed by a row over an anonymous two million pound donation to the Labour Party. Sizeable donations were supposed to be transparent and reported.

CHAPTER 15

2001: Another Labour Landslide. More Bovine Carcasses. 9/11

I drove to Sky News Westminster bureau in Millbank ludicrously early on January 2nd. Prostitutes were still plying their trade on Caledonian Road at five o'clock in the morning. I picked up where the previous year left off: Labour's mystery two million pound donor. The pressure was on to name the donor. I cut packages all morning, and again all afternoon once the identity of the donor was finally released. It was millionaire publisher Paul Hamlyn. Two days later, Labour revealed that it was receiving another four million pounds, half from Lord Sainsbury and half from Christopher Ondaatje. This time, the party offered the information freely, although *The Economist* had the names and was about to publish them. The Conservatives said the donations revealed that Labour relied on a small number of very large donors. As with divisions over Europe, the words pot, kettle and black again sprang to mind. Labour said forty per cent of its funding came from individual donations, thirty per cent from trade unions, twenty per cent from large single donations and ten per cent from commercial activities.

The row over the cost of the Millennium Dome was also continuing. I interviewed PY Gerbeau, the dome's chief executive. It was announced that the Millennium Stadium in Cardiff would host the FA Cup Final while the new Wembley Stadium was being built, so I did a PTC at the venerable old stadium with its famous twin towers before it was demolished.

The Department of Health reported on serial killer Harold Shipman, who had been sentenced to life twelve months earlier for the murder of fifteen of his patients. Now it was revealed that he might have killed at least two hundred and fifty and possibly more than three hundred, mostly elderly women. I did lives at the Health Department. Three years later, Shipman hanged himself in his cell at Wakefield prison.

There was still no date for the general election, but early in January, Tony Blair was pelted with tomatoes in Bristol, William Hague launched a poster campaign, Charles Kennedy was firing up the Lib Dem troops. The early election skirmishing had already begun.

A few days later, William Hague made a speech supporting the new American missile ballistic defence shield ('son of Star Wars'). It was untried, untested and would cost forty billion dollars. I packaged that with reaction from Iain Duncan Smith (for) and Menzies Campbell (against) and a PTC at the Ministry of Defence.

MPs finally voted to ban fox hunting by three hundred and ninety-nine votes to one hundred and fifty-five, and also rejected a proposal to allow licenced hunting. I did a piece on the continuing sanctions against Iraq, ten years since Saddam Hussein had invaded Kuwait precipitating the first Gulf War. Ten years! Where had they gone? Tony Benn addressed a rally of anti-war protestors in Trafalgar Square. Tony Blair made a speech on inner-city regeneration before we went with him on a walkabout around a housing estate in Stepney. Not only Blair but also John Prescott, Alistair Darling, Stephen Byers and Mo Mowlam. I cut several two-minute packages. I had so much material I could easily have filled half an hour.

I had a six-minute package running a week later, a very long piece even for Sky News. Peter Mandelson had resigned from the cabinet for the second time. As so often, it was not the original misdemeanour or indiscretion but the subsequent attempt to cover it up which had led to a ministerial resignation. He had got Chris Smith to unwittingly lie for him and had misled Alastair Campbell, a very big mistake. The issue was passports-for-favours for the Hinduja brothers, sponsors of the dome. The Curse of the Dome had struck again! At lunchtime, Mandelson emerged from 10 Downing Street and announced his resignation. We had been waiting in the freezing cold street for two hours since the eleven a.m. Lobby briefing at which Alastair Campbell had said that the situation was still unresolved, hardly a ringing endorsement. We correctly took that to mean a resignation was imminent. Peter Mandelson blamed the media, which was a bit rich coming from him, but it later emerged that he had not, in fact, helped Srichand Hinduja's application for a British passport or made any representations on his behalf. Before he resigned, Peter Mandelson took Northern Ireland questions in the House for the last time and sat next to an exhausted-looking Tony Blair at PMQs. It was the most memorable image of the day. Blair paid tribute, Hague stuck both boots in.

There was still no election date although we expected it to be in May, but on January 25th Labour unofficially lit the blue touch paper. I had begun the day at the Home Office for a briefing on asylum seekers. The annual figures were up, but all they wanted to talk about was the fall in numbers month-on-month for December. I interviewed Minister of State for Asylum and Immigration Barbara Roche (who was also, at that time, my local MP), Ann Widdecombe for the Tories, a spokesman for the Refugee Council, did a PTC at the Home Office and packaged for lunchtime. Then, in the evening, Labour delivered a booklet, *The Choices for Britain*, to be delivered to all party members with a personal message from Tony Blair urging them to counter voter apathy. Labour felt that the Conservatives were somehow trying to persuade voters not to bother to vote, believing that the Tory core vote would turn out and was much more reliable than the Labour and especially Liberal Democrat cores, which many believed were soft. *The Choices for Britain* sent a clear signal: the general election starts here.

The Mandelson affair continued. It was rather stupidly dubbed 'Mandygate' by the tabloids. Whatever the subject of my live two-ways, for more than a week there was always a question thrown at me about Peter Mandelson. The focus shifted onto Leicester East MP and Minister of State for Europe Keith Vaz. Had he helped the Hinduja brothers with their passport applications? In a Commons written statement, Barbara Roche revealed that Vaz had contacted the Home Office to ask when the Hinduja brothers could expect a decision on their applications. Vaz had known the brothers for several years. By now, Tony Blair had asked Sir Anthony Hammond QC to carry out an inquiry into the whole affair. The Tories, using Parliamentary privilege, claimed Vaz was guilty. We had to be far more circumspect as we reported the story. Later, in March, Vaz admitted that he had made representations on behalf of the Hinduja brothers and others. In the government reshuffle after the general election he was sacked or stood down from (versions vary) his position as Europe minister.

Peter Mandelson was in his Hartlepool constituency a few days later and gave his first interview since his downfall, to BBC Radio Cleveland. He planned to stand again in Hartlepool in the general election. He did so, and won with a handsome majority. Before the election, in March, he had been exonerated by the Hammond Inquiry's report.

William Hague and Michael Portillo held a press conference to promote an increase in state pensions. They were talking directly to their core voters. Secretary of State for Health Alan Milburn held a press conference on the future of the NHS, Labour's key issue. There was a political row when the Lord Chancellor, Lord Irvine, hosted a Labour fund-raising dinner for lawyers. The Conservatives demanded his resignation on the grounds that the Lord Chancellor should be seen to be politically neutral. This went nowhere, not least because, in reality, the Lord Chancellor is a cabinet position and is always a political appointment. The Lord Chancellor is appointed by the monarch on the advice of the prime minister. Little known fact: Technically, the Lord Chancellor as the highest-ranking Great Officer of State nominally outranks the prime minister!

One afternoon in late February, the government announced a three pence per litre cut in petrol prices. The fuel protests had been going on for too long. The announcement came at four fifteen p.m. The government spin doctors clearly had their eyes on the BBC *Six O'clock News*, not on our *Live at Five*. I scrambled together a package followed by a live from our Westminster studio, with more carefully constructed packages for six p.m. and nine p.m., both followed by a live two-way.

A case of Foot and Mouth Disease was discovered in Essex, although the diseased pig had come from a farm in Northumberland. By the beginning of March, the disease had spread to Devon, Cornwall, north Wales and southern Scotland. Nick Brown at the Ministry of Agriculture Fisheries and Food was holding regular briefings. He looked increasingly uncomfortable, some said shell-shocked. For several days I attended these briefings and did lives outside the Ministry every hour all day long and into the evening. The Ministry was burning infected cows and sheep. More than six million were eventually killed before the disease was finally brought under control at the end of the summer. Meanwhile, the news was full of shocking images of piles of burning animal carcasses. Most of them were perfectly healthy.

Spurred on by the Conservatives, farmers were up in arms, with both painting the Labour government as anti-rural, a city versus countryside narrative. Nick Brown was looking more dishevelled and sounding more ragged. Government competence in general was now under the spotlight. The briefings coming from Number Ten and MAFF were not always entirely congruent. Tony Blair began a series of visits to farms to try to repair the damage. The army got involved in an operation commanded by Brigadier Alex Birtwhistle, who I had once trained. He was very media-savvy and media-friendly. I take no credit for that. Well, maybe just a little.

Questions were being asked. Why were we so severely damaging our tourism industry, for example in the Lake District, to protect a relatively small export market? And there were stories that some farmers were ignoring the disease and possibly even deliberately spreading it to cash in on government compensation payments. The NFU strenuously denied that this was happening. The government was under pressure to postpone the general election. It was put back a month. I interviewed John Major on this. He was starting to find his feet in his new role of elder statesman.

Other stories that March, and there were other stories, included packages on the Budget and an interview at Carlton House with Foreign Secretary Robin Cook and his Polish opposite number. The Lords voted to overturn the fox hunting ban, so that battle was still being fought. But at the end of March and into April I was still covering the Foot and Mouth outbreak. The government's own numbers were far worse than had been expected. I was also reporting on speculation about the date of the general election.

I packaged the launch of NASA's Mars Odyssey, though sadly from London not Cape Canaveral. The following Sunday, the *News of the World* had really not very interesting so-called revelations about Sophie, Countess of Wessex, but their story acted as a springboard for me to do a piece about the conflict between being a member of the Royal Family and having a career, and about the wider issue of the Civil List. I interviewed Jeremy Corbyn at 11.54 a.m. and we had to hot-roll the interview live into the news at twelve o'clock.

More Foot and Mouth Disease. Tony Blair was in rural Durham. The question now had become about whether or not to vaccinate against the disease, and how that would be resourced and implemented.

The Tories had problems of their own. The Campaign for Racial Equality had produced a Race Pledge which they wanted politicians to sign. Michael Portillo refused to do so. I packaged the story and did lives all afternoon and evening. Two days later, I interviewed Michael Howard about it. The Conservatives failed to kill the story, and a week later, I was still interviewing people about it, this time union leader Bill Morris, Conservative peer Lord (John) Taylor and Conservative MP John Townend who had added fuel to the fire when, referring to a speech by Robin Cook, asked if the British were 'a mongrel race'. William Hague stepped in. I interviewed him at Conservative Central Office. Townend was forced to apologise, but the damage had been done. Meanwhile, I was still doing pieces about FMD and on the general election campaign, both of which frequently made the lead story.

The traditional May Day riot failed to materialise when police contained several thousand cold, wet and miserable protestors at Oxford Circus, denying their perfectly legitimate right to protest in order to prevent civil disorder. The race issue as still plaguing the Tories. Conservative MP Laurence Robertson was forced to apologise for publicly supporting John Townend's remarks and adding a few equally inflammatory comments of his own. He had a choice, to publicly apologise or have the Conservative whip removed. It has to be said that since then Robertson, the MP for Tewkesbury, has campaigned against racism, in particular racism in football.

May 3rd would have been election day but for the outbreak of Foot and Mouth Disease. Tony Blair held a press conference at Number Ten at which he said the disease had been conquered even though the crisis wasn't yet completely over. He officially launched Labour's election campaign a few days later. I packaged that complete with interviews with William Hague and Charles Kennedy for balance, as we are required by law to observe. I packaged PMQs that week and hoovered up all that day's election activity, a long package that led Sky News all day and all evening. William Hague had performed well at PMQs, not that it made any difference. Tony Blair seemed a bit out of sorts, subdued, not quite firing on all cylinders.

I packaged the election campaign almost every day for the next month, usually the lead story. On May 14th Blair was in Scotland, Hague in Wales and Kennedy in Cornwall. We had reporters with each of them, but I was taking in the words and pictures to create a coherent overall package. Sometimes I got out on the road to cover a walkabout or a rally. Labour put out an impressive PEB (Party Election Broadcast). For my report on it, and in the interests of impartiality, I interviewed Douglas Alexander (Labour), Phil Willis (Lib Dem) and Michael Ancram for the Conservatives.

The Conservative PEB was bleak and depressing, focusing for some inexplicable reason on the dangers of the early release of prisoners. It was, in any event, completely overshadowed by a promise of twenty billion pounds in tax cuts by Shadow Secretary to the Treasury Oliver Letwin. Some leading Conservatives were talking about eight billion pounds in tax cuts. Confusion reigned and Labour made hay. For my package I interviewed William Hague, Shadow Chancellor of the Exchequer Michael Portillo and Chancellor Gordon Brown, who I later replaced with excerpts from a speech by Tony Blair in Leeds. Politicians also sometimes get 'big-footed'!

On May 16th, Labour's manifesto launch was completely overshadowed by three events which, in normal times and with a stronger opposition party, should have caused any government a big problem. Jack Straw was booed, heckled and slow hand-clapped at the Police Federation annual conference in Blackpool. That played neatly into the Conservative law and order narrative. Worse, Tony Blair was berated by a woman, Sharon Storer, outside a hospital in Edgbaston. She was complaining that there was no bed in the bone marrow unit for her partner. It went on for far too long in full view of the cameras. Blair's minders couldn't really usher him away as she was blocking the hospital entrance. She declined his offer to go inside and discuss it in private, away from the cameras, accusing him of being all talk and no action. "You don't do anything to help anybody." Blair looked badly shaken.

As if that wasn't bad enough, far worse was to come when John Prescott sprang into action. With a left jab! Whichever way you cut it, punching voters is really not a good idea, especially if you are the deputy prime minister. In Rhyl, he had been egged by a protestor sporting a very outdated Chris Waddle-style mullet. The egg wasn't thrown, it was slapped onto the back of Prescott's head with some force. John Prescott always had a short fuse. He was half comedian, half bully. He was also, it was said, from a normal working-class background. If someone hit you, you hit them back harder. There followed a few seconds of the two men grappling before they were separated.

Reaction to this bizarre event was mixed. While some thought it an obvious case for immediate resignation, others were more tolerant. Some even found it hilarious which, in some ways it was, but the violence, the Prescott Punch, was clearly wrong. Prescott himself adamantly refused to apologise. Several commentators, including Sky News political editor Adam Boulton, went into full righteous indignation mode. Violence was absolutely not acceptable. Not only that, but this from a deputy prime minister whose government had been moralising on yob culture and anti-social behaviour. Maybe, some joked, Prescott should be issued with an ASBO (Anti-Social Behaviour Order), a rather gimmicky attempt to cut down on yobbish behaviour introduced by the Blair government three years earlier.

Labour decided to tough it out. Most people, it seemed, sympathised with Prescott who had, after all, been physically attacked. Tony Blair came out with 'John is John', like a father apologising for a naughty child. He needed John Prescott. He was the conduit to the trade unions and motivated the party faithful. He waved around Labour's pledge card and sold the brand of 'Tony'. John Prescott was also very often the peacemaker between Tony Blair and Gordon Brown.

The curious incident of the Prescott Punch blew over, but it had enlivened an otherwise lacklustre election campaign, an election everyone knew Labour was going to win.

I returned to more mundane (and peaceful!) election coverage, pulling together and packaging the main events of the day. A row over National Insurance contributions went on for days. On May 22nd, I had extra-long packages on whether or not Britain should join the Euro. The main interview was with Margaret Thatcher saying, "No to the euro". We must "Never give up the pound". She was, I think trying to sound Churchillian ('we shall fight on the beaches' etc.), but without being unkind, I thought she had lost the plot and was sounding increasingly out of touch. It made for yet another lead story. In all, I packaged the lead story for fifteen days, with stories on the other days that weren't quite strong enough to make the lead.

While Gordon Brown and Alistair Darling were battling with Michael Portillo and Oliver Letwin over the issue of National Insurance contributions, Tony Blair was busy visiting hospitals and schools and giving speeches on health and education, sharply focusing on Labour's key election message: 'schools and hospitals first'.

On some days, I was packaging every hour all day, often turning around press conferences almost as they happened. We would often take them live, and my job was to package an instant summary of what had just been said for the top of the next hour with, later, reaction from the other parties. It was hard work and seemed relentless, but I loved reporting every twist and turn, every nuance, of the election campaign. It was political history in the making.

A not untypical day, in this case May 26th, saw me doing lives from a morning Labour party conference, going straight from there to do lives from at a Lib Dem press conference, packaging for lunchtime and then accompanying Margaret Thatcher on a walkabout (Save the pound! No surrender to the euro!).

There were race riots in Oldham, an issue which had been brewing there for weeks. Petrol bombs, bottles and bricks were flying. The same day, I had covered a William Hague speech in Darlington. Just a quiet Sunday, then! The election was less than two weeks away. The opinion polls showed Hague and the Conservatives were doing even worse than just days before. Their popularity had actually fallen from an already very low base. I packaged that.

On May 29th, I covered a Tory rally in Brighton, with speeches by William Hague and John Major and took into my lead story package an interview done by Adam Boulton with Tony Blair, and at a Lib Dem Rally in Edinburgh a speech by Charles Kennedy. Political balance box ticked!

Adam, the best in the business, did an interview with William Hague on May 31st. Hague was hopeless on the key question of his promised tax cuts and where the money was going to be saved. It was an inept performance, under relatively little pressure from Adam. I had already done a few election interviews that day, with Alan Beith, Damian Green et al., but my package for the evening was centred entirely on the William Hague interview and the Conservatives tax plans.

William Hague's mantra was so many 'days to save the pound', with the day number inserted counting down to election day. He and his party were claiming that the Blair government, if re-elected, would join the euro. They knew, as we all did, that Gordon Brown would absolutely forbid it, but they had presumably been told by focus groups that 'saving the pound' resonated with the voters. Both strategically and tactically it failed badly. Instead, the spotlight was firmly fixed on the party's shambolic tax plans.

Margaret Thatcher was out campaigning every day, which I thought might be doing William Hague more harm than good, Labour had already released a poster of Hague's face with Thatcher's hair. She too was still banging on relentlessly about the evils of joining the euro.

Only the *Daily Mail* and the *Telegraph* were supporting the Conservatives. Some newspapers had been keeping their powder dry but on Monday, 4th of June, just three days before the election, *The Times* and *The FT* declared firmly for Labour. Do newspaper endorsements affect the way people vote? Probably not, but they certainly affect the zeitgeist and the morale and motivation of party workers and activists.

On election days, we are bound by law to avoid reporting on any actual politics. We are allowed to film the outside of polling stations and party leader casting their votes, and that was my package which ran all day until the polls closed at ten p.m.

Everyone expected Labour to win, the only question was by how much. It was another landslide, with a huge overall Labour majority of one hundred and sixty-six. The Conservatives won one seat in Scotland, where they had been completely wiped out in the 1997 election. Among the new intake of Tory MPs were the party's bright stars of the future: David Cameron, George Osborne and Boris Johnson. Notable retiring departures included Edward Heath, Michael Heseltine, John Major, Paddy Ashdown and Tony Benn. My friend Bob Smith held on to his seat in Aberdeen, but former ITN colleague Hugh Pym failed in his bid to become an MP. Both were Lib Dems, who had gained six seats taking them to fifty-two.

William Hague resigned the next morning. He looked shell-shocked, as did all around him. The Labour campaign had not been that good, but the Conservative campaign had been a disaster. Wrong message and the wrong leader. William was very clever and could be very funny, but none of that registered with the electorate. I covered his resignation and did a package on who might be the next Conservative leader, the runners and riders.

The Tories were in total turmoil. To be on the wrong end of two election landslides resulted in deep psychological damage and even existential doubt. For the next few months it felt like we, in the media, were asking the questions a properly functioning Opposition ought to have been asking. As if they didn't have enough problems, Ann Widdecombe announced that she might run for leader.

Tony Blair reshuffled his cabinet the next day. I packaged that as the lead story all day. The big change was Robin Cook, demoted from Foreign Secretary to Leader of the Commons. He was not happy. He was replaced by Jack Straw, with David Blunkett promoted to Home Secretary. Tessa Jowell, who I liked and got on with very well, was the new Secretary of State for Culture, Media and Sport. Tony Blair seemed keen to promote more women. Margaret Beckett was the new Secretary of State at DEFRA (Department for the Environment, Food and Rural Affairs), Estelle Morris became Secretary of State for Education, Patricia Hewitt was the new Secretary of State for Trade and Industry, Helen Liddell was the new Secretary of State for Scotland and Hilary Armstrong was the new chief whip.

I had been working flat out for a month, as had we all. I had had the longest run of lead stories I had ever enjoyed and, the joy of working for a twenty-four-hour news channel, they had mostly been very substantial packages far longer than could be accommodated by the limited running time of terrestrial news bulletins.

The next couple of days involved wrapping two political stories into one package: Tory leadership speculation, and Tony Blair's junior ministerial appointments, always a good opportunity for us to spot who the government saw as potential rising stars.

Late June, and a week in Pathos, Cyprus, a quick family holiday to decompress. Beaches, fish restaurants, the Roman mosaics, the Tombs of the Kings. There was a karaoke night at our hotel. After much persuasion and against her better judgement, Marion sang 'Moon River'. It was exquisite. The tourists were treated to a professional performance and loved it. Karaoke it wasn't. Maddie, who had just turned three, found a pretty pebble on the beach and I said she could take it home. "Yes, Daddy. It was lost but I've rescued it."

We had had such a good time that we booked another break almost immediately. In the first week of July we were back in Tunisia. In effect, this was a two-week summer holiday just divided into two parts. Sandy beaches, a tranquil turquoise sea and the best two restaurants in Hammamet,

Chez Amchour and Barboarossa, above the Medina, overlooking the little harbour. The George Sebastian Villa, which was now Hammamet's cultural centre, was so beautiful I wanted to live there.

I was also back to media training various clients, notably Brigadier Peter Wall who would go on to become CGS (chief of the general staff), head of the army. Others included Microsoft, a travel company, Bacardi, the RNIB, BT, various regional health authorities and another week at the UK Defence Academy in Shrivenham. I also helped Barnardo's with their media messaging.

Back in the saddle at Sky News, my package of the day posed the question, should Lord Archer, Jeffrey Archer, be stripped of his peerage? Archer had been convicted of perjury and attempting to pervert the course of justice and been given four years. I interviewed Baroness Emma Nicholson, who wanted to know what had become of the millions of pounds Jeffrey Archer had raised to help the Kurds in Northern Iraq. She claimed they had received almost nothing.

The television satire programme *Brass Eye* created a storm with an episode called 'Paedogeddon', which mocked the way the press exaggerated the issue of paedophilia. Thousands of people wrote in to object, more than for any previous television programme. The tabloids attacked *Brass Eye*'s creator and presenter, Chris Morris. The Minister for Child Protection, Beverley Hughes, described the show as "unspeakably sick", and cabinet ministers David Blunkett and Tessa Jowell waded into the row, Blunkett's spokesman saying the Home Secretary was "dismayed" and Tessa urging the ITC (Independent Television Commission) to change its rules. Chris Morris himself was not saying anything, which left a gaping hole in my package. No one was defending him or his programme.

Into August, and a story about BSE in sheep. I tried not to over-egg it. I didn't want to scare people. I did a package on homelessness, which was getting worse. The Queen Mother celebrated her one hundred and first birthday. I thought Princess Margaret was looking very ill. She died the following February.

That weekend, I cut a package on tours of Parliament, which was fun and looked very good. It ran all day, while I was busy doing entirely unrelated interviews with Northern Ireland First Minister David Trimble, Ben Gill of the NFU and Bruce Kent of CND. The Ben Gill interview was for yet another Foot and Mouth Disease package which ran the next day, and there was a story to report on random drugs and alcohol testing at places of work.

At DEFRA (which we called Defcon 4!), the new Secretary of State Margaret Beckett gave a briefing and I interviewed her afterwards. There were to be three separate inquiries into the outbreak of Foot and Mouth Disease but, crucially, no public inquiry. There were more asylum seeker stories to be reported and yet another government inquiry, announced by Environment Minister Michael Meacher, after water in Camelford, Cornwall, became contaminated with aluminium sulphate.

When the Tory leadership ballot papers were sent out, I interviewed Ken Clarke live. Surely they would elect their best potential leader this time? I packaged the Conservative Party leadership contest for several more days in late August.

I once again media trained Premier League referees, eight of them, and once again urged them to give post-match interviews, but that particular piece of advice once again fell on deaf ears.

The asylum seekers' story took a new twist in early September when the French opened a second refugee centre outside Calais, even though Home Secretary David Blunkett had asked them to close the existing one. It was an open invitation for illegal immigrants to attempt to get to Britain. We had night-time shots of dozens of them trying to get through the Channel tunnel. Utter madness.

A day covering the TUC annual conference in Brighton. There were rumblings, more than rumblings, of discontent. They felt the Labour Party leadership had been ignoring them since 1994. Since they paid so much to fund Labour, they believed their policies should become the Labour government's policies. The problem was that many of the TUC's policies would almost certainly render Labour unelectable.

I was in Germany the next day when al-Qaeda attacked the World Trade Centre twin towers in New York. Like everyone else, we watched the television in disbelief. The senior officers we had been working with (colonels and brigadiers) immediately returned to their army bases as the security alert hit the highest level. We were watching both CNN and Sky News. CNN had reporters running around like headless chickens shouting, "Oh my God! Oh my God!" Sky's coverage from the streets of New York was far more measured, calm and articulate. But it was very difficult to process what was happening. It seemed unreal, like something out of a Hollywood disaster movie. Once we got over the initial shock and absorbed the fact that this was actually happening, it became obvious that 9/11 was a huge event, the worst terrorist attack ever. It was also immediately clear that the Americans would react and want to respond, but how, where and against whom?

There has been so much said and written about 9/11, especially the shock of the second plane, that there is little worthwhile to add here.

Tony Blair was in Brighton to give a speech to the TUC. He was due to talk about the euro. He seemed to want to join, but was being blocked at every turn by Gordon Brown. But the issue of the European currency had paled into insignificance after the attack on New York. The speech was handed out in written form (he attacked some of the TUC's more extreme policies, while the euro was an issue on which Blair and the unions were in broad agreement) and instead said a few words about the attack on the World Trade Centre, describing international terrorism as the "greatest evil" in the world and offering sympathy and, crucially, unconditional support to the Americans before heading straight back to London. There was that unforgettable image of the look on George W Bush's face when, while visiting a school, an aide came in and whispered in his ear to tell him what was going on.

After 9/11, Tony Blair's Premiership was defined by Iraq. Not the minimum wage, independence for the Bank of England, Sure Start, money for schools and hospitals or the successful military interventions in Kosovo and Sierra Leone. In fact, Blair wanted to intervene in Darfur. I knew from my senior military contacts that they had been asked to war game intervening in Darfur and he had been told that it would be impossible.

That same day, in northern Afghanistan, two al-Qaeda suicide bombers, posing as a Belgian television crew with a bomb hidden inside their camera, killed Ahmad Shah Massoud, 'the Lion of the Panjshir', who had fought the Russians to a standstill and, subsequently, kept the Taliban at bay. A true hero, his death was a great loss to Afghanistan and the world. Of course, it got almost no news coverage. All eyes were on New York.

The next day, NATO invoked article five (that an attack on one was an attack on all NATO members). The Tory leadership result was postponed for twenty-four hours (it hardly seemed to matter). We were now seeing the planes hitting the towers from all sorts of different angles, the images of people running away through the smoke and flying debris, and those chilling images of people jumping out of the upper stories of the towers to their deaths. Tony Blair had chaired a Cobra meeting the evening before. Security was stepped up at Heathrow, Canary Wharf and elsewhere, and at British Embassies. There were to be no flights over London. We managed to get back to Heathrow from Germany without incident.

The Conservative Party leadership result was announced. As with Hague, the party had voted for the anyone-but-Ken-Clarke candidate, this time Iain Duncan Smith, 'the quiet man', which was very obviously an extremely poor choice. Clarke's position on Europe had once again stymied his ambition to lead his party, and maybe, the country. Personally, I have no doubt that the Conservatives would have fared far better in 2001 and 2005 with Ken Clarke at the helm.

Tony Blair threw himself into an international diplomatic mission, visiting more than twenty countries before Christmas, to build a coalition behind the Americans. There were voices in America calling for Iraq to be punished, but what had 9/11 to do with Iraq? Should we be taking much stronger military action against the Taliban in Afghanistan? The problem was that 'international terrorism' is such an elusive enemy.

Tony's Travels, as they became known, kept us busy. He was bouncing between European capitals and the United States. In one week, he was in Berlin, Paris, Washington, New York and finally Brussels. In France, President Chirac was supporting military action in Afghanistan but not Iraq. For weeks, there was only one story.

Jack Straw went to Tehran, the first British foreign secretary to visit Iran since 1979. The annual party conferences were to be cut short, Parliament was being recalled for a two-day emergency debate. All of this and other 9/11 fallout kept us all very busy for the rest of September. Tony Blair added fuel to the fire of the speculation that some sort of military action was imminent when he said, after meeting Chirac in Paris, "Within the next few days". But he had been referring to diplomatic efforts not military action.

Blair went to Moscow, Islamabad and Delhi. The main purpose of the trip was to get Pakistan onside. His visit to Pakistan was considered potentially dangerous and was taken despite security advice not to go. Delhi was included after the Indian prime minister had complained that to visit Pakistan but not India would be taken as an insult. I did packages and lives. He returned on October the 6th and the general mood, even expectation, was that there would be military action, possibly as soon as that night.

The next afternoon, I was doing lives from Downing Street. It was quiet, the lull before the storm. American and British attacks by air and cruise missiles on Afghanistan went in just after five p.m. Tony Blair did a live statement at six forty-five. I continued doing lives in Downing Street until eight p.m. when Adam Boulton took over and I switched to packaging the story. Although this wasn't yet entirely clear, it was the opening salvo of the coalition invasion of Afghanistan.

And that was the rest of October, lives from Downing Street as events in Afghanistan unfolded. I wasn't on the front line but I was, at least, on the political front line. Of course, to know what was really going on you needed to be on the inside, in the room. As journalists, even with the best and most helpful contacts, we only ever had glimpses of what was really happening.

There were other stories to cover, most notably the IRA declaring that the armed conflict, The Troubles, in Northern Ireland was finally over. They were fully decommissioning at last, putting their weapons beyond use and moving beyond the armed struggle. Rebel Labour MPs, the usual suspects, were speaking out against the bombing of Afghanistan.

Tony Blair's travels continued, taking in Britain's friends in Oman and Jordan, the less than friendly President Assad, dictator of Syria, and Israel where the subject was, as ever, the treatment of the Palestinians with both sides, Sharon and Arafat, refusing to compromise. When he returned, some in the press were hailing the Middle East trip as a success, others (with their own agenda) were branding it a disaster.

Benjamin Netanyahu arrived in Downing Street on November 1st with a ludicrous amount of security. I also interviewed Tam Dalyell who, with other Labour rebels, was trying to force a Commons vote on the Afghanistan bombing. They'd be lucky to get into double figures. I was live in Downing Street every hour all day when Tony Blair hosted Chirac and Jospin, Schröder, Berlusconi as well as the Spanish, Dutch and Belgian prime ministers, a kind of informal European summit. It was an assessment of the current situation in Afghanistan to ensure that everyone was still fully on board rather than providing any dramatic development or announcement.

A week later, the BBC's John Simpson liberated Kabul! Or so he seemed to be claiming. The city had fallen, and in marched John like Lawrence of Arabia entering Damascus! He had always been brave and intrepid but also seemed rather bombastic and slightly preposterous, especially dressed in a burqa.

The Taliban had fallen but, as it is easy to see in retrospect, October 2001 was far from the end of the Taliban or of the suffering of that beautiful country.

David Blunkett introduced a new anti-terrorism bill in the Commons. Only five MPs voted against it. I had to interview former Radio One DJ Simon Bates about paedophile Jonathan King who was to be sentenced the next day after being convicted of child sex abuse. He had sexually assaulted five boys. He got seven years.

Blair versus Brown, the TB-GBs, continued to rear up as a story, there were briefings, counter-briefings, followed by denials of any briefings at all! There were clearly policy differences if not personal antagonism, but somehow a prime minister and chancellor seemingly so at odds worked well. An example: On November 22nd at the lobby, Alastair Campbell downplayed the differences between the two men on the very day before Tony Blair gave a speech in Birmingham extolling the virtues of joining the euro, something Gordon Brown was implacably against. I did lives on this both the day before and on the day of Blair's Birmingham speech.

I reported on government guidelines to avoid deep vein thrombosis on flights. That same day, at the end of November, the sad news came from Los Angeles that George Harrison had died of Cancer. He was only fifty-eight.

There were other stories to cover in December. The BUPA hospital in Redhill was to be used by the NHS. Another health story when Health Secretary Alan Milburn announced billions more to fund the NHS. I had interviews with both Alan Milburn and Tony Blair and on any other day it would have been the lead story, but the Taliban surrendered the city of Kandahar, their last remaining urban stronghold. The government was defeated in the Lords again, this time it was the anti-terrorism bill. There was a leak which suggested that Special Branch had been tipped off before the Omagh bomb of August 1998. The anti-terrorism bill was finally passed and given Royal Assent. I packaged that all day. The Lords' objection had centred around the draconian nature of the bill, the speed with which it had been rushed through Parliament in the wake of 9/11, and the fact that some sections of the very long bill didn't directly address terrorism at all and were in contravention of the European Convention on Human Rights. The Anti-terrorism, Crime and Security Act 2001 was eventually replaced by the more measured Prevention of Terrorism Act, 2005.

At the end of the year, for Christmas, we went on holiday to Havana, Cuba. But the story of that would require at least a chapter to itself.

CHAPTER 16

2002: Jennifer Jane Brown. The Wobbly Bridge. The Queen Mother.
Raine Spencer's 'toyboy'. Saddam Hussein Playing a very Dangerous
Game. The 'Dodgy Dossier'. John Major and Edwina Currie! Meeting
Bill Clinton. Cherie Blair and Carole Caplin

The first big shock of 2002 came on January 7th. Gordon and Sarah Brown's baby daughter, Jennifer Jane, died in hospital in Edinburgh. She was just ten days old. She had been their first child and had been born seven weeks prematurely, weighing just two pounds and four ounces. It was an unspeakably sad moment. I wanted to send condolences but didn't for two reasons. Firstly, I didn't want to intrude on what was obviously a time for closest family and friends. Secondly, because I didn't want them to think that I had an ulterior motive, a journalist somehow attempting to curry favour. This sounds silly in retrospect, but I've always been poor at dealing with bereavement. There are never the right words. A friend's mother died not long ago. 'I am so sorry for your loss' felt so utterly inadequate. Just days before, the Browns had looked so happy cradling their beautiful baby. With a baby girl of my own, who was now three, I wept for them.

As well as covering politics for Sky News, I was busy that January media training a range of corporate clients, the highlight being three days in New York for an international bank. There was a viewing platform to look at Ground Zero, but we sneaked up onto the roof of the Marriott Hotel from where we had a much better view directly onto the gaping hole where the Twin Towers had stood. On January 29th George W Bush delivered his 'axis of evil' speech.

There were packages on Trident submarine HMS Vanguard in Devonport for a re-fit, a piece on eating disorders, and another marking the fiftieth year of the Queen's reign, a two-minute-thirty-package which worked out at about thirty seconds per decade! Succinct didn't even begin to describe it.

My story on mercenaries included an interview with Lt. Col. Tim Spicer, the founder of Sandline International which had been mired in controversy for its activities in Papua New Guinea and Sierra Leone.

I was live in Downing Street when Jo Moore finally resigned. She was Transport Secretary Stephen Byers' special advisor who had sent a notorious email on 9/11, saying it was 'a good day to bury bad news'. The only surprise was that she hadn't been sacked months earlier. The government wanted to give the Territorial Army reservists a bigger role with more responsibility, four years after cutting TA numbers from sixty thousand to forty thousand. I said it felt like they were trying to fit a gallon into a pint pot.

I had two camera crews to cover the re-opening of the Millennium Bridge. It had become known as 'the wobbly bridge' as it swayed in even the mildest breeze. Now, the problem had been fixed. I was live at the bridge all day, with live interviews with architect Sir Norman Foster, the project manager, and live vox pops. Some people preferred the pedestrian bridge when it had swayed in the wind. Linking St Paul's Cathedral to Tate Modern, it had already become a favourite but also something of a national joke. Now, of course, we take it for granted and those early teething problems are long forgotten.

Other stories that spring included a piece on homelessness with Stephen Byers and Louise Casey, a package on child soldiers in Africa, Education Secretary Estelle Morris addressing the NUT conference in Bournemouth, and Defence Secretary Geoff Hoon spoke on the thorny issue of women soldiers fighting on the front line. He was against it.

The Queen Mother died on March 30th. She was one hundred and one. She had passed away in her sleep in Windsor. I was sent at once to Buckingham Palace to do live two-ways. Rather oddly, I also did a live for Fox News in New York. It felt like a cliché to say it, but it did feel like the end of an era, she had been born in 1900 into a very different world. I spoke about her unique contributions, continuity, her role during the Blitz and her more recent manifestation as grandmother of the nation. She was immensely popular, as was shown by her lying in state in Westminster Hall when two hundred thousand people filed past over three days and her funeral on April 9th when a million people lined the streets.

Tony Blair went to Crawford, Texas in early April for a meeting with George W Bush at his private ranch. The Americans were clear in their ambition to get rid of Saddam Hussein.

Health and education loomed large as issues for the rest of April. The RCN (Royal College of Nursing) held its annual congress in Harrogate. Tony Blair was doing interviews that day on health, but was being rather evasive about Iraq. I had the lead story, with contributions from Charles Kennedy and David Davies for political balance. Education stories included an interview with Estelle Morris on teacher shortages, and a crackdown on bad behaviour in schools. I interviewed her again a few days later for a government report on teachers' workload. The teachers and their unions were lucky to have such a sympathetic education secretary.

The local elections were on May 2nd. Governments usually take a hammering in mid-term local council elections, but the Blair government got off comparatively lightly. There was a story that Tony Blair claimed to have seen legendary centre forward Jackie Millburn play for Newcastle United, which was unlikely since Millburn's last game for Newcastle had been in 1957. The newspapers were characterising this as Blair lying to suggest he was some sort of ordinary bloke, in touch with the people and so on. Downing Street dismissed the story as an 'urban myth'.

A North Sea gas rig was evacuated after a fishing boat crashed into it (how do you do that? Those rigs are enormous). No one had been hurt. The pictures came in, precisely one minute seven seconds of pictures. I had to use every frame to make the story into a tight package. Tony Blair gave a speech setting the mood music on a vote on joining the euro, effectively though unofficially launching the Join campaign.

Labour seemed to have a schizophrenic approach to the euro. For Tony Blair, it seemed a political project, a closer-knit European Union. For Gordon Brown, it was economic anathema. Joining the euro would be an economic catastrophe and he set out stringent economic conditions, criteria which were basically impossible to meet.

I packaged Stephen Byers' speech to the train drivers' union ASLEF (the splendidly-named Associated Society of Locomotive Engineers and Fireman) conference in Scarborough, and interviewed Bob Crow the general secretary of the RMT (the national union of Rail, Maritime and

Transport workers), who was his usual left-wing firebrand self. I also did a piece on drugs in schools. The government was against them!

Iain Duncan Smith criticised the government's handling of the asylum seekers issue, playing to the Conservative/*Daily Mail* core. I interviewed Camelot chief executive, Diane Thompson. Their slogan was 'it could be you'. She admitted that the likelihood of it actually being you was astronomically slim. The brilliant newsroom satire *Drop the Dead Donkey* used to refer to playing the National Lottery as 'paying the moron tax'!

Tony Blair went to Rome for what was being described as an 'historic' NATO summit. That was widely taken to mean that NATO would soon be taking military action against Iraq. In the event, it signified nothing of the sort. Russia had attended and the summit established a new NATO-Russian council set up by the NATO secretary-general, our old friend George Robertson. In that respect, it could be said to have been historic.

In the cabinet re-shuffle at the end of May, there was a lot of sympathy for Stephen Byers when he left his job as transport secretary, though not in those newspapers which had been crucifying him for weeks. He had resigned the day before the re-shuffle to spare Tony Blair having to sack him. He was replaced by Alistair Darling. Having already had the lead package for several hours as the changes emerged, I did a two-camera interview with Darling at two thirty p.m. which Sky News aired in its entirety at half past the hour for the rest of the day. I also had the lead story at the top of every hour! Paul Boateng became Britain's first black cabinet minister, at last.

The government announced tough new measures on illegal asylum seekers, basically saying they would be deported before they could appeal against their deportation. Kowtowing to the *Daily Mail* agenda?

We had enjoyed Tunisia so much the previous year that we had another week there in June, visiting familiar places.

Back in London, and in Trafalgar Square doing lives with rowdy England fans after a 3–0 win against Denmark in the World Cup. We were 3–0 up by half time so, for once, we were able to watch England without having a nervous breakdown! I got absolutely soaked and accidentally slightly hurt when some good-natured but rough fans decided they wanted to throw me into one of the fountains. I suppose doing the live two-ways absolutely drenched made me look part of the event.

There were claims in the Sunday papers that Number Ten officials had tried to find Tony Blair a more prominent role at the Queen Mother's funeral. This was aimed at both Tony Blair and at Alastair Campbell. Number Ten was outraged and denied it in the strongest possible terms. I remember Alastair Campbell dismissing it as "complete bollocks". Despite there being no new developments this story, or non-story, kept me busy for three days.

Normal service was resumed on day four when Tony Blair delivered the keynote speech at a conference on crime. People remembered Blair's promise that Labour would be 'tough on crime, tough on the causes of crime' as he tried to wrest the law-and-order agenda from the Tories all those years earlier. Now, he was expected to live up to that promise.

The National Audit Office reported on the 2001 outbreak of Foot and Mouth Disease. It had cost the country eight billion pounds. Sir John Brown's report concluded, in lessons to be learned, that there needed to be more thorough contingency planning and that the national ban on animal movements should have been implemented sooner. This was worthy though less than riveting, but important enough to merit a package which I tried to make as interesting as possible.

London Mayor Ken Livingstone was accused of a domestic assault during a birthday party in north London which he'd attended in May. He denied the allegations. I did lives at the Greater London Assembly which was questioning him before heading to Tufnell Park and the flat where the party had taken place. His future as mayor hung in the balance. He claimed to be the victim of a newspaper smear campaign. A report by the Standards Board for England cleared Livingstone of any wrongdoing. He went on to win re-election two years later, after being admitted back into the Labour Party.

I had breakfast with Raine Spencer, Countess Spencer, stepmother to Diana Princess of Wales. The circumstances were rather unusual. My wife Marion opened the Harrods sale, and sang two arias. Enrique Iglesias was top of the bill. Afterwards we marched through Harrods for an hour in the wake of Mohamed Al-Fayed and a pipe band. The entourage stopped and talked to shoppers every few minutes, and to pose for the dozens of snappers. I hung back and chatted with the Harrods PR team through whom I'd got Marion the gig. Breakfast was in the Georgian Room and I was placed next to Countess Spencer. Al-Fayed told her he had brought her a "toy boy"! She was interested in my work covering politics, very interested in Marion, and told me about a trip she had taken to Iran. I thanked Al-Fayed for giving Marion the opportunity. He was very charming.

Next day it was back to reality and the HSE (Health and Safety Executive) report on the Potters Bar rail crash of two months earlier. Seven people had been killed and more than seventy injured when a train had derailed at high speed. The points had been poorly maintained. I interviewed Alistair Darling at the Department of Transport and packaged the story. In the United States, it was Independence Day. People were nervous, fearing another major terrorist attack.

Lord Woolf, the Lord Chief Justice, held a rare press conference. I packaged that and also interviewed Jack Straw, now the Foreign Secretary, about supplying arms to Israel via a third country and his forthcoming trip to India and Pakistan. I packaged the election of the general secretary of the AEEU (the Amalgamated Electrical and Engineering Union). Left winger Derek Simpson beat Sir Ken Jackson, the incumbent and Tony Blair's 'favourite trade union leader'. There were four recounts. They both received more than eighty-nine thousand votes, Simpson eventually won by just four hundred. I doorstepped the meeting of the union's executive committee which then refused to ratify the election after Jackson raised ballot-rigging allegations and demanded a fresh vote. Six left wingers walked out. It was an utter fiasco and made a lively package for Sky News. It was like an Ealing comedy.

Iain Duncan Smith re-shuffled his shadow cabinet. Theresa May became party chairwoman, David Davies was demoted (seen as a threat by IDS?). I packaged that with interviews with May and former party chairman Michael Ancram. I was regularly packaging PMQs on Wednesdays. Duncan Smith was certainly no William Hague. He had the debating skills of a wet fish, the charisma of a damp sponge.

In August, before our family holiday in France, Saddam Hussein was once again playing his dangerous games. He invited UN weapons inspectors for talks, as opposed to allowing them to actually do their jobs. For my package, I interviewed former ambassador to Iraq Sir John Moberly, who was a font of knowledge and insight. Libya was also bubbling away beneath the surface. Foreign Office minister Mike O'Brien went to meet

Colonel Gaddafi in the Libyan dictator's famous tent. I packaged that and did live two-ways. Before escaping to France, two more stories, on food labelling and A level results. In Soham, Cambridgeshire, police still had no useful leads in the search for two missing ten-year-old girls, Jessica Chapman and Holly Wells, who had been not been seen for eleven days. Hundreds of police and local volunteers had been searching for them. It was heart-breaking to see their distraught parents appealing for help.

Of course, two days later it got far worse when the bodies of the two girls were discovered. Just a few days earlier their killer, school caretaker Ian Huntley, had given media interviews. He had told Sky's Jeremy Thompson that he still held 'a glimmer of hope' that the two girls would be found. He was sentenced to two life sentences with the High Court later recommending he serve forty years in prison.

Back from France in early September, my first job was to cover a Tony Blair press conference. He was just back from the sustainable development Earth Summit in South Africa, but there was only one topic of conversation, Iraq. He was adamant that Saddam Hussein must allow full weapons inspections if Iraq wanted to avoid war, and that Britain would stand beside the United States, preferably with a UN mandate. He was passionate, but this was not a popular message. The majority in the country was against a war in Iraq, and George W Bush was unpopular in Britain with many regarding him, wrongly, as some sort of village idiot.

After a short break in Barcelona, I covered Tony Blair's speech to the TUC in Blackpool. September 11th was the anniversary of the 9/11 terrorist attack. Tony Blair was meeting Northern Ireland Chief Constable Hugh Ord and, later, the SDLP leadership in Downing Street. On a quieter news day I would have packaged that, but not on this day. We were wall-to-wall covering 9/11 one year on. The next day, I was live in Downing Street when Tony Blair met Charles Kennedy and, later, Iain Duncan Smith to update them on Iraq and the plan to recall Parliament. On September 23rd, Blair briefed the cabinet on the latest on Iraq, which gave me the lead story all afternoon and evening. Robin Cook and Clare Short were vociferous in their opposition to any military action. Blair's position seemed to be that we would support the United States no matter what, although he wanted any military intervention to be mandated by the UN. His support for Bush was being ridiculed in the newspapers, and the undercurrent of anti-American feeling in the country was growing stronger.

The next day, the Commons sat in emergency session. Tony Blair presented the now infamous 'dossier' of evidence against Saddam Hussein with the claim that the Iraqi dictator did, in fact, possess an arsenal of WMD (weapons of mass destruction). Blair was persuasive and convincing, the dossier less so in my opinion even at that time. I cut a long five-minute package updated each hour all evening with a shorter version for the next morning's *Sunrise* programme.

On the train to Blackpool for the Labour Party annual conference on September 28th and one of those completely jaw-dropping moments. I was sitting with Sky News political editor Adam Boulton when Philip Gould, Tony Blair's pollster and a key member of his inner circle, came bouncing up to us in a state of great excitement. "Have you heard? John Major and Edwina Currie!"

We had no response. It couldn't possibly be true. But it was. John Major who, as prime minister had led an almost evangelical moral crusade, 'Back to Basics', had had a four-year affair with Conservative MP Edwina Currie! Within thirty seconds, Adam's phone rang and he was live on the phone into Sky News while I was sitting opposite him and desperately trying to keep a straight face.

That evening in Blackpool, I did short interviews with Tony Blair and John Prescott, and we filmed a meeting of union leaders in a smoke-filled ground floor hotel room through the window from the street before they spotted us and shut the curtains. A bit of exclusive video on the eve of conference, always good value, and a chance to speculate on what The Brothers might be plotting.

The answer was their opposition to the PFI funding for hospitals. I covered that debate, and in the evening once the hall had emptied, did a PTC for the next morning's *Sunrise* package standing on stage at the podium. We would never have got permission to do this had we asked, so I didn't ask! They loved it back at base, Labour MPs thought it was hilarious, and the BBC demanded to know why they hadn't been given permission to do that as well!

The government was defeated on the PFI issue, but won the debate on Iraq. Gordon Brown gave a passionate speech, as ever, invoking the spirit of Nye Bevan. Also as ever, it was eclipsed by Tony Blair's calm, measured leader's speech the next day. Wittingly or not, they were a great double act.

Bill Clinton was the conference guest speaker, the star turn, and like Mandela before him, caused quite a stir in Blackpool. He wasn't doing interviews, but I got to meet him at the Imperial Hotel and he stopped to chat. We talked briefly about Iraq and his total support for Blair's position. I had with me two female producers, one of whom had worked in war zones. When Clinton shook their hands they almost fainted! One of them actually said she was never going to wash her hand again! I turned to them and said, "What the hell is wrong with you two?" I don't know what that thing is that Clinton has, some kind of animal magnetism, but I wanted some!

After I had cut and sent the conference package of the day and sent a piece previewing David Blunkett's speech the next day for *Sunrise*, we headed to the Northern Lights reception where, among those chatting and drinking, were Tony and Cherie Blair and Bill Clinton with his friend, the actor Kevin Spacey. Spacey was Hollywood royalty at the time.

The Blunkett piece ran all morning, we carried his speech live and interviewed him live. I doorstepped Estelle Morris after her speech. The Tomlinson Report had just been released. There had been a massive cock-up in the marking and awarding of grades for A levels. Bill Clinton's speech was by turns decisive, profound and funny if a little cheesy. Of course, he received a rapturous standing ovation. The Labour Party faithful were completely smitten.

Little Sarah Payne had been abducted and murdered in July 2000. She was just eight years old. The case had captivated the country. Her killer, Roy Whiting, had been convicted and sentenced to life in December 2001. He had a previous conviction for kidnapping and sexually abusing an eight-year-old child. Sarah's mother, Sara Payne, had launched a campaign, 'Sarah's Law', to allow controlled access to the sex offenders register so that parents would know if a registered sex offender was living in their area.

Sara Payne was at the Labour conference in Blackpool, lobbying for the law to be changed. I interviewed her on the penultimate day of the conference. She was convinced that such a law would have saved her daughter's life. The counter argument was that such a change would force paedophiles underground which would make it harder for the police to find them. Moreover, they could become the victims of vigilante attacks.

345

In August 2010, the Home Office finally approved a modified scheme which would allow parents to enquire about a named individual who had regular access to their child.

The Labour Party conference ended with a Tony Blair press conference. He took an hour of questions, but revealed nothing new. The main issues were foundation hospitals, and of course, Iraq. He defended what would later be described as the 'dodgy dossier', claiming that Saddam Hussein did have WMD ready to use.

At the Conservative Party conference in Bournemouth, Theresa May's speech ("the nasty party") included what was interpreted as a thinly veiled attack on party leader IDS (In Deep Shit, according to the *Daily Mirror*!). Was his leadership doomed so soon? Would there be a leadership challenge next spring? Who would wield the knife? David Davies? Or Ken Clarke, Liam Fox, Oliver Letwin? The Conservatives seemed in total disarray.

I covered the meeting of the Fire Brigades' Union when they voted by a ratio of nine to one to go on strike. Estelle Morris told the House that some A level results, fewer than two thousand, would need to be upgraded. At PMQs the next day, Duncan Smith said that the A level results were 'not worth the paper they're printed on', which addressed what the Conservatives were portraying as government incompetence but offered no reassurance or support to worried A level students and their parents.

Estelle Morris resigned as education secretary. It was a sudden announcement, though insiders told me she had been contemplating it for some time. She said that she did not feel up to the job and that she'd felt happier and much more effective as a junior education minister. This was an extremely rare admission for a politician to come out with. Estelle had always been far too modest. She hadn't been a bad education secretary, far from it, but had become overwhelmed by the A level marking fiasco and the failure to meet the government's own literacy and numeracy targets.

Tony Blair had a row with French President Jacques Chirac over the Common Agriculture Policy which quickly became public. There seemed to be nothing Chirac liked better than to have a row with the Americans or the British, the 'Anglo Saxons', but they were usually kept private, behind closed doors.

The government announced a plan to abolish higher-rate tax relief for wealthy pensioners (very Labour), and in a speech in Birmingham, Gordon

Brown announced a crackdown on people who were claiming unemployment benefits but refusing to take a job (which seemed straight out of the Conservative party playbook but actually resonated across party lines).

We had several bites at the IDS leadership issue in November. He was doing TV interviews, and each seemed even worse than the last. But our focus for the latter half of the month and into December was on the firefighters' strike and the deployment of the army in their so called 'Green Goddesses', old Bedford lorries built in the 1950s.

The Firefighters' Union, the FBU, was demanding a thirty-nine per cent pay rise. As far as I'm concerned, our firemen and women are all heroes. They were under paid at the time, and had a lot of public sympathy. But to demand so hefty a salary increase was widely seen as completely unrealistic.

John Prescott and Gordon Brown were leading for the government in the FBU dispute, not directly involved in the talks at first, but making statements in the House to keep MPs informed and urging the firefighters to return to work. On November 22nd, I was convinced that the FBU would suspend an eight-day strike, the latest in a series of walk outs, but the government in the shape of John Prescott said 'no deal' so the strike went ahead. Prescott was becoming directly involved in the talks to resolve the first firefighters strike for twenty-five years, which he described as 'unnecessary and unreasonable'.

After several days in early December covering the fire strike, a strange story which also lasted for too long. The *Mail* was attacking Cherie Blair's friendship with Carole Caplin, whose boyfriend was a convicted conman, Peter Foster, who claimed to be the Blairs' financial advisor. He wasn't. However, he had helped Cherie Blair buy two flats in Bristol. She denied this at first, but had to make a public apology. Her tearful statement came on December 5th, on the day the *Daily Mail* ran nine pages on the story which had already been front page news for almost a week, lazily dubbed 'Cheriegate'. We had been lied to for nearly a week. It is always the lies and attempted cover up.

The following week, I was still doing lives in Downing Street on the Cherie Blair story, with a bit of light relief provided by Michael Heseltine calling on IDS to resign as Conservative Party leader. There was another statement of contrition from Cherie Blair, this time delivered in the Atrium restaurant in 4 Millbank, where we, the political units from Sky, ITN and the BBC regularly ate, drank and gossiped. It was pure theatre. It had become an even bigger story. I was doing six-minute packages with live two-ways off the back of them.

The story was still going (still!) a week later when Peter Foster made a statement on camera in the Atrium at ITN's building in Gray's Inn Road. I was doing long lives outside the ITN building in Gray's Inn Road where I used to work, which felt very strange. A lot of people popped out to say hello, which was very nice of them. Among them, Angela Frier, cameramen Mike Inglis, Eugene Campbell and Alan Thompson, and reporters Terry Lloyd and Harry Smith. That was December 16th, the story had been running for more than two weeks. Downing Street had failed to shut it down and the *Mail* was like a dog with a bone.

Two more stories before the year ended. There was a row over whether or not the England cricket team should go to Zimbabwe for the cricket World Cup the following February, and Nicholas Winton, the 'British Oscar Schindler', was knighted, finally, at the age of ninety-three. His was the most incredible story. He had rescued six hundred and sixty-nine children, most of them Jewish, from the Nazis in Czechoslovakia and arranged transport to get them to Britain. His role in rescuing the children had been largely unknown until 1988. He had never spoken about it in public or demanded any recognition. He probably deserved sainthood rather than just a knighthood. Former Labour MP Lord (Alf) Dubbs had been one of the children Nicholas Winton had saved from the Nazis. We spoke to him, in a pub in Keswick in the Lake District, and got a satellite dish to his home so that he could go live into *Live at Five*. His interview and his recollections were vivid, evocative and very moving.

I had been already covering a lot of politics for Sky News. Now, I was covering political stories almost exclusively until I was officially appointed Sky News political correspondent. But those years, dear reader, the premierships of Tony Blair, Gordon Brown and David Cameron, are the subject of the next book, *More When I Stories*, available now in all good bookshops.

Glossary of Terms

As Live: As it sounds, a live two-way recorded and used in later bulletins as if it was live.

Central Lobby: Between the House of Commons and the House of Lords and accessible to the public.

CCO: Conservative Central Office.

Doorstep: Waiting for someone in order to throw a question at them. Often involves hanging around in the cold and rain.

Doughnut: A live by the reporter before and after his/her package.

Embargo: A story that can't go to air or print until an agreed time.

Grab: Sky News jargon for a soundbite.

Live or Live Two-way: The reporter is answering the presenter's questions live.

Live at Five: Sky News flagship programme.

The Lobby: The Parliamentary lobby, briefings usually conducted by the PMOS which political journalists, with the correct accreditation as lobby correspondents, attend.

Millbank: 4 Millbank, the Westminster broadcasting centre where the Sky News, ITN and BBC political units and studios are based.

Package: A television news reporter's report.

PLP: The Parliamentary Labour Party.

PMOS: The Prime Minister's official spokesman/woman.

Pool or pooled: An interview or pictures shot by one broadcaster and shared with all other broadcasters.

PTC: Piece to camera. The bit in the reporter's package where the reporter appears on camera.

RTS: The Royal Television Society which holds annual awards for the best of television news.

Sign-off: At the end of a package the reporter says his/her name, organisation and location eg. "Glen Oglaza, *News at Ten*, Berlin".

Soundbite: The part of a recorded interview which gets on air, usually ten-fifteen seconds long.

Strap: Also called a Super or an Aston, the written text along the bottom of the screen identifying the person being interviewed.

Tease: A promo telling you what story or stories are coming up.

Ticker: Moving text along the bottom of the screen with the latest news headlines, also called a crawler.

Track and rushes: A reporter voice over and accompanying pictures to be edited together back at base.

Underlay: Video voiced over live by a presenter. Also called overlay.

The Usual Suspects: Labour rebel MPs during Tony Blair's premiership. Jeremy Corbyn was invariably among them.

Vox Pop: Vox populi. When a reporter talks to members of the public, usually in the street.

VT Editor: Video tape editor.

5:40: The ITN early evening news back in the day. Huge audiences.

News at Ten: ITN's flagship programme and the highest rated news programme in the UK when I worked there.